learning from delhi

learning from delhi

dispersed initiatives in changing urban landscapes

edited by Shamoon Patwari and Bo Tang
written by Maurice Mitchell

ASHGATE

Published by
Ashgate Publishing Ltd
Wey Court East
Union Road
Farnham
Surrey
GU9 7PT

Ashgate Publishing Company
Suite 420
101 Cherry Street
Burlington
VT 05404-4405
USA

www.ashgate.com

British Library Cataloguing in Publication Data
Mitchell, Maurice.
    Learning from Delhi : dispersed initiatives in changing
    urban landscapes.
    1. Architectural design. 2. City planning.
    3. Architecture--India--Delhi--Designs and plans.
    4. Architecture and society.
    I. Title II. Patwari, Shamoon. III. Tang, Bo.
    720.1'03--dc22

Library of Congress Control Number: 2010935101

ISBN 978 1 4094 0102 5 (pbk)

Mixed Sources
Product group from well-managed forests and other controlled sources
www.fsc.org Cert no. SA-COC-1565
© 1996 Forest Stewardship Council

Printed and bound in Great Britain by
MPG Books Ltd, Bodmin, Cornwall.

Contents

Part 3: A Catalogue of Selected Student Schemes and Live Projects

Preface

As a young person embarking on a career in architecture in the late 1960s, I found the allure of the Architectural Association's then School of Tropical Architecture, led by Professor Otto Koenigsberger, with its celebration of difference and tantalising offer of an experience of the other, profoundly compelling. At the time, lectures and seminars by Babar Mumtaz and Pat Wakely analysed buildings which responded to different exotic climates without the use of industrial technology, and Bernard Rudofsky's book, *Architecture Without Architects*, displaying whole landscapes of mud architecture, fired the imagination of my group of college friends. Responding to this stimulus at the end of our first year of study, we bought an old ambulance from Clapham Motors and drove to Morocco to work with Jean Dethier in Tinezouline, a village constructed from rammed earth in the Draa valley.

The AA Tropical School has now transformed itself into the Development Planning Unit at University College London and opportunities to study and work in unfamiliar contexts are offered more widely in schools of architecture. Paul Oliver's MA in the Vernacular Architecture of the World and Nabeel Hamdi's work at the Centre for Development and Emergency Practice (CENDEP), both at Oxford Brookes University, have been seminal in this regard. In addition the enthusiasm and imagination of young architecture students for the subject is channelled today through such organisations as Architects Sans Frontières and Architecture for Humanity.

The enthusiasm and optimism first experienced during these early days and consolidated later during more prolonged periods of work in Ghana and Southern Sudan provided me with the confidence to both practise and teach the architecture of rapid change and scarce resources, not just as a peripheral subject within the broader culture of architecture, but as something central to it.

Returning annually to Delhi since 2002 with increasing numbers of self-selecting, energetic and engaged architecture students from London Metropolitan University, I have, over this period, also experienced the enthusiasm of young people within the illegal settlements of this thriving city and sensed their optimism. Unencumbered by the baggage of the past they are keen to be directly involved in the upgrading of the infrastructure, public spaces and amenities of their respective communities.

Since the 1960s the debate within architecture in the UK has moved on from demonstrating and calculating the contextual response of buildings to climate, through to broader issues of how to fit proposals to local context whilst at the same time being mindful of more strategic, global concerns. Over this period, the worldwide shortage of energy supplies and the degradation of the environment; rapid globalisation accompanied by wholesale urbanisation; the warming of the planet together with more recent doubts about the sustainability of the current financial system have all had, and will continue to have, an impact on the direction of the profession and the place of architectural education within it.

In situations of rapid cultural and technical change where resources are scarce or limited, the ability to produce appropriate design ideas is likely to become increasingly relevant and is steadily moving up the professional agenda of the Royal Institute of British Architects.

The initiation and resolution of architectural propositions within a complex and constantly changing landscape will, as ever, depend on the enthusiasm, optimism and engagement of the young, who if they are exposed during their period of architectural education to meaningful issues and real situations will have the opportunity to do their most relevant work in the years immediately following their qualification. Such an education and early experience is likely to provide a solid and confident foundation for a fulfilling professional career.

During eight years of engagement by the studio, Delhi has expanded to surround existing villages, left marginal land to be occupied illegally by perhaps 40 per cent of urban migrants, built a metro system from scratch and struggled to provide for its urban poor. This book records the part that this city has played in the education of architectural students from London Metropolitan University at the start of the 21st century. It reflects on some of the issues emerging and catalogues some of the resulting schemes and live projects.

Maurice Mitchell
March 2010

Acknowledgements

This book is the product of the collective effort of those who studied in the studio from 2002 to 2010 but its roots go back to students who came to the studio before 2002 expressing the desire to go and learn from India. We would never have undertaken the journey if students hadn't been curious and intrigued, as well as demonstrating a desire to go there, sufficient to find the funding for their own field trip. The credit goes not just to those students who won prizes in the studio but to all those ex-students who are now out there earning a living in today's difficult conditions using the skills and insights gained in the studio. Without their hard work, sensibility and graphic representations this book would have been impossible.

We would never have gained access to study sites in Gujarat and Meerut without the chance visit of Sourabh Gupta to London Metropolitan University in 2001. Particularly during the early years, Sourabh and his Delhi architectural practice, Archohm, managed by Mohit Mathur facilitated, commented upon and encouraged our work. Archohm also provided post qualification employment in Delhi for a number of our students.

Since 2004, Professor Ashok Lall, who has kindly written the foreword to this book, has been our academic mentor and guide in India. His students at the TVB School of Habitat Studies have shared some of our fieldwork and Ashok himself has been the external examiner for our MA, travelling backwards and forwards between Delhi and London to give valuable comments on our work. Staff involved with the studio at TVB School of Habitat Studies included Neeraj Manchandra and Professor Krishna Menon and Arunava Dasgupta. It is a great sadness that the TVB School was forced to close in 2007 but its alumni still provide a rich network of architectural culture in Delhi and beyond.

Through Ashok we were introduced to Dr Renu Khosla, Director of the NGO CURE who have given us unparalleled access to disadvantaged, illegal and poor communities in Delhi and Agra since 2006 and has facilitated, and continues to facilitate, our studies and live projects there. Those working at and for CURE who have participated with the studio include Shveta Mathur, Manish Kumar, Rajesh Kumar, Geetika Jaswal, Nandita Gupta, Bashobi Dasgupta and Ajit Seshadri of the Vigyan Vijay Foundation.

Ben Derbyshire, Director of HTA Architects here in the UK, has been a great support to the work of the studio since 2007 including offering prizes and funding for our exhibition of student work in Delhi in November 2009. Through Ben we were introduced to Sandra Wolton who has proved an essential communication link with the NGO ARPHEN, our client and facilitator for the live community classroom project in Navi Mumbai. Staff at ARPHEN include Mr Sirodkar, P. K. Nayak, P. Sarathchandran, Kulsum, Raju, Prachi and Mukhesh.

Professors Neerja Tiku and Aruna Grover at the Delhi School of Planning and Architecture (SPA) hosted and Alex Burton of HTA facilitated our exhibition of student work in November 2009. SPA gave us a tremendous welcome at very short notice.

Without Robert Mull's enlightened management of ASD, the studio could not have operated in the way it has and might very well not have been able to operate at all.

Robert's recent creation of the Projects Office as an architectural practice within ASD provided a unique structure in architectural education which allowed our live projects to flourish under the tolerant direction of Anne Markey.

A special thanks to Bo Tang and Shamoon Patwari, who went through the rigours of the studio for both of their 4th and 5th years and then became Architectural Research Assistants within the Projects Office applying the lessons of the studio to design and build all the live projects and manage all the summer surveys funded by the Water Trust.

Without the thoughtful help of former students Emma Curtin and Stefanie Rhodes who commented on the text in draft there would be many more errors. Bo and Shamoon's help with laying out and formatting the book was invaluable. All images have been acknowledged in the caption where possible. Errors in the text and any image formatting blunders that remain are my own responsibility.

Finally, but perhaps most essential to the development of the ideas represented in this book through the painstaking yearly round of field trip and academic exposition, is the support and encouragement of my teaching partners, Robert Barnes, Francesca Pont, Annika Grafweg and Carsten Vellguth who have all travelled with the students to learn from India.

Forewords

Over the past decade a new awareness has emerged in both academic and professional communities across the globe. The communication revolution has made all of us more aware of the processes of change in the rest of the world and the relative ease of travel has enabled a growing number of academics and professionals to see and experience the reality of different places first hand. I think that, as a result, this has engendered a growing sense of a common and shared humanity – an instinctive reaching out and holding hands at times of need – and of a readiness to share good fortune and exchange ideas. One can also sense a new universalism of values in the making, led by the perception of the global susceptibility to climate change and environmental degradation, to support greater equity and dignity across nations and within societies. Even if it is a romance, it is fully worth its while.

This is a significant counterpoint to the dominant themes of globalising markets and cynical realpolitik. We heard the contrapuntal chants of this romance at the Copenhagen Summit last December. The chorus rose and was heard everywhere.

The new universalism I refer to is seeking to be heard in the discussion over the evolution of academic disciplines and professional conduct in a globalising world. Architecture is no exception. In the case of architecture, it is important to recognise that the new universalism is to be distinguished from the heyday of the modern movement – of Le Corbusier in India and Louis Kahn in Bangladesh – or the universalism of today's global markets with postmodern heroes marking distant territories with their distinctive flags. In such events the signification of a transcending modernity or of technological prowess can be seen to descend, as it were, from a superior realm of creativity with its grand narrative.

The new universalism adopts a diametrically opposite position. It has its roots in the 1960s, when John Turner was working with the barriadas of Peru, when John Habraken sought to make industrial production responsive to individual needs and when Christopher Alexander delineated the spatial codes of stable social structures. The 1960s and '70s were also the postcolonial era when climatology, intermediate technology and housing for the poor were formulated in the West into postgraduate courses for professionals and officials from the third world. Following on from this through the '70s and '80s, and I can speak of the Indian experience here, new schools of architecture in the developing countries developed curricula based on the same concerns, with an added dimension of evolving cultural identities from rich vernacular traditions.

From the 1990s onwards much of the developing world changed dramatically. The liberalisation of economies to attract global capital and their integration into international trade has brought about rapid economic growth. This growth is characterised by an urban-centric economy of, on the one side an enriched middle class, and on the other a proliferation of unorganised settlements of poor migrants into big cities. The surge of upmarket urban development under an 'international' business model has been attracting the attention of the professional community away from the critical issues of sustainable habitat and spatial justice. But it is commendable that the schools of architecture, certainly in India, are paying serious attention to the new challenges of increasing income disparities and environmental stress.

In the academic institutions of developed countries, amongst their students and young professionals, there is a complementary concern and interest that is also becoming evident. I refer to my recent experience as a member of the jury for the Holcim Awards for Sustainable Construction, which has a global reach. The awards have a 'Next Generation' category for students and young professionals. There has been a stream of entries such as the one from Germany, proposing an in-situ redevelopment for slum communities in Mumbai, or the one from Finland proposing a model of urban regeneration in Shanghai to preserve cultural and social continuities. The Awards bear witness to the intellectual contribution of such work.

Maurice Mitchell's work as a teacher is part of this new universalism.

What we witness in Maurice Mitchell's work of several years with students of architecture is the new universalism holding its ground and establishing its place in the wide spectrum of architectural education. The learning of architectural design and its pedagogy, based as it is on the atelier model, acknowledges that the methods of design would be found according to the purposes of design. In its 'bottom up' approach Mitchell's studio provides a much needed interrogation of the dominant narrative of 'futuristic' design where resources are usually taken for granted or are conjured up as 'cutting-edge' and 'hi-tech' fixes where the user–client becomes a spectator. It tests the work of the designer and the role of the professional in the current context of development, which he aptly describes as a condition of 'rapid change and scarce resources'. It develops a responsive design methodology – of learning to work across cultures by building human bonds; of mapping the informal and latent resources within 'disadvantaged' communities and instigating innovation within the limits of available resources through the physical act of making. Above all, it directs the imagination into an empathetic capability to express the aspirations and new identities of community through an architecture of positive change. Imagination, by definition, cannot be constrained, what matters are the purposes to which it chooses to apply its freedom.

Professor Ashok Lall
New Delhi
March 2010

Our Department at London Metropolitan University is committed to finding ways of reconnecting students with their duties as citizens first and professionals second. We test this commitment with the simple question: to who or what do you owe your 'duty of care'? The answers are as varied as our many teachers and students. But over the past ten years, the work of Maurice Mitchell, his colleagues and his students has played a key part in this agenda: first during their work in Kosovo in the immediate aftermath of the war, and more recently in India which is the work documented here.

The work has many implications for those taking part and those benefiting directly from its outcomes, but I want to focus on the effect it has on the students. By the time an architectural student reaches the later years of their education they have become experts in the mediated, specialist culture of architecture but have become distanced from their direct responses to more humble situations and people. The work in India lead by Maurice Mitchell, helps students to refocus and find more visceral and accountable ways of working. Students are reanimated by their experience and find a renewed confidence in their ability as proto-practitioners.

In every case their experience in Unit 6 informs their future practice. Some students return to India and work in ways related to their experience as students. But of course, the majority return to more conventional forms of practice closer to home. All carry with them the gentle bravery formed in India, which helps them to become more effective in engaging with and finding practical responses to social deprivation and inequality wherever they find it. We can hope that in time these graduates will begin to find new ways of dealing with the pressing social issues we face in Britain. This will be one of the hidden but intriguing legacies of the work contained in this book. Perhaps in the next one we will be Learning from Hackney or West Belfast?

On behalf of the University I want to thank all those who have contributed to the work in India. To Maurice Mitchell, his teaching colleagues and our partners in India, but most of all to our students whose optimism, clarity and pragmatism are a source of immense optimism for the future.

Professor Robert Mull
London Metropolitan University
June 2010

Introduction

The inflexibility of modern urban planning, which seeks to determine the activities of urban inhabitants and standardise everyday city life, is challenged by the unstoppable, unplanned growth of illegal settlements. This is a global phenomenon (Davis 2006). In rapidly expanding cities, issues of continuity with local traditions, local conditions and local ways of working are juxtaposed with those of abrupt change due to emergency, modernity, environmental degradation, global market forces and global technological imperatives. These often combine to make efforts by the authorities to control urban growth by physical planning, redundant as soon as master plans are published.

In most developing world cities there is little social welfare and almost no attempt at social housing. The urban poor must still house themselves with little or no state help to procure land or infrastructure. Not having a legal existence, 'slums' are automatically swept away to create a 'tabula rasa' prior to a complete new build for those who can afford the full cost. The notion of upgrading the existing built environment has hardly entered the official planning vocabulary.

Since 2002, both Diploma and latterly Degree students from London Metropolitan University Department of Architecture and Spatial Design have produced their portfolio schemes from research work generated during an annual 14-day November field trip to India. Work is focused on situations where rapid cultural and technical change is affecting traditional or transitional communities who have access to only limited resources. Sites have included post earthquake desert locations in Gujarat, under-serviced urban slums in Delhi, dense traditional city landscapes in Meerut and the integration of Marwari nomads into a settlement in Agra. This has proved a stimulating and provocative academic learning environment producing a range of innovative work. One of the students involved, Angela Hopcraft, won runner-up for the RIBA Silver Medal for the best UK diploma portfolio in 2006 and Valerie Saavedra Lux, a degree student, won RIBA Bronze Medal Commendation for her portfolio.

In the course of this enterprise, links with Indian non-governmental organisations and architectural schools have developed providing a wealth of opportunity for further work. The first live project based on studio work and funded anonymously, to provide sanitation to a low income urban village in Agra is now nearing completion. Two other live projects: for primary education in a stone quarry near Mumbai and for a housing cooperative in northwest Delhi, are ongoing.

The course has been groundbreaking and innovative in this area in that it seeks first to understand the cultural and physical patterns of old city labyrinths and illegal urban settlements before, and as an aid to, intervention. Extended physical and cultural surveys which update the 'diagnostic' surveys first employed by Patrick Geddes in the early 20th century are carried out by the students. By understanding the historical, cultural and physical factors which underlie the current city fabric, students are able to propose and validate a range of schemes from simple conservative surgery carried out by the community alone, to working alongside cultures of resistance to provide alternatives to planned projects. They have also shown how major infrastructure projects can be tweaked in practice to add greater potential to those who use them. Students design using a narrative approach to frame, capture and harness (however fleetingly) moments from the everyday to use as building blocks for their imagined proposals. Their schemes show how an untidy mix of the old and the new, of memory and aspiration can, in a spirit of experiment and curiosity, give unique identity to place.

Part 1: Setting the Scene
traces the background to the studio work and reviews working methods in two chapters.

Chapter 1: Field Research
reviews fieldwork booklets produced by the students and the scope and relevance of this empirical enterprise for the architectural investigation of the everyday.

Chapter 2: Methods (and Modernity)
investigates the narrative methodology of the studio and sets it within a historical and creative framework. It constructs the theoretical context within which student endeavour is initiated and supported.

Part 2: Essays
reflects back through a series of essays on themes which have emerged from the work of the studio in India.

Chapter 3: Delhi's 'Slums': Red Lines and High Walls
reviews the historical development of a range of illegal settlements in Delhi and reflects on the different ways that city dwellers without adequate means have provided themselves with shelter.

Chapter 4: The Waste Pickers of Panchsheel Vihar
focuses on the historical landscape of a part of the fourth (of seven) cities of Delhi. It shows how the physical landscape has been recycled a number of times and then describes the current inhabitants: a community of Waste Pickers within which students have sited a number of schemes. This chapter speculates on the extent to which the re-use and recycling of waste can provide an opportunity for social mobility in the waste picking community.

Chapter 5: Havelis and the Conglomerate Matrix
reviews the growth of traditional and unplanned urban settlements in India and characterises the physical morphology of such settlements. It then describes the values and qualities associated with this urban form and compares them with those associated with more recent modern urban morphologies.

Chapter 6: Urban Nomads
reviews the everyday working lives of the Marwari community in Agra. The Marwaris are an example of a number of wandering peoples who supply urban markets and provide pavement entertainment n India who are steadily being encouraged to become

sedentary. The chapter discusses issues of cultural and physical integration with the wider urban community within a rapidly changing urban context. It assesses the unusual short life building fabric employed by the Marwaris to construct their shelters and looks at appropriate shelter provision for the future.

Chapter 7: Climate, Density and Construction

looks at how, within contemporary illegal and unplanned settlements, comfort and conviviality are mixed within the dense urban landscape. It goes on to describe the emergence of a particular 'slum' house type and assesses its role in the alleviation of physical discomfort and overcrowding. It finishes by describing the adoption and adaption of this type of house design within a cooperative housing scheme in a resettlement area of Delhi.

Chapter 8: Place, Space and Services

explores emergent urban place-making within the context of inadequate urban sanitary provision. It reviews the process of place-making during the implementation of an alternative low-cost community sanitation initiative derived from student schemes and now being transformed into reality.

Chapter 9: The Relevance for Architectural Education in the UK

summarises the pedagogy discussed in the book and its application to the live projects which have been derived from studio work. The chapter also explores the relevance of the studio's approach within the debate about architectural education which is currently underway within the architectural community in the UK.

Part 3: A Catalogue of Selected Student Schemes and Live Projects

annotates selected student schemes for review within the critical framework of the essays in Parts 1 and 2. The schemes in this catalogue are derived from a careful study of both the immediate physical landscape and particular sociocultural context of the situation first experienced during the annual two-week field study. This context is recorded during the field study so that it can be used later as a resource in the student's scheme design. In addition the legitimacy of the scheme proposals are derived directly from this study rather than from building codes or planning guidelines. Proposals are always intended as an 'improvement' as defined by the ambition and needs of the individuals and families who occupied the study area bounded by the place-making potential of the site itself. Usually, at the very least, the current meagre supply of public space was enlarged and access to clean water supply and individualised sanitation increased.

Nearly all the settlements studied were illegally occupied. With the exception of the live project in Kuchhpura, Agra any attempt to realise any of the hypothetical student schemes would have fallen foul of the ownership question and might have lead to the displacement of the community studied: the opposite of the intended outcome. Thus, students regarded the people they studied as their clients and assumed for the purpose of their schemes that owner occupation would somehow be achieved, often sketching out an optimistic scenario of how this might happen.

Cities are in a process of constant renewal. The piecemeal re-use and adaptation of the existing urban fabric in an attempt to match the changing aspirations of its inhabitants is cost effective, environmentally sustainable and appropriate.

Learning from Delhi is about the application of the architectural imagination to the process of changing and upgrading particular urban settlements in northern India. It is also a testimony to the value of linking real, live projects with architectural education in the studio for students studying in the UK. The methods and working techniques employed, however, have relevance for educationalists and architectural practitioners who are trying to 'think global and act local' whilst operating with few resources in rapidly changing cities throughout the world.

chapter 1

Field Research

Every year since 2002, each cohort of students have produced a booklet of their two-week fieldwork in India. This chapter reviews the scope of this work and its relevance for the architectural investigation of the everyday.

So why does a studio in a UK school of architecture base its design projects in low income settlements in India?

Students measure and document the physical and cultural context, interact with local residents, experience culture shock and, in the process, learn how to make Kanda and organise cricket games. Confronted with the difficulty of communicating without knowledge of Hindi or Urdu, students often have to rely on methods of non-verbal communication based solely on the profound richness of their raw observations. At first these attempts to communicate might prove difficult. How do you explain non-verbally that you are not a government worker, that you are here for purely educational purposes and do not intend to interfere with the running of the community? Sometimes such issues have been solved by simply arranging introductions to community representatives via a local non-government organisation, and occasionally this has been necessary for effective working. However some of the most insightful exchanges are those organised directly by the students themselves, often with the help of curious, energetic children but without direct, outside help.

Because of the language barrier and the lack of familiarity, students have to listen, question and decipher much more intensively than they would have had to do for a project based in London:

Surprises lay behind every physical or metaphorical corner. It is easy to take the environment and culture for granted in your own society – working in India was a wake-up call. Maybe some of us went with the intention to change the world with big gestures. Yes, the settlements have problems with their sanitation systems, few children go to school and the health care is often basic. But more importantly we encountered an extraordinarily rich and hospitable culture and people (Note 1, p. 3).

As part of their fieldwork students are asked to propose a design idea, a metaphor which would lead later in the year to an individual studio design project. A collection of some of these design ideas, which provide a powerful summary typology of the students' spatial experience in India are summarised in this chapter, but first: a review of both the physical mapping and cultural exercises undertaken by the students to construct an understanding of place and space with some theoretical grounding for the methods employed.

student measuring levels with a homemade theolodite
Edward Ridge

Mapping: Physical Surveys

(1) Accuracy
Right from the start of their field trip, students are usually worried about the accuracy of the maps they produce. In Agra they had the benefit of a government map drawn for tax purposes which they found, when checked on the ground, to be highly inaccurate. Another base map had originally been drawn by the women of Kuchhpura to keep track of pregnant mothers and newborn children and proved more reliable. In South Delhi the Delhi Jal Board (Water Board) was able to provide an accurate map of the area of investigation which failed completely to represent the unauthorised settlements under

first viewing points for sketch survey Soami
Nagar Camp
Yanira de Armas-Tosco

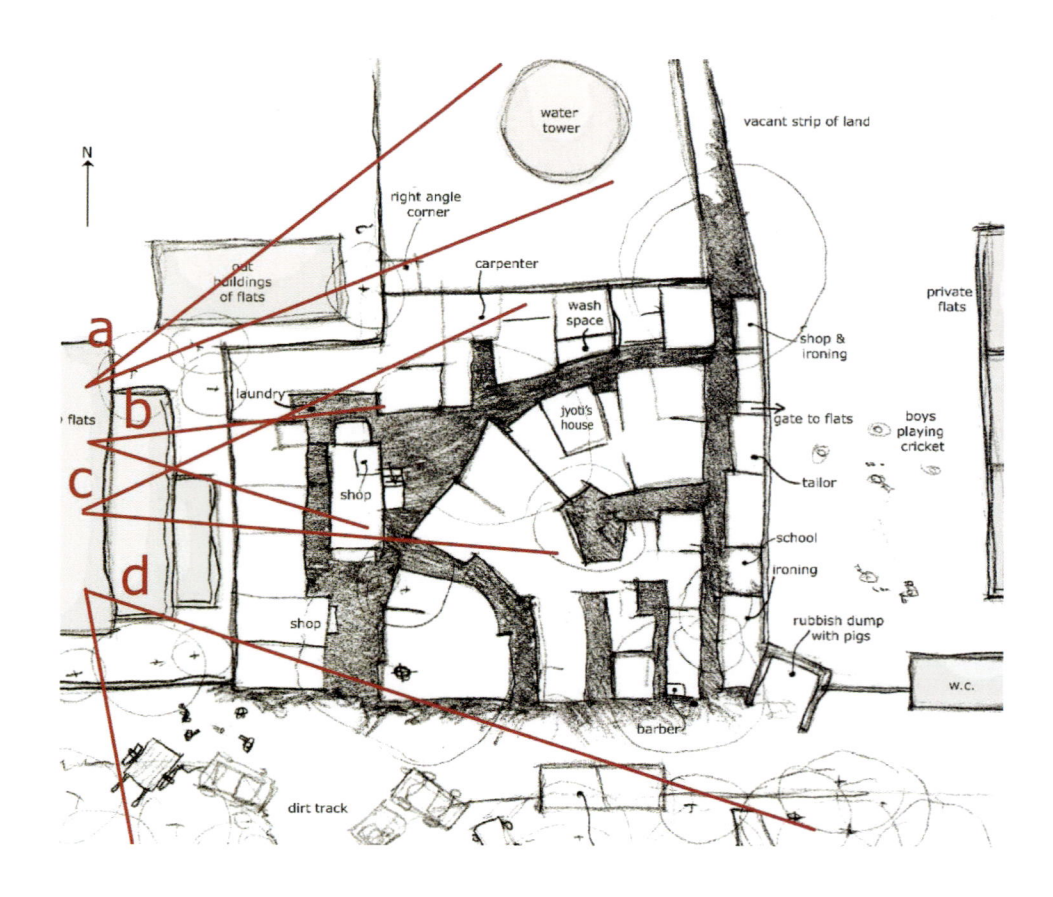

study. They were just left as blanks on the sheet; a form of contemporary 'terra incognito' waiting to be explored. In Meerut, students obtained a detailed map of the old city drawn up by the colonial authorities towards the end of the nineteenth century and still being used today by the Meerut City Council: very accurate, but also out of date and missing a century of change.

In the last few years the availability of Google Earth has transformed the students' ability to set out the main vectors of the unauthorised and previously unmapped settlements but even here buildings are often obscured from the satellite camera by tree canopies and the image resolution is often insufficient to pick up the details of place even at the strategic level.

In fact, on the ground, students have made every attempt to measure accurately but this was always a real challenge given very little surveying equipment and no previously established fixed coordinates. To overcome this, a range of innovative surveying tools was developed by the students including trundle wheels, theolodites, measuring sticks and the calibration of elevational photographs by including a measured child, Souraj, in each image. But this would not do for long distances:

The longest road was almost a mile long … then a boy on a bicycle rode past … he agreed to measure the road's length using the revolutions of the front wheel. A small crowd formed. Chalk outlines at the start and finish were drawn to make it seem more like a race. Later we referred to Google Earth and found our measurements spot on (Note 1, p. 33).

One particular survey of the Soami Nagar J.J. (Jhuggie-Jhonpri) camp by Yanira de Armas -Tosco (2004 and 2005) was begun with the misapprehension that the area being

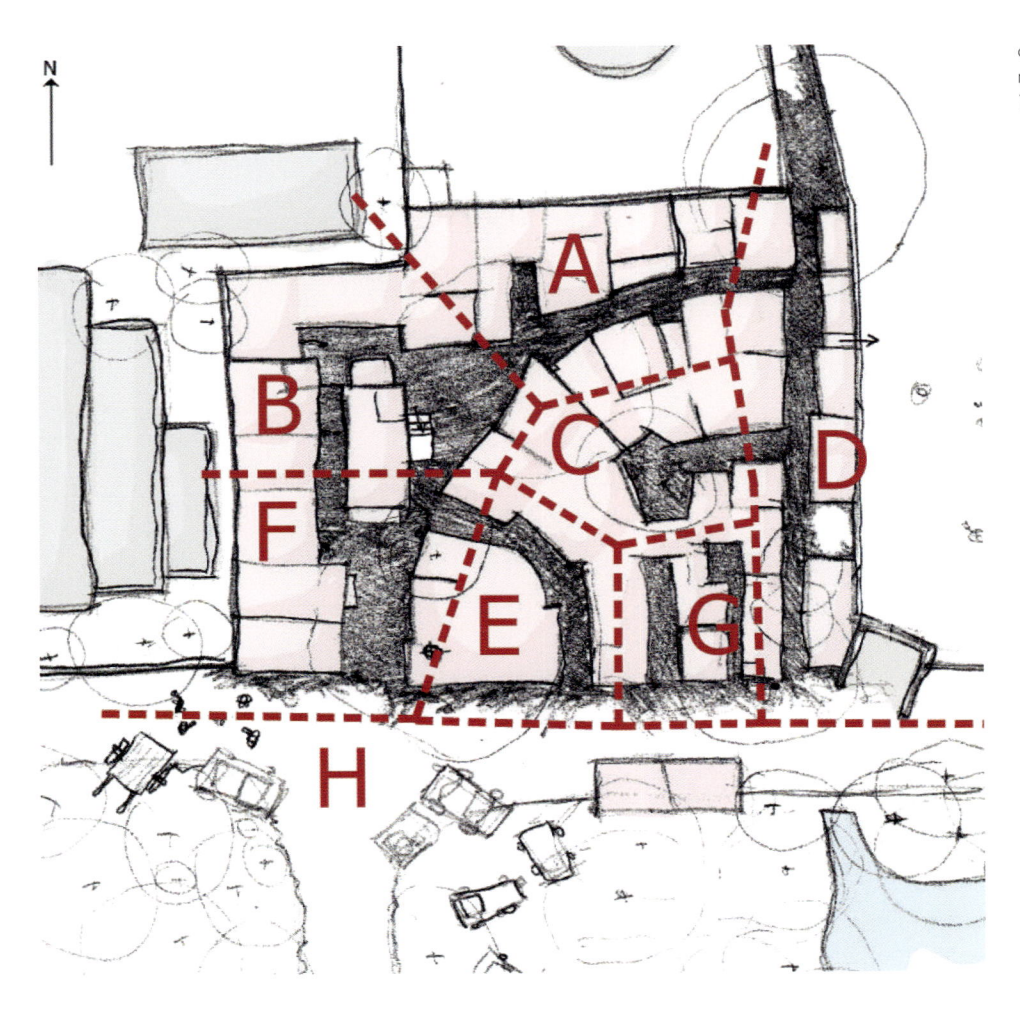

division of Soami Nagar Camp into
neighbourhood survey areas
Yanira de Armas-Tosco

measured was roughly square on plan but as soon as the team began assembling their
information they noticed huge flaws and began once again, using the geometrical analysis
of compass bearings taken at height, to give an overall framework to their more detailed
survey measurements, methods pioneered by the early surveyors of colonial India (Keay
2000):

Bearings of major landmarks around the site were taken using a compass. There were very few
sightlines through the camp so we had to climb trees and stand on roofs. Even then the density
of the tree cover made it difficult to be accurate. Bearings were also taken of the direction of
every street and all major walls to help tie all the detailed information together.

Overall street dimensions were then taken on the ground with a long measure which we
constructed out of knotted string and some sticks. A detailed survey for each street was then
carried out using a tape measure. Cross and diagonal check measurements were also recorded.

Information on the internal layouts of the houses was recorded along with the locations of beds,
cookers, coolers and TVs (2).

Returning in 2005, Yanira found that there had been many alterations and extensions to
the settlement in the intervening year. Some dwellings had grown a storey and temporary
dwellings had been rebuilt in more permanent materials. The settlement seemed to be
growing and changing before her eyes. Added to the student-led imperative for accurate

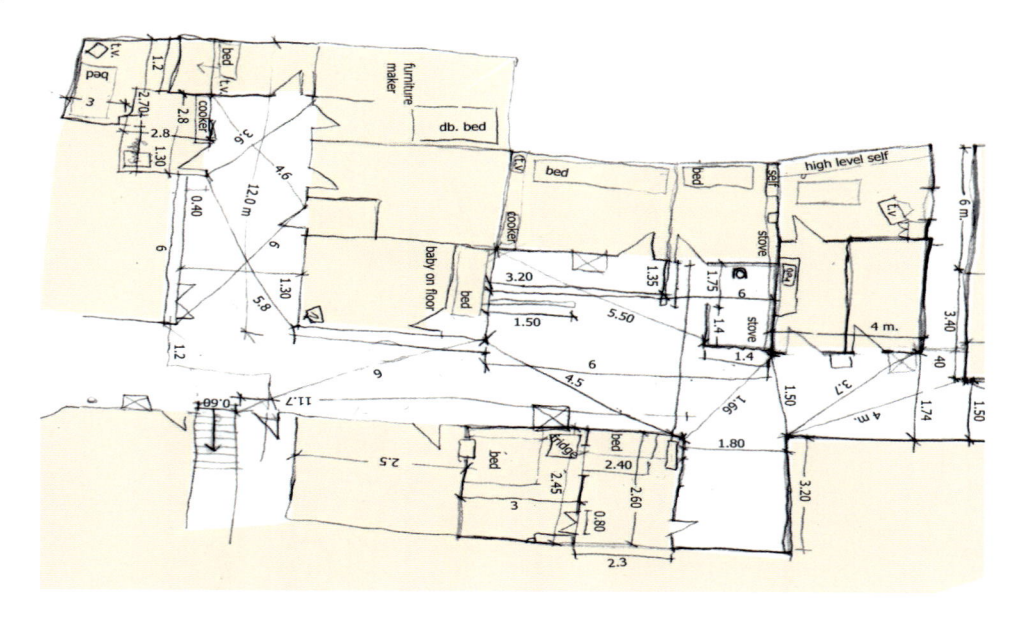

representation in three dimensions was the need to record a 4th dimension: the speed of change.

Students were concerned to record as real and precise a set of physical dimensions as possible despite the rapid changes and the ephemeral nature of some of the objects and spaces they were measuring. It was sometimes hard to make judgments about appropriate scales to represent recorded measurements: when to focus down and enquire further and when to pull back and take a more strategic view. Given that in many cases settlements were being mapped for the first time and that the non-government organisation with whom the studio was working was likely to make use of their maps, students were concerned about their own responsibility for the accuracy of their surveys:

We are designing small projects on sites in four, unauthorised settlements based on our analysis, physical records and interaction with the residents. The information we collected is purely for this purpose. It is not sufficient or appropriate for official purposes and even though we have made every effort to ensure that it is precise, we cannot guarantee this (notes 1 and 3).

Learning from examples of student work from earlier years, more recent students have been able to perfect their hands-on survey techniques. Mapping the densely packed, multi-storied and crowded building mass of Chirag Delhi offered one of the greatest challenges.

Here, the tightly-packed and irregular buildings were criss-crossed by a web of narrow streets and alleyways. In response to the size and complexity, a team of six students, worked in pairs surveying at different levels of detail. Detailed surveys of the main squares were linked by a spider's web of triangulated measurements taken along the alleyways:

This involved recording all the distances that made up the perimeter of the chowks using a measuring tape and marked up string for the longer spans. This was always a challenge as we were often the centres of attention, but soon the local kids became a cooperative rather than a disruptive influence on the measuring. By triangulating distances we were then able to pinpoint the location of trees and other structures within the chowks. We took level heights we could

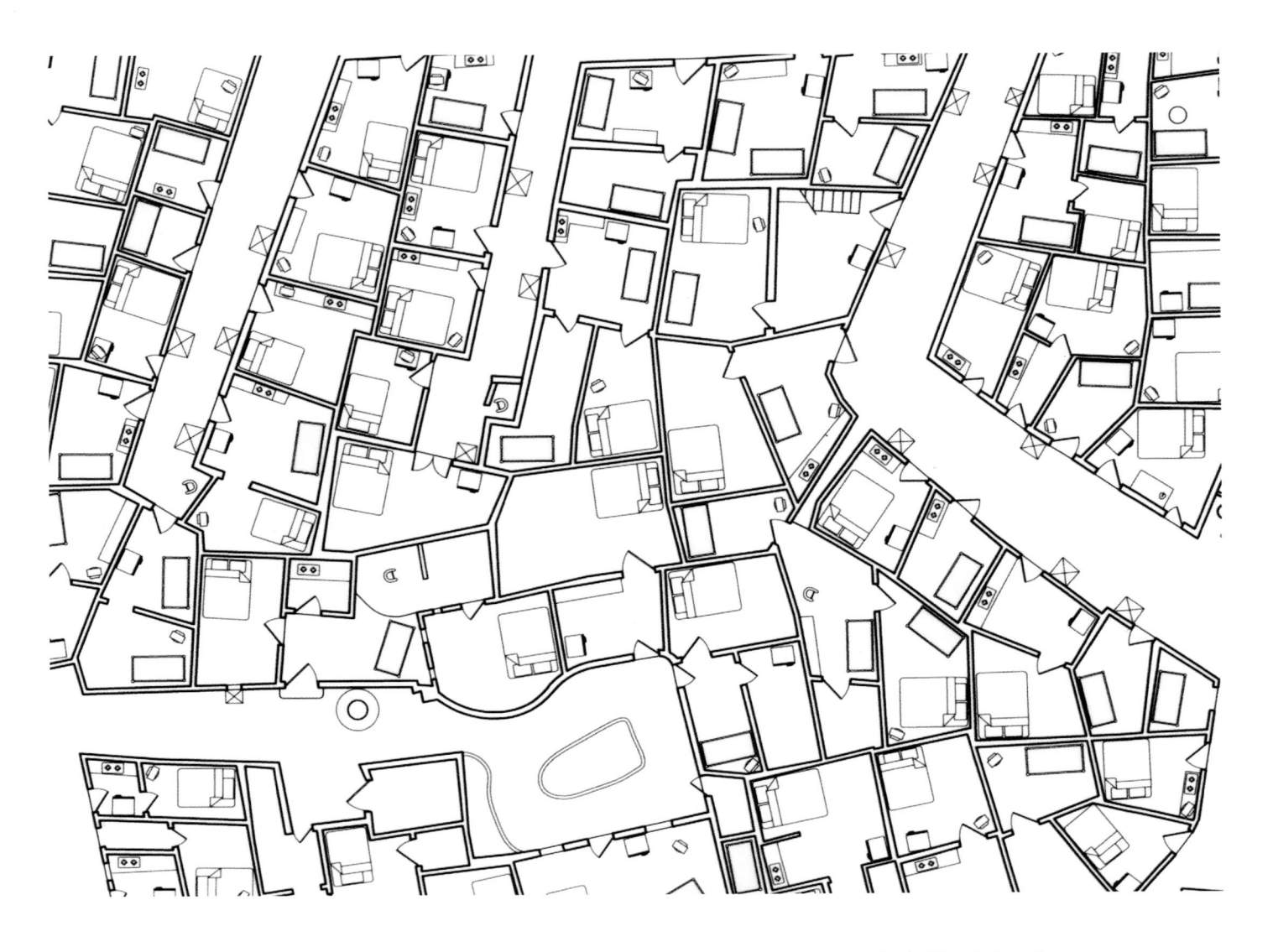

detail of Soami Nagar Camp survey
Yanira de Armas-Tosco

reach with the tape to inform sections and elevations [recorded in photographs] around the perimeter and later using an inclinometer to take several key block heights from surrounding buildings. By staggering readings to get around corners, this tool allowed us to track the change in levels from the central Dargah chowk to the town's perimeter. By pacing out distances and sketching while walking we managed to piece it together bit by bit. We also found that by accessing rooftops we were able to develop the map more accurately and add information covering building heights (2).

The supposed reliability of measurements is in contrast to the immeasurable qualities inherent in recording cultural exchanges covered later. Sometimes the two went hand in hand as a clear task of measurement often provided access to the community.

… every single family welcomed us into their houses to measure and Rahul was able to interview many people while Helen and Yanira ran around with the tape measure (2).

(2) Morphological Tales

Nick Maari recognised in the topography of the poor, illegal and overwhelmingly Sikh, East Delhi settlement called Kalyanpuri Block 19/20, which he surveyed in 2007, the physical expression of what Evans has called 'the terrors of over communion' (Evans 1997, p. 42). In Delhi he felt that the main issue was that:

right
overall plan of Soami Nagar J.J. Camp
Yanira de Armas-Tosco
facing page
mapping Chirag Delhi
Amy Penford and Emre Turkmen

There was too much of everything going on, too much noise, too many people, too many cars, too many rickshaws, too much poverty, too much extravagant wealth and too much garbage (4).

Nick's original impression was that Block 19/20 was a typical example of a poor, gated community where the lowest class was hidden away from the middle and upper classes. But as the survey progressed the emerging patterns revealed a more complex, and at times sinister, narrative.

Kalyanpuri Block 19/20 is discussed in more detail in Chapter 3, however it is sufficient here to state that it consists of a walled enclosure packed with single-roomed houses served by a maze of narrow winding alleys. In 1984, following the murder of Mrs Gandhi, the then Indian prime minister, by her Sikh bodyguards, there was a period of intense communal rioting in Delhi. The riots were at their worst in the Kalyanpuri area and many of the members of the Sikh families in Block 19/20 were killed. This event has scarred the lives of the current inhabitants and explains the continued presence of the perimeter wall. The justification for the construction of this defensive and impenetrable maze provided students with an insight into the topographical implications of separation by caste, class or wealth. The desire to seal off difference was matched by the opposing wish of the victims for safe retreat behind a solid wall.

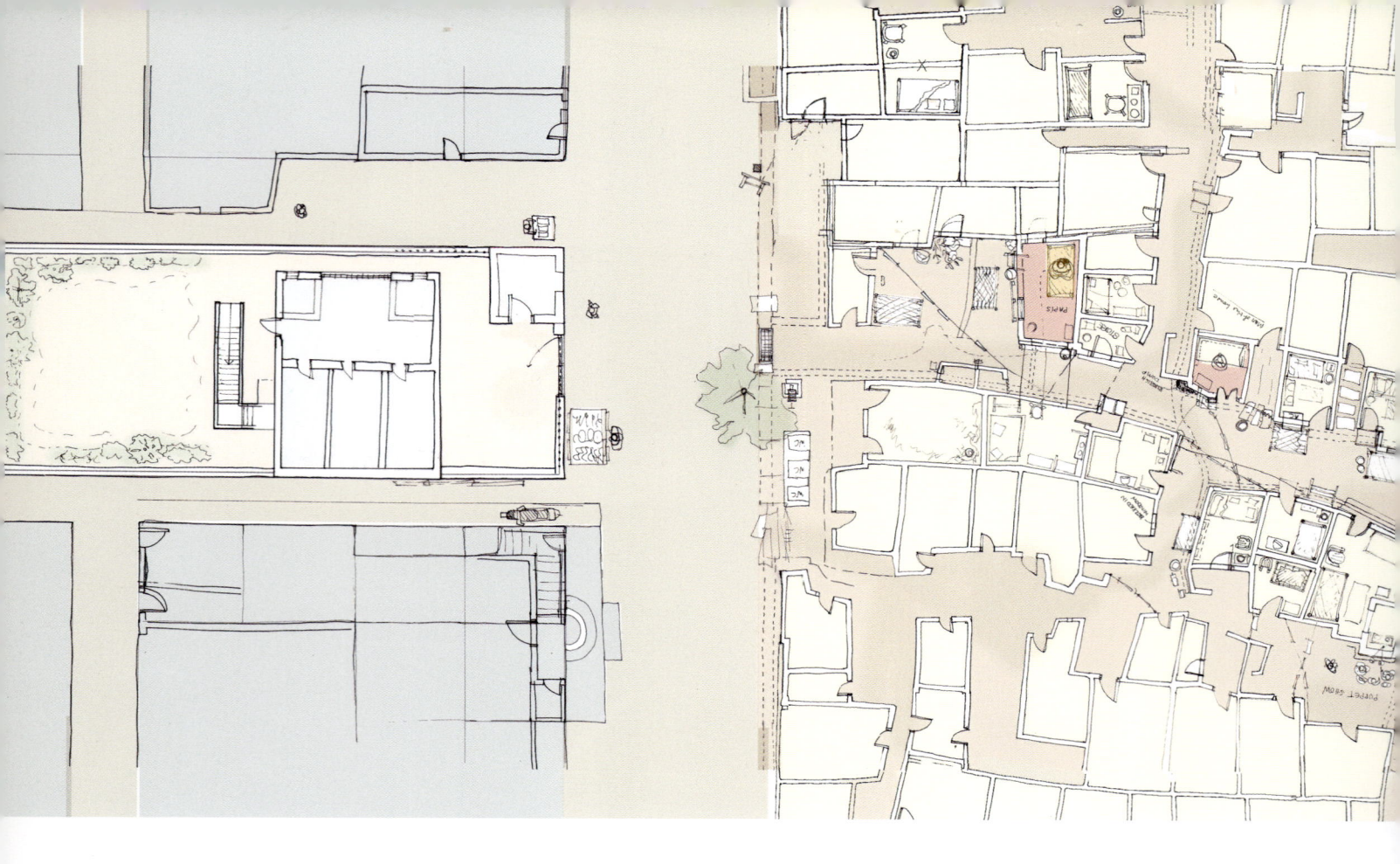

Just as an eye irritated and plagued by a piece of grit will encapsulate it in a soft sheath of frictionless excretion, so human beings will deal with others of their own kind by whom they feel threatened by enclosing them in inoffensive brick – and doing so with a natural lack of remorse that tempts us to believe that this behaviour too is biologically sanctioned (Evans 1997, p. 42).

Within the enclosure, clusters and terraces are assembled from single celled habitations, one per family, and each approximately 2.5 x 3.5 metres in plan, surrounded on three sides by adjoining walls and opening on to an alley or court from the fourth side. All communal activity takes place in the alley. All spaces are multivalent, not differentiated according to function. The primary physical threshold is at the entrance to the settlement, at the wall: not on entry to the alley or the room, where boundaries are flexible according to the time of day and individual routine, established by custom, convention and symbol.

(3) Two Examples of Psycho-geographically Discovered Space in Meerut

Example (1) Rooftop Realms

In Old Meerut (2003) students lived in a traditional family haveli (see Chapter 5) and had access to the roof. Finding it difficult to navigate the narrow streets to locate potential sites, Carolos Efstathiou and Konstantinos Poulopoulos, encouraged by a nimble neighbour, chose to survey the adjoining rooftops instead. An excerpt from their daily diary indicates the other-worldly experience of this survey:

Rooftop walk at sunrise; monkeys; misty views of distant towers; old broken down shelters being taken away; alley jumps; guide shows footholds; walk on parapets like cats as roof unsafe;

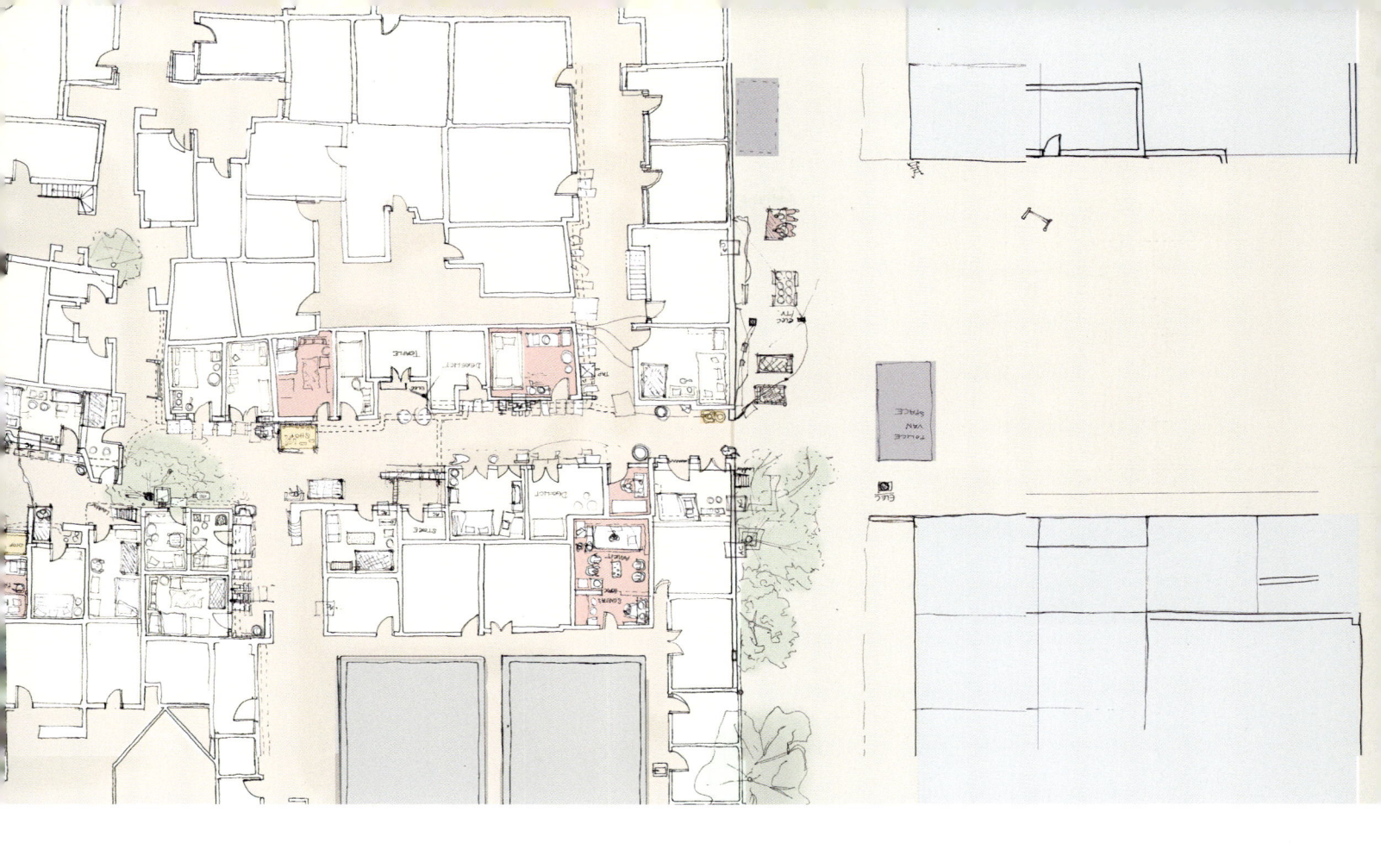

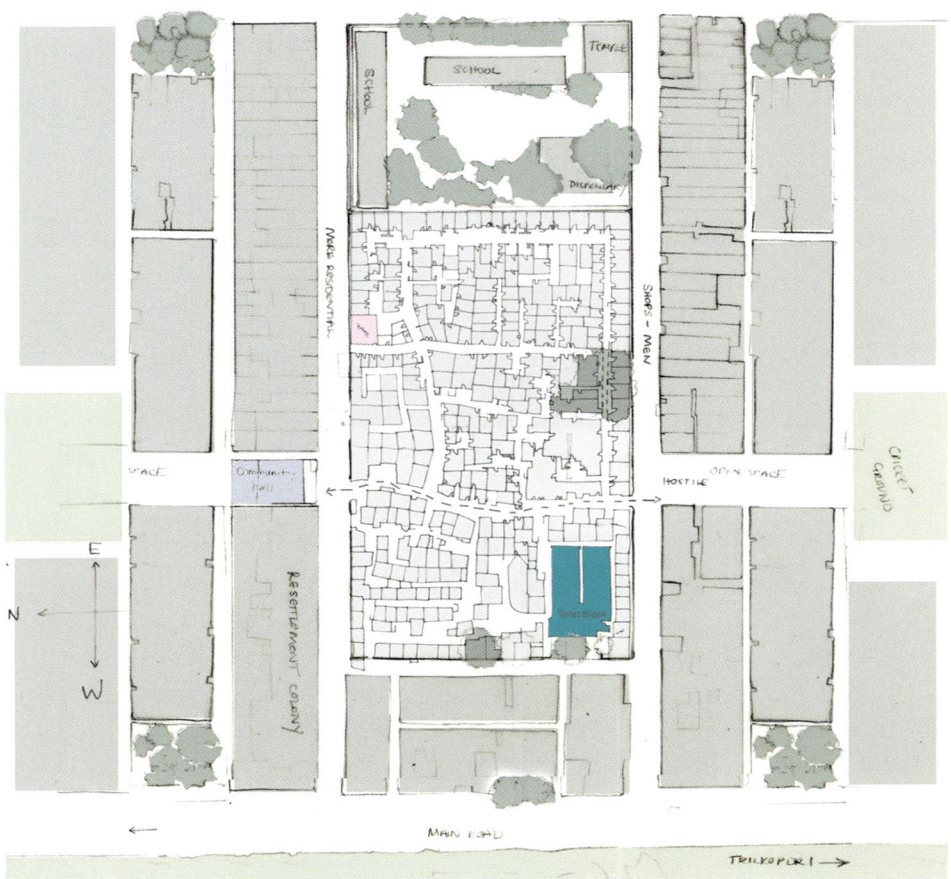

main image
plan of only the lane through Kalyanpuri Block 19/20
Amelia Rule
left
overall plan of Kalyanpuri Block 19/20
Amelia Rule

above
surveying Meerut Rooftops
Carolos Efstathiou and Konstantinos Poulopoulos
right
Meerut rooftop survey drawing
Carolos Efstathiou
below
children bound by friendship and family playing
on a rooftop realm

pigeon fancying; kite festivals on August 25th and June 16th; bet of RS 3,000 on cutting kite strings; network of paths; people at different heights (5).

Whilst it was possible in theory to access most of Old Meerut in this way by jumping over the narrow alleys below; in practice, passage was limited by the necessity to obtain the permission of the house owners and occupants living below, as well as the need to navigate crumbling parapets. So the resulting map represented friendly rooftop territory surrounding the haveli, a common ground amongst neighbours. Sometimes the boundaries were those between rooftops owned by proprietors of competing pigeon flocks or kite enthusiasts but more often they were defined by ties of friendship or family. So this survey delineated a geography of space bounded as much by social linkages as by physical limits. Within this concept of the social bounding of space was an idea about a type of space which was larger than the haveli but smaller than the neighbourhood; one of many such potential sites dotted around the rooftops of Meerut.

In naming these rooftop realms and postulating a potential array of such spaces the studio might be accused of commodifying the previously ephemeral. In Henri Lefebvre's terms, students were in danger in explicitly representing these previously hidden or undefined spaces, of turning them into objects for everyday consumption by defining their form and structure in order to allocate a useful function (Lefebvre 1997, p. 33). This rush to functionality has proved to be reductive, producing banal repetitive proposals.

The best student schemes were produced, however, by those who were able to sustain the experiences of their early surveys, reserving any attempt at proposing function, preferring instead to simply record the spaces as revealed by their five senses with a view to sharing this experience with others. This emphasis on the representation and communication of the lived experience of physical landscape, of discovering the unique within the everyday whilst at the same time holding back on functional exploitation, seems to be a precondition for design quality.

Example (2) The Depression: combed street boundaries and watersheds

In order to understand the meaning of apparently unique physical events within the landscape, more detective work is sometimes required particularly when trying to understand how such physical anomalies come about and whether causal processes are still in motion. Upscaling to the general from the particular and using the specific as a metaphor for general application is only remotely possible if these processes have triggered similar events elsewhere.

Seeking to escape the claustrophobic streets and unbelievably dense population of Old Meerut, Eunah Kim chose to investigate the more recent settlement of Brahmpuri built around a series of streets radiating to the south west from the base of the low hill on which the old city stood and parallel to the main Delhi road. Branching out at regular intervals, on both sides of these residential streets were a series of dead-ended lanes. Wandering down these lanes Eunah discovered a steep sided depression about 2.5 metres lower than the surrounding land which marked the end of four or five cul-de-sacs on both its northwest and southeast sides. Intrigued by the 'depression', she mapped the contours, noticing that houses were constructed on the cliff edges with raised floors to make them level with others in the higher lanes. From conversations with residents she found that the whole of Brahmpuri was liable to flooding. In the monsoon season the

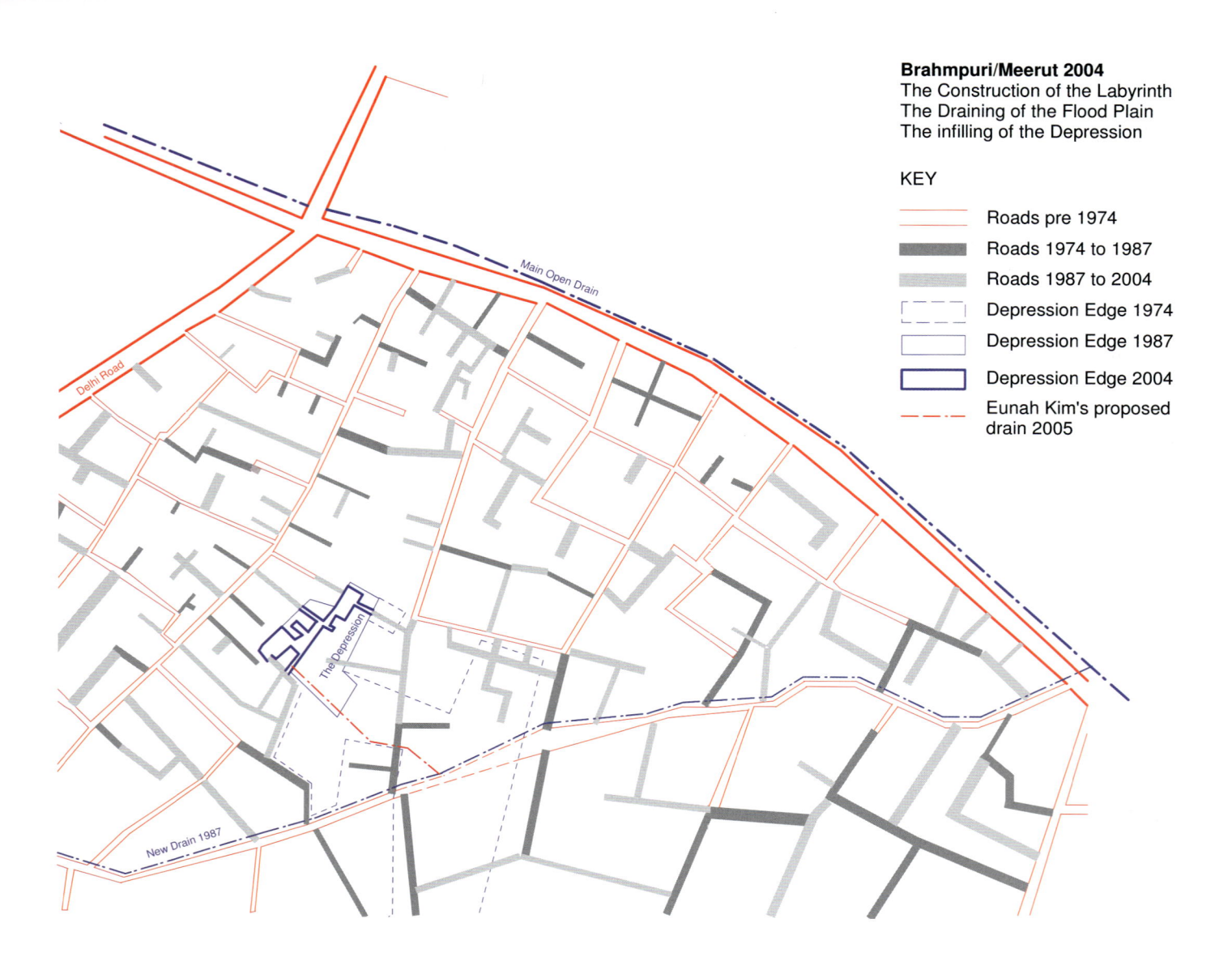

Brahmpuri/Meerut 2004
The Construction of the Labyrinth
The Draining of the Flood Plain
The infilling of the Depression

KEY

———	Roads pre 1974
▬▬▬	Roads 1974 to 1987
▬▬▬	Roads 1987 to 2004
⌐ ¬	Depression Edge 1974
☐	Depression Edge 1987
☐	Depression Edge 2004
– · – ·	Eunah Kim's proposed drain 2005

A walk down the dead-end lanes of Brahmpuri
Eunah Kim

main drain around the base of the Old Meerut hill blocked and inundated the hinterland. Whilst, because of its relative height, Old Meerut was known for its healthy atmosphere, these undulating back lands had apparently always been low lying and malarial. For this reason, even though Meerut is one of the most densely occupied cities of India, this land had been left untouched whilst surrounding higher land became densely occupied. Eventually, in the early 1970s population pressure was such that residential development had begun without the infrastructure necessary to avoid annual flooding.

However, the city authorities were struggling with the problem and a relief drain had been constructed in 1984 which moderated the annual flood. Eunah obtained access to maps which showed Brahmpuri in 1973 and 1984. She updated these maps to show the situation in 2003. It became apparent that the primary streets giving access to the settlement had been built on low 'ridges'; and in their turn the secondary lanes had been laid over top-fill, raised up above the floodplain to reduce vulnerability and abruptly truncated when they reached the edge of the 'depression'. In 1973, in the early years of settlement, the 'depression' had been much broader and had gradually been filled in, raising the land above flood level and occasionally allowing through lanes to connect the parallel streets, helping to unify the settlement.

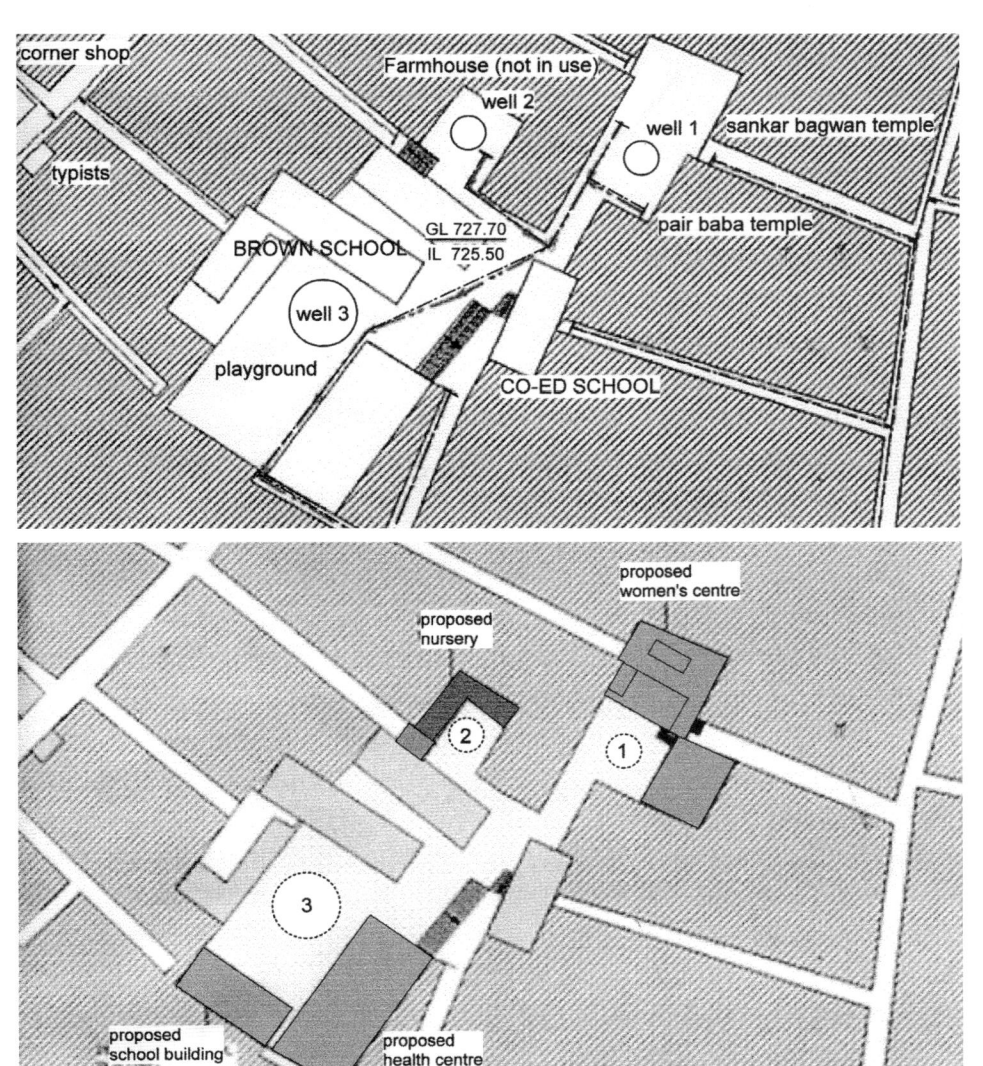

top
Venetian well and drainage scheme for the 'depression'
Eunah Kim
bottom
stitching dead-ends together with new community buildings
Eunah Kim

Eunah, by dint of careful enquiry and judicious choice of survey method, had uncovered a unique moment in the physical history of Brahmpuri. The last vestiges of the depression were about to be smoothed over. If this happened all traces of the original flood plain would then be removed; the pattern of development would be regularised and one part of Brahmpuri would end up being much like the rest. Eunah's scheme was based on her sensitivity to the unique qualities of place latent in the remaining part of the 'depression'. This was an accessible, but car free sectional idea where drinking water shortages could be alleviated by collecting rainwater and where the scale of the remaining 'depression' suggested occupation by a community sized institution rather than the projection of the surrounding residential lanes. This particular opportunity would soon be lost, however, if infilling continued, but could easily be realised if only the depression were to be adequately drained by a short length of pipework to the nearby City Council relief drain, now available to the southeast.

Is this unique moment quite so unique, and is there an opportunity for place-making based on the physical characteristics of 'depressions' found elsewhere?

Himanshu Parik, the India group Director of Buro Happold Engineers has described how

there is a strong correlation between the distribution of the natural watersheds in a city and the areas inhabited by the poorest sections of the population:

New York also has the same pattern, except that on the natural drainage path you'll see Harlem, Queens, Bronx ... the distressed areas have a habit of being very closely associated with natural drainage paths ... the rivers, the streams, the creeks, the lakes, the ponds (Parikh 2004).

When, in mainstream developments, natural falls are ignored, ground is levelled and a planned carpet of settlement is laid out with mains water and sewerage lines, the resultant cost in pumping stations and treatment plants is very high. If, on the other hand, there is no attempt to provide a 'tabula rasa' and if both the settlement and infrastructure lines are laid out to fall with the land then trenches need be no more than 1.5 metres deep without the need for pumps. Parikh sees the poorer areas built later along the watersheds as an opportunity to service both the slums themselves and the earlier more regularised developments cheaply and efficiently. Seen in this way the poorer neighbourhoods are not parasites; they are city changing devices.

The sectional idea: dramatic height changes in dense urban neighbourhoods; may not facilitate car use but it does have other advantages. Once cleaned up, well-drained landscapes provide opportunities for water collection and storage. This water can be distributed to households in times of drought and be employed to green the city. Speaking of his work in Indore, Parikh describes how, after installing drains which followed the landscape:

... the riverbed started drying up because it was largely sewerage and rivers in India only flow in the monsoons. The rest of the year, they are dry and the bed is in fact drying up. We cleaned up the bed and started building dams so that when the monsoon comes you can catch it and at least then you have water during the monsoons and then afterwards you have a series of ponds and the city changes (Parikh 2004).

The discovery by Eunah Kim, through a heightened sense of curiosity, of a locally ignored but intriguing physical 'depression' led not only to her discovery of a set of architectural attributes associated with the space itself but also to the gradual realisation that such insights, given more strategic or even global concerns over car use, water consumption and public space within the city would have application elsewhere.

Cultural Exercises

The very act of measuring space, itself a performance by the students and entertainment for the local people, often provided the key which opened the door on a whole range of cultural exchanges giving insights into the relationship between people and space.

Sometimes sporting, drawing or language exchange events were explicitly organised by the students to provoke such cultural exchanges. Almost daily, students were invited into homes for tea and occasionally for a meal. Some students were invited as guests at weddings or to other festival events. Female students would be of particular interest to the women of the community and would often individually be invited by them to visit their homes and perhaps stay overnight. There they might dress up in traditional clothes and discuss their different life experiences.

Occasionally, students would organise the construction of a small, temporary structure or otherwise make minor changes to a building or space which would in itself provoke discussion and exchange.

(1) The Energy of Children

The catalysts for such exchanges were almost invariably the children of the community. Joanna de Berry has described how 'especially in a rapidly changing and dynamic city, young people's perspective on everyday life is very different to that of adults' (de Berry 2004). Working for Save the Children she got the children of Kabul to draw their own maps which illustrated their ambitions for a better life, their heightened fears over safety, especially the dangers of vehicular traffic, and their ways of interpreting and navigating the physical landscape. She shows how particular places, where accidents or other acts of violence have happened, can have a ghost-like quality provoking the children's terror. Many of these findings were confirmed in the previous work of the studio in Kosovo (Mitchell 2003) and indeed in India, albeit in a form modified by the Indian context.

Whilst not having had to face the extremes of war experienced by the children of Kabul or Kosovo, the children of the north Indian slums which the students studied have experienced their own ghosts:

A commuter train running along a track bordering Ambedkar Camp in Delhi would appear silently through the morning mist at one time of the year killing children defecating on the lines spreading terror and providing legendary escape stories ... Students pulled out a screaming eight-year-old child, who was waste deep in a black water drain in Jagdamba Camp and

the ghost train, Ambedkar Camp
Stephen Chown

washed her down ... Children pointed out the danger and helped fill in a large, collapsing communal septic tank in the illegal settlement of Block 19/20 Kalyanpuri (4).

Despite these hazards children have actively taken on roles and responsibilities to help sustain themselves and their families. Alongside adults, they too confront and overcome obstacles and in so doing make changes to their surroundings.

(2) New Routes, Realms and Gateways
For example, children have provided new access to the walled-in Jagdamba Camp. Home to 6,000 slum dwellers, this illegal settlement is lodged in a half-kilometre-long natural drainage channel running west to east between two retaining walls which are about 40 metres apart. The settlement has just two entrances, both pedestrian only: one at the west end and one at the east end. Children have burrowed away under the enclosing walls and in one case have completely broken down part of the wall giving access to unoccupied woodland to the north. They have colonised this forest for play space and forged a new, but hidden route to the main road.

In another example, children led students up a wobbly bamboo ladder, above the dense, narrow alleys of the largely single-storey slum settlement of Kalyanpuri Block 19/20 to experience the long rooftop views. This was a novel world where you had to be nimble to follow your guide, jumping from roof to roof, shouting to other children several blocks away, eventually chasing each other whilst at the same time avoiding lines of laundry and piles of firewood. Here, kites were flown and pigeon lofts were located. Here also students discovered isolated bamboo shacks inhabited by older people hiding from the hustle and bustle of life on the streets.

children with bat as trophy, Khirki Mosque
Amy Penford

(3) Separation

In contrast to the children studied by de Berry, those befriended by the students seemed to be culturally and economically divided from one another. Even in the bottom of the dried-up moat of Khirki mosque where the children loved to play cricket, boys from different sides of the mosque did not play with each other. Students organised a joint cricket game intending to bring these disparate groups together. From this game a conversation developed about the surrounding spaces, about the bats and squirrels that lived in the mosque and the flock of parakeets which would land from time to time in one of the courts. To help with communication, students began to draw these animals and birds, inviting the boys to comment and contribute when suddenly:

… one of the boys ducked in to the Masjid [mosque] and returned with a bat in his hands. He proceeded to spread its wings. Half shocked and half grasping for the camera [the students] photographed the moment. The Khirki boys were so impressed at the reaction that they paraded the bat like a trophy. Terri [one of the students] had intended to discuss the squirrels that lived in the mosque walls but stopped her drawing hand on the paper as she felt that a helpless squirrel might be the next target. This commotion however did bring a trio of sisters over to us – Jyoti and her sisters Roshni and Dupika (note 2, p. 10).

Young girls tend to stay with their mother at the threshold to the house or visit each other at their homes, so involving these three girls in the conversation was an unusual event which led to an invitation for tea by a young woman in a turquoise blue sari and a red choli who was passing by at the time:

… she took us through a gate which said KK44 Painter and was the same blue as her sari. We went up a set of concrete steps and on to an outside terrace … we entered her nine square metre room, the entire apartment … she took a gas burner from the corner out onto the terrace … she showed us how to make masala chai … adding the different ingredients in turn … she had a beautiful set of matching cups – green with a chocolate brown rim … served on a stainless steel tray … her sister appeared from nowhere in a green sari with a pink choli. We talked about her job, her family and her daily routines (note 2, p. 10).

Once above school age, boys and girls did not generally play together. State schooling itself, intended in most societies as a great leveller of social and wealth divisions, often remained divisive and conformist. In the process of organising drawing sessions for the children of waste pickers and their neighbours in Panchsheel Vihar, students found that waste picker children were not admitted to the local school. When asked to draw their immediate environment and the changes that they would like to see, schoolchildren drew rather formalised images of idealised houses with pitched roofs (seldom seen in Delhi) set in a mountainous landscape inhabited by colourful symbols of trees and birds. The waste

picker children however aspired to the multi-storied concrete residential blocks which surrounded their cardboard shacks and without the benefit of formal education drew these realistically, and really quite accurately, but in monochrome without the benefit of a natural landscape.

(4) Spatial Provocation

Direct short term intervention within particular spaces was adopted by the students as a means to encourage debate about the importance and characteristics of the space: its occupation and potential.

One of the earliest attempts by the students at using making as an exploration of space occurred in Datrana, a desert village in Gujarat in 2002 (note 6, p. 17). The village had been damaged in an earthquake in the previous year and subsequent building repairs by outside agencies had increased the availability of materials readily available for construction. Observing that the provision of shade and sun protection in public places was key to understanding its use throughout the day, students devised an idea for a bender-type canopy using hooped reinforcing rods with a fabric cover.

The main square, mostly inhabited by men had various shaded areas and little unoccupied space for an on-site investigation ... we discovered four lakes just beyond the periphery of the village. Two lakes were totally dried up ... the last lake was a hive of activity with four wells, each of which was constantly crowded with women collecting water and washing their clothes on the stone sill of the well ... Following a translated discussion we understood that they had a desire for a shaded place adjacent to the well (note 6, p. 17).

But although children and some women joined the students under the canopy, which had been built to a brief and at a location discussed with the women, a few days after construction nobody seemed to use the structure. One woman explained that they just did not have enough time to sit down in the shade!

Such well-intentioned interventions can have unintended consequences. CURE, the Indian NGO with which the studio has worked for a number of years, described to the students an exercise which they organised to clear a piece of open ground in the centre of Katra Wazir Khan in Agra, on which the children played, in order to provide a cleaner and safer environment. As soon as the land was cleared however, the owner, who up to that point had been untraceable, fenced it off, attempting to deny public access. Fortunately the children dug under and jumped over the fence reclaiming the use of the land but the experience inhibited future group action.

On the whole, short term, reversible, exploratory interventions have proved less threatening and provided a more optimistic focus for discussion about spatial and infrastructural alternatives. One such example was the painted wall.

Tim Sanderson and Eoin O'Keefe (2005), LMU students working with Soni Meera and Czaee Malpani from the TVB School of Habitat Studies Delhi, recognised the importance of the west entrance to the linear Jagdamba camp mentioned above. This entrance lane is where the neighbouring, gated middle class community and poor Jagdamba mix; the poor serving the rich. Laid out in an ad hoc manner along the northern perimeter wall, are market stalls and tradesmen's booths mixed with reclining cows and stored bicycles. At first students distributed chalks for children to draw on the wall which they did enthusiastically. The resulting graffiti was quite extensive however and the students felt obliged to clean it up. So they set to and painted the long stretch of the wall:

Now the street is clean and the wall is blue. [It] has transformed into a more inviting space to walk through. The day after the wall was painted charpois were brought into the walkway where women and their babies slept. [It became] an extension of their homes as living space ... To celebrate we organised a street party ... Men and children danced and the women of the JD camp watched (note 7, pp. 26–9).

For a few days this squeezed narrow space, previously neglected but now recognised as an essential space of entrance, meeting and exchange was the focus of community endeavour and a celebration which crossed boundaries of caste and wealth. The conversations and working relationships developed between students and local people during the course of these events enabled a greater understanding of the historical development of the site and its perceived problems; of social mobility and commercial exchange; of educational, age and gender divisions and allowed the students to begin to explore the possibilities inherent in the situation. The insights gained from this particular exercise combined with the students' measured surveys grounded their future design work and became a reference point to test their ideas as they began to emerge later in the academic year.

A similar exercise in spatial exploration by spectacle originated in what began as a modest drawing competition organised by students for Bouvra Chowk [public square] (8) in Chirag Delhi but later snowballed into a major event. The chowk is dominated by two large trees which provide shade over two raised concrete platforms and a disused covered well. The drawing exercise was primed with a small group of 4- to 6-year-olds but

children drawing with students, Panchsheel Vihar
Hiromi Yang

later in the day older school children returning home from school joined in so that by the evening there were about 150 children taking part.

Residents were bemused at our own notions of drawing and representations of everyday life. They were particularly curious as to the rope frame we rigged up hung from the surrounding balconies so as to set up a web on which to hang the children's drawings. Young and old enjoyed the event which was made especially lovely with the aid of ranguli (Indian dry paint placed in patterns on the ground) and candles as darkness fell. After we departed the children got caught up in the wave of high spirits and decided that they wanted to keep their drawings and paintings. Before long the entire show was dismantled. The ropes were taken down for use as washing lines. The whole event gave us a great understanding of the differing concerns of the people of Chirag Delhi in the face of a totally different set of cultural and economic parameters (note 2, p 17).

Despite the preponderance of rigidly enforced caste boundaries in Chirag Delhi, the social relationships initiated during this exercise were maintained and extended over a number of years of study by successive student cohorts allowing them some quite remarkable access across gender and privacy boundaries.

Perhaps because this is one of the few chowks accessible by ambulance, a total of three separate doctors' surgeries ply their trade from the buildings on the constricted perimeter of Bouvra Chowk. For this reason, when comparing the characteristics of Bouvra Chowk with other public open courts in the urban village, students working there casually re-named Bouvra: the 'medical' chowk. Men (and cows) tend to congregate in the chowk

more than women, playing cards and gossiping whilst relaxing on the concrete plinths. One man set up a table to iron clothes for a living whilst watching over the few cars which are parked there.

At first it was difficult even for the female students to talk to women. However, eventually the hospitality of families occupying three old havelis forming one side of the chowk enabled one student, Anja Theis, to construct extensive tree diagrams of the family connections within. In conversation with doctors and women, from a wider reading of the literature (Macpherson 2007), and more particularly from her family tree diagrams Anja concluded that there was evidence of female foeticide if not infanticide. This led to a project based on providing improved and more transparent birthing procedures within this particular community. Anja's knowledge of the problem was, of course, informed by the general literature as well as the physical morphology of Bouvra Chowk but her passion for the project was driven especially by her particular knowledge of the families' blood relationships and her sense of individual discovery.

Other notable cultural exercises carried out by the students are mentioned elsewhere in this book. These include the construction by Angela Hopcraft of a community canopy from scrap timber downstream of Jagdamba Camp (Chapter 2); the fabrication of a mobile stall with the nomadic community of Marwari Basti in Agra (Chapter 6) and the penetrating success of Anthony Corke's cricket match (Chapter 2) in Kuchhpura nearby.

(5) The Role and Popularity of Physical and Cultural Surveys

The study of poor and unfamiliar city environments is becoming increasingly popular within architectural studios as a means to generate knowledge and understanding of some of the most important issues facing the world today: those of sustaining and improving the quality of livelihood, family and community in a situation of rapid cultural and technical change with scarce resources. The techniques of physical and cultural survey reviewed above offer only a small contribution to the range of survey methods available.

A more extensive set of methods is offered by Babar Mumtaz (Mumtaz, undated). In order

drawing of Jagdamba Camp entrance wall
Tim Sanderson

to 'read' the city, Mumtaz offers techniques of Local Area Analysis in four stages: Windscreen Survey or Reconnaissance (overview); Detailed Examination (building conditions, commercial activity, service infrastructure, social facilities, open space etc.); Listening to Stories (no subheadings) and Assembling the City (land use, buildings, services incomes, environment and land value). The survey methods described here engage, expand and privilege the 'Listening to Stories' section of Mumtaz's notes. Treating the existing physical reality as a resource, students are present on site for long enough to offer provocative engagement with local people, breaking through mysteries and memories, hidden lives and illicit trades to uncover the everyday practices and narratives that usually remain hidden below the gloss of our preconceptions. Students also have time during the field trip to go some way towards exploring with residents what is possible through action as well as words.

(6) Developing a Design Idea using Transitional Metaphors

Scaling up any findings from such a local investigation to validate strategic interventions is always problematic but repeated field trips to the same or similar locations in Delhi has helped to firm up findings and sort out the general from the particular. Investigating and imagining the other is not only an aesthetic tool and a moral imperative, but also a deep and very subtle human pleasure. Once such essentially qualitative experiences are recorded, students are asked to come up with a design idea: a metaphor and a location which can be used to encapsulate and transfer experiential qualities glimpsed and expressed in the survey, together with associated quantitative insights, into a project proposal.

Not yet ready to design, to begin the process of fitting the idea into a changed context,

students leave India at the end of their field trip having coined a phrase (the metaphor), written a short paragraph of explanation and chosen or created a single image; all as a bridge from field research into project design. This task serves as a future memory aid and also as a tool for privileging qualities which students wish to transfer from the field. Alongside this they are asked to choose a site which they will have measured: the location of their future project proposal.

In carrying out this short task of metaphor construction students are asked to hold back on describing or proscribing a precise function for their site: the basis for most architectural briefs and perhaps also the basis for Lefebvre's accusations of 'reductive commodification through the over focus on function' mentioned above (Lefebvre 1997). Instead, students are encouraged to encapsulate a 'design idea' into a transferable experiential package which is intended to carry over the enthusiasm, curiosity and commitment of the student from collecting to creating. The best metaphors hold up right to the end of the design process maintaining the student's passion for the subject and providing guidance throughout the academic year on the project's boundaries. Original metaphors are not rigidly enforced, however and judgement is needed as to when they should change as the design process develops and the original (poetic) insight is lost.

A metaphor is a word or phrase given to an object or idea to which it does not literally apply (9). There has been an increasing interest among commentators in the role of metaphor in concept construction and whilst metaphor is a device of the poetic imagination studies have found that its use is all pervasive in constructing everyday concepts. So the use of metaphor is related to the construction of meaning rather than

painting the entrance wall part one
Tim Sanderson

the understanding of absolute truth as espoused by scientific method. This does not mean that scientific methods, categories and models should be abandoned but rather that even technical and scientific communication are, in reality, constructions and are bound together by metaphors. Metaphor is a double imaginative act of outreaching and combining and is linked closely to the process of learning and discovery: making analogical leaps from the familiar to the unfamiliar: rallying imagination and emotion as well as intellect (10).

The deeper reality of human dwelling is that it thrives on creative metaphoric disclosures and decays when such powers degenerate into mechanical repetition (note 10, p. 7)

In a classic example, Christopher Alexander uses metaphors of pattern in constructing names for places (Alexander 1977; 1979). The language he uses to name a space or type of space is key. Examples include, in no particular order:

Connecting to the Earth; Terraced Slope; Sleeping to the East; Street Windows; Trellised Walk; Waist High Shelf; Half Open Wall.

In the assembly of his pattern language Alexander includes form but tries to avoid

allocating function and prefers to focus on other, less measurable, architectural attributes. Here are a few examples from studio work. Students have not found the task of metaphor construction easy and very few have come up with a sustained example. Most student metaphors have some allusion to function which is difficult to remove from a contemporary student's list of priority concerns:

Laundry and the Little Ones: Nicole Bruun Meyer (2007), Sonia Camp, Delhi: Although laundry is a function, the reference is to a spectacular wall of washing drying across the front of a house. The project eventually focused on spaces where children could play safely whilst their mothers worked.

Women's Workshop Terrace: Simona Grimaldi, Mehrauli, Delhi (2008): refers to the combination of a sectional idea, on a steep cliff on site and her social programme derived from her cultural exercises.

Some are mostly driven by social concerns:

If you really care for us, then help us: Judith Ben-Tovim, Panchsheel Vihar, Delhi (2005): Comment abstracted from cultural exercises with waste pickers.

painting the entrance wall part two
Tim Sanderson

A Happy Space: Toshitsugo Matsumura, Jagdamba Camp, Delhi (2005): Enlarged chowks for the drainage community based on his happy experience in the camp.

Also, a large number of projects struggled with the separation between genders, castes, and between rich and poor and tried to frame their projects so as to bring people together:

A Way Through: Amelia Rule, 19/20 Kalyanpuri, Delhi (2007)
Living in Close Quarters: Nisha Kurian, 19/20 Kalyanpuri, Delhi (2007)
Emerging and Connecting Communities: Katherine Edmondson, Jagdamba Camp, Delhi (2008)
Breaking Through to the Other Side: Audrey Lematte, Panchsheel Vihar, Delhi (2008)
Breaking Down Boundaries: Natasha Reid, Panchsheel Vihar, Delhi (2008)

Some preferred to write a story which would lead to a project by completing the narrative:

The Goat Herder and the Haveli: Shamoon Patwari, Old Delhi (2008): Reconstruction and transformation of an old Haveli.

Others used a formal device both literally and metaphorically:

A Doorway: Je Ahn, Kuchhpura, Agra (2006): Access to independent work for village shoemakers oppressed by factory work.
The Lantern: Marco Sosa, Marwari Basti, Agra (2006): Amenity building for nomadic community.
The Wall: Nicolas Maari, 19/20 Kalyanpuri, Delhi (2007).
Snakes and Ladders: Simon Elliston, Mehrauli, Delhi (2008).

The last two examples both deal with problems of separation and connection in society and in formal language.

Some were purely experiential:

Room with a View: Jaroslaw Engel, Kuchhpura, Agra (2006): Accommodation for tourists in an existing village with a view of the Taj Mahal.
A Sense of Calm: Huw Trevorrow, North Jagdamba, Delhi (2008): An experience in the under-occupied wooded land adjacent to the very dense illegal settlement.

entrance wall painted
Tim Sanderson

Transforming Lefebvre's description of everyday commodification (Lefebvre 1997, p. 34), the legibility of forms inscribed within structures (the infrastructure) should not be ordained only or even primarily by function, but by qualities which are informed by the five senses and transposed to the drawing board by metaphor from recorded experience. Only then, as part of the process of design, should such forms be tested by imagined use and their potential for adaptation by future successive occupants explored.

Students also collected information under the other headings listed in Babar Mumtaz's piece on Local Area Analysis listed above (Mumtaz, undated) but this was overlaid with the insights provided by the physical surveys and cultural exercises which informed metaphor construction. This rich seam of material was mined, using the methods discussed in the next chapter, to generate student design projects for the remainder of the academic year.

Notes

(1) Agra Narratives: Agra Field Trip Booklet, November 2006.

(2) Dispersed Initiatives in Changing Urban Landscapes: Delhi Field Trip Booklet, November 2004.

(3) They had no such inhibitions when it came to interpreting their cultural exercise: 'our cultural exercises and observations however are subjective'.

(4) East Yamuna Exchanges: Delhi Field Trip Booklet, November 2007, p. 47.

(5) Notes from survey diary: Carolos and Konstantinos, November 2003.

(6) Landscapes of Change: everyday conversations in space and time: Gujarat Field Trip Booklet November 2002.

(7) Delhi Dialogues: Field Trip Booklet, November 2005.

(8) Summary of tutorial notes 2004 and 2007.

(9) *The Concise Oxford Dictionary*, 6th Edition, 1976 (London: Book Club Associates).

(10) Union of International Associations: web site databases: http://www.uia.org/metaphor/metacom_bodies.php?kap=2 5/01/2003.

chapter 2
Methods (and Modernity)

More Tweak than Tabula Rasa

Looking and listening, coherently recording physical and cultural landscapes, identifying patterns, recognising the richness of this raw material as a basis for innovation rather than nostalgia and then postulating change. More often 'Tweak' than 'Tabula Rasa': this is the work of the studio.

(1) Looking for the Unique within the Everyday: A Narrative Technique

'A mind which focuses on finding the particular within the everyday and discovering its resonance within the global has become almost a cliché within cultural studies and commonplace for commentators on the global humanitarian agenda' (Hamdi 2004). But the world is changing fast. It never stops and by the time we have explicitly interpreted today's everyday, things have moved on without any informed architectural input. The challenge here is to take forward ways of understanding and interpreting the world generated by cultural commentators such as Raymond Williams (Harvey 1996) and Michel de Certeau (Highmore 2006) in such a way as to curate a healthy architecture which recognises the special within the ordinary. It is with this intention that the studio endeavours to understand the places studied and with this understanding to construct meaningful architectural proposals.

Within the context of rapid change, the urgent demands of the moment coupled with the obfuscation of official statistics have meant that the humanitarian aid community have had to develop techniques for the rapid appraisal of communities and their immediate physical environment (Chambers 1983). These appraisal methods provide an intriguing precedent for the mapping techniques employed by students which are introduced in the previous chapter and discussed again below.

Originally developed to enable farmers to share knowledge and work out solutions to problems of soil conservation communally, 'Participatory Rural Appraisal' is a mapping technique which has revolutionised the 'bottom up' approach to community empowerment. Maps made from chalk, seeds, sticks and coloured stones are located in the village square. Often of a surprisingly high graphic quality they make individual knowledge explicit for the benefit of the whole community. Different age and gender cohorts, young men and old women for example, can show clearly their different viewpoints set out on the ground in front of them. This can often stimulate more positive discussion than a mere verbal exchanges: the image of the map itself having its own transformative power. Positive images such as these are needed if communities are to share an optimistic common purpose. They tie in to the notion of the non-verbal path described by Diderot (Sennett 2008, p. 95) as available to artisans: of showing rather than telling. In this way the visual material produced by the students and catalogued in Part 3 stands alone: pieces of work generated from the process of research (curiosity, experimentation and reflection), devised by each individual student. Chapters 3 to 9, on the other hand, are essays about the context and discourse surrounding the work produced rather than a replacement for, or a description of these stand alone architectural pieces.

(2) Looking For and Establishing Patterns: An Inductive Technique

At the same time as looking for the culturally unique within the everyday, students need to observe, record and understand the changing physical landscape. The layers of material which make up the physical landscape move over one another and 'loosely' interact to provide a particular inhabited place at any one time and then dissolve again. Techniques of recording and

measuring the outside of Khirki mosque with Raja
Amy Penford

interpreting this interaction are required to inform a way of making an architecture specific to place and time. Attributes of architectural time are understood and reinterpreted after assembling a painstaking record of the physical evidence. These attributes include: continuity and change, mobility, fluency and permanence; Kuchha (temporary, short life, reducing in value) and Pukka (permanent, finished, increasing in value); the raw and the cooked, the rug and the picnic (1), retrofit and post-hoc installation of infrastructure.

Whilst we are all becoming more and more aware of the reductionism inherent in a standardised response to a rich local scenario, we are also clear that the more particular the analysis, then the more specific the intervention required and the shorter the time there is to act meaningfully. The insights revealed by the students suggest a craftsperson's way of working as explored by Richard Sennett rather than that of a mainstream architectural office worker (Sennett 2008); a question of needlework rather than the operation of a loom.

Within the studio, over the years, various methods of analysis and action have been explored. These are laid out as if on a market stall each year for students to take up as and when they are required, to help provide a provocation for their own work. This section reviews the theoretical background to these methods of recording and interpretation of specifically local physical and cultural singularities and links this to the resulting student work illustrated later.

Architect as Detective

For UK students travelling to India for the first time, ordinary life in illegal settlements is unfamiliar and bewildering. As soon as the student starts to make a physical survey of such a settlement and interview the occupants, assumptions are made, preconceptions are confirmed or accommodations made to these preconceptions. Gradually, in practice, a working understanding of the nature of the settlement and its inhabitants is formed by the student. This understanding is shared with peers whilst at the same time being accommodated to the peer group's understanding. In turn this is mediated by the various group member's own survey work and preconceptions.

(1) The Observer and the Observed
Students aim to improve their theoretical understanding of the relationship between what they are seeing locally both to w der global factors and to other similar situations elsewhere in the world. In this way they search out useful precedents for understanding and action.

As part of this process, students are made aware of the importance of considering the observer's standpoint as well as that of the observed. They become conscious of the inherent danger of seeing the unfamiliar 'other' through western eyes and of imposing an alien set of values and judgments; as portrayed so effectively in Edward Said's classic book *Orientalism* (Said 1978). However, in spite of its dangers, objectivity is impossible as the student's own sensitivities are the lens through which experience is processed. How can this reality be transformed from a liability into an opportunity?

To help come to terms with this challenge students are introduced to the Leibnitzian Conceit (Harvey 1996, pp. 69–76) (Vidler 2000, pp. 219–33) and the concept of the Monad, wherein Leibniz postulates that everything you need to know about the world is concealed within a seed (the Monad). To a lesser or greater extent each Monad will mirror (or contain the information, the 'DNA', to mirror) the universe. The conceit referred to occurs when you treat yourself as the Monad (as in the phrase, to know the other: know yourself). This approach leads back to Eurocentrism and the construction of the oriental 'other' referred to by Said. Instead, as a studio, we try to focus on the particular physical and cultural entity (the settlement) which is being studied. Within the settlement students look for the clues (seeds) to assemble (propagate) a 'watertight' case (architectural idea).

Beyond these caveats what is perhaps even more significant for architectural practice is that students understand the 'fundamental impossibility of measuring without intervening and thus changing that which is being measured' (Harvey 1996, p. 56). So the nature of the fieldwork carried out by students is already an intervention: a more or less invasive interrogation of the physical and cultural fabric of the chosen settlement. Regular surveying procedures coupled with imaginative cultural exercises re-enact everyday life and provoke a response for the record. The resulting architectural project becomes the denouement: established with a measure of authoritative finality even if within a limited time frame until appealed.

How then to study such places? How should students approach the struggle to construct an architectural imagination which allows them (to paraphrase Harvey 1996, p. 14) to contemplate (their own and the studied settlement's) embeddedness in space, time, nature and place?

(2) Tradition and Modernity: The Hotel Lobby

A way of dispelling the bewilderment experienced when being dropped in an unfamiliar place can be found in the parable of modernity entitled 'The Hotel Lobby' by Siegfried Kracauer (Kracauer in Leach, ed. 1997).

... modernity was characterised by a form of transcendental homelessness, which was embodied in the hotel lobby, where silence reigns and where guests bury themselves in their newspapers to avoid exchanging glances.

The author compares this space (the hotel lobby) with that of a church which could equally be a metaphor for all entrenched traditional social structures such as those embodied in caste. Here everyone knows their place. In church, temple and mosque, the priest officiates making everyone's position in the cosmos absolutely clear. For Kracauer the church is synonymous with such traditional spaces. Here I would like to suggest that it is also appropriate to link it to spaces with which the observer is familiar and confident.

Compared to this, the only person capable of making sense of the hotel lobby (or in our case the unfamiliar situation) is the detective who constructs a form of reality by questioning seemingly unrelated individuals to make a case which will stand up in court. The detective has privileged access (having the right to question and accuse) despite their version of reality being clearly just one of many. Each enquiry shines a spotlight which focuses and bounds the constituent parts of that constructed reality into a resolved piece: the case which the court will legitimate.

As a stranger to the community the student has the potential to occupy a role similar to that of the detective. Thus, in the same way as a court case is constructed by police and lawyers, familiar (modern) reality is constructed and then re-constructed in their final project by the students. According to the physical and cultural context within which the action takes place (the settlement), project boundaries are drawn by the student observer who is informed by her own interpretation of the physical evidence and the testimony of the characters (witnesses) involved. In effect this reality is only made explicit when mediated by a person such as an architect who has privileged access (like a detective in a criminal investigation) and who has constructed (made a case (detective) or drawn (architect)) a representation of that reality.

(3) A Series of Moments

The idea of a spotlight creating a boundary for the investigation was explored by Edward Hopper in his paintings at night, most famously 'Nighthawks'. But his array of sketches and paintings of 'Office at Night' and indeed another series entitled 'The Hotel Lobby' show a more protracted obsession with characters and their role playing in a tightly defined space. The works display a touch of the Leibnitzian Conceit, mentioned above (Wagstaff, ed. 2004):

Hopper's paintings do not report an actual event in the world but rather stage a re-imagined event in narrative pictorial terms ... (his) desire was to reach a kind of plausibility ... a painterly manifestation of Goethe's 'reproduction of the world that surrounds me by means of the world that is within me'.

An early instance of an attempt to construct and communicate a reality from the complex confusion of everyday life is to be found in the work of the early nineteenth-century French novelist, Stendhal. This is particularly so in his autobiographical novel *The Life of Henry Brulard* (Stendhal 1995). The story is made up of a series of sharply observed 'images' or 'mental pictures'. This graphic record is not open to contradiction: the pictures it contains are private and deemed to be utterly reliable (2).

Whilst these 'images' are clearly constructed from memory they do provide the certain building blocks that make up Stendhal's story. Physical definition of the places where each incident takes place is not only described in the text but is also illustrated with a freehand sketch. This highlights the physical elements important to the story and the positions of the characters taking part. Each sketch includes an annotated key covering the memories and desires of the author that are linked to buildings and objects in the sketch. Within the main text the description of each 'mental picture' records a range of disparate sensations (touch, smell, sight and memory) related to the precise moment in time recorded. This is not so much to guide a narrative plot, which is actually quite disjointed, but to provide the reader with a focused sense of the same reality in that place and at that time as constructed by the author. Questioning the objective truth of the 'image' is beside the point as the elements used by the author to construct the 'images' are mostly not capable of scientific measurement. The powerful effects of such annotated sketches are for the reader 'genuinely poignant in their particularity'.

But Stendhal's method of working with 'mental pictures' can help with another of the problems inherent with student work today; that of the hegemonic outsider and the dangers of Said's Orientalism. Instead of making pretence at objective study, negating the prejudices of the observer, Stendhal's 'mental pictures' are constructed from the particular standpoint of the author himself looking back on his life from a particular time and place in his life. Stendhal's method of representation specifically includes this standpoint in time and place. Physical and cultural attributes are combined as an interplay between the observer and the observed. Students are required to invent and implement both physical and cultural surveys which attempt to mirror this approach. Sketches, maps, collages and other drawings are produced which reveal 'mental pictures' where the student's own senses and memories are engaged alongside those of community members. Diverse viewpoints are acknowledged and challenged as part of the process of research and design.

(4) The Derive

Between 1957 and 1969 the Situationists, a group of artists in Paris, were trying to develop a culture of resistance to the urban habits and myopic assumptions involved in living and working in the city. They proposed a series of playful acts called 'Derives' designed to provoke random behaviour in those affected. The Situationists built on the nineteenth-century Parisian figure: the 'flâneur': a gentleman who, not having to earn his living (a new and spreading phenomenon at that time), could wander freely through all neighbourhoods experiencing the various sights, smells and sounds for the pleasure of the experience. The 'flâneur' was thus the first 'psycho-geographer' mixing the senses with spatial geography in an urban wanderlust. Guy Debord, perhaps the principal member of the Situationist International described the Derive as a process by which people:

... drop their usual motives for movement and action, their relations, their work, their leisure activities and let themselves be drawn by the attractions of the terrain and the encounters they find there (Andreotti and Costa 1996).

Techniques used to stimulate a Derive were quite random. They might include making decisions as to a route by the throwing of a dice or observing the reactions of passers by when you scrub the pavement with a toothbrush.

Representations of derives were named 'detournements': psycho-geographic maps made from found materials with the original meanings of these materials subverted. Situationists believed that psycho-geography could be mapped to create a new understanding of the city.

Unit 6 challenges the conventional understanding of Delhi by studying places which are often not formally recognised by the Delhi authorities and are sometimes liable for demolition as part of urban resettlement programmes.

In order to do this effectively, students have adopted and adapted some Situationist mapping methods. So that in addition to the hard measurements gained through physical survey, these alternative methods allow engagement with the sensual, social and political aspects of the places being studied. Examples of these Cultural Exercises, such as playing cricket on the beach behind the Taj Mahal, are described later and in the previous chapter on field research.

So, in a similar way to the Derive, Cultural Exercises are used in the studio to briefly change the way the urban environment is used and perceived. This can stimulate discussion within the local community and by representing such survey work in portfolio and exhibition can encourage debate in the broader academic and official communities.

(5) Validity, Legitimacy, Characters, Friends

Whether such records of place are as deeply personal as those of Stendhal and Hopper, or as random as the 'flâneur', they can act as methodological precedents for the study of complex places which are unfamiliar to the observer. This in turn can lead on to their effective representation by the student to a wider audience.

Papi, the protector and gatekeeper
Amelia Rule

However, if the reality so constructed is to lead to an accepted programme of action then it has to be legitimated (made plausible: cf. Hopper above). This is especially so when designs are progressed remote from the situation. Effective representation, advocacy and performance are essential to achieve a sufficiently broad consensus for action. Drawings and other project material needs to be of high quality, attract informed debate and communicate effectively. Projects also need to be presented well in exhibition, lecture, seminar, booklet and/or portfolio.

With these tools for communicating and demonstrating findings and ideas, the studio is able to engage in a legitimated critical discourse with other interested individuals and organisations. This discourse also adds validity to the projects.

A similar process of legitimating student projects is used in Robert Mull's Free Unit at London Metropolitan University where students undertake a design project set up by themselves alone. Here students are required to compile a critical cultural framework by choosing 12 'friends' of the project. With some knowledge of the particular situation the 'friends' are required to comment on the proposals as they emerge and eventually take part in assessing these proposals.

During their intensive field research, Unit 6 students choose individual characters they have encountered to act as witnesses to the progress of their design work. Sometimes students keep in touch by email, sometimes they intuit witness responses, re-inserting them back into the finished design to test cultural fit.

In some cases, Unit 6's partner Indian NGO CURE occupies a comparable and complimentary role to the community characters. In a series of email workshops, issues relevant to both student projects and CURE's work in the settlements, is explored.

By focusing on particular people students can avoid generalised assumptions based on a wider sample. Concentrating on individualised characters enables students to see wider issues through the lens of the everyday lives of these real people. Here is a brief description of one of the characters in Amelia Rule's study of Kalyanpuri:

Papi is the Protector and Gatekeeper for Kalyanpuri Block 19/20. Domineering and matriarchal she sits all day long dressed in a glistening shiny sari in sumptuous splendour on a cushioned charpoi in a broad brick painted recess at the entrance to the bazaar street keeping an eye on what is happening, checking to see that no-one enters the settlement unwelcomed. The narrowness of the street enables this form of casual surveillance ...

From these observations the variables of place definition and transformation were acquired. Notions of entrance, a woman's role in space, the position of strangers and the role of colour and dress were all highlighted and given a role. Just as Hopper trained the spotlight on his characters and Stendhal portrayed his moments in space time by describing what he sensed, annotated with a sketch, so Amelia was able to begin her narrative exposition of place with text and image.

In this way, just as a novel can get to the heart of a situation in a more direct and evocative way than a social survey, student schemes can creatively pick up the general through the particular. Individual characters are the key. Their idiosyncrasies, aspirations and inspirations are at the heart of a student's design programme.

Example (1) Playing Cricket on the Beach: Anthony Corke's Cultural Exercise

Being a sport obsessive, Anthony packed his cricket bat and 'whites' as soon as he signed up for the 'India' studio. Once arrived at Kuchhpura, as an outsider (the detective) he noticed immediately what he considered a great paradox. The village was populated almost exclusively by Hindus yet it was founded on, and was still the home of the functioning Humayun's Mosque (3). Conversely, the next settlement to the north of the village consisted of a Hindu temple backing on to a Muslim community. Intent on exploring this paradox, Anthony organised a cricket match between a combined Kuchhpura community team and the London students. Both the Hindu and Muslim religious leaders and two university-educated sisters living in the village, helped to organise the game. A village artist produced posters, advertising the event. Played on the river sands opposite the back of the Taj Mahal, the match changed the function of this space for the day. In this way and in the manner of the Derive, Anthony's intervention stimulated unusual behaviour and provoked an unpredictable outcome. The students were roundly thrashed largely through the efforts of the combined community's secret weapon, the spin bowler. This quiet man emerged from the Muslim community previously unbeknownst to the Hindus. His actions spoke louder than his words.

main image
the cricket gamer
Anthony Corke
above
the spinner
Anthony Corke

But the silent spinner was just the first of Anthony's characters to emerge through the organisation and acting out of this event. The cricket match shone the spotlight on other people who became key to the construction of Anthony's project programme enabling him to weave a narrative web and define a site for his project.

We have already been introduced to the two religious leaders, the two sisters, and the artist. Next came the sisters' father, a surveyor, who had produced a scheme for the irrigation of a field to the northern edge of the village which faced on to the Muslim settlement. Anthony proposed that fallow patches of this field be used for regular cricket matches: the place of play rotating with the crop cycle. The penultimate character was the son of a wealthy local doctor, nicknamed 'the godfather':

... he runs a number of businesses throughout Kuchhpura, employing many people, running carpentry shops, shoe makers, farmers and tuk tuk drivers. He was also responsible during the course of this work for the training and employment of a number of young people (4).

What was more, he owned the land for which the surveyor had produced his scheme. The last of Anthony's nine characters was named the apprentice: a boy who helped every day with the physical survey of the streets and houses of the village and who was very keen to learn from the experience:

... most of the children lost interest after a few hours of following us around. He, however stayed to help us throughout the day. In fact he would be waiting for us every morning at the entrance ready to start surveying again ... he learned how to draw and measure very quickly ... he was one of the brightest sparks in the village (4).

During the course of the survey a potential building site was identified: a patchwork of almost rectangular sites backing on to one another across the terraced streets and adjacent to the new cricket field. So the cricket match (cultural exercise) evolved into a programme for a vocational school on this patchwork site run by a set of trustees partly from the village and partly from outside.

The revelations of such cultural exercises are a far cry from absolute truth (religion: the traditional space) or even from the results of the scientific examination of objective data (the deductive, reductionist space of the master plan). They are just a way to provide sufficient meaning in a complex (modern: the hotel lobby mentioned above) situation to allow practical action (the meaningful student project) to take place.

So student research as described here is not used solely to construct a brief, but also and far more significantly, to provide the physical assemblies and cultural metaphors for an architectural proposal.

Architect as Author

The interrogation of place and the construction of meaning referred to above can shift seamlessly and easily into a process of design. Just as a legal case is prepared by assembling a host of small details into a coherent whole, so narrative exposition can be translated into creative work. Students use just such a narrative approach to frame, capture and harness (however fleetingly) moments from the everyday to use as building blocks for their imagined proposals. Their schemes show how an untidy mix of the old and the new, of memory and aspiration can, in a spirit of experiment and curiosity, give unique identity to place.

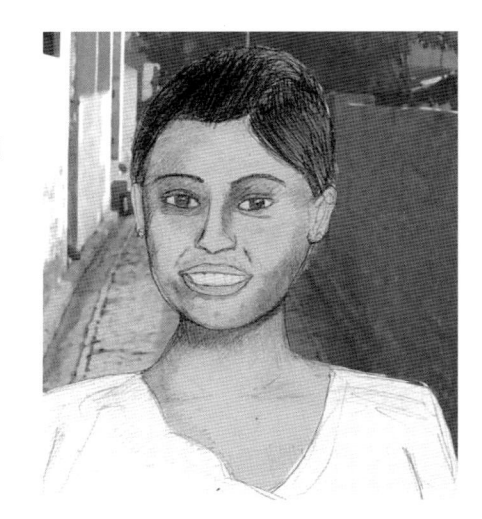

(1) Narrative Juxtaposition

When recording a place, opportunities for transformation are always in mind. Seeing a place as a stage set within which individual characters act out a drama can provoke the imagination and facilitate architectural remodelling. Even the record of a single observed moment can be imaginatively extrapolated into a series of events in a constructed narrative.

The characters in some of Hopper's paintings scream out for this treatment, challenging the observer to look again, put aside first impressions and really think what might be going on. Alternatively, they play on the observer's curiosity, inviting her to step inside the picture frame and become involved. In a technique akin to a filmic transformation of still photography, one recorded moment can become a story by imagining what went before and after. This imagined narrative can be used to test the spatial infrastructure leading to further experimentation and innovation by the student. New and adapted spatial configurations will in turn suggest further narrative manipulation. This is a cyclic process which in successful schemes leads to a coherence recognisable as a meaningful piece.

the two sisters and their father the surveyor,
Anthony Corke

(2) Disjunction between Activity and Space

Bernard Tschumi (Tschumi 1994) develops techniques for the narrative transformation of space that celebrate the disjunctions inherent in Stendhal's method of assembling powerful but disparate 'images' dotted through space time. With Tschumi however, the disjunction is not between each 'mental picture' but between the physical space and the use to which that space is being put. He shows how this disjunction can be recorded and reinterpreted to produce 'cumulative meaning'.

Using a tripartite mode of notation, discrete moments in time are assembled by making separate representations of events, sequences and spaces for each moment. These moments are then reframed (subjected to addition, compression and insertion) to provide a newly configured sequence of spaces. In this process of transformation successive sequences are subject to 'zooming' (changes of scale which focus down on particular elements) and

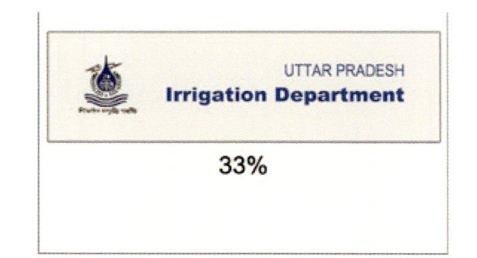

33%

combined 67%

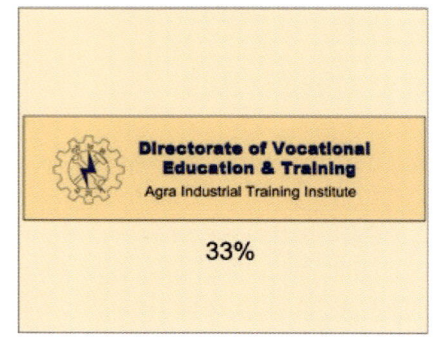

33%

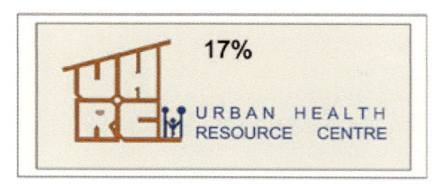

17%

COMMUNITIY LEADERS

17%

BOARD OF TRUSTEES

The principal trustees are chosen from residents of Kuchhpura as local users must always be given priority. The Hindu priest and the Imam from the mosque represent the village. I would prefer that a secular representative was chosen in line with the Indian constitution but the two priests are the most prominent figures in both communities and have the largest number of contacts. External trustees might be appointed by the NGO CURE and should not be biased. Their primary function should be to spot any internal inconsistencies. This is important to sustain the integrity of the Kuchhpura Vocational School.

the apprentice and the godfather
Anthony Corke

transgression (testing by subjecting proposals to an unexpected act or use).

Tschumi (Tschumi 1996) has a fascination with limits. If architecture is a continual process of making, where does it stop, particularly when applied to an existing cultural and physical landscape? In a sense, to suggest an answer, the making of landscape never stops but any particular construction of meaning as well as artifice will have its boundary. The edges of that making process and its interaction with its neighbours are as fascinating and challenging as its core. If, however, architecture is dumb, just infrastructure, and meaning is provided by occupation (the inhabitants' interpretation) then the opportunity for surprise and unpredictable performance (occupation) is perhaps strongest at the edges.

As an extreme example, look at the case of Beirut. In 1992, the urban landscape had been torn apart by gunfire. Opposing sides in the civil war, occupying these redundant building shells, faced each other across the rubble of the green line. Little did they know that this boundary or limit to their area of control would become the one area of neutrality after the war and would blossom into a large, linear urban park where all sides could stroll, promenade their families or just walk their dog in peace.

46

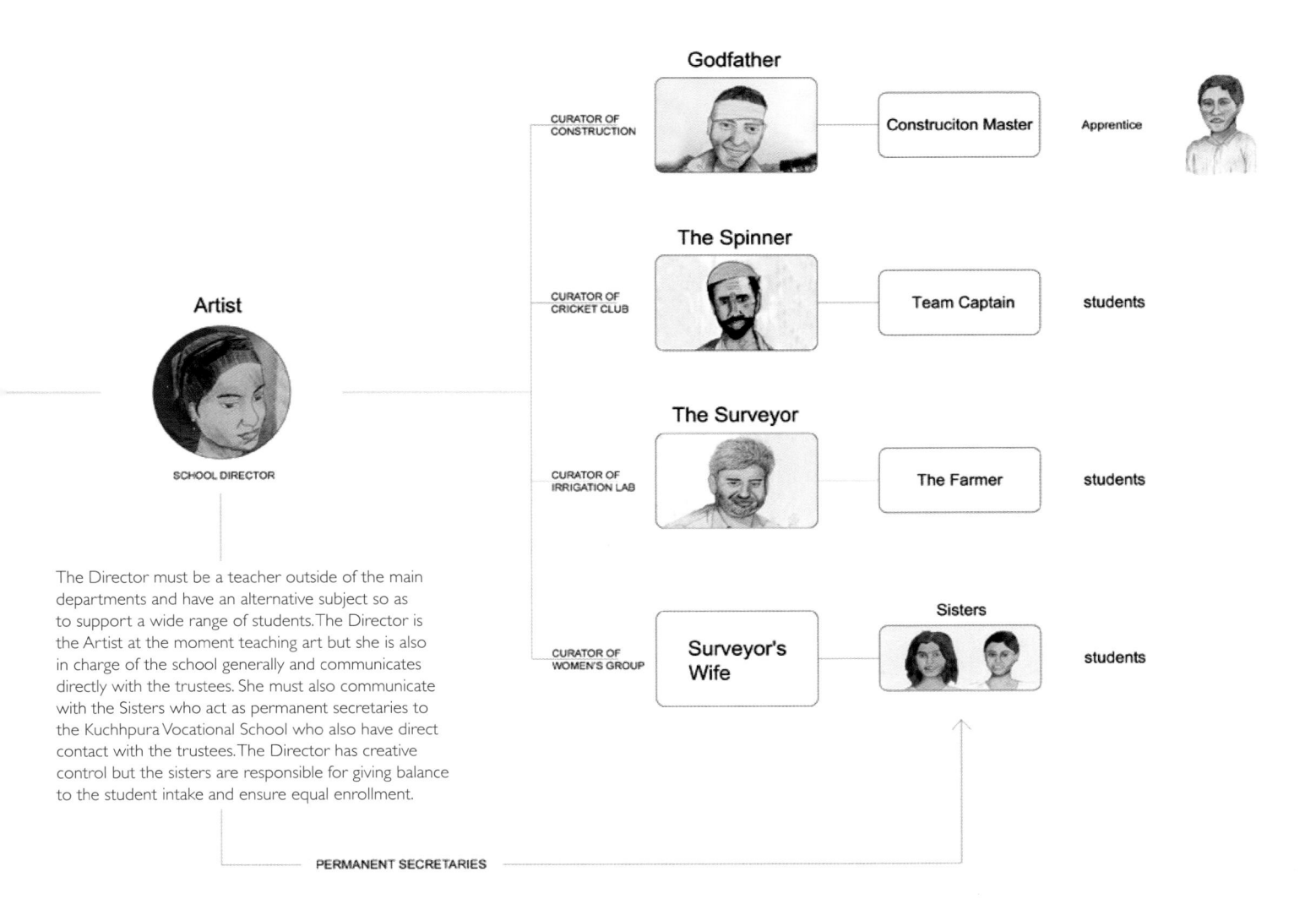

Godfather

CURATOR OF CONSTRUCTION

Construciton Master

Apprentice

The Spinner

CURATOR OF CRICKET CLUB

Team Captain

students

The Surveyor

CURATOR OF IRRIGATION LAB

The Farmer

students

Artist

SCHOOL DIRECTOR

Sisters

CURATOR OF WOMEN'S GROUP

Surveyor's Wife

students

PERMANENT SECRETARIES

The Director must be a teacher outside of the main departments and have an alternative subject so as to support a wide range of students. The Director is the Artist at the moment teaching art but she is also in charge of the school generally and communicates directly with the trustees. She must also communicate with the Sisters who act as permanent secretaries to the Kuchhpura Vocational School who also have direct contact with the trustees. The Director has creative control but the sisters are responsible for giving balance to the student intake and ensure equal enrollment.

In such a way, entrenched artifice becomes redundant and as a surprise throws up new, more hopeful, activity at its edges. Students have sought to become familiar with the cultural and physical patterns of old city labyrinths and illegal urban settlements before, and as an aid to, intervention. The consideration of edges and boundaries and the opportunities they offer for new typologies is key to many student schemes. These range from simple conservative surgery carried out by the community alone, to working alongside cultures of resistance in order to provide alternatives to top down over determined planning. They have also shown how major infrastructure projects can be tweaked in practice to add greater potential to those who use them. Unlike masterplanning this way of working does not seek to lay down a fossilised grid within which inhabitants must fit themselves. In contrast, it seeks out the left over gaps, marginal land, 'terra incognita' and morphological interstices to plant the seeds of the new.

organisational chart of proposed Kuchhpura Vocational College
Anthony Corke

Example (2) Angela's Widows' Refuge

The narrative for Angela Hopcraft's scheme (2005) for a widows' refuge in the Jagdamba settlement camp had two generating narratives. The first came from a brief moment, fleetingly observed, but profoundly affecting. Whilst lining up for water at a government tap, a widow,

proposed new east entrance to Jagdamba camp
showing widows' refuge on the left
Angela Hopcraft

recognisable by her shaven head, was pushed to the back of the queue. This act, distressing enough in itself, led to Angela researching the place of women in camp society and that of widows in particular. She discovered that whilst some Hindu temples provided refuge to widows, they were still stigmatised and left in poverty. Interestingly, she also discovered that blacksmiths had a traditional role in society as protectors of outcasts. As a consequence of her investigations her scheme was for a secular institution where the entrance was approached past a terrace of blacksmiths' workshops. In such a way, imagined narrative led to the beginnings of formal grouping.

The second generating narrative was more purposefully, if not painstakingly, constructed. The students devised an exercise intended to encourage cultural exchange with local people through hands-on making. Angela imagined an exercise for the construction of a lamella roof canopy from previous experimentations in Wales with waste material (see later in the chapter). From this process and the conversations it generated, she was able to highlight the lack of any public space within the community sufficient to accommodate communal activity. Angela's scheme took on the challenge of providing a new way in to the settlement which would also be linked to a larger public space for health days, educational activities, community meetings and celebrations.

So these are the spatial issues driving the scheme at both the infrastructural and building scales within which the new institution should fit. Firstly, and rather symbolically, the site included the water and sanitation facility where the original incident in the queue had occurred provoking research into the condition of widows. This government facility was to become redundant with the provision of piped water and internal toilets to each household within the settlement. Secondly, settlement level was a full storey below the surrounding road network. Improved pedestrian access and a new public entry space were needed. Thirdly, the

images showing gridshell construction in
Jagdamba camp
Angela Hopcraft

new institution building itself would be required to offer a protective environment with a clear separation between inside and out. Finally, as if by complete serendipity, there happened to be, at the edge of the site, a lush walled garden which no one seemed to own or use.

A three storey courtyard (haveli) type, appropriately scaled, could provide a protected home but what about the rest? The narrative: 'entry to the settlement'; had to play alongside 'widows' protection'. A new public entry space and steps were proposed to sweep past the refuge at first floor level. Underneath and within the privacy of the refuge, the widows' narrative was extended both to include access to the walled garden and to provide a space for interaction with the community: a nursery perhaps. At the western junction with the camp itself, leftover space was transformed into a larger chowk, providing the largest public/market space in the community. The whole was tested as an assemblage through drawings. These represented a range of activities taking place not only within the terms of the two extended narratives but also by hypothesising cataclysmic events such as flooding and riot. As a result an impluvium was added by cutting a hole in the first floor settlement access. This cast light into the community interactive space below and shed water into cisterns buried in the floor.

Thus two spatial narratives, extrapolated from a moment and a cultural exercise respectively, were used to generate a building proposal. By a process of addition, insertion, rescaling and testing, this building proposal was adapted to fit the existing urban landscape morphology. Further images of this project can be found in Part 3.

Architect as Craftsperson

(1) Hand to Eye: Resistance, Ambiguity and Arousing Tools

In his book *The Craftsman* Richard Sennett (2008) throws a refreshing new light on both meaningful toil and fashionable competition within the architectural profession. According to Sennett, cooking, playing the violin and making architecture are all examples of crafts which involve the skill and coordination of both the hand and the brain. In order to acquire the

knowledge and competence necessary to practice such crafts, 10,000 hours of application are required for an individual to fully translate healthy obsession into rounded performance. One of Sennett's key insights is his explanation of how the satisfaction which he calls the 'sentiment of competence' can be achieved through such craft skill.

Sennett's philosophy resonates within the interstices of current urban practice which is bogged down in a swamp of strategic initiatives and policy one-liners. He sees the discovery of resistances in the urban fabric as an opportunity. He revels in working with ambiguity within a difficult context. None of these curious drivers work well when being led charismatically from the front but do, on the other hand, engage the imagination, skills and experience gained from a long and reflective apprenticeship.

Being a craftsperson also requires an ability to operate experimentally within a particular set of (often changing) conditions, to suspend the desire for closure and to take responsibility for the results of your work. For this reason, a key element in the pedagogy of the studio is to introduce elements of innovation into the building technology involved in the proposed design. Following Sennett, the studio also values precedent, anticipates the implications of proposals as they are developed and accepts a duty to the wider public.

During the nine days of immersion in field work in India, methods of construction are observed and understanding is gained of the conditions and processes involved. The building types observed may be vernacular developed through long tradition or a very local creative response. On returning to the studio, the observed construction methods are re-examined by analysing photographs taken and sketches and measured surveys made during the fieldwork. Back in the studio they are made more explicit and coherent through detailed drawings. Precedent is sought out from relevant literature provoking curiosity and adaptation of the original recorded crafting process. Ideas are further refined through modelling, both in the Department's workshop and at a larger scale during a 4-day field trip to the Centre for Alternative Technology, Wales.

section showing gridshell erected to the east of Jagdamba camp in use as a market canopy
Angela Hopcraft

It is this process of innovation by experimental modelling which turns the imagined making/ designing process from a technical task (turning a finished design into a realised building by the application of a known technology) into a craft. Thus, the making of the building is integrated with, and very much a part of, the design process. In this way proposals are crafted not through imitation but by a dogged process of trial and error, balancing resistances in the worked materials with appropriate accommodations in methods and ambition.

(2) CAT Workshops

In a crafted model the choice of material to be worked determines the skill set to be developed. During the CAT workshop, students are restricted to the choice of just one material for each building element modelled. By limiting material choice students are guided and bounded by the physical properties of the chosen material in the crafting of their pieces.

Thus the form of the building element is approached by finding out (asking) what the material will let the student do in the manner of Louis Kahn (Cruickshank 1992). In the following quotation Kahn describes limiting the material for wall construction to brick:

And if you think of Brick, for instance,
and you say to Brick,
"What do you want Brick?"
And Brick says to you
"I like an Arch".
And if you say to Brick
"Look, arches are expensive, and I can use a concrete lintel over you.
What do you think of that Brick?"
Brick says:
"... I like an Arch".

Design does not predate building. It evolves in tandem. The CAT workshop provides students with the opportunity to design and make buildings using materials found on site or available locally. Skills are site based, focusing on those of mason (wet trades) and carpenter (dry trades). It consists of periods of practical work alternating with seminars where the work in progress is discussed. At each of these seminars each student group is asked to consider and communicate their answers to the following questions:

(1)   what did you intend to do?
(2)   what did you actually do?
(3)   what problems did you encounter?
(4)   what accommodations to these problems did you make?
(5)   what do you intend to do next?

So, over the course of a few days a building evolves through a hands-on, cyclic process of experimentation and focused group criticism followed by modifications to the original proposal.

Consideration of how to join the individually crafted building elements is not allowed to determine the size and scale of the elements themselves. Joining of coherent elements comes after the making of each element. Elements can then be joined directly, one to another (as in a brick wall) or be spaced apart and independently supported to provide new transitional spaces (loft, conservatory or lobby) between constructed elements. Alternatively, small two-dimensional elements might be assembled together in an array and fixed back as a cladding to a primary structure via a mediating or secondary structure. Whichever way is chosen, the final decision as to the juxtaposition and joining of elements to form buildings is made after

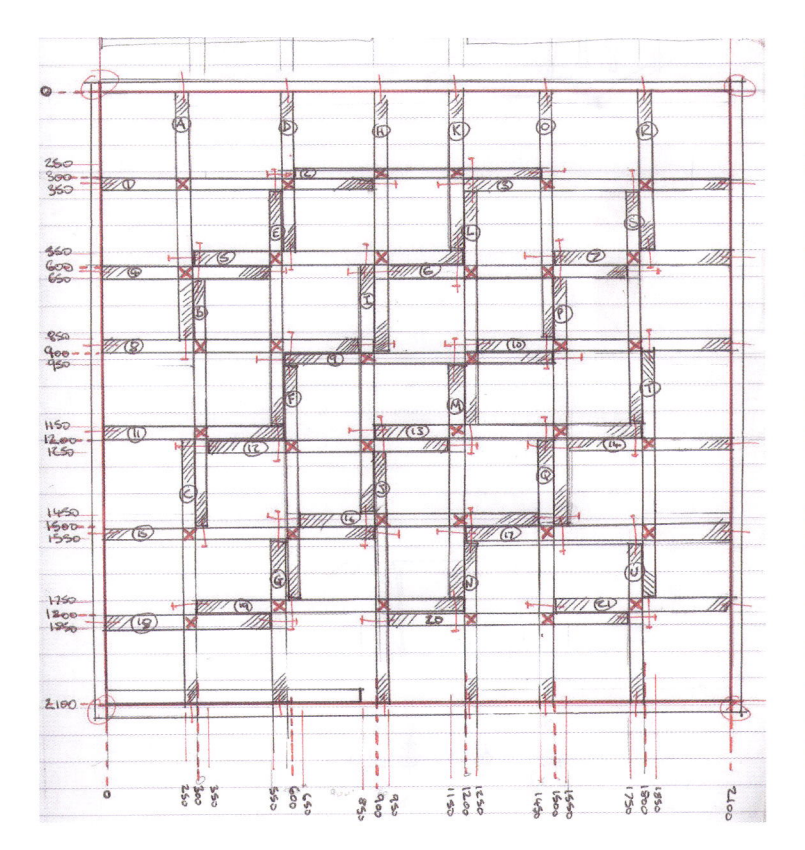

the integrity and coherent construction of each element has evolved from the process of experimental making. So the building is made from the raw material upwards.

As the course progresses and the skills, ambitions and interactions of the students become clear; a built form evolves which is quite unique. The final product, which is left standing as students leave is more a large-scale model than a finished building. Its form, never predictable at the start of the process is a way of learning about the process by which technology and human agency are transformed into a culture of making.

The seeming triviality of the objects being made is banished within the group as the work proceeds by constant self-conscious communication and iterative endeavour. Meaning is attached to the building elements being made by clearly identifying prototypes and other precedents. This consolidates the learning process.

In a situation of rapid change and scarce resources builders, occupants and designers are often the same people and building work is carried out over a long, if not continuous, period of time. In this context it is this newness or uniqueness of innovation, responding to the changing circumstances with immediacy and originality which allows a rapid response. Available skills, habits and resources are adapted efficiently and effectively to making places in an unfamiliar context.

(3) New Materials

Materials which are newly introduced to a particular context either by chance or design can have a profound effect on the normal way of doing things. They can enhance the appropriate use of local materials or hinder it by making a local technology redundant. Usually the

left
on site student sketch of proposed scrap timber floor
CAT, Wales
right
scrap timber floor
CAT, Wales

LARCH POLES AS PRIMARY STRUCTURE.

BIRCH SECONDARY ROOF STRUCTURE

SLATE WINDOW SEAT

GAP BETWEEN RESTORED WALL AND NEW PATH.

MOSS CLADDING

LARGE CRATE

WET LAID VOUSSOIRS

DRIED VOUSSOIRS

EXISTING EARTH + STRAW WALL SURROUNDS NEW STOVE

NEW SLATE PATH AND STEP.

sketch of student construction; CAT, Wales, *Edwhite Pe*

introduction of nails, wire and bolts alongside traditional string and rope is an enhancement. It can multiply structural possibilities with pole frame technology for example. So the studio explores the value added to creativity in a particular context by considering the introduction of low-cost, lightweight, loose fit, factory made materials which behave reliably.

In addition, some traditional materials such as brick (under pressure because of improved pollution controls), and bamboo (suddenly popular globally), have reinvented themselves to meet contemporary conditions. Students have embraced these changes and explored the possibilities opened up by these improved traditional technologies.

Other traditional materials such as newly harvested timber have generally been replaced by steel (in the form of small angles) and reinforced concrete. The everyday combination of such materials to form new assemblages to fit the contemporary context becomes evident during surveys and is a continuing subject of student curiosity.

The ubiquitous Indian red sandstone continues to be both cheap and available and students have enjoyed exploring the possibilities of locally crafted stone in their schemes.

(4) New Techniques of Representation

Many other studios at ASD have based their work on the innovative possibilities opened up by the computer generation of images. Modelling on computer has enabled new material and complex structural concepts to be formulated and tested easily and quickly with profound implications for the form of new buildings. Despite the huge processing power of computers, however, design by computer alone, whilst boosting the speed of calculation, also serves to increase the separation of the head from the hand. The learning and skilling which the hand acquires through repetitive action is replaced by computer drawings. These appear more finished and streamlined than the reality which they purport to represent. Sennett calls this condition a form of 'mental impairment' (Sennett 2008, p. 52).

Whilst making full use of digital drawing techniques, the studio encourages hand drawing and sketching, painting and rendering. The studio also employs a wide range of pragmatic modelling techniques combining full size structures at CAT with card, plaster, plywood and hardwood working models made in the Department's workshop. This process of making is interrogated and extended using photography, computer generation and collage.

(5) Global Precedent

Attempts to 'improve' traditional technologies worldwide have generated a plethora of guidance publications (from the stabilisation of earth to the recycling of tin cans for roofing). The Green Movement, desperate to save energy and reduce carbon emissions, is provoking a rethink of how we make our physical landscape inhabitable and use our resources sustainably. NGOs such as Development Workshop (5), working with a humanitarian agenda in the field of human settlements have provided numerous precedents for live project work. In a parallel development other architectural studios such as Rural Studio in Alabama (Dean and Hursley 2002) have begun working with live projects within deprived communities to improve architectural education. Precedents such as these have informed debate on what is possible in the studio.

Students have been particularly alive to new possibilities, derived from research around the world, inherent in the use of:

Bamboo, on site plasterwork, Eucalyptus poles, local treatment of black and grey water, recycling of and alternatives to fired brickwork, improved rammed earth or earth block technologies, insulated (with waste paper bundles) roof canopies, solid first floor construction with minimal use of Portland cement, rainwater catchment, treatment, storage and distribution, appropriate and sustainable sanitation. Examples of these newly-developed experimental technologies can be found in the following chapters and in Part 3.

Summary

Changes occurring on the other side of the world can have unforeseen consequences which impact on small relatively discrete communities. Architects, in response, are urged, in the words of Patrick Geddes (Stephen, ed. 2004), to 'think globally and act locally', to carry out a 'diagnostic survey' followed by 'conservative surgery'. However, beyond this, in order to make meaningful proposals in unfamiliar, but somehow strangely interconnected contexts architects need to broaden the skills and sensitivities which over determined, capital intensive, time specific, product driven initiatives tend to ignore or reduce to a meaningless minimum.

This chapter has reviewed the methods used in the studio to redress that dearth of appropriate skills and sensitivities. From Hopper's 'Spotlight' and Stendhal's annotated sketches to the randomness of the Situationist Derive and Tschumi's narrative drawings,

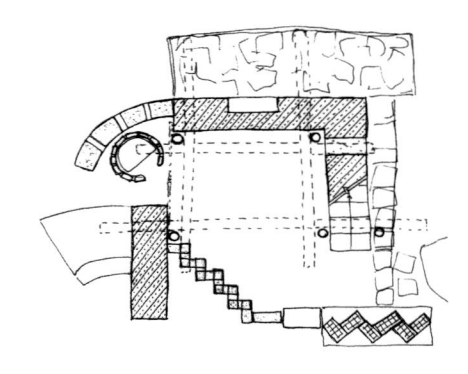

plan and description of student construction
CAT, Wales
Maria Smith

I can't help but compare it with Winnie the Pooh. I read Winnie the Pooh before all important exams, it focuses my mind and sets my priorities straight. It heightens my thoughts and awareness of what at first seem like small things that then reveal themselves to be innate and crucial.

I have borrowed from Winnie the Pooh, A.A. Milne's use of capitalising concepts, affording them to proper noun status. This has allowed me to trace the instances of things and places happening over the course of the few days in which we made an Outside, a Doorway and an Inside. A Staircase, an Upstairs, and therefore a Downstairs; et cetera.

these sensitivities have been extracted from literature and published architectural drawings. Collected together and combinec with Richard Sennett's pragmatic philosophy of developing craft skills through hard work and reflection, these ideas have formed the basis for students to operate effectively as architectura detective, author and craftsperson.

The aim and anticipated result of all student work within the studio is to make appropriate proposals for individually crafted buildings which fit snugly within their chosen context. The methods described above are intended to support this ambition.

Notes

(1) Both of these terms are used by Professor Florian Beigel and Phil Cristou of ARU in their teaching in Unit 1 at ASD, London Metropolitan University. In their study and conceptualisation of 'mat' buildings and landscapes they suggest to their students that they design 'the rug and not the picnic': leaving the props (furniture and fittings and even elements of the building) for the activities to be provided and positioned by the occupiers themselves rather than specified by the architect who simply provides the infrastructure (the rug) to support a diverse range of changing activities. The reference to the raw and the cooked is a metaphor of the extent to which raw materials have been worked on, in the process of making buildings. Claude Lévi-Strauss refers to the raw, the cooked and the rotted (Sennett 2008, p. 129) in a metaphor for cultural production and decay.

(2) Introduction to Stendhal (1995) by J. Sturrock, pp. xviii–xx.

(3) Located in the centre of Kuchhpura, Agra, Humayun's Mosque was built in 1530 at the start of the Mughal period. Whilst in ruins, the mosque is still in use and has recently been the subject of conservation and repair by the Archaeological Society of India. The mosque was built before the village, which is clustered around it.

(4) Field Trip Booklet: Agra Narratives, 2006.

(5) See www.dwf.org.

chapter 3

Delhi 'Slums': Red Lines and High Walls

A Landscape of Walls

(1) Legal Walls: The Story of Lal Dora

In older parts of Indian cities where settlement has preceded the making of planning laws and centralised building ownership registration, rules are applied (like mains servicing) retrospectively. This originated with the classification of land in rural areas as either agricultural or 'abadi' (village settlement). 'Abadi' was originally a Persian word derived from the root 'ab' (water) and meant increasing population and prosperity in a town or district presumably because of the presence or availability of water (Kumar 2002). 'Abadi' areas were made exempt from regulation such that organic patterns of settlement were maintained and were able to become denser without obtaining government permission.

In Delhi there is a system of 'lal dora' (literally 'red line': meaning the area which has a red line drawn around it) which allows the government to declare older settlements as 'abadi' or 'urban villages' exempt from planning and building law. This is sometimes used to include overspill within the 'lal dora' boundary. Hence South Delhi has an array of these urban villages which are steadily being engulfed by both planned 'colonies' and completely illegal settlements.

Within the area originally enclosed by the walls of old Jahanpanah (the fourth city of Delhi, see Chapter 4 for fuller description of the cities of Delhi) there are a number of such urban villages which have been granted 'lal dora' status including Lado Serai, Khirki Village and Chirag Delhi. Holding planning law in abeyance has created an opportunity for urban villages to specialise in particular commercial activities without government control. Chirag Delhi, for example, boasts a range of metalworkers operating from workshops embedded in the north wall. Here, encroachment on footways has proceeded to such an extent that there is very little public open space remaining within the settlement. A zone surrounding the settlement on three sides was reserved for public space and in 2005 a substantive tall house, built in this zone in contravention of the policy, was being demolished by the authorities.

Without the protection of 'lal dora', settlements in south Delhi which have not been approved as part of the masterplan are strictly illegal and theoretically liable to be demolished at any time. In the past when the possession of a legal address was necessary for voter registration, the security of tenure essential for a sense of social, economic and educational stability was almost impossible for such inhabitants. More recently production of a ration card, issued to all Indian nationals, has been accepted as one of the 17 documents which can be used to establish identity for voter registration. This means that in practice, for the larger, more established slum settlements, eviction and demolition are unlikely to happen as residents can elect politicians 'en block' to protect their interests and keep the bulldozers at bay. However, the smaller illegal settlements called J.J. camps (Jhuggie-Jhonpri) are still vulnerable to the forced removal of their populations to resettlement areas outside the city.

(2) City Walls: Chirag Delhi

The walls of Jahanpanah, the fourth city of Delhi, were built in 1326–27 and surrounded a huge area which stretched from the 'lofty' (Ibn Battuta, quoted in INTACH 1996) city ramparts of Lal Kot in the south west to the military complex of Siri Fort in the north east and originally enclosed a forested landscape consisting of Neem, Kikar, Peepal and Banyan trees interspersed with a few agricultural holdings. It seems that this enclosure was originally reserved for the pleasure of the sultan Muhammad Tugluk, perhaps allowing him to hunt and build a palace in peace.

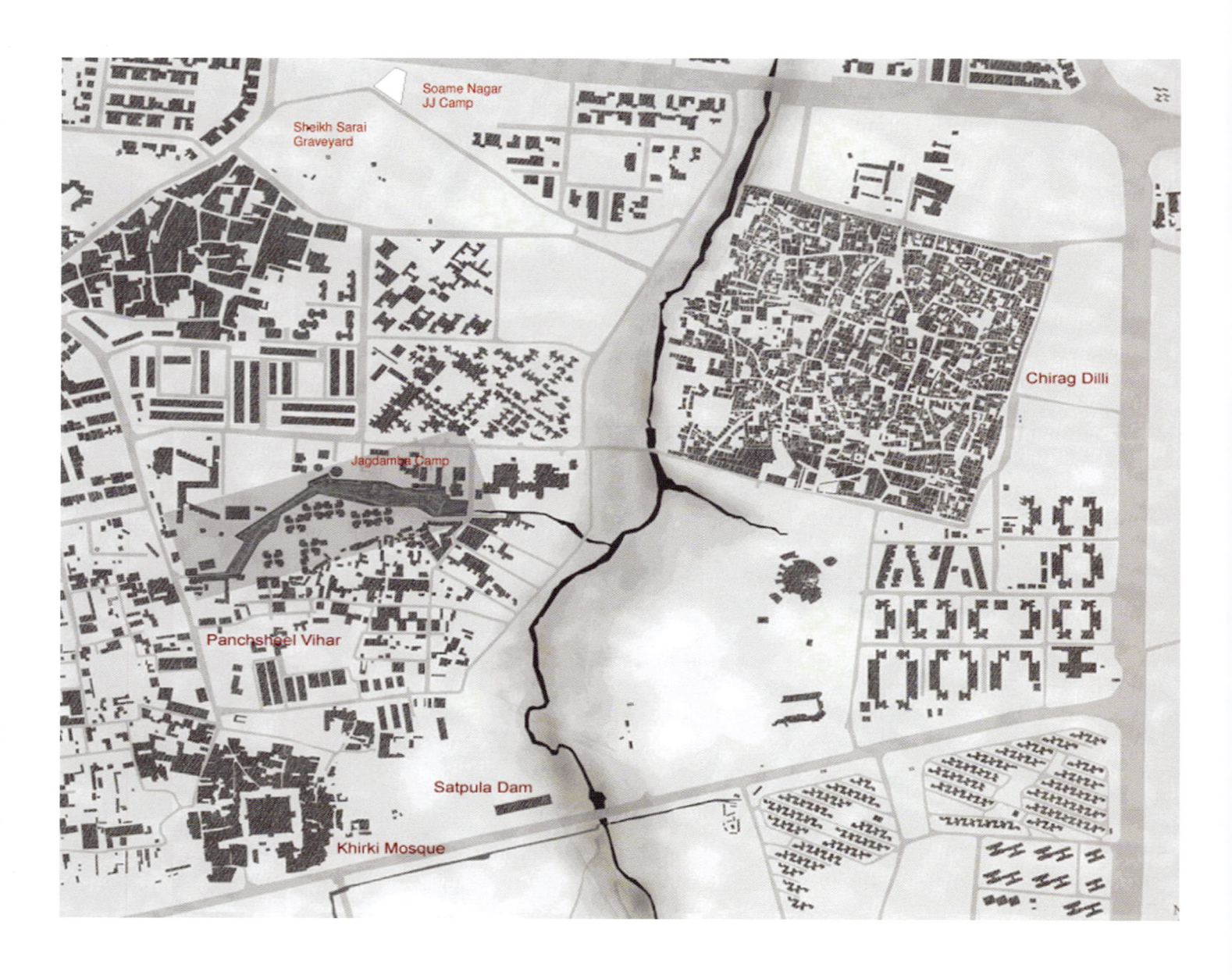

plan of part of south Delhi showing location of
Chirag Delhi and Jagdamba Camp
Angela Hopcraft

Within this vast enclosure were a number of noted monuments including the Dargah (or tomb complex) of Naseruddin Mahmud, the last of the three great Sufi saints of north India. Along with the few agricultural settlements these religious institutions and monuments were protected by the city walls from external interference providing pleasant, relaxed, almost bucolic, surroundings.

The fame of Naseruddin Mahmud's tomb as a place of pilgrimage spread over the centuries and gradually the tombs of further notables were added to the complex. In 1729, as a mark of respect for the Sufi saint, the Mughal Emperor Mohammed Shah Rangila built the walls which now mark out the urban village of Chirag Delhi encapsulating a large tract of land surrounding the Dargah shrines. These walls describe a 400 × 400 metre square on plan and are bounded on the west side by the nallah (Barrapullah stream).

The enclosure was entered by a gate on each of the four sides which had semi-octagonal and circular bastions crowned by domed 'chattris' (canopies) at the corners (quoted in INTACH 1996).

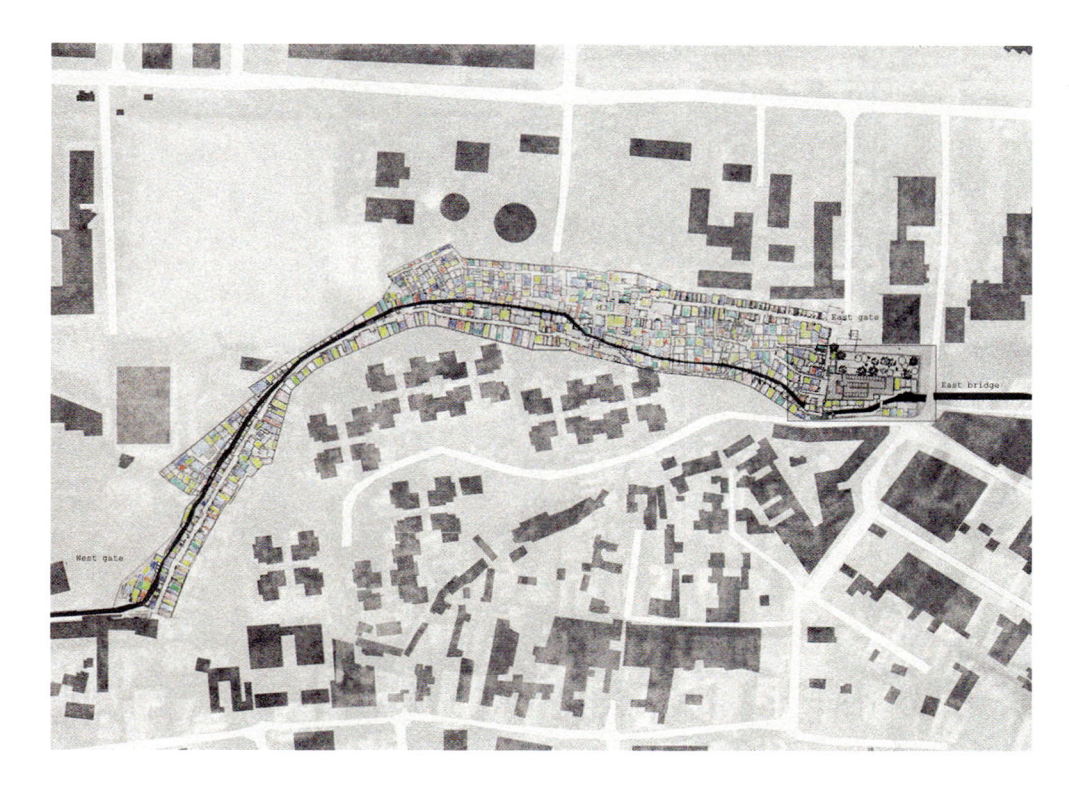

Once more, just as in the case of the walls of Jahanpanah itself, but at a smaller scale, the settlement walls were built before the bulk of the settlement was begun as an attempt to preserve the unique atmosphere of the place. In 1739, a pilgrim described how:

The pleasantness in the vicinity of the mausoleum is akin to (heaven) and the atmosphere around his resting place is like an avenue in paradise ... Caravans of pilgrims arrive from dawn till sunset and setting up their tents in the shadow of the walls they amuse themselves. The place is a spectacle of musical assemblies of good cheer and from every corner sounds of (musical instruments) emanate.

But in 1761 the function of the walls changed. During the invasion of Ahmad Shah Abdali of Afghanistan, the population of the surrounding areas fled to the protection of Chirag Delhi (1) and the urbanisation of the settlement began in earnest. Instead of packaging paradise for royalty or pilgrim, the walls became the protector of an increasingly dense urban population which now, as an urban village, enjoys the protection of 'lal dora'.

As a result, a dense settlement with a distinctive morphology within the hybrid landscape of south Delhi has developed over the succeeding years unchecked by government regulation. The spatial configuration of Chirag Delhi is a coherent example of a contained, dense, urban built matrix which is legally constituted outside of mainstream development. The opportunities and issues related to the future of Chirag Delhi are discussed in Chapter 5.

(3) Retaining Walls: Jagdamba Camp

Jagdamba camp is built on marginal land straddling a tributary of the same nallah which forms the western boundary of Chirag Delhi. With a population of about 6,000 in 2005 this settlement is a 500-metre long by approximately 40-metre wide, linear slum.

rooftops of Jagdamba Camp
Studio Booklet Appendix 05/06

The original inhabitants were building tradesmen and labourers who came to find work in the construction of the nearby Apeejay public school and stayed on to build other planned communities nearby. They never left as employment continued and the settlement expanded along the stream bed.

By defining the edges of the land they were developing with solid brick retaining walls, workers were also circumscribing the marginal land on which they were squatting. The marginal land is sunk by as much as four metres in some places but even so these retaining walls have had to be raised several times to obscure any view of the vertical growth of the settlement from the surrounding legal neighbourhoods. Sometimes the wall is even topped with chain linked fencing laced with exotic plants. As long as Jagdamba was out of sight, it was out of mind.

So, confined by long unbroken walls to the north and south prohibiting entry to the planned, legal, modern housing of its neighbours, there are just two entrances to Jagdamba, both only pedestrian: one to the northeast and one to the west. In November 2005 the local inspector of police said that they rarely entered the settlement as there has been no trouble. He is concerned however about the lack of easy access in case of fire, riot or other emergency.

The natural drainage channel upon which Jagdamba sits is one of Delhi's main outfall sewers. As such it is prone to flooding for one or two weeks in the rainy season and on other occasions when there is heavy rain combined with blockages in the drain. In such cases the inhabitants move their goods up to the first floor and wait for the water to subside. The settlement pattern is comprised of small, one, two and three-storey brick houses either backed up against the long retaining walls or placed back to back in an extended terrace over the sewers. The settlement is served by two tight, narrow, linear, parallel, pedestrian footways. There is a profound lack of public space. The water supply is turned on for just two hours a day and there are public toilets and showers at the eastern end of the settlement. When water becomes available the whole settlement turns out to wash down the pathways, clear out the rubbish from the stream and fill a multitude of plastic containers with water supplies for the coming day.

(4) Two Walls and a Pig Fence: Soami Nagar

The Soami Nagar J.J. camp is located in a small, triangular piece of land separated from legal housing by two high brick security walls; one facing north east and the other north west. To the south however the camp is open to the unmade up Sheikh Serai Road which in turn borders a forested graveyard surrounding an ancient mosque. So whilst the camp can be entered on foot from the north along the Outer Ring Road at the apex of the triangle, vehicular traffic deposits residents along the southern edge where mechanics mend old cars and basic sanitary facilities have been provided by the city authorities.

Whilst the economic health of the J.J. camp residents depends on providing services to their middle class neighbours, their use of urban space is negotiated with those using the road edge and by extension, the Waqf Board, which runs the mosque.

The mosque itself was built to house the late 14th-century tomb of Sheik Zainuddin and came to include a small madrassa or religious school. Before partition in 1947, a large area surrounding the mosque including the graveyard had come under the control of the Waqf Board. In 1960, the Delhi Development Authority (DDA) made a deal with the Waqf board which involved the release of the eastern part of the land for development as a cricket pitch for general use by the surrounding population. Much later in the 1990s, and again with the agreement of the mosque authorities, the western end of the mosque lands were turned into Andolan Park: one of the few formal public spaces in the area where large weddings and festivals are regularly celebrated.

Starting in the late 1980s, the Waqf Board began to rent out plots of land along the edge of Sheikh Serai Road to the north of the mosque, facing the Soami Nagar J.J. camp. At the same time four families built their houses within the walls of the mosque compound. Then, as middle class housing and flats were developed along the Outer Ring Road to the north, the J.J. camp lodged itself in a leftover piece of land between two sites. The foul and waste water from this camp was dispersed into a cesspit within the graveyard. By 2005, commercial activities included two car workshops, a farm, recycling yard and tea stall. All paid a small variable rent to the mosque. There were no piped water or sanitary facilities built specifically for either the commercial strip or the houses located within the mosque so all shared the minimal communal facilities built for the J.J. camp on the roadside. Furthermore residents of neither the J.J. camp nor the commercial strip were ever given security of tenure nor were they allowed to erect a permanent structure.

Psycho-geographically, the southern boundary of the settlement is not the road, which is calm and convivial, carrying minimal vehicular traffic but rather a line drawn in the forest at the back of the commercial strip. Here the mosque authorities, having released land for parks and commerce over the years since Independence, are finally feeling the need to protect the

ruined mosque to the south of Soami Nagar J.J. camp

the historic development of the Sheikh Sarai
graveyard to the south of Soami Nagar J.J.
Muhammad Akmal

graveyard from further incursion. But this time the threat is not from human encroachment but from foraging pigs. The pig is anathema to Muslims and in some countries it is forbidden even to pronounce its name. However the J.J. camp is made up of people from diverse cultures. Some eat pork and farmed pigs are left to graze on rubbish dumps and scrub land. The idea of pigs grubbing up roots amongst the overgrown graves is understandably unacceptable and thanks to the installation of a ring fence, the mosque, madrassa and graveyard are now pig free.

The combined settlement of J.J. camp and commercial strip provide a balanced work/ life environment settled comfortably in the interstitial spaces left over by the planners and suitably adapted to those neighbours with whom its residents can engage.

(5) Backs to the Wall: Kalyanpuri Block 19/20

Whilst Kalyanpuri Block 19/20 is nowhere near the other three settlements mentioned above, being in East Delhi beyond the Yamuna flood plain, it is worth mentioning here because of speculation about the way in which its organic settlement pattern developed. Just as the landscape of walls in south Delhi provided protection and privacy to insiders and outsiders alike so the more recent defensive nature of settlement at Kalyanpuri Block 19/20 provides harbour to its inhabitants.

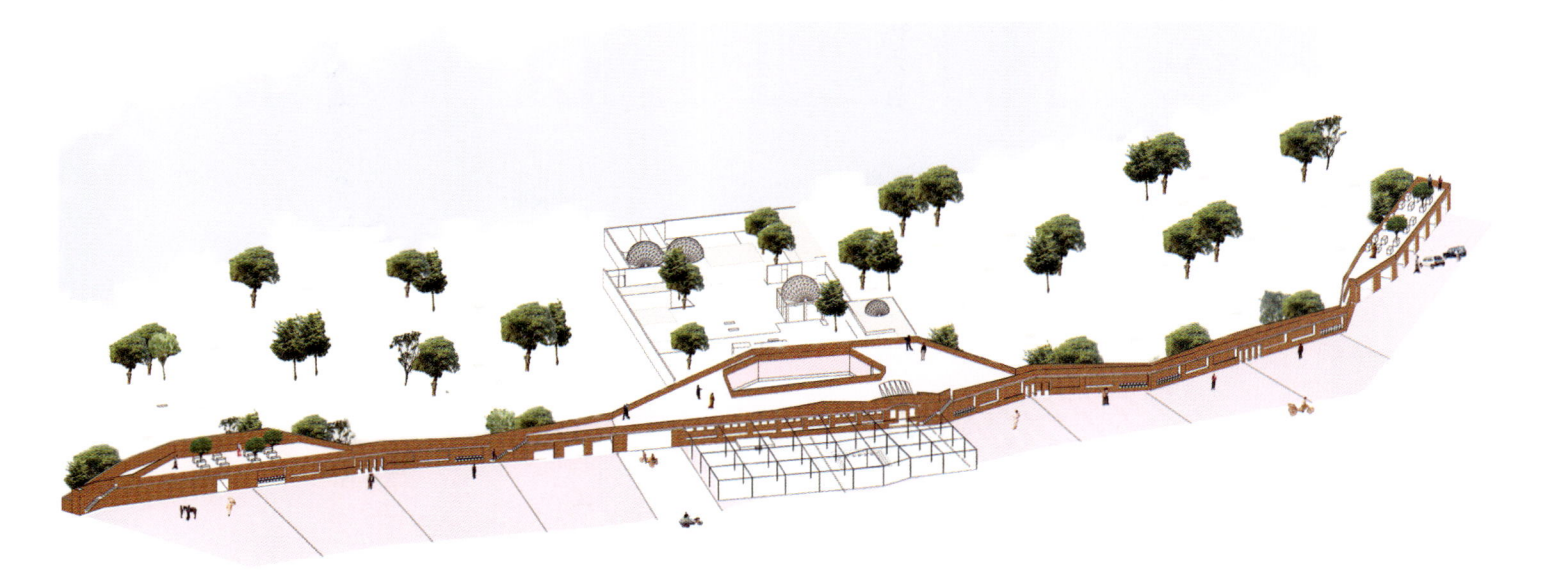

scheme for rebuilding the pig fence as a
service wall
Muhammad Akmal

The rectangular site (approximately 60 × 90 metres), was originally planned as a piece of open ground within a grid development of back to back resettlement terraces. The number of houses provided for the Punjabis, moved from central Delhi in the 1970s, was insufficient and this piece of ground acted as an illegal overspill. It seems that the boundaries of the settlement were developed first. Single-storey, one-roomed houses were built in terraces with their backs to the outside creating a fortress frontier. Within the enclosure, protected by the encircling terraces, clusters of rooms were quickly assembled around small courts. Over the years these clusters were enlarged and eventually nudged up to face the terrace lines leaving a tight, densely packed, if claustrophobic, array of alleys and courts. This must have provided some sense of security to the Sikhs who were the victims of Delhi-wide rioting in 1984 following the assassination of Mrs Gandhi by her Sikh bodyguards leaving one generation of Kalyanpuri's population decimated. In 2007, five or six recognisable clusters of housing existed within the perimeter penetrated by cul-de-sacs in the manner of 'mohallas' (neighbourhoods) aping the more traditional urban fabric of Old Delhi.

The settlement is still hardly more than one storey high and there is but one entrance to the settlement on each of three of the four sides which can always be barricaded in times of trouble. There is just one through street, named the bazaar street by the students, with one entrance at either end. These entrance zones are overlooked and activities monitored by particular individuals who make it their business to know what is going on so that they can forestall any trouble (see quote from Rule 2008 in Chapter 2).

At the southern entrance students also recount how several women sallied forth to provide protection from youths jostling them on the main street, driving the young men away and urging the students to come within the settlement where they would be safe.

Life within Walls

How do such settlements operating under these different legal and planning constraints function on a day to day basis?

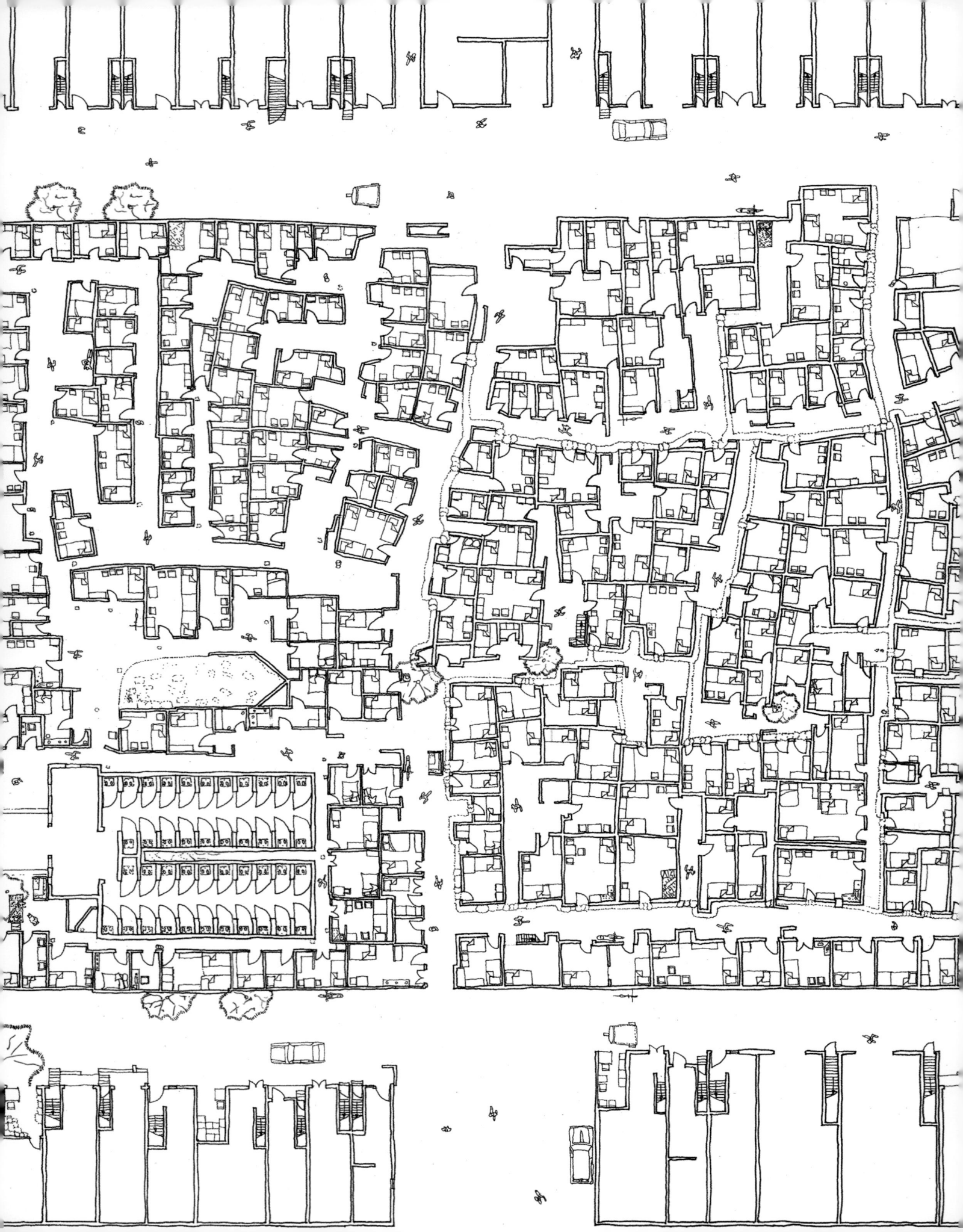

(1) Water, Sanitation and Health

The most all-pervading problem in most settlements is the lack of adequate supplies of clean water and basic sanitation. This seemed to trump all other causes of distress and disease within the population and was the most intractable. Medical services were sufficient to highlight the morbidity caused by waterborne diseases but not adequate to treat them. The real solution, the provision of networked mains, was beyond the means of local organisation and required government intervention.

The Delhi Jal (Water) Board provides settlements with mains water for between two and five hours a day supplemented by borehole wells which often run dry, and need recharging with ground water. Government inspectors checked these wells and sometimes found them to be contaminated.

Communal toilets, when provided, were always too few and only functioned if there were one or two full time attendants keeping the premises clean and charging a small fee. They were often located a considerable distance from the home.

(2) Education and Rights

Perhaps the poorest settlement mentioned above is Kalyanpuri Block 19/20. Here primary schooling was not available to all children without payment and at least one woman was reputed to have sold a kidney to pay for her child's education. With the exception of Chirag Delhi, schools, clinics and shops are mostly located outside the settlements but there is some evidence of self-help groups tackling issues of health and education within the settlements. For example Soami Nagar had both a small shop and nursery provision provided by two women who looked after children whilst the parents worked.

(3) Social Spaces: Chowks and Otlas

All the settlements were almost completely pedestrianised. Even when a car or motor bike was able to penetrate a little way into the settlement the narrowness of the pathway was such that pedestrians took priority. This made for a very relaxed atmosphere in the winding lanes especially where each house had an otla (raised entrance space) where residents sat and chatted to their neighbours and those passing by. Children playing in the streets were safe

above
wall along southern edge of Kalyanpuri Block 19/20
Jonathan Turney
facing page
detail from plan of Kalyanpuri Block 19/20
Nicolas Maari

young children with books in an alley in
Kalyanpuri Block 19/20
Eureka de la Cruz

from traffic but might be vulnerable to injury from storm drains and loose electricity cables. Whilst there remained in Chirag Delhi a few old chowks or squares, usually centred on a tree, a redundant public well and a raised sitting platform; dedicated public space was always difficult to find and unless actively occupied, vacant lots were liable to disappear overnight due to further encroachment. This left most settlements with an array of badly-paved alleys down which ran open drains perhaps channelled to one side. In the poorer settlements these alleys acted as living rooms and kitchens. In Jagdamba children ran around at will; in and out of the rooms which faced the alleys so that when opened, doors and alleys acted as one space.

(4) Zoning by Ethnicity, Religion and Caste

Settlements were often zoned according to ethnicity and religion. Chirag Delhi, the oldest and most established was occupied like an onion in layers with the Jains and Brahmins (priests) in the centre, surrounded by the Baniyas (merchants) and Jats (farmers). Separate areas were reserved for the Khumaris (potters) and Punjabis whilst the poorest castes were located in the west along the boundary with the nallah where the original wall had disappeared and the land was lowest.

(5) Public, Secular, Liminal Space

Secular and commercial space was reserved for the outside. The walls of Chirag Delhi had been remodelled to provide commercial property with shops and even mechanics' garages to the rear without too much concern for caste. The strip of land just outside the walls provided a secular 'liminal' space where everyone could mix freely: where sports were played and markets had been established.

In his essay 'Medieval Reservoir and Modern Urban Planning: Local Society and the Hauz-i-Rani', which focuses on the historical development of part of the South Delhi suburb of Saket nearby, Kumar (2002) describes the function of such secular liminal spaces:

[they ease] the differences between communities, presenting an opportunity to strangers to establish acquaintances outside their familiar social realms. The free access and unstructured nature of ... activities [places] no premium on class or confessional differences. For the moment people [are] accepted as individuals and not as extensions of their separate social worlds. On the contrary, the process of fraternisation provide[s] the opportunity for doubting the validity of the many inherited clichéd sentiments about unfamiliar people. Not only [is] this ... secular and democratic, but it could also ... [prove] to be an agent for neutralising a potential class and communal polarisation between neighbourhoods.

It is noticeable that the 'liminal' public space associated with the essentially Hindu Soami Nagar J.J. camp was the roadside to the south and had been secured by arrangement (perhaps unselfconsciously) with the Muslim Waqf Board. This paralleled the more formal agreements between the Waqf Board and the Delhi Development Authority to release land for the cricket pitch and Andolan Park. In the Jagdamba camp, public space was limited to the two entrance spaces to the north east and west, both long and thin, like extended funnels channelling people in and out of the settlement. However they each performed differently. Whereas the western entrance doubled up as a linear market the eastern entrance became the site for another linear activity: the occasional community queue: whether for free medical check ups or for the distribution of food stuffs. Both entrances performed secular functions and might therefore be classed as liminal spaces. But here the linear regimentation of the settlement plan is continued to the entrance spaces: long, straight, parallel walls, terraced dwellings, queues and lines of stalls.

(6) Gendered Space

In the closed world of Kalyanpuri Block 19/20 the Sikh inhabitants had some measure of security but the only public space was within the confines of the narrow alleys immediately outside the one-roomed apartments. Here, the alley space became gendered: swapping from female during the day to male in the evening when the father came home from work. Privacy was provided by hanging cloths on lines and alternating activities behind this screen between cooking and washing during the day and laying chairs for relaxation in the evening. As the alleys were shared these normal family activities were open and neighbours would join in the daytime chores and evening chats. Immediately outside the settlement however, this gendering of space was noted on a larger scale. The brighter, more colourful street along the northern edge occupied mostly by women working on their doorsteps appeared more convivial and could be contrasted with the southern edge where youths hung out jostling those who passed by on their way to and from school and men scurried around operating small business from the ground floors of the houses across the street.

(7) Other Worlds

Most of Kalyanpuri block 19/20 consisted of just single-storey dwellings with the roofs

left
children drawing in Bouvra Chowk, Chirag Delhi,
Studio Booklet 04/05
right
the other world of the rooftop

providing another world for children to play, allowing them to shortcut between the alleyways below and to perform games of run and jump over parapets. Accessed by bamboo ladders from the outside, occasional lightweight first floor rooms were built on the roof, providing hideaways for older people to sleep away from the bustle of the family. Alongside these rooftop retreats were bamboo perches, needed for pigeon competitions, and kites trapped in the suspended cocoons of electricity wires.

But in difficult times rooftops have provided a more compelling purpose as alternative streets in the sky. Sam Miller describes how, as a journalist, he covered the riots in East Delhi in 1992 (Miller 2009 p. 259). He arrived in the district of Seelampur just after the mob killing of Muslim residents had taken place:

I saw, to my amazement, that the uneven rooftops of Seelampur had become an elevated walkway, busy with silent shuffling pedestrians. The streets may have been empty, but dozens of people were moving around, carrying provisions and keeping watch on what was happening below. They were making preparations for the possible return of the killers by fortifying their rooftops.

How do people, present in the city without adequate means, acquire shelter?

Delhi's population has grown from 800,000 in 1941 to a little over two million in 1954 and again to over 13 million today. The authorities only managed to build a little more than one million homes during this period (2). After Independence in 1947, Delhi experienced a huge influx of

using washing to provide privacy screening in the alleys
Amelia Rule

migrants, which still continues today. Statistics from 2003 show that of the 500,000 people who migrate to Delhi each year, eighty per cent end up in illegal settlements or dwellings; by 2015 India's capital will have a slum population of more than 10 million (Davis 2006, p. 18).

Referring specifically to Delhi, David Drakakis-Smith (Davis 2006, p. 10) describes a pattern of city development which he calls rural/urban hybridisation which consists of a rich diversity of human habitat:

... the distinction between what is urban and rural becomes blurred as cities expand along corridors of communication, by-passing or surrounding small towns and villages which subsequently experience in situ changes in function and occupation.

This diverse landscape has been incubated in an array of physical and cultural walled enclosures and has been engulfed by the modern phenomenon of planned expansion following successful economic development. However the planned settlements are just as liable to be walled and gated (controlling access and protecting the middle class inhabitants) as the traditional and illegal versions. Secular liminal spaces exist between the walled enclosures offering the opportunity for free association outside familiar social constructs. Davis asks whether these are just transitional

WE FOR YOU

THE 'WE FOR YOU' NGO MANAGED TO CONSULT WITH 210 PATIENTS IN ONE DAY.

THE BIGGEST PROBLEM IN THE CAMP ARE WATER BORNE DISEASES, LIKE DENGUE.

4 PATIENTS HAD TUBERCULOSIS

2 PATIENTS HAD LEPROSY

2 PATIENTS HAD A SEXUALLY
TRANSMITTED DISEASE

health day held by medical NGO in Jagdamba
Camp entrance space
Tim Sanderson

landscapes or new forms of urbanism (Davis 2006). Either way, it is in the interest of all inhabitants of Delhi that the plight of slum dwellers is addressed. This means the provision by the city as a whole of legal access to land and services.

Legal tenure, whether complete ownership or recognised tenancy, is almost impossible for those without the means to pay. Historically some rights might be acquired through protracted occupation but registered title requires positive, recorded, recognition by those in power. The modern requirement for further permissions related to use, aesthetics, health and safety create barriers which make it virtually impossible for the urban poor to house themselves without some relaxation of these property rights, planning rules and building regulations. For the effective use of scarce resources it actually requires more from the authorities than relaxation. If the efforts of the poor to house themselves are to be supported then the schemes of the planning authorities should follow the patterns of occupation laid out unself-consciously in illegal settlements rather than seek to parachute in a grid of alien requirements or blight the efforts of the actual occupants by denying recognition to their pragmatic efforts.

At the moment in Delhi whilst it is widely recognised that the lack of adequate legal social housing is of primary concern, there is very little discussion of the concept of upgrading, of even legally owned and constructed property, let alone any concept of squatters acquiring ownership rights to their already constructed dwellings.

The Delhi Development Authority (DDA) has been responsible for low cost housing provision since 1968 and has re-housed thousands of people by providing resettlement colonies. The DDA provision has never kept pace with demand and focus has always been on the clearance of high value land or land with a perceived public purpose such as that required for the Commonwealth Games 2010. At their inception, colonies are seldom supplied with clean drinking water or mains sanitary facilities risking degeneration of the fabric and spread of disease. The legal resettlement colony of Kalyanpuri had to wait 13 years for such service provision.

Currently the DDA relies on the provision of out of town resettlement colonies to relocate squatters pending demolition of their more central 'slum' settlements. These new colonies are almost always sited away from employment opportunities and without adequate services leaving their new occupants with no option but to drift back to the city in order to find paid work (Shirangan 2000).

There is an overriding advantage for low income communities to live near their place of employment. Once relocated to a resettlement colony the family provider would often have to spend the daily wage merely on the cost of transport to make the return journey to the city centre and their job. It is not surprising therefore that many people sell their allocated resettlement plot, despite the subsidies, and return to live in an informal settlement close to their place of employment (Rule 2008, p. 2)

Whilst Fernando de Soto has advocated giving land title to squatters in order to enable development funds to be secured on its value; others have claimed that this benefits absentee landlords rather than the poor occupiers themselves (Davis 2006). This is borne out by the fact that without control of plot transfer, low income residents of successful DDA resettlement schemes usually sell on their plots to higher income groups and again return to the 'slum'.

But there are other forms of tenure in common based on the law of Co-operatives and Trusts and of philanthropic key worker housing (e.g. the Tata Group's worker housing) which have pointed the way elsewhere and which might be used as a precedent in India. Cooperatives insist on the continued residence of their members, buying up property from members who leave, thereby avoiding slum landlordism. Fortunately, the new Delhi 2021 Master Plan published in 2007 to regulate the haphazard development of the city has gone some way to recognise such alternative forms of social housing:

... it will leave in place the present strategy of relocating slums from 'areas required for public purpose' and allow specific sites to be upgraded in-situ while other slums will be left 'to continue'... In the meantime a search for a third and hopefully successful step is underway. This will include 'a cooperative resettlement model' with obligatory 'resettlement rights for the residents on sites with relatively small clusters' rather than very large resettlement sites, which risk becoming a planned slum if not serviced properly (Rule 2008, p. 2 and Shirangan 2000).

These mechanisms require concepts of common ownership based on a secular understanding of rights and responsibilities rather than adherence to familiar social norms based on faith or caste. By supporting upgrading initiatives in existing illegal settlements close to centres of employment and by enabling new cooperative residents to maintain control over house improvements; homes can be adapted to a changing way of life. Studio involvement with CURE in initiating a pilot housing cooperative in the resettlement colony of Savda Ghewra is discussed in Chapter 7.

Notes

(1) BBC News, 'Why so much of Delhi is illegal'. 4 February 2006. http://news.bbc.co.uk/1/hi/world/south_asia/4665330.stm.

(2) During Partition in September 1947, the 'huge open grassy space, the size of twenty football fields' enclosed by the walls of the Purana Qila, the Old Delhi Fort, was home to 'tens of thousands of desperate Muslims' providing another example of enclosing walls providing temporary protection during invasion and civil strife rather than fortifying an existing urban settlement (Miller 2009, p. 93).

chapter 4

The Waste Pickers of Panchsheel Vihar

Recycled Landscapes

In the 14th century, to the south of modern Delhi, the Barrapullah stream, a tributary of the Yamuna was dammed at Satpula. In this way the Tughlaq dynasty provided drinking water and a moat for their fortress city Jahanpanah (meaning literally 'the shelter of the world'). Jahanpanah was the fourth city of Delhi and its new walls enclosed the virgin scrub and woodland between Lal Kot, the first city, and Siri Fort, the third city. The Satpula dam formed part of these walls but still allowed the stream and floodwaters to pass through to the broad, enclosed flood plain within (Peck 2005). At the same time nearby, just inside the walls, but above the flood plain, an experimental mosque called Khirki (1375; the mosque of windows) was constructed. It was built using stones recycled from 27 Hindu and Jain temples destroyed by the first Muslim rulers. The plan of this mosque was highly unusual (a cruciform plan with four internal courtyards instead of one central court). The mosque was abandoned within just a hundred years as it divided the faithful into four small groups rather than combining prayer sessions within one common space.

The city walls of Jahapanah have all but disappeared, their building stones reused by future generations: that is, apart from the Satpula Dam itself. This stone wall still holds back the silted up stream and distributes water through its seven arched weirs.

Prior to Independence in 1947, a small number of buildings around the abandoned mosque were occupied by Muslims and Khirki mosque was used occasionally as a baithak (community gathering space). With Partition in 1947, all Muslims abandoned Khirki leaving the mosque eerily vacant. Home to a myriad of circling bats, it still survives almost intact. It appears as if sunk in a crater; a neglected monument, protected now by the Archaeological Society of India, surrounded by a taller substantial mini townscape which is raised above the ancient domed edifice by countless layers of waste from seven centuries of subsequent occupation.

surveys of Khirki mosque and surroundings
Robert Johnson, Amy Penford and Terry Whitehead

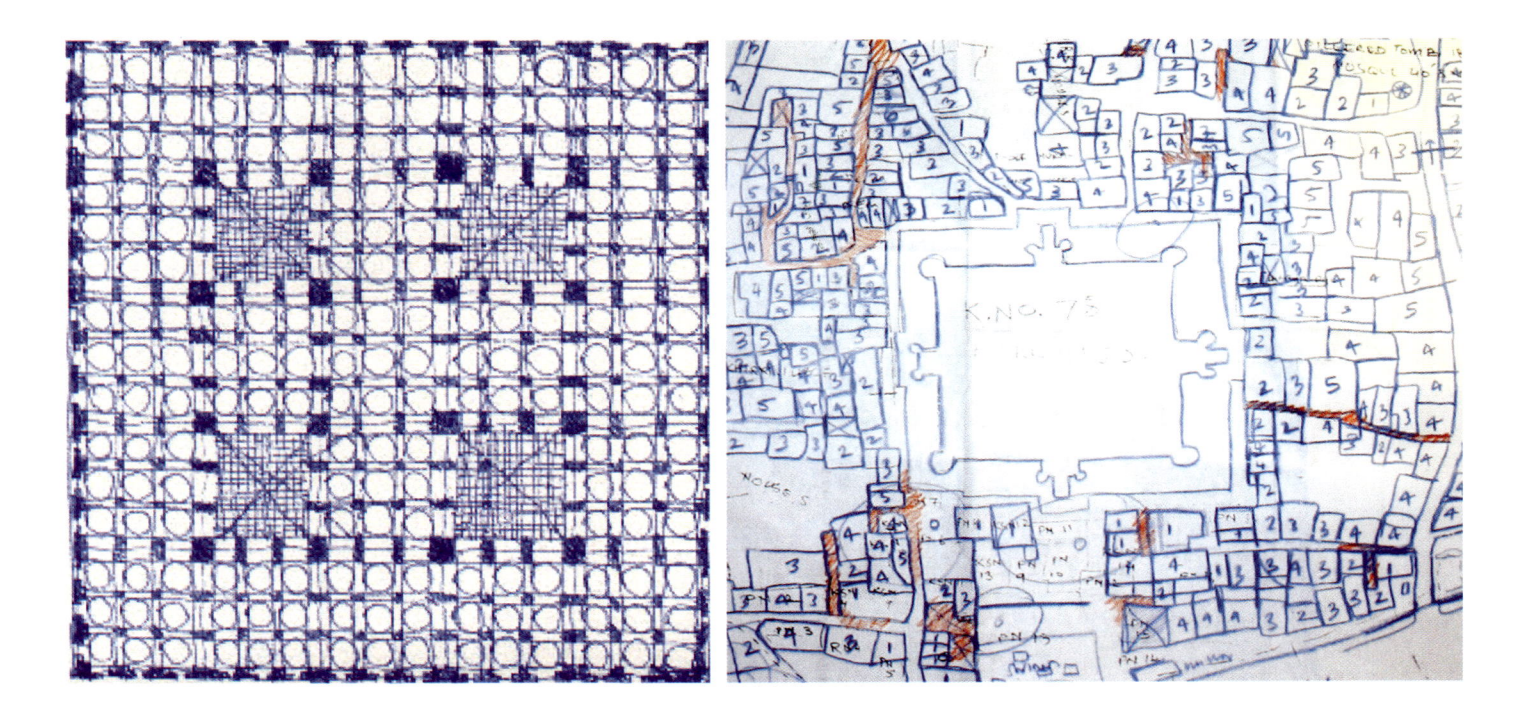

The seven cities of Delhi
Shamoon Patwari from map (Mani 1997)

1 Lal Kot
2 Siri
3 Tughlaqabad
4 Jahanpanah
5 Feroze Shah
6 Indrapat
7 Shahjahanabad

A Yamuna river
B New Delhi
C Chirag Delhi
D Panchsheel Vihar
E Khirki Mosque
F Satpula Dam

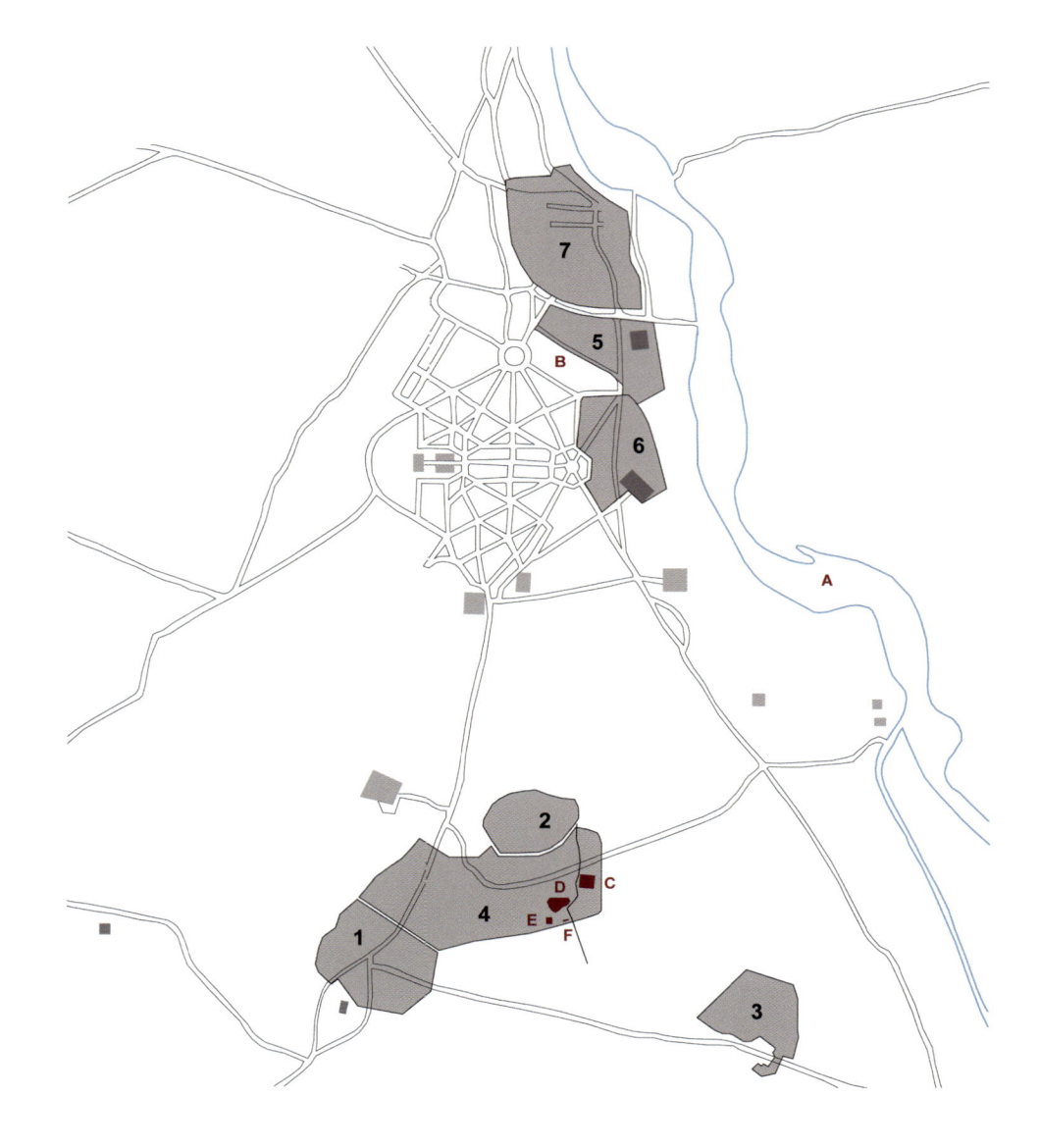

interior view of Khirki Mosque

1380

1755

1947 Partition

1975

1984

1996 - Present

Thus, the empty but intact mosque, visited only by tourists, stands as an example of communal space built with materials recycled from previous generations. It was abandoned early on in its life as its design did not encourage communal prayer and was then used briefly as a community space. It is now left empty because there is no perceived need for space shared by the local community.

About 250 years ago, Hindu peasants moved in to farm the flat lands known as Panchsheel Vihar to the north of Khirki village and mosque and stretched eastwards merging into the flood plain of the Barrapullah stream. Over the succeeding years, ownership of the farm land was established by the Hindu farmers and as a consequence the plot boundaries were clearly defined. Then in the 1980s, land reforms allowed owners, on payment of a government tax, to register land ownership and divide up their agricultural plots. Some plots were rented out as small farms to new migrants but the pressure for housing was such that rents became too high for the land to support subsistence agriculture. In any case by this time the stream had been transformed into a highly polluted, slow moving, black effluent running slowly into the river Yamuna. It is now simply referred to as the nalla.

The authorities have never given permission for the construction of any privately owned buildings in this area. Whilst land ownership is fully registered, private building construction in the south Delhi suburb of Panchsheel Vihar has always proceeded illegally. Even before the 1980s, land reforms the flood plain of the 'nalla' to the east of Khirki and Panchsheel Vihar had been used as a dump site for building debris brought to the site from Delhi and New Delhi. Consequently the land surface of the flood plain has been raised above the flood waters. As a result the second wave of residential buildings was about 600mm higher than the original ground level. The new service roads were also built on ground made up with building debris whilst unused plots and backlands between the made-up roads remained at a lower level.

above
student analysis of the growth of Khirki Village
Sam Bentil-Mensah
below
the edge of Khirki village by the nalla showing the layers of waste on which much of the village is raised

sketch of basement workshop below the level of
the raised road
Nat Horner

From an analysis of surveys of Panchsheel Vihar compiled by students, it appears that the new plots were first serviced by unpaved roads extending at right angles to the primary through routes. At any one time each of these roads stopped suddenly at the end of the development. So from the air, the pattern began to appear as a series of roadway trees (or back to back coombs) with the dead ends of their branches eventually being stopped randomly against the backs of the plots of adjacent development trees.

Eventually, by repeatedly breaking through, pedestrians linked up arbitrarily adjacent 'road trees' across the unmade, uneven backlands. Similarly such preferred pedestrian lines linked one or two previously insignificant dead ends (of 'road trees') to meet the main tarmac perimeter roads over undeveloped plots. This ad-hoc linking up added character and dimension to the urban spaces and with it came the explicit gift of identity to the previously unselfconscious layout of the settlement. The backland spaces involved provided some of the most interesting sites for student speculation.

In 1999, tarred roads were introduced in some parts causing ground levels to rise a further 300mm in places. This has left the earliest buildings up to one metre lower than the adjacent road; requiring visitors to duck down in order to negotiate the entry threshold. Being so much lower than the surrounding ground level can be a disaster for residents of the humblest, single-storey buildings closest to the nalla. In the absence of a comprehensive surface water drainage infrastructure, heavy rainfall in August and September often sweeps into these dwellings, with no means of exit for the muddy deposits except evaporation and ground seepage. This leaves the residents temporarily homeless and their possessions permanently damaged.

Whilst the ground slopes naturally towards the nalla, running north down the middle of the flood plain, subsequent dumping of waste, both generally and within each plot, has resulted in a very uneven and loose fill. Excavation to provide foundations for substantial new buildings must go much lower than this fill. Plot developers to the west of the settlement, furthest from the 'nalla', where flooding is least likely, have exploited the filled ground to invent a new room type. By scooping out the rubbish and hardcore from the foundation level upwards and establishing the ground floor two or three steps above ground level, a semi-basement can be provided. Approached by ladders or stairways leading steeply downwards from pavement level such basements make pleasantly cool and evenly top-lit workshops. The tranquil, secluded comfort of basements sited on flood plains, is reminiscent of the semi-subterranean arrangements in some traditional Baghdadi courtyard houses sited within made-up ground next to the river Tigris.

Clearly, there is a general tendency for the ground level to rise, for the flood plain to be encroached upon and for the natural water course to be canalised. During heavy rains, in the absence of a neighbourhood surface water strategy, puddles in the roadway and indeed on any exposed ground surface are filled in locally. This further contributes to the general rise in ground level.

Despite the fact that the land is overlaid with 900mm of building rubble, it is still classified by government as agricultural. This situation is so entrenched that until recently no established owner even bothered to apply for a building permit. Thus, because of this fossilised zoning rule, the provision of piped public services to houses by government is almost totally lacking. As a welcome response the more wealthy residents have banded together to provide, at their own expense, feeder connections to government sewers and water mains on the periphery of the settlement.

Excavation for the retro-fit of piped services is made easier by the looseness of the fill. However despite pressure from residents for the settlement of Panchsheel Vihar to be 'regularised': a formal process by which such well-built neighbourhoods are given retrospective legality, the government has still not acceded and any connection to mains services remains frustratingly illegal. The remaining marginal land adjacent to the nalla is itself now used as the channel for a major piped water main which has in turn (2008) been overfilled by excavated material from the nearby new metro line tunnels. The canalisation of the nalla is almost complete.

Most recent migrants to Panchsheel Vihar have come directly from the poor rural areas of Bihar and Uttar Pradesh in search of brighter opportunities. They live alongside the more established middle class residents.

Dwellings are characterised by two classes of construction. Kuchha construction is temporary, made of short lived materials where occupation is ad hoc, piecemeal and largely tolerated without permission from the authorities. Pukka construction on the other hand is more permanent and carries with it implications of the need for approval and legal ownership of the land.

Many of the poorer migrants live in the south and east of the settlement, on the edge of the marginal flood plain in kuchha hutments. Their livelihoods are based on the sorting of waste materials collected from the more middle class households and from industry for sale to middlemen. These lower caste families are the waste pickers of Panchsheel Vihar living at the heart of a rapidly changing physical landscape on the scraps left over from the lives of their more affluent neighbours.

A study of these waste pickers offered an opportunity for speculation on the part of several students. They identified potential for the waste pickers' activities to extend beyond their current scope of sorting waste to include processing it and producing goods. Could the recycling of community refuse, rather than just involving collection and sorting activities be the basis for the acquisition by waste pickers of new craft skills that would transform their livelihood opportunities? Could an understanding of the current pragmatic use of space and materials by waste pickers lead, through design, to the potential for viable permanent residence in Panchsheel Vihar? Could these opportunities lead to greater acceptance of waste pickers and their children within the wider community?

The Waste Pickers

The waste pickers are of the lowest caste, traditionally fated to deal with the waste of Indian society. They are almost totally uneducated and lack formally recognised skills. They live in and amongst the sorted and unsorted rubbish which they collect. Materials such as newspapers, cardboard, jute sacks and bottles are sorted according to type and size and then bundled up for onward sale to middlemen. Despite having a legal right to primary education, waste picker children have real difficulty in gaining access to the local schools for largely cultural reasons. Most children stay with their parents, sorting waste. Dwellings are assembled on the internal perimeter of the sorting yards and are the embodiment of kuchha (see above). Waste pickers live and work in the same place for a short period and

model of waste picking yards on the edge of the nalla in Panchsheel Vihar
Judith Ben-Tovim, Christina Monteiro, Sam Bentil-Mensah and Hiromi Yang

then move on to another vacant plot as the first is developed, wrapping their lives in the debris of the surrounding community as they go.

New Delhi is a rapidly growing city and the demand for new pukka housing on legally recognised holdings is palpable. The settlement of Panchsheel Vihar, surrounded on three sides by middle class neighbourhoods (and on the fourth by the broad flood plain of the nalla) mostly with legal title to both land and buildings, is no exception. The government vision, as perceived locally, is to import a 'Manhattan skyline' and this unstoppable higher rise pukka juggernaut has already breached the boundaries of the district. New middle class residential developments on former waste picker plots are springing up to the north, west and centre of the district. Inexorably waste pickers' yards are being driven into the southeast corner: the last remaining kuchha neighbourhood.

Students studied the settlement of Panchsheel Vihar in general and the lives of waste pickers in particular in November 2005 and November 2008. There are a number of rich local spatial and material strategies and issues embodied in the everyday life of the waste pickers which resonate in these student schemes.

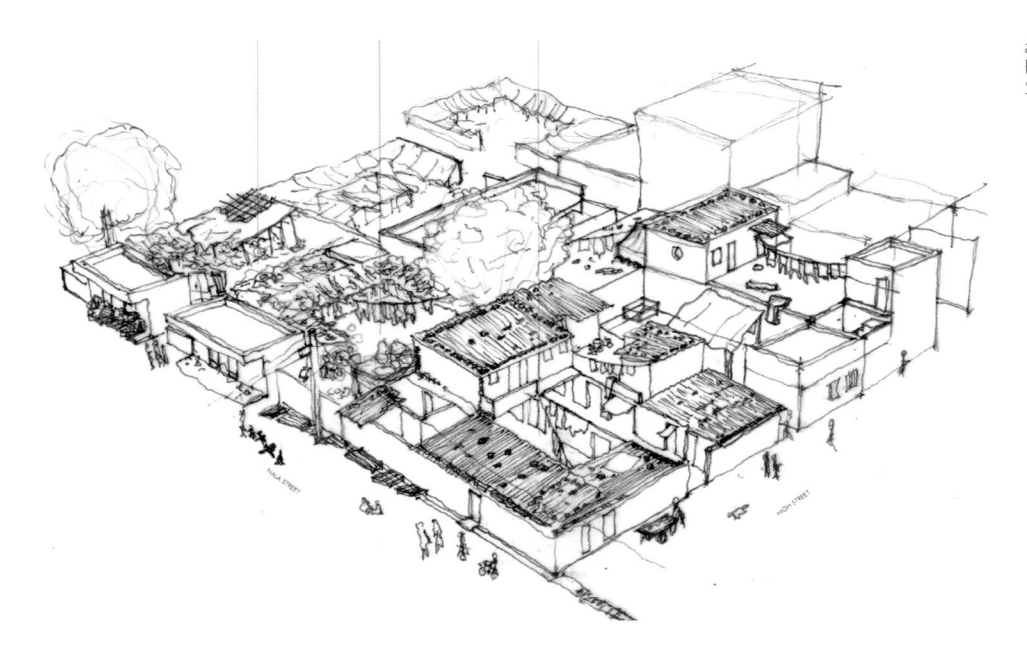

axonometric sketch of waste picking yards,
Panchsheel Vihar
Sam Bentil-Mensah

(1) The Use of Courtyards as Communal Live/Work Yards

There is a long history of the use of courtyards in the urban history of Hindu and
Mughal architecture in India. However, with the rise of modernism in the dying days
of colonialism and then through Independence and beyond; bungalows, villas and
then apartment buildings have become the established norm for new legal pukka
construction. Nevertheless, in a country where the provision of ordinary public space is
often limited to roadways, the private courtyard still acts as a mediating transitional type.
The characteristics of courtyards foster communal living, group security and the multi-
functional use of space. They continue to provide efficient shelter for those without the
resources, the education or the inclination to operate formally in the more individualised
secular world of the air-conditioned apartment.

But cultural values have been attached to these two opposites. Whereas shared
communal courtyards might be cool and secure, they are also regarded as congested,
dirty and regressive. Individualised apartments on the other hand need to be gated for
security and artificially humidified and cooled for thermal comfort but have the sobriquet
of being clean, tidy and progressively modern (Ben-Tovim 2007).

The majority of the recycling yards are spaces where work and living co-exist. Yards are
usually surrounded by a high solid wall with just one entrance for security and privacy. At
the centre of the open yard the waste is piled up and sorted. It may be covered with nets,
corrugated sheets or plastic fabric to stop the waste blowing away and to protect the
sorters from the sun. Around the inner edge of the yard, leaning up against the wall are
kuchha constructed of frames made from bamboo or Sheesham poles, sometimes two
storeys high, clad with cardboard, tin sheets or plastic tarpaulins attached with shredded
inner tube from bicycles. Each room is about 2.5 × 3 metres and is the home of one
waste picking family. In some cases there are two yards adjacent to one another: one for
dwellings and the other for sorting.

So long as courtyard housing and communal living is regarded as fundamentally
undesirable, then as the kuchha courtyard plots become developed into pukka, flatted

apartments so the waste pickers will have to move out and continue their nomadic existence elsewhere. But if the safety, flexibility and passive climatic response of courtyard houses can count for more than the negative factors seen to be associated with communal living, there is no reason why courtyards cannot become respectable urban prototypes for permanent settlement by picker communities.

(2) The 'Pukka'/'Kuchha' Juxtaposition and the Question of Change

The binary classification of buildings and materials (pukka/kuchha) has made it easier to dismiss the poorer and more temporary dwellings as undesirable. This, in turn has made it more difficult to integrate new ideas and recycled materials into mainstream construction. However, continuing change in the availability and status of materials allows some scope for new ideas and for waste pickers to move into their production and use.

Fired brick, a solid pukka building material, has been formed traditionally from clay soils such as those found in the Yamuna flood plains around Delhi and fired using coal or firewood. This continues to be a huge industry employing millions of workers in a process of small-scale, informal, locally-organised production. It is still the predominant mainstream building material in India. Such fired brick production uses increasingly scarce amounts of biomass and fossil fuels, has a prominent carbon footprint and a nasty tendency to pollute the atmosphere. Whilst, on the one hand, attempts to increase the efficiency of brick kilns are proceeding, on the other, recent anti-pollution legislation has banned such industrial activity taking place within one hundred miles of Delhi. This has increased prices and intensified the search for alternatives including recycled, bricks and fly ash bricks. To make such bricks, fly ash (a pozzolanic residue from power stations); lime (a by-product of the acetylene industry); and gypsum (a by-product of chemical plants) are combined in a process which does not require thermal energy (Knippers 2008). The recycling of materials from the demolition of old houses provides a continuing supply of fired bricks to the poorer settlements. Writing of his experience in Ahmedahbad, Knippers (2008) writes that these houses are:

... dismantled layer by layer. The materials are sorted, cleaned and sold ... roughly 85% of the bricks recovered in this manner found their way as building materials into the slums, whereas elements such as used doors and windows were sold to people of higher income.

As mentioned earlier, Panchsheel Vihar has been a dumping ground for waste building rubble since the 1980s and this continues to provide a rich source of fired bricks for recycling. However the practice of re-using building materials goes back much further. It continues a long and rich tradition stretching back to the 14th century and the construction of the Khirki mosque described earlier.

Unlike fired brick, bamboo is a traditionally kuchha material which grows throughout India except in the hot deserts of Rajasthan or the cold mountains of Ladakh. Bamboo's temporary status is related to its susceptibility to insect attack and difficulty with junctions and joints. New treatments can give bamboo a life of at least 40 years provided buildings are designed with appropriate details at ground and eaves level whilst grouted and bolted joints have proved effective. Having found ways of changing the performance of bamboo, what remains is the need to promote an equivalent change in the perception of bamboo to that of a pukka building material:

Examples from the last ten years demonstrate the enormous potential of bamboo as a building product. But because of the lack of standards and regulations relating to this material, legislation limits its application. To make bamboo accessible to a broader public, further efforts need to be made in the fields of basic research, teaching, product development and marketing (Knippers 2008).

Visions of the flood plain landscape changing from smoking brick kilns to rustling, shaded bamboo groves drove several student schemes. The relationship between the supply of and demand for construction materials is changing due to the political and environmental factors already described. New or reinvented building materials could soon become commonplace. Exploiting their experience in dealing with Delhi's waste, the waste pickers of Panchsheel Vihar could begin to focus on producing and working with such new and

sketch of waste picker housing, north Panchsheel Vihar
Nat Horner

right
cardboard bundles used to form waste picker house
below
two-storey waste picker house with bamboo framework above sorting yard

recycled building materials. Even within the mainstream multi-storey concrete and brick dwellings of the middle classes there is potential for the creative involvement by the occupiers in a process of retrofit and adaptation. Moveable and temporary shutters, screens and pergolas together with experimental water catchment and heating devices can all be made from recycled materials and components.

Nevertheless, it is clear that if waste pickers are to expand the scope of their involvement from sorting to manufacture then their new products will need to have a reliable and predictable performance. This is essential if such recycled products are to gain a status comparable to their brand new, pukka equivalents.

(3) Communal, Public and Individualised Spaces

Walking in amongst the roads and alleyways of Khirki and Panchsheel Vihar it is difficult to find designated public space, set aside for the public to enjoy and maintained by the municipality. There are however, many leftover spaces where access is possible if not encouraged.

The nalla: home to a landscape of dispersed thorn trees is a toilet for the poorest and their established daily rituals make it possible for male and female, young and old to make use of this facility with some privacy. Here, footpaths provide shortcuts to other settlements and pigs recycle organic waste. Where dwellings butt on to the wasteland, children play along its edges but keep quite close to their homes. Amal, whose parents are waste pickers, explained his need for public space:

The only space we have available to hang out is the jungle (nalla) which is overcrowded and means we cannot play any cricket (1).

Hidden, onion-like, by layers of later buildings, the Khirki Mosque roof is a surprise: a wide

right
Khirki Mosque roof
below
recycling fired bricks during the
demolition of a pukka house

open landscape in its own right. Groups of dome summits ripple over the empty, ancient deck in stark contrast to the cramped dusty alleyways below. Standing on the roof, looking in every direction you can see the terraces and rooftops of houses where people are sitting, washing or hanging clothes, eating or drying food, playing cards or sleeping. People prefer to meet the public at the threshold to their house or hail them across the rooftops rather than make use of the roof of this old, empty mosque.

Apart from the courtyards within the waste pickers work/life accommodation, in Panchsheel Vihar and Khirki as a whole, there was a lack of transitional, semi-public space, within the house: space, that is, which might be shared by several occupants. Each room was generally a separate tenancy. Newly-constructed pukka tenements were accessed by corridor only, without any other shared space. The absolute divide between inside and outside was exemplified when one of the students was invited to have tea with a resident of Khirki:

… each home we were guests in was immaculately clean and organised despite a shortage of space … after having carried an empty plastic bottle with me for hours in the vain hope of finding a bin, I was invited into Jyoti's house for tea. She spotted my unwanted luggage and made a gesture to take it from me … To my surprise she just opened her front door and threw it out on to the pavement in front of her own home (2).

It is not clear whether waste pickers regularly trawled the streets to pick up such bottles or indeed whether they have agreements with households to collect waste but what is clear is that what little non-private space remains is regarded as a depository and that this is fertile ground for the pickers.

Students picked up the need by vulnerable groups such as waste pickers, who depend on the public realm for their income, for a more variegated and sophisticated spatial strategy. Instead of all public places being regarded as potential depositories of rubbish for

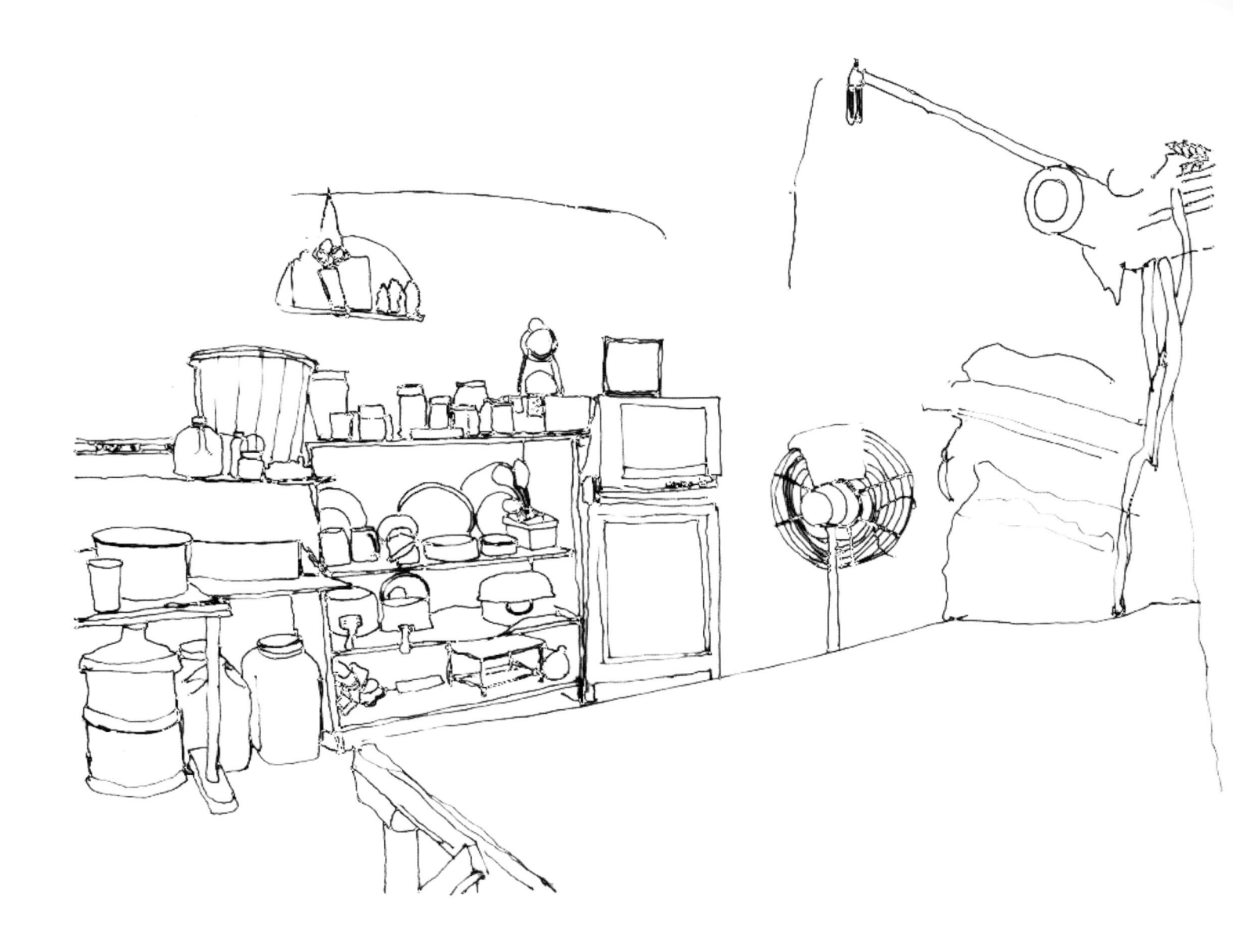

example, public spaces could be made 'accountable' and managed responsibly according to their use. Rubbish could be deposited at particular times and places and collected regularly.

student sketch of waste picker's house interior

A clearer spatial definition of the thresholds between room, courtyard, entrance transition and street for example, would ease movement and foster conviviality in multi-occupied space. In addition a more subtle spatial definition within what remains of the public realm, a definition made evident by practice rather than that provided by high walls and doors, would go some way towards modifying the negative effects of the absurdly rigid dichotomy between public and private spaces evident in modern society.

(4) Climate, Waste and Space: Yards, Courts and Havelis

New Delhi has a composite climate with a broad seasonal range. A very hot dry season runs from April to mid-June with some diurnal range (difference between day and night temperatures). This is succeeded by a hot, humid, monsoon season from mid-June to September with little or no diurnal range. A comfortable autumn is followed by a short, cool, dry winter from November until February with a high diurnal range. This leads back gradually to the full heat of April with a gentle spring season.

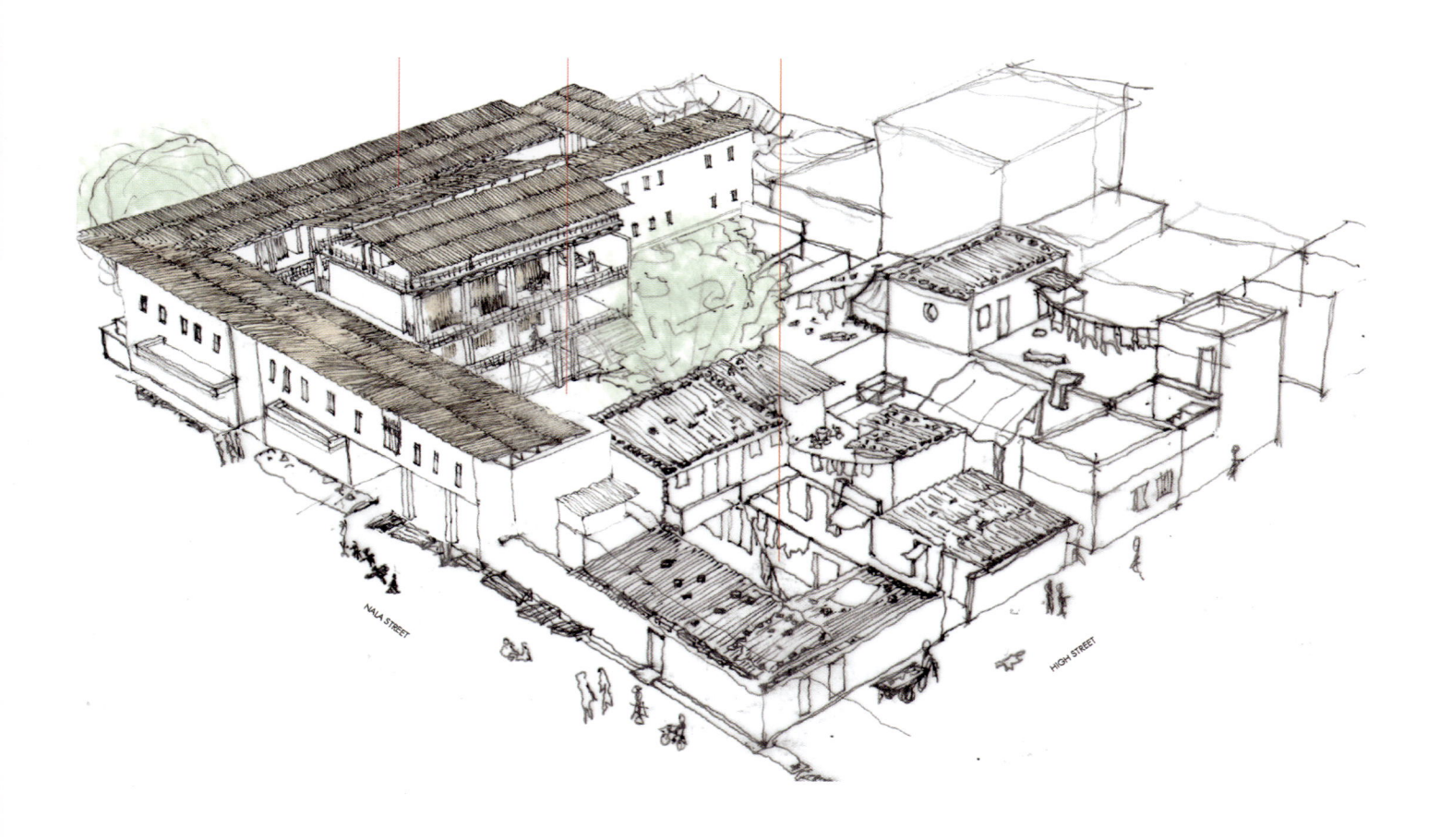

proposal for improvements to existing waste picker yards to provide permanent workshop/houses
Sam Bentil-Mensah

Where there is a diurnal range, it is possible to use the thermal mass of materials such as brick to moderate the temperature swing. Rooms are closed down during a hot/dry May day then opened up for cooling at night whilst sleeping on the roof. Winter energy is collected by opening up rooms to the sunlight during the day to help give an inner warmth at night when sleeping inside. The monsoon is the most difficult season within which to provide comfort passively as only cross ventilation can modify the heat and humidity.

Some of the climate modifying characteristics of courtyard construction are to be found in the waste pickers' yards. These courtyard types indicate a progressive development from:

– yards which typically consist of a brick perimeter wall supporting one-storey lean-to temporary structures with waste and sorting activities based in the centre to
– courts which have single storey brick rooms around a courtyard where the primary function is dwelling and major sorting activities are excluded to:
– 'havelis' where the perimeter structures are two or even three storeys; where every room is accessed from the central courtyard and where this courtyard acts with the form of the whole building as a more sophisticated climate modifier.

Yards are generally very hot and uncomfortable during extremes of climate but rooms, brick perimeter walls and working areas are mostly shaded from the direct rays of the sun. Paper and cardboard, sorted and packaged for onward sale are used as temporary building materials to provide thick-baled insulated cave-like structures for some families. All that is lacking for thermal comfort in most seasons is a substantial airflow over the body.

left
proposal for bamboo walkways leading to work/
live accommodation across the nalla, *Cristina
Monteiro*
right
proposal for a bamboo and waste paper bundle
roof pergola, *Nat Horner*

If courts become restricted in size, and even reduced to just corridors, then their function as open living space becomes cramped and eventually unusable and the opportunity for both horizontal (during the monsoon) and vertical ventilation (in the hot/dry season) is severely restricted. In houses which function well as passive climate modifiers windows are kept small to exclude reflected light and walls become perforated (jali walls) to permit ventilation whilst maintaining visual privacy.

As courtyard housing develops vertically, ancillary spaces are added such as shaded balconies and rooftops which provide a buffer zone around the thermally massive core. Doorstep otlas become the preferred relaxing place where occupants can stretch out in full view and watch the world go by. If the courtyard happens to be on the western perimeter of Panchsheel Vihar where there is a lower risk of flooding then it may include cool basement rooms (see above).

Students found that their study of the development of the waste pickers' courtyard typology revealed a way of building which enabled construction to be phased according to available resources and requirements. Given security of tenure students also discovered the seeds of a material and spatial strategy that extrapolated the waste pickers' existing kuchha methods to provide safe, comfortable and pukka courtyard town houses.

Staying put by turning waste into an opportunity

Establishing permanent settlement for the waste pickers would require not only a spatial and material strategy, but also an improvement in education and livelihood skills and the development of higher-paying jobs to support better living and working conditions.

At a global level, waste management and recycling is increasingly recognised as necessary both to control pollution and conserve scarce natural resources. The techniques of waste pickers in collecting, sorting and re-assembling useful waste into bundles for re-use or reprocessing is a phenomena which is gaining prominence, sophistication and respectability worldwide as part of the emergent green revolution.

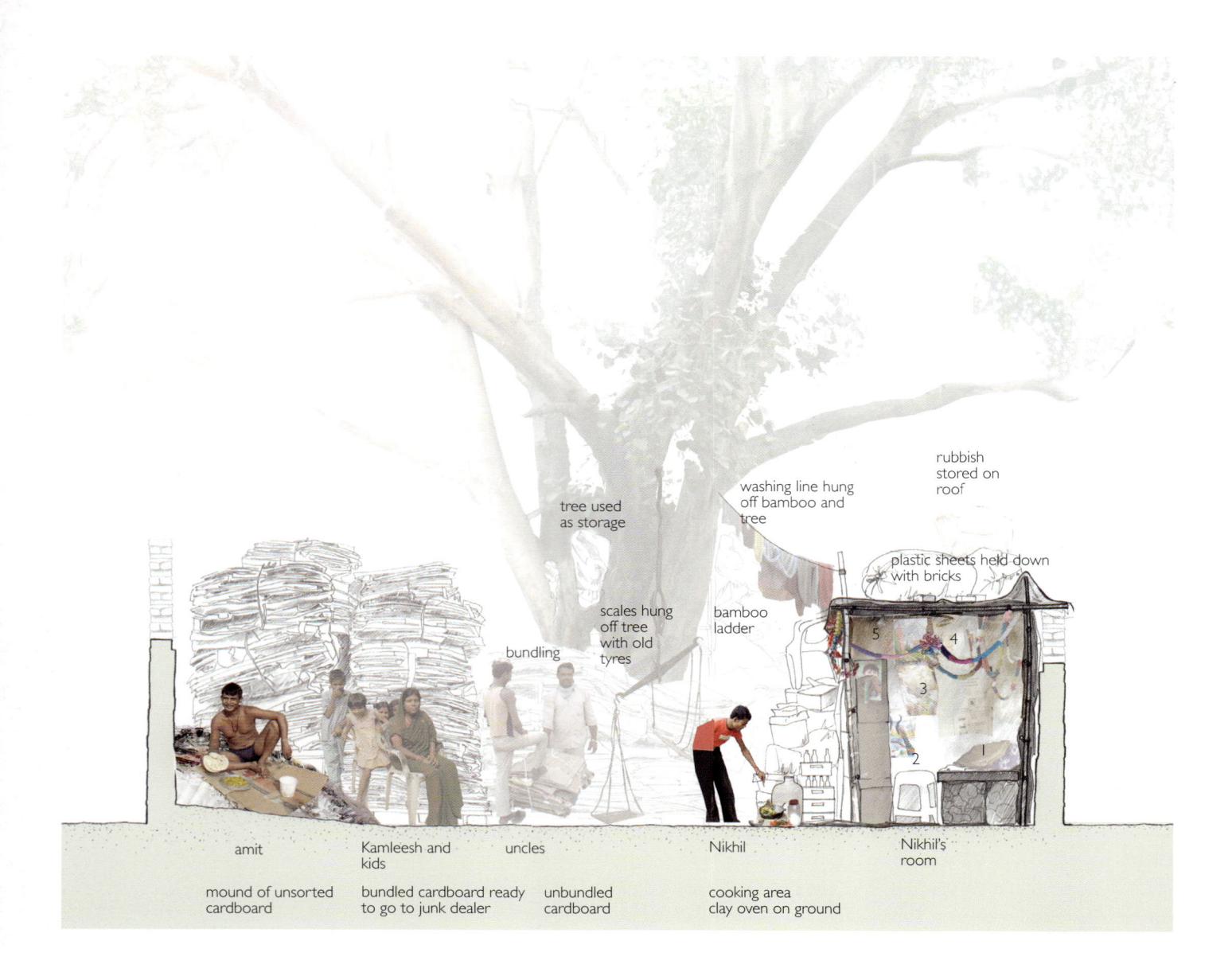

Labels on illustration:
- tree used as storage
- washing line hung off bamboo and tree
- rubbish stored on roof
- plastic sheets held down with bricks
- scales hung off tree with old tyres
- bamboo ladder
- bundling
- amit
- Kamleesh and kids
- uncles
- Nikhil
- Nikhil's room
- mound of unsorted cardboard
- bundled cardboard ready to go to junk dealer
- unbundled cardboard
- cooking area clay oven on ground
- 5
- 4
- 3
- 2
- 1

analytical sketch of waste picker yard
Natasha Reid

Nikhil's room construction:
internal items

1 bed: board with boxes under
2 plastic stool holds open door
3 Disney posters
4 garlands
5 light bulb

Instead of being sold on to middlemen, as is the current practice, could the repackaged waste of Panchsheel Vihar become the raw material for a range of new local live/work light industries which might support an improvement in local material well being? Rather than being considered as operating on the margins of society, could the Delhi authorities accept the construction of permanent, multi-occupied, live/work courtyard houses as a viable urban building type? Could the waste pickers play a part in developing a more convivial public realm where space is more accountable and use is more diverse and open to all?

Several student schemes in Part 3 explore these possibilities.

Notes

(1) Delhi Dialogues: Field Trip Booklet, November 2005.
(2) Ibid.

chapter 5

Havelis and the Conglomerate Matrix

The student schemes illustrated in this book are a contribution to a debate which is taking place at a global level (Davis 2006) about upgrading illegal settlements as opposed to demolishing them and resettling the occupiers. Contributors to the debate aim to treat the people who live in illegal settlements, in extreme but ubiquitous environments, as clients rather than as victims or passive recipients of welfare. There is always a choice and the authors of the schemes in this book have chosen technologies and spatial strategies which emerge, amongst other things, from their study of Indian urban precedent.

In order to inform such an approach, this chapter examines three examples of Indian urban fabric that have emerged over many centuries, adapting, decaying and becoming more dense through time. The intense vernacular morphologies of old Meerut, Old Delhi and the 'urban village' of Chirag Delhi are studied within the context of their surrounding hybrid contemporary landscapes. The chapter explores continuity and change in physical response to changing patterns of occupation in this sometimes overdeveloped physical fabric and introduces the thinking behind student schemes which have been located within them.

The concept of Conglomerate Ordering as defined by architects Peter and Alison Smithson (Smithson 1993) is introduced as an aid to reflection on this mature physical fabric. By comparing traditional and modern Indian architectural landscapes and their inhabitation, lessons can be learned which improve understanding of the formation and resource value of contemporary illegal urban settlements where the vast majority of urban migrants reside (the subject of Chapters 3 and 7). Apart from its intrinsic appeal, this knowledge is a necessary precondition for any architectural intervention which relies on incremental upgrading as a tool for development.

view over the dense Meerut city matrix to the Victorian clock tower

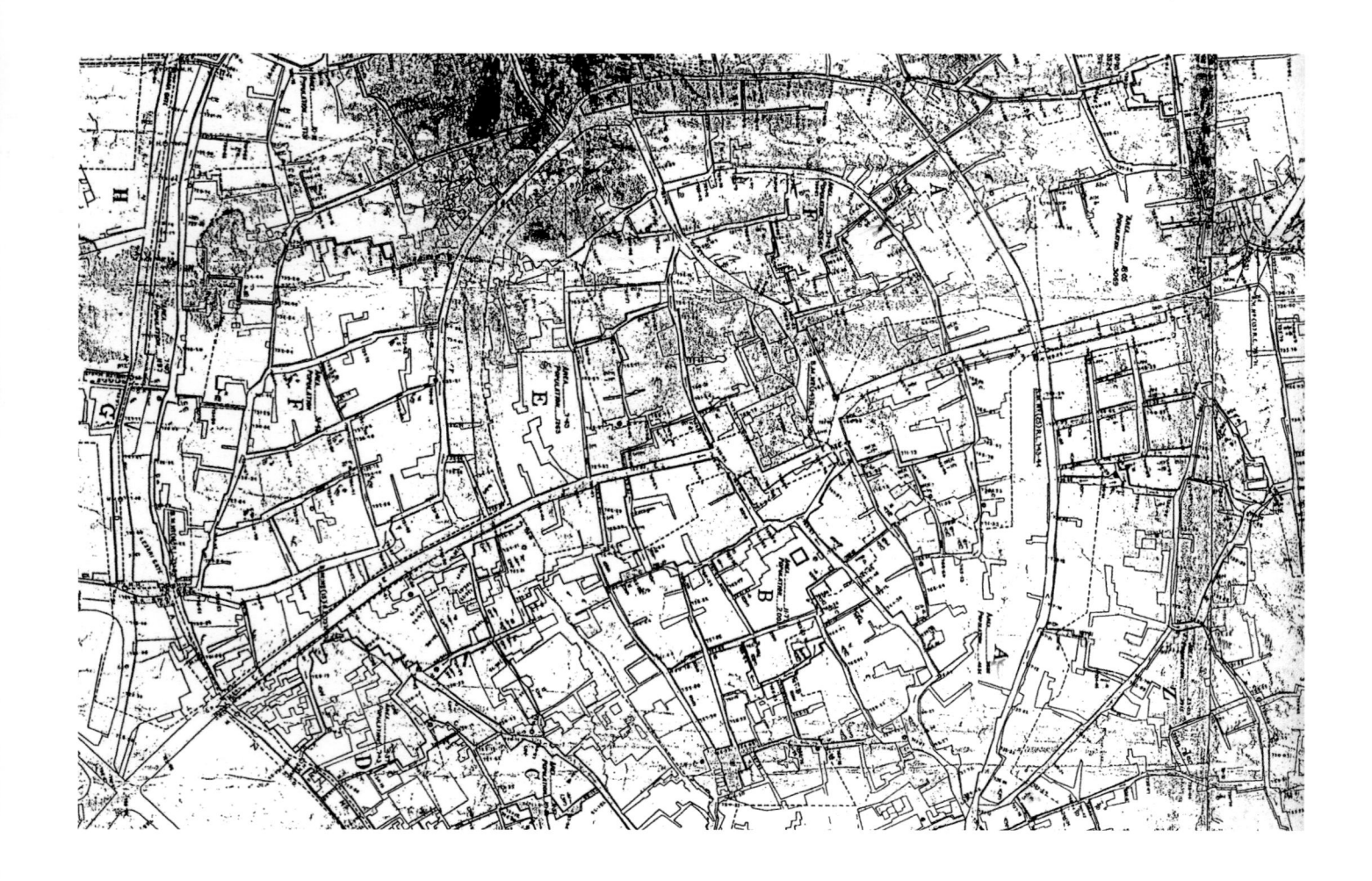

Old Meerut

Built on a low, circular hill, the ancient heart of Meerut (1) is ideally placed for effective surface water drainage. Narrow, irregular paved alleys snake out radially from the Jama Masjid at the top of the hill to discharge into the larger modern drains contouring around the base below. Thronged with crowds of people, bicycles, scooters, carts and rickshaws travel these lanes but cars can barely penetrate. A complete overhaul of the alley paving and surface drains was completed recently leaving these narrow passageways, the public sinews of the old town, clear and functioning. Once the main gate under the Victorian clock tower located at the bottom of the hill on the line of the earlier city walls is left behind, a stranger is soon lost in these twisting lanes. However, whilst the long view is absent throughout, if you remember to walk uphill at every turning point and cross roads then the end point will always be the mosque at the top. Similarly, escape is guaranteed by returning downhill.

Behind the continuous façades of the alleys and streets, is a dense mass of building, three and four storeys high, punctuated as if cut out from above by rectangular courtyards. The majority of these courts are a central focus for large havelis (courtyard dwellings) divided by shared party walls, within the building mass, which are entered through often grandly decorated gateways punctuating the continuous street frontage. However these public façades also open on to shops (which spill out on to the street) and provide access to temple courts, mosques, schools, a church and a multitude of workshops including the famous Meerut Scissor Factory. Despite a balance in numbers between the Hindu and

map of old Meerut
from print given to students by authorities

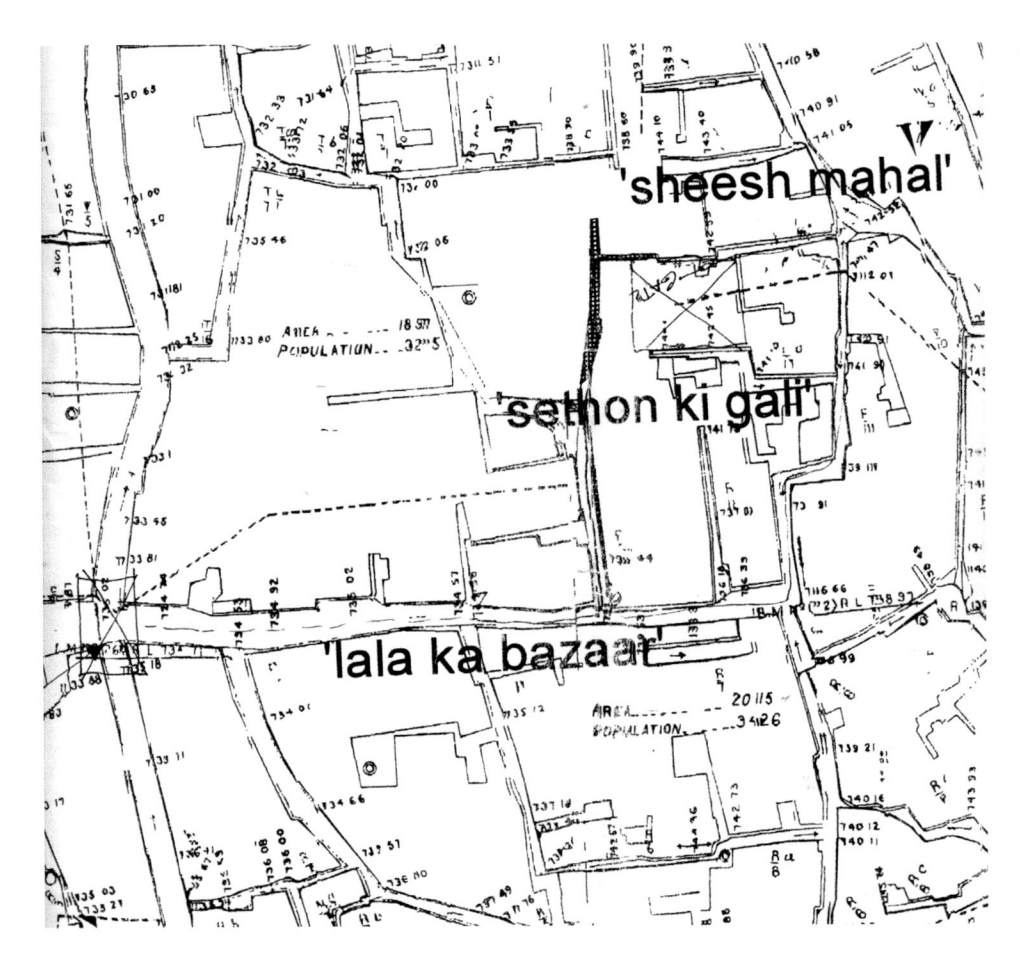

Muslim communities in old Meerut there are still tensions between the two even today. There have been numerous riots which have erupted in recent years within the building mass and its girdle of lanes. These disturbances have resulted in police lock downs and curfews.

Once through the wall and into the haveli, the dust, hustle, noise and brightness of the street is left behind. Pushing through a quieter interior world of mottled light and protecting shade, the visitor can at last enter the family courtyard which is usually organised formally with some degree of symmetry in its façades and formal hierarchy in the size and positioning of the surrounding internal spaces.

All ground floor rooms are entered through the court whilst access to rooms on the upper floors is from balconies or terraces which overhang it. Activities which take place within the court change with the ritual of everyday family life just as the sky above changes with day and night, sun, cloud and rain. In contrast, the arched walls and paved floor, overhanging balconies and relative positions of entrance and main room appear fixed and unchanging.

Roofs are a different world. With sufficient care taken to avoid unsafe and dilapidated surfaces, it would be theoretically possible to scramble over the undulating landscape of flat roofs and crumbling parapets to reach nearly any part of old Meerut if only all your neighbours would allow it. This territory is however, shared with families of feral red-bottomed baboons who scavenge from rooftop to rooftop without seeking such

permission. An unexpected close encounter with these super-strong and well-established inhabitants is best avoided. Despite having to share the roof zone with baboons the tranquillity afforded by being lifted clear of the public crowds and the family chores, during the evening coolness, is profoundly relaxing. A refugee escaping from the closed world within the building mass emerges on to the rooftops to experience a long panoramic view over the urban roofscape stretching into the dusty distance suffused with the sounds of the call to prayer and the occasional smells of cooking and jasmine. But enjoying the roofscape is not always a solitary experience. Competitions between neighbouring pigeon keepers are common place, often a daily occurrence. The aim is to entice members of another flock to join yours when they circle together overhead or simply to catch individual doves in traps attached to tall, bamboo poles. Lofts and perches, the paraphernalia of such avian tournaments, litter the landscape as they have for centuries.

Perhaps the most popular entertainment which connects the open space of the rooftops with the narrow world of twisting lanes is that of the kite flying competition. Layers of ground glass are pasted on to the kite strings making them razor sharp. At festival times hundreds of hopefuls launch their kites, jousting with each other with the aim of cutting as many rival strings as possible. Downed kites tumble into the lanes below and are retrieved as trophies by young boys. A similar situation in Afghanistan is described in Khaled Hosseini's popular novel (Hosseini 2003):

Soon, the cutting started and the first of the defeated kites whirled out of control. They fell

from the sky like shooting stars with brilliant, rippling, tails showering the neighbourhoods below with prizes for the kite runners. I could hear the runners now, hollering as they ran the streets. Someone shouted reports of a fight breaking out two streets down ...

haveli courtyard, old Meerut

(1) Conglomerate Ordering

Without a superimposed grid or any other form of self-conscious planning, the old city of Meerut and the havelis within it demonstrate a clear sense of what Alison and Peter Smithson have termed 'conglomerate ordering' at both the city and building scales. They describe a range of buildings (Smithson 1993):

where it is possible to find oneself in a hidden, almost secret place: yet one is never afraid: an inner-self reassures: I can always find my way back ...

This sense of a place being ordered whilst still having the capacity to overwhelm engages the senses in a way which is more difficult to find in over-determined, planned, modern cities. Rather than buildings being objects on a gridded tray, spaces are experienced as three dimensional assemblies, over time, of fabric, worn and stained by layers of continuous usage:

We may not be able to see where we are, but [we] can nevertheless navigate through our capacity to feel light and warmth and wind on our skins; sense the density of surrounding fabric; know that behind that wall are people; smell who has been here, or where someone has gone.

A building of the Conglomerate Order has spatial presence – more awesome than object presence – something not remotely reducible to a simple geometric schema or communicable through two dimensional images.

The Smithsons list a range of other characteristics of Conglomerate Ordering which relate to its domination by one monolithic material (the matrix) and its ability to accommodate continual change within this matrix provided the 'convention of use' of the matrix is maintained. The thick heavyweight horizontal nature of the matrix gets thinner and lighter as it gets higher (but not very high), and allows daylight to penetrate from above.

(2) Patterns of Occupation

The private and homely experience of the interior of a haveli within the building matrix, is in stark contrast to the often unpredictable nature of events which take place in the alleyways outside. Running along the lanes and byways which penetrate the building matrix, inhabitants move in droves between home and school, workplace or market. They avoid becoming lost in the claustrophobic crush by familiarising themselves with a regular route taken at a particular hour: for whilst the lanes are crowded and bustling during most of the day, at night time, when quiet descends, they are only filled with empty echoes. Take a wrong turning or travel at the wrong time and you can find yourself in an unfamiliar landscape: desolate and strange. Shops, colourful and welcoming when open will be closed by steel shutters out of hours. At which time, prompted by your lonely footsteps, prying eyes might peer out at you through jalis and spy holes. Writing of Allahabad, a North Indian town similar to Meerut at a time of curfew, Rai (1998), describes the uncanny anxiety which can be provoked within such narrow lanes:

... the crowd vanished, and the girl found herself in a lane ... The houses had such an eerie look – their doors and windows were like tightly clenched jaws – she couldn't be sure if anyone lived in them ... (the girl had in fact passed through that lane endless times. God knows why the same lane seemed totally unfamiliar today.)

... After a few minutes it became clear that the houses around her were not as deserted as they seemed. Behind every little slit in every door and window there were faces glued to them.

Until a generation, ago each haveli would be home to one, large, extended family with each family sharing the same cooking facilities and often eating together. Rooms were not differentiated according to their usage but rather according to their thermal comfort characteristics at different times of the day and in accordance with the importance of the activity and its spatial requirements. The equipment needed for living was minimal and consisted of charpoys (lightweight timber bed frames), masands (reclining cushions) and other such moveable furniture. Whilst the main ceremonial room, often sited across the courtyard from the entrance might contain more formal western style tables and chairs, these were hardly ever used except on formal occasions.

More recently, younger generations of the old established families have moved outside old Meerut to take advantage of better work opportunities and to further their education. This has left a significant proportion of the building matrix under-occupied and behind the alley walls parts of the fabric are decaying and even collapsing. In this context poorer migrants have rented rooms on the ground floors whilst older family members have retreated upstairs. This process of shrinkage and renewal of the conglomerate urban matrix is even more pronounced in Shahjahanabad, the walled city of Old Delhi, where decay and crumbling brickwork are a constant feature behind the enclosing walls of the bazaar.

above
narrow old Meerut alley
facing page
landscape sketch of narrow lanes and alleys, old Meerut
Youjung Park

left
rooftop kite flying
Bo Tang
facing page
sketch of old Meerut street
Youjung Park

Old and New Delhi: The Conglomerate Order Contained and Fragmented

(1) Shahjahanabad

Running from Delhi Gate to the famous Jama Masjid, the narrow bazaar street, lined with shops called Chitli Qabar cuts through centuries-old mohallas (neighbourhoods) which are in turn penetrated from all sides by galis (dead-end lanes) giving access to havelis. This part of the conglomerate urban matrix has withstood the depredations of the British after the 1857 rising. This contrasts with the situation nearer the Red Fort and around the later Victorian railway station where huge swathes of Shahjahanabad were swept away for defensive or engineering purposes in an attempt to contain and sanitise what the authorities could neither control nor understand (Hosagrahar 2005).

However those mohallas which survived the nineteenth century clearances, now suffer decay from within. Originally comprising an Emir's palace, Daryaganj mohalla situated on Chitli Qabar Bazaar, included a series of:

... pavilions and units connected by courtyards. The haveli included a grand gateway with guards and musicians, an audience hall to receive visitors, a women's quarters, a library, a bath and a mosque ...

together with rooms and workshops for retainers and service personnel. The mohalla was later divided into a number of smaller, more compact, havelis for wealthy merchants and their families. Typically, such a haveli might consist of a grand entrance from the bazaar leading to a more public men's court protecting a smaller women's court, each surrounded by pillared spaces. The roof would consist of a large terrace with a sleeping pavilion. But by the early twentieth century most havelis had been reduced to one courtyard with a more modest street entrance and:

... stairs next to the entrance [which] led up to the women's quarters. Windows on the upper level opened on to a screened balcony that overlooked the street.

So as time moved on, the urban matrix became denser and the occupied compartments smaller.

(2) Colonial Delhi: A Landscape of Bungalows

Meanwhile, outside the dense conglomerate matrix of Old Delhi, colonial, residential areas such as the Civil Lines just to the north, were constructed on totally different principles with a density of occupation reduced by a factor of 80 (King 1984, p. 59). Set within spacious compounds, the bungalows of the ruling classes were surrounded by lawns where parties and receptions were held. Instead of each room being entered from a multi-purpose courtyard as in a haveli, the rooms of the bungalow were arranged in a linear fashion with the public rooms at the front, the more private bedrooms above and the servants' quarters at the back. In the bungalow, the division of space according to function was strictly enforced with rooms crammed with heavy furniture (sitting, dining, cooking, sleeping). The extent to which room function and furnishing has become specialised in this way has been called a measure of their 'criticality' (Grover 2002). Thus instead of an undifferentiated dense horizontal conglomerate matrix punctuated with courtyards set on a low hill, colonial residential areas consisted of detached bungalows set in a rolling garden landscape.

Whilst contiguous courtyard houses provide light and air to the inside of the dwelling, with the only long view being from the rooftops, bungalows look ever outwards on sometimes up to four acres of dedicated lawns and shrubs. Shielded from their neighbours by vegetation, detached in their own grounds, bungalow residents could console themselves with the thought that they were masters of all they surveyed.

To counter this binary morphology there is at least one point of similarity. The haveli entrance threshold space or 'otla' where occupants and friends might gather to chat and watch the world go by might be compared with the 'front of house' bungalow verandah where guests were received and relaxed evenings spent in conversation.

(3) New Delhi: Plotted Developments

With the construction of Lutyen's New Delhi from the 1930s onwards, colonial Western style patterns of residential culture became the norm for newly-planned authorised developments. Still teeming with life, but car free, Old Delhi remained and continued to operate as it always had done within its conglomerate matrix. Further south in New Delhi and its extensions, the more modern, watered, sanitised and electrified neighbourhoods were accessed by a growing network of dual carriageways. Since Independence, even further south than New Delhi, to the west beyond Karol Bagh, to the north behind the Civil Lines and across the Yamuna to the east, these vehicular highways have been extended, stretching out over the virgin landscape, lassoing existing established settlements and parcelling out previously agricultural land into brand new urban territories. These new territories have been sub-divided into serviced 'plotted developments' served by surfaced feeder roads. Delhi's growth has been so rapid that these feeder roads often have no names and the plotted developments, having no history, are known only by block numbers.

Unlike the sparse and simply furnished rooms within a haveli where charpoys and cushions are moved around as necessary, middle class housing in Delhi tends towards the western pattern with the hallmarks of high criticality: specialised function and large heavy furniture. However, the extremely low densities of the Civil Lines and the bungalows of New Delhi had to be tightened up when translated to the later plotted developments. In the design of new semi-detached and row houses, individualised lawns were discarded in favour of public 'greens' which in practice were prized rather for bestowing status than for any actual community use (Grover 2002). The space in front of each house is now hard paved to park a car rather than grassed over as a pedestrian welcome mat. Joint family occupation is quite popular and in this case different nuclear families within the same extended family will occupy different floors which have separate access for servants and guests by means of an external stairway at the front of the premises. Internally another more private staircase allows the family to move freely between floors. The family itself is served by individualised private rooms, bathrooms and a family room usually with a television next to the kitchen. Verandahs have been replaced by balconies and terraces above ground level and in contrast to the rest of the house these spaces can maintain low criticality, being used for occasional cooking, sleeping, drying clothes and relaxing. Over the years boundary walls have been raised to improve security, terraces have been enclosed with steel bars and grills (jaals) and in some cases apartment blocks have been sealed off in gated clusters controlled by uniformed guards.

Old Delhi showing location of Chitli Qabar Marg and the mohalla
Bo Tang and Shamoon Patwari

1 red fort

2 jama masjid

3 chitli qabar bazaar

4 daryaganj mohalla

proposed site

railway

green areas

old Delhi blocks

new city blocks

historical sites

(4) Old Delhi Now: Re-inventing the Conglomerate Order

Compared to this, the crumbling building matrix of Old Delhi suffers from the shrinking cities syndrome found in Eastern Europe after the fall of the Berlin Wall. Shahjahanabad is now regarded by much of the educated middle class as irredeemably insanitary and far too overcrowded for effective functioning. At various times in recent years, in an effort to maintain a sustainable use for the haveli, some of the ground floors have been turned into workshops or more usually, warehouses.

In 2007, Bo Tang and Shamoon Patwari investigated a prime example of just such a mohalla which was crumbling from the inside out. This is located towards the Delhi Gate end of Chitli Qabar on the north east side. The bazaar along Chitli Qabar Bazaar itself was fully functioning and very crowded. Most of the havelis within the mohalla were more or less densely occupied but there were three extensive areas behind walls set just one building unit behind the bazaar which were accessible to the public through gateways from the bazaar.

Within one site the government was in the process of building a school (MCD primary school Daryaganj). The half-completed school buildings had been carefully constructed not only so as to avoid the sacred and protected Banyan trees which once stood in the vanished haveli courtyards, but were also set back all round from the adjacent building matrix. The resultant formal contortion was a clear rejection of the morphology of the conglomerate matrix, (a square peg in a larger polygonal hole) leaving the school, rather out of place, detached and alone in its plot.

The second site had been partially occupied by a dilapidated row of single storey structures, one of which was home to a women's organisation concerned with getting children into pre-school. Without sufficient outside funding such temporary usage can only scratch the surface of the site potential.

On the third vacant lot, a large, ancient haveli (the Baq'ullah Khan haveli) had once stood with a Jamun tree at its core, but two generations ago, its upkeep became prohibitively expensive for the family who owned the site and it was donated to the government. Later the government struggled to maintain it as an industrial school (Dastary Government Industrial School) but abandoned the attempt in the 1960s when new pollution laws made this impossible, leaving the fabric to decay irretrievably. Squatters have occupied the remaining three storey entrance building. The open site itself has now become a consolidated platform of dense building rubble topped off with regular deposits of waste. A rag picker comes twice a week to sort out the pickings which include waste paper, fabric offcuts and car headlights. Bo Tang (2008) describes how in November 2007 vegetable trimmings dumped on the site were being fed to a herd of goats by the local 'crazy man' Rizi. After feeding, the goats would perch, comfortably, on high stone ledges left protruding from the last vestiges of the ruined haveli. To guard against the cold winter nights, the goats were clothed in old jumpers and tailored sacks.

Bo Tang and Shamoon Patwari (2007–08) sited their schemes on this third site. In attempting to repair and regenerate the conglomerate matrix they each maintained a large, inner open space, knitted local workshops/memory archive/waste sorting facility and a restaurant into the existing fabric and introduced a new taller haveli form with its own inner court on a smaller footprint than the old haveli. Squatters would now be offered work and kites would still be flown from the roofs. However, in addition, a more

global aspiration centred on accommodating visitors to the 2010 Commonwealth Games (Shamoon) and providing an international summer school and all-India college (Bo) was to be employed to raise expectations beyond the current claustrophobic crumbling landscape.

external access for servants and guests

Having produced a landmark guide book on the fascinating range of diverse habitats walled up behind the decaying mohallas of Old Delhi, Lucy Peck (2005) has speculated on what will become of them once the wholesale markets leave. She anticipates this will be an inevitable move if the remarkable growth in India's economy continues:

... what will happen to the thousands of buildings that are left empty? ... as shoppers are provided with more modern facilities elsewhere, the importance of the old city will fade. It is obvious that the problem is a difficult one and, sadly, a short term pragmatic solution will not be one in which the architectural heritage of this area is considered.

Students have taken a more optimistic view in preparing their proposals for the mohalla adjacent to Chitli Qabar Bazaar. As a tool for scaling up, perhaps their approach can be used to re-invigorate the diverse range of secret worlds which Lucy Peck has helped to uncover elsewhere in Old Delhi.

Many have seen the picturesque amongst the decrepit but, putting aside such nostalgia, the ability of the conglomerate matrix to renew itself after decay and neglect should not be underestimated.

Chirag Delhi: The Conglomerate Order within the Hybrid South Delhi Landscape

In Chapter 3, the growth of Chirag Delhi from a walled Dargah sanctuary to a dense urban village with lal dora status was reviewed. Later in Chapter 3, it was suggested that the growth of the modern 'slum' settlement of Kalyanpuri Block 19/20 with its perimeter

rubble of collapsed building, Chirag Delhi 2008

single-roomed terraces surrounding discrete single-roomed clusters which were in turn penetrated by dead-ended alleyways might provide a model for understanding how the conglomerate matrix originally developed in mature, dense, urban villages such as Chirag Delhi.

But what of Chirag Delhi now? What are its morphological characteristics and its future potential? The physical limits of the settlement are defined by the old walls on three sides and the Barrapullah stream (nalla) on the fourth: the boundaries of the lal dora delineation. The building height is determined by the number of storeys people are prepared to climb without a lift to reach their room, often up to seven.

There is nowhere else to go and the density of the settlement is perhaps as high as it is practically possible using currently available technologies. Within the settlement, there are a number of small open public places (chowks) which are increasingly encroached upon. The students found that these chowks had different functions and named them accordingly. For example Bouvra Chowk, characterised by the students as quiet, laidback and safe, was called the Medical Chowk by students because two doctor's surgeries and a pharmacy were located there and it was one of just two chowks accessible to small ambulances. The only other vehicular access is to the Bazaar and Dargah chowk. Apart from the lanes leading to these two chowks the alleyways are too narrow to admit motor transport other than motorbikes and motor scooters. Even so alleyways and chowks are still being encroached upon to squeeze the last square metre of space for the built matrix.

As you penetrate deeper into the maze of lanes, so the ownership becomes more established and the buildings higher and more dense. Neighbourhoods are grouped according to caste with the Brahmins and Jains, the higher castes being more centrally located surrounded by the Jats and Jatavs of the Kshatriya caste. Along the southern wall and on the western nalla edge are lower caste Kumars (potters) and refugees from the Punjab and Pakistan. Much of the economic and commercial activity is located along the edges making use of easier vehicular access. At the base of the high northern edge is an array of metal workshops whilst along the southern façade, under some of the apartment blocks, semi-basements have been dug and a series of motor garages and mechanics workshops installed. The western edge, which is the least developed and is at a slightly lower level still, has some potential for densification. It is here that the most recent migrants have settled and the Kumars have their pottery kilns.

So in Chirag Delhi the physical fabric is powerfully associated with the established and entrenched social hierarchy. Later immigration has loosened these associations only slightly but more seriously, has added to social tensions. Outsiders provide income for established landlords whilst at the same time being blamed for congestion.

Mixing residential, commercial and even light industrial activity together legally is only possible because of Chirag Delhi's lal dora status and would not be allowed in adjacent, modern, mainstream legal colonies.

In the centre, old havelis can still be found owned by long established Brahmin families. Slowly but surely however, these courtyard houses are being changed beyond recognition. No longer are such havelis fully occupied by an extended family. Some rooms have been left to crumble whilst others are let out to smaller nuclear families. Occupying families add rooms and adjust the layout to accommodate a greater density of occupation

survey drawing the ruin of Baq'ullah Khan Haveli, *Bo Tang*

without any intention of respecting the original courtyard layout. This endangers not only the coherence of the resulting structure but also the spatial presence necessary for a coherent conglomerate ordering. Elsewhere, total demolition of a haveli is followed by a reinforced, concrete-framed multi-storey block maximising floor area to the detriment of passive thermal comfort provision. Building collapse for lack of engineering skill or poorly sourced materials is relatively commonplace.

Example (1) Pau Ling Yap's Women's Rooftop Refuge

Pau Ling Yap (2008) studied Kumar Chowk (labelled Male Chowk by the students and characterised as noisy, exciting, colourful and sweaty), lying just south of the Dargah. Kumar Chowk was fully occupied by mostly unemployed and often inebriated men.

Badam is the concierge of Kumar Chowk. He is the oldest man with the authority to control the proceedings including chasing away the naughty children. The rowdy men playing cards also have a dominant presence. There are four groups of players and they are territorial. All other activities like food stalls have to be set up in accordance with the pre-established territories of the players. There is also another group of men who sit and drink tea (chai). They are usually passive but when the occasion arises they also have the authority to control the situation (3). Women were to all intents and purposes excluded from meaningful engagement with activities in Kumar Chowk:

[A woman's] role is confined to the house. Outside the house they tend only to be seen in the narrower streets where they can disappear quickly indoors. If they watch the street from the terraces they move back quickly into the darkened interior if caught watching (3).

Pau Ling developed this sectional idea of spatial use being divided vertically. The ground plane containing shops and open space was male dominated with the upper floors and roof plane being female territory. The further up from the chowk, the more private and female the spaces became. She combined this idea with the findings from her conversations with a local doctor and families in the surrounding houses that alcoholism in men was a prime cause of family break up.

interior ground floor view of self help multi occupied town house infrastructure
Paul Harvey

By assembling lightweight steel bridges joining adjacent rooftops she proposed a network of high level escape routes for women fleeing alcoholic husbands. Rooftop garden, library and refuge places provided sanctuary and neighbourly support. In time, Pau Ling envisaged a comprehensive network of high level pedestrian routes providing a safer alternative to the ground plane for women to visit each other.

Examples (2) and (3) Dealing with Density

Students concluded that the historic urban village with its Sufi Dargah had the potential to attract many more pilgrims and tourists from all over India and beyond. However visitor numbers were inhibited by Chirag Delhi's lack of open space, difficult access, poor accommodation and sometimes oppressive congestion. At the same time, poverty and unemployment within the population needed to be addressed by providing more educational opportunities.

Providing more space by turning back the tide of chowk encroachment and improving pedestrian access was a focus for several student schemes. Reducing density in the chowks however, required building more densely elsewhere.

Paul Harvey's scheme provided for an infrastructure of multi-occupied, cooperatively-owned, four-storey, framed courtyard town houses to replace the existing kuchha housing along the western edge of Chirag Delhi. In this way he was able to widen and improve an existing access route from the west to the Dargah providing a linear market and refurbishing lesser monuments along the way. Providing more public space in the centre whilst increasing density around the periphery would result in a doughnut/saucer/stadium/colosseum model for the whole settlement.

Henry Lau proposed tackling encroachment and density chowk by chowk. Testing out his ideas in Kumar Chowk, Henry introduced lift technology to allow him to propose a seven storey tower to house those displaced by enlargement of the chowk. When applied to Chirag Delhi as a whole such an approach would result in a landscape of towers; each tower being associated with its own wider, improved chowk.

scheme for a pilgrims' rest house and library
Toby Pear

Example (4) Toby Pear's Library and Pilgrims' Accommodation

Toby Pear (2008) noticed that the management of the Dargah, the prime visitor attraction compared badly with its sister shrine in nearby Mehrauli. He proposed the upgrading of the Dargah buildings to provide a library and visitors' accommodation together with the paving and shading of the Dargah Chowk itself.

Derived from his study of conglomerate ordering within Indian paintings, the arrangement of shrines within the Dargah and more general concepts of space in traditional Indian architecture (Pandya 2005), Toby introduced an idea which he called 'terra incognita' which helped occupiers to navigate through complex spaces. Without a rigid grid or the organisation of a building around a courtyard it is difficult to locate yourself within the conglomerate matrix by memory of your route alone. Without an organising idea the area off route was terra incognita. Toby introduced the idea that the matrix was made up of both objects and spaces. At different scales spaces could be within objects and objects could be within spaces. Knowledge of within which space the object was located or within which object the space was located assisted understanding. Named spaces and objects could be assembled within one another rather like a set of Russian dolls. High points, rooftops and towers within the matrix helped overall orientation.

Toby assembled his library and accommodation buildings within a site space made up of the Dargah Chowk and an adjacent demolished ruin. The accommodation was arranged around a courtyard in the form of a dharamsala (pilgrims' rest house). Within the library

Brahmins
With access to education, wealth and politics

Jats
Comparable living standards as the Brahmins, but of lower caste

Jatavs
Considers themselves *Kshatriya Shiva Gotra*
(Lineage from Lord Shiva)

Punjabis
Indo-Aryan people native to the Punjab region,
consists of multi-religions, subdivided into many castes if Hindu

Kumars
Traditionally potters, progressive & hardworking group

Jains
Non-Hindus, followers of Jainism

Balmikis
Hindu religious group who rejects the caste system
Members revere Valmiki as the incarnation of God

Pakistani refugees
Mostly Hindus who fled Pakistan post 1946 India-Pakistan
partition, seeking the safety of religious majority

Qureshis
Pakistani Muslims tribe

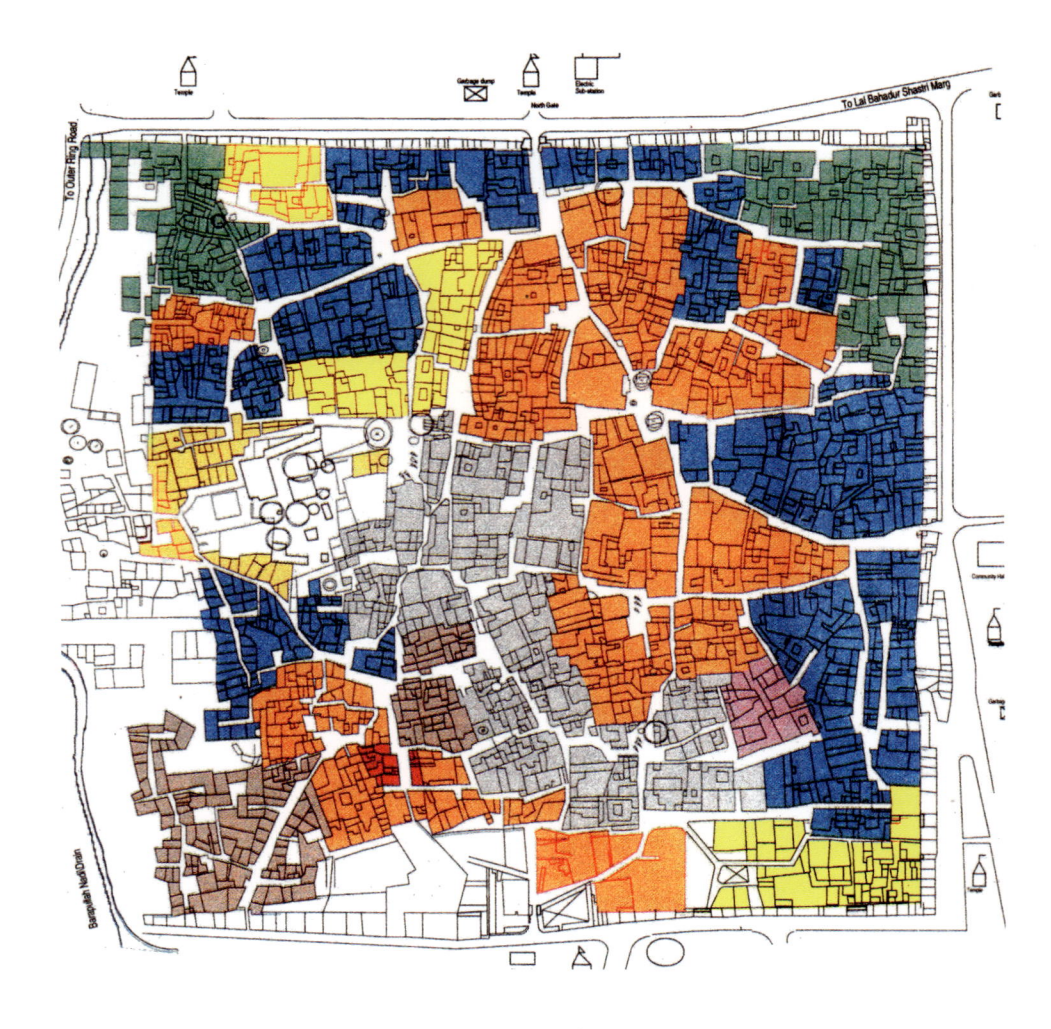

map of Chirag Delhi showing location of
population according to Caste (4)
Pau Ling Yap after an illustration (INTACH 1996)

complex was a courtyard and the library itself was cooled by a wind tower. From the top
of the wind tower the sister shrine in Mehrauli could just be made out in the distance.

The Conglomerate Matrix and the Modern Vernacular

The process by which the conglomerate matrix is renewed has been practised to
perfection over the centuries in Meerut, Old Delhi and in countless other North Indian
cities. It involves encroachment, appropriation, redefinition and reconstruction mostly by
the residents themselves. This process has a continued lease of life amongst 'slum' dwellers
elsewhere in Delhi where it makes possible the illegal inhabitation of marginal land located
within the interstices of planned growth, where 80 per cent of the migrant population
lives (Davis 2006, p. 18).

One such settlement is Ambedkar Camp (also discussed in Chapters 7 and 8) located in
the Jilmil Industrial Area of east Delhi sandwiched between the Grand Trunk Road and
the main railway line to Kolkata. This is one of a number of camps housing migrants who
first came to work in the surrounding steel industries, an industry which is now in rapid
decline, killed off by new pollution laws. Threatened with eviction by those who wish to
develop the land in association with the new metro line which now connects the area
to central Delhi, the inhabitants of Ambedkar camp are desperately poor. Despite this
situation people are not only surviving but steadily expanding their settlement whilst at
the same time imbuing it with coherence and identity.

The first settlers built along the more diagonal pedestrian pathways originating from the temple chowk in the northeast corner of the site. Most houses are single-storey except for those facing onto a strip of land between the settlement and the railway, which in November 2007 students labelled the High Street. This area is cool and pleasantly shaded. It serves as a communal area and gives the settlement an attractive focus. The settlement is unusual amongst illegal settlements in having such a space for everyone to share. The houses and the pedestrian lanes leading off this space display a combination of attributes, some of which have emerged from the conglomerate matrix whilst others echo the more recent legal plotted developments. They have both been adapted for use in the camps.

(1) Room Morphology

Single-storey houses consist of just one room adjoining other similar rooms on three sides with just one side facing the street. Rooms are plotted without internal courts. Lanes are however, limited to pedestrian use and the built matrix is continuous between lanes. These rooms are refuges from everyday life and are usually quiet and modestly furnished without significant criticality. Despite being cramped, dark and poorly ventilated, rooms are kept very clean as you would expect when private space is so scarce.

(2) Otlas: Entry Threshold

Entry thresholds within a traditional conglomerate matrix are usually raised three or four steps above the flood line and are provided with raised sitting spaces (otlas) over a surface drain. Within Ambedkar's lanes there was no room for a raised platform and inhabitants had to rely solely on the drain to protect them from floodwaters.

However, the whole frontage was used for household chores. Cooking and cleaning took place here so that these lanes functioned like communal work rooms during the day and swiftly changed into places for neighbourly conversation in the evening. Due to the

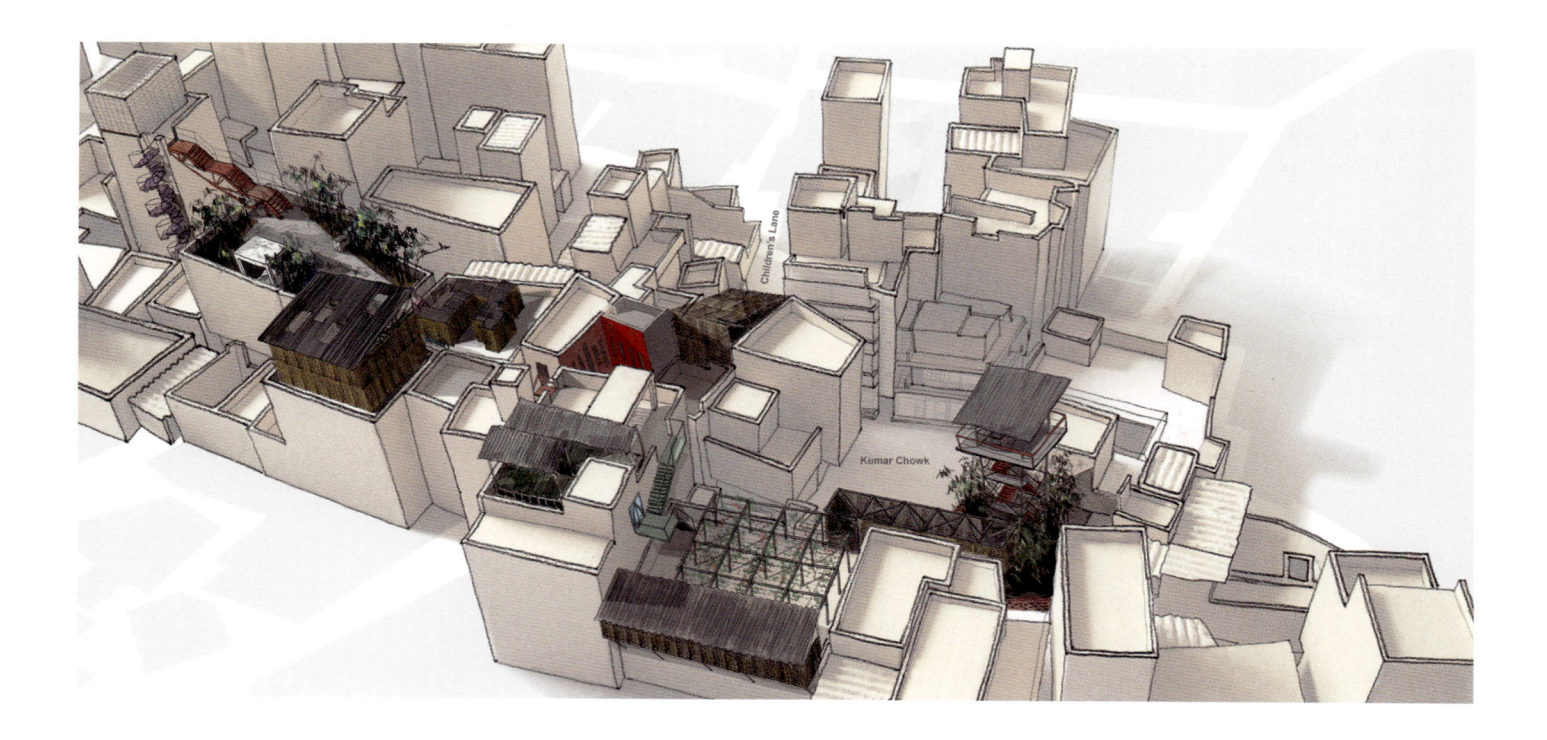

rooftop scheme
Pau Ling Yap

including:

peeping bridge
six types of steel stairs
watch tower in garden with jali walls
shaded pergola
breezy platform handicraft space
mysterious passage screening place
mystical cavern
playful education space
top-lit dance space
zen garden
bird space

compactness of the layout, division of space according to gender was more difficult than in the traditional matrix but was sometimes switched in the same space depending on the time of day. The two-storey houses which faced the High Street had raised the pavement along the frontage providing a mix between a verandah and an otla. As well as giving entry to ground floor rooms, this platform over the drain, whilst being clearly within the curtilage of the dwelling, was also the base of the stairs to the upper floor; the site of a grocery/tobacconist's kiosk and also a place to store a charpoy (bed) and a range of water containers.

(3) Building Up: A Second Floor

Owners of havelis in Old Delhi had in the past taken full advantage of planning rules to build temporary pavilions or 'barsati' structures on the roof (Hosagrahar 2005, p. 155):

Customarily, a 'barsati' was a light structure or open pavilion on top of residential structures used for sleeping in the summer. However, 'barsati' structures were routinely converted or constructed as complete rooms for living. Gradually this expanded to become a whole additional floor.

Upper floors on houses in Ambedkar bordering the High Street have been developed in this way. Elsewhere (5) I have described how single-storey roofscapes in Kalyanpuri Block 19/20 (a comparable illegal settlement in east Delhi) had become both playgrounds for children and the site of retreat shacks for the elderly. Such 'shacks in the sky' start off as lightweight pole structures covered with thick mats and polythene sheet, accessed by bamboo ladder and opening on to flat-roofed terraces. These upper rooms are later transformed into solid brick structures with corrugated sheet roofs stretching across the full extent of the floor below. Access is via a steel or stone stair on the outside of the dwelling.

All the houses in both Ambedkar and Kalyanpuri Block 19/20 lack the private courtyards present in the traditional matrix. To make up for this in two-storey dwellings; terraces and balconies have been added at the upper level to accommodate outdoor family living, comfortably above, but overlooking and within easy communicating distance of the street.

(4) Materials of Construction: Brick, Steel, Stone and Bamboo

Having space as a resource almost as scarce as cash, thinness in construction has been a driving force. The architect Laurie Baker (Bhatia 1991) has made a career by taking a minimalist approach to low-cost brick house construction in India. He has shown how thin brick walls, penetrated by jalis (arrays of small openings giving ventilation whilst maintaining privacy) can be constructed with many fewer bricks than in larger houses. Many of these lessons have already been learned by trial and error in the new settlements.

Perhaps one of the most significant characteristics of the new settlement materiality which marks it out from both the conglomerate matrix and that of its plotted successor is in its use of cementitious materials. In both old Meerut and Old Delhi, haveli walls are rendered and flat roofs screeded with a lime stabilised mix. Although more expensive, Portland cement has replaced local lime cements in mainstream construction because of its improved strength and durability. In the new settlements, to avoid this expense, external renders have been omitted leaving the brickwork exposed or 'fair faced'. This presents itself as a vertical array of distinct textured rectangular surfaces framed by corners and penetrating floors. Some of these surfaces are painted in bright colours and regularly re-painted at festival time.

In another cost saving measure, haveli style first floors supported by timber beams have not been replaced by the ubiquitous reinforced concrete slab floors seen in plotted developments but by an ingenious array of small steel beams supporting red sandstone slabs: thus limiting the use of expensive Portland cement to mortars and thin floor screeds. Overhanging balconies on upper floors are made possible by cantilevering the steel beams supporting the stone slabs a little way out over the brick walls (also discussed in Chapter 7). Whilst such overhangs were commonplace within the haveli where they were supported by carved stone brackets they are banned in plotted developments. Such overhangs give depth to the otherwise thin walled facades. Because of its durability, Portland Cement is often used in screeds to protect pathway surfaces. There is evidence in Ambedkar that brickwork laid to camber and fall is being used partly as an underlay and partly as a replacement layer to further reduce the need for concrete.

Whilst, because of the scarcity of hardwood, the timber columns, beams and joists and lintels of the haveli have given way to the steel joists, doors, windows and staircases of today; these items are still manufactured and fabricated locally. Metal doorways are very robust, yet easily allow ventilation. People feel very secure behind them (Rule 2008). Stairs can either be of stone, often cantilevered out from the wall with no handrail, or steel, fabricated out of an array of small sections. Steel stairs can be either straight or spiral but are usually much steeper than the masonry version (2).

Summary

Despite the need to conserve space which has often led to walls being only one brick thick, there is still a sense of depth, heaviness, surface texture and worked materiality which resonates with that found in the old matrix of Shahjahanabad. Ambedkar is plotted, but not in such serried ranks as the legal plotted developments. This is because the pre-existing, criss-crossing pathways were taken as early frontages in the same way as the original settlers in old Meerut built their first dwellings along pre-existing routes.

Just as with the conglomerate matrix, the materials of construction evident in Ambedkar are 'grounded in our shared existential reality' (Pallasmaa 2005). They are natural materials: brick, stone and bamboo all capable of expressing 'their age and history, as well as the story of their origins and their history of human use'. Often they are constructed by the occupants themselves and express their particular obsessions and desires.

The students who have schemes presented in Part 3 which are intended for locations in Old Meerut, Old Delhi, Chirag Delhi, Ambedkar or Kalyanpuri Block 19/20 have looked, listened and learned from the physical and cultural situation they found in their fieldwork. They have attempted to bring out in their proposals the inherent architectural potential of both the site and the cultural situation they have chosen to explore.

Notes

(1) Meerut is about 50 kilometres northeast of Delhi in the state of Uttar Pradesh. The age of the city has been traced, through excavations, to the time of the Harappa civilisation (2500–1600 BC). From the 12th century onwards, Meerut was an affluent town secured within the confines of a city wall. The old town has a population of about 1.5 million which is now outnumbered by the more modern expansion around the foot of the hill. The population is made up of approximately even numbers of Muslim and Hindu. During the colonial period, the British established a large military garrison encamped in the nearby cantonments and in 1857 the Indian Mutiny (or First War of Indian Independence) began here.

(2) Further discussion of building materials in India can be found in Chapter 4, Waste.

(3) From notes on Pau Ling Yap's drawings (2008–2009).

(4) Drawing adapted by Pau Ling Yap from maps in INTACH (1996).

chapter 6

Urban Nomads

There are a number of wandering peoples who typically supply India's urban markets and provide pavement entertainment. Economic changes, cultural factors and land scarcity are steadily encouraging these groups to become sedentary. This essay reviews the everyday working lives of the Marwari community in Agra and discusses issues of cultural and physical integration with the wider community within a rapidly changing urban context. It assesses the unusual short life building fabric employed by the Marwari to construct their shelters and looks at appropriate amenity building provision for the future.

Marwari Basti: Views of a Camp

At Agra, before sweeping south and then east past the Taj Mahal, the Yamuna river runs under three bridges and past an array of Mughal ruins on the eastern bank. These monuments are almost empty being only populated by the occasional tourist and a few self-appointed guides. The gaps between them are mostly hidden by trees. When viewed from a boat floating down the river, these tombs, palaces and gardens provide a breathtaking panorama. Close up, however, behind the curtain of riverside foliage, a series of poor, but bustling and well-established settlements can be seen. They thrive on what remains of the steel industry and employment in the roadside plant nurseries and ice-making factories. But there is another type of settlement and another type of people living amongst these forested ruins.

Just to the south of the last bridge before the river turns east towards the Taj, are the dhobi wallahs (laundry workers). Their colourful rectangles of laundered fabric, stretched out to dry every day on the river sand are visible on Google Earth. Moving east from the riverside laundry through an extensive grove of eucalyptus trees, the Google Earth satellite can pick up the solid brick houses of Shambhu Nagar, but not the site of an old British Army encampment just beyond. This jumbled collection of low mud walls and tarpaulin-covered timber pole frames is now home to a community of Marwari and is called by its neighbours 'Marwari Basti' (or Marwari settlement).

the dhobi ghat (riverside laundry)
Bo Tang

However, the settlement is known to the Marwari inhabitants themselves as Indra Nagar. It is the only Marwari settlement in Agra but just one of many spread out across India, east and south from the Marwari original home in northern Rajasthan. Since Mughal times Marwari have developed a reputation as wandering traders and more recently as successful businessmen. In this respect they share this reputation for nomadic business acumen with the Lebanese in coastal West Africa, the Jews in Europe and the Hausa in the Sahel across the sub-Saharan savannah of Nigeria, Niger and Mali.

Dressed in clothes which are distinctive in style and colour, the Marwari community's income is dependent on products crafted in the settlement including bamboo stools and glass religious lanterns. Perhaps the most ubiquitous products are however, whips made from scrap leather, a by-product of Agra's leather industry. These artefacts are sold by the Marwari to tourists outside the Taj Mahal and Agra's Red Fort.

In addition to the manufacture of whips and glass lanterns, several families have cockerels trained for fighting. Fights take place in Delhi where a winning cockerel can fetch as much as Rs 5,000. Although labelled a nomadic community, a large majority of the inhabitants is engaged in craft work and remains at home. The community is however, still dependent on a few more nomadic members who travel to maintain connections with other Marwari communities, buy scrap materials and sell goods further afield.

A typical family house, rectangular in plan, consists of painted earth walls, waist high at the sides with full height (perhaps 2 metres at the apex) gables at either end. The pitched polythene roof is often independently supported on a pole framework. The entrance to this single, private family room is by an opening in one gable end and sometimes light is also admitted through ventilation holes in the side walls. In front of the doorway is a semi-private raised earth veranda used for cooking, craftwork and receiving guests. There are two more durable houses in the community built of concrete blocks. The largest has a stone flat roof and is painted yellow and set apart from the others. This is the house of Bhima, the chief or elder. Bhima is often away, travelling between different Marwari communities. Whilst he is away his house is closed up. Close to Bhima's house is a private open space tightly surrounded by a living fence of eucalyptus trees. This garden contains a house, typical of most in the settlement and a private toilet: the only such toilet in the settlement. It is at this house that Guru Ram Das stays, when he visits the settlement every couple of years. It is his toilet and his open space where he receives guests and supplications.

Generally, clean water provision and sanitation is very limited. CURE (2) have provided a number of standpipes which discharge into open grey water channels which run across the sloping ground towards the river. The trees and shrubs in the land around the settlement are used to give privacy sufficient for the area to be used as a toilet without further screening.

There is little or no formal public space in the settlement. However the open spaces do have a strong character and identity which is reinforced by the many small Hindu shrines built by the community. There is also a modest community temple masonry platform and shrine at the northern entrance to the settlement under a large spreading banyan tree. Here, for two hours a day during the week, children of all ages receive some schooling.

This community is quite different from the other riverbank neighbourhoods in terms of both shelter provision and cultural expression. Physically, unlike other more established settlements the houses are temporary and the land is not owned by the inhabitants. But, unlike other slum settlements which the students have studied, there seems to be no drive by the Marwari to build permanently or to obtain title to the land. The Agra local authority allows the Marwari to live at Indra Nagar provided that they do not build permanently. Under state law, dwellings are regarded as temporary because their materials of construction (earth and framed tarpaulin tents) are temporary, requiring regular repair and renewal. Thus a relatively refined house type has evolved which both suits the specialised life of the Marwari and their legal position. Prior to Independence in 1947, such groups were 'notified' by the colonial authorities (see below) stigmatising them as criminals to be avoided by the rest of society. Whilst such ostracism is no longer legitimised, the residents of Marwari Basti still suffer prejudice from other riverbank communities. The Marwari community appears to thrive on its in-between status.

Keeping itself apart from others, the community has also learned to benefit culturally from its evolving homogenous identity by presenting this as a unique selling point to tourists. The Agra Marwari have developed a livelihood based not just on the artefacts they produce, but also on the distinctive culture within which these products are made.

Nevertheless links with the outside world have to be established for survival: links to tourists to maintain a livelihood; links to other Marwari through their wandering elder (Bhima); and links to local politicians to reinforce and support their right to stay. The

map of dhobi ghat, Shambhu and Indra Nagar
Bo Tang

☐ Proposed Zones
☐ Existing Areas

PROPOSED KEY

Bamboo roof shelter
Brick dwelling
Brick Sanitation tower
Allotment and toilet

Vertical Reed bed

EXISTING KEY

Thatched dwelling
Brick Structure
Tented Dwelling

Concrete structure
Powerline
Washing line
Fabric drying

Marwari are not without means, nor are they totally powerless in establishing these relationships. Bhima's house is modern and permanent, square and solid. Not only is it more expensive but it also breaks the mould of the established mud and fabric prototype: perhaps evidence of a greater wealth and a hidden desire for more permanent settlement. Similarly the support of the Marwari is clearly valued locally, as students have observed a politician within the settlement during election time handing out cash to Marwari families in order to secure his vote bank.

This unusual set of circumstances raises a number of questions relating to the provision of urban amenities and services for urbanising nomadic communities generally and the development of an appropriate architectural response.

How has this distinctive identity come about and what role does it play in the urbanisation process? What are the mechanisms by which the identity of an urbanising nomadic community is reinforced rather than dissipated within the wider more anonymous individualised urban culture? How is this reflected in the architecture of the Marwari both in Marwari Basti and elsewhere? What lessons can be learned from studying the Marwari that can provide insights into other urbanising nomadic communities? What architectural inputs are most appropriate to support such urbanising nomadic communities in the take

up of urban amenities such as education, health and access to livelihoods?
These are the questions reviewed in this chapter. First of all however some explanation of how travelling communities such as the Marwari came to be set apart from the rest of Indian society and in Agra achieved their present status as hawkers of whips and lanterns.

Denotified Tribes

To those who are settled in one place, wandering strangers, particularly those who appear poor and needy (and perhaps dress differently) are easily made the object of suspicion. As far back as the early nineteenth century, the British colonial authorities took advantage of these suspicions to control the extensive new road network in India. The scapegoating of wandering peoples by the settled communities was accepted in order to justify the regulation of their movement. For example, the *Thuggee Act* of 1836 criminalised an entire community by constructing an image of that society based on low caste and false hereditary myths and also by exaggerating the prevalence of known acts of violence. This was so successful that even today the word 'thug' is synonymous with someone engaging in wanton violence for its own sake. The *Criminal Tribes Act* of 1871 formalised and extended this process to a much wider range of nomadic and marginalised communities (about 150). Under this Act, the Governor General was empowered to label or 'notify' groups of wandering peoples so that individuals were regarded as criminals just by nature of their membership of such a 'notified' community.

Whilst this notorious Act was repealed soon after Independence in 1947, the damage had already been done. Whole peoples had been set apart from mainstream society and classified as different, difficult and dangerous (D'Souza 2001).

Under the post-Independence constitution large numbers of nomadic communities and artists who were once classified as 'notified' were now called Denotified Tribes (or DNTs) and have special status. Following the repeal of the 1871 Act, the government of Bombay appointed Dr K.B. Antrolikar to report on ways to improve the quality of life of the DNTs. He eventually made 69 recommendations which included the provision of education and livelihood training. Very few, if any, of his recommendations saw the light of day.

A new constitution and the repeal of the 1871 Act has not however, removed settled people's prejudice against the 'denotified tribes'. In the years since independence their separate identity has not only been maintained but reinforced. Peripatetic settlements such as Marwari Basti are located in little clusters on the outside of cities. Situated on marginal land they are swept away when the construction of permanent settlements for the middle classes begins. Nomadic communities are characterised by their different behaviour (wandering Pardhi groups are described as 'bubbling and boiling'); by their colourful clothing; by their pseudonyms (Riksha after Rickshaw or Biscuit after a type of trick (D'Souza 2001, p. 153)). Each community is likely to have a reputation for a particular ability or skill: Pardhis for trapping quails for example; the Bajana tribe for playing musical instruments; the puppeteers of the Kathputli colony, Delhi who are descended from the nomadic tribes of Ghatt, Gujarat and the Rajasthan and Harvana deserts (Sosa 2008, p. 127) or indeed, the Agra Marwari for cock fighting. Whether or not the current inhabitants of Marwari Basti are descended from a previously 'notified' group, their different behaviour still marks them out from the rest of urban society. Students report from conversations with residents that children from Marwari Basti who have

Eucalyptus tree

Pipal tree

Neem tree

tree types making up the forest behind Dhobi Ghat and surrounding Shambhu and Indra Nagar
Bo Tang

previously attended mainstream school have had to leave due to intolerable prejudice and discrimination from teachers and other children. In contrast, children from neighbouring Shambhu Nagar attend mainstream school regularly.

Born with this separate identity, an identity on which the community's livelihood depends, it is almost impossible for an individual to escape. To do so a person must somehow obtain an education and a job in mainstream society. Then she must change her name and place of residence so that the new neighbours are ignorant of her origins: a task which can only be achieved at best over a few generations. In this way communal identity is both a survival mechanism and a trap.

The Denotified and Nomadic Communities Rights Action Group, founded in 1998 to lobby for the rights of such groups has found that the differences between travelling groups is so profound that it is very difficult to present a common platform (Devy 2005). However, at a convention in 2005, the one statement all nomadic communities could agree upon was that the 'primary mission of the predatory state is sedentarisation of the subject'. Thus there is a deep-seated resistance to the government's efforts to settle nomads permanently: resistance to the very idea of the state interfering in the nomadic way of life: to taxation, registration and government control and perhaps also to inappropriate educational programmes. It is no help to have clean water and access to health care if your opportunity to make a living is curtailed. Whilst individuals do sometimes manage to move out and join a mainstream community (D'Souza 2001, pp. 131–6); as a whole nomads want to remain as nomads even if that means remaining cash poor.

For some groups of Marwari however, reinforcing group identity has become a 'unique selling point' and has lead to untold wealth in a globalised world rather than a life of poverty in a marginal city settlement.

Marwari Identity

Hardgrove (2004) argues that the idea of a Marwari is a subjective construct rather than referring to either a precise geographical homeland or even a linguistic grouping. She gives

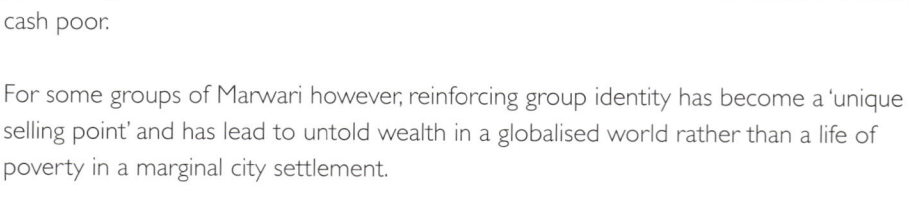

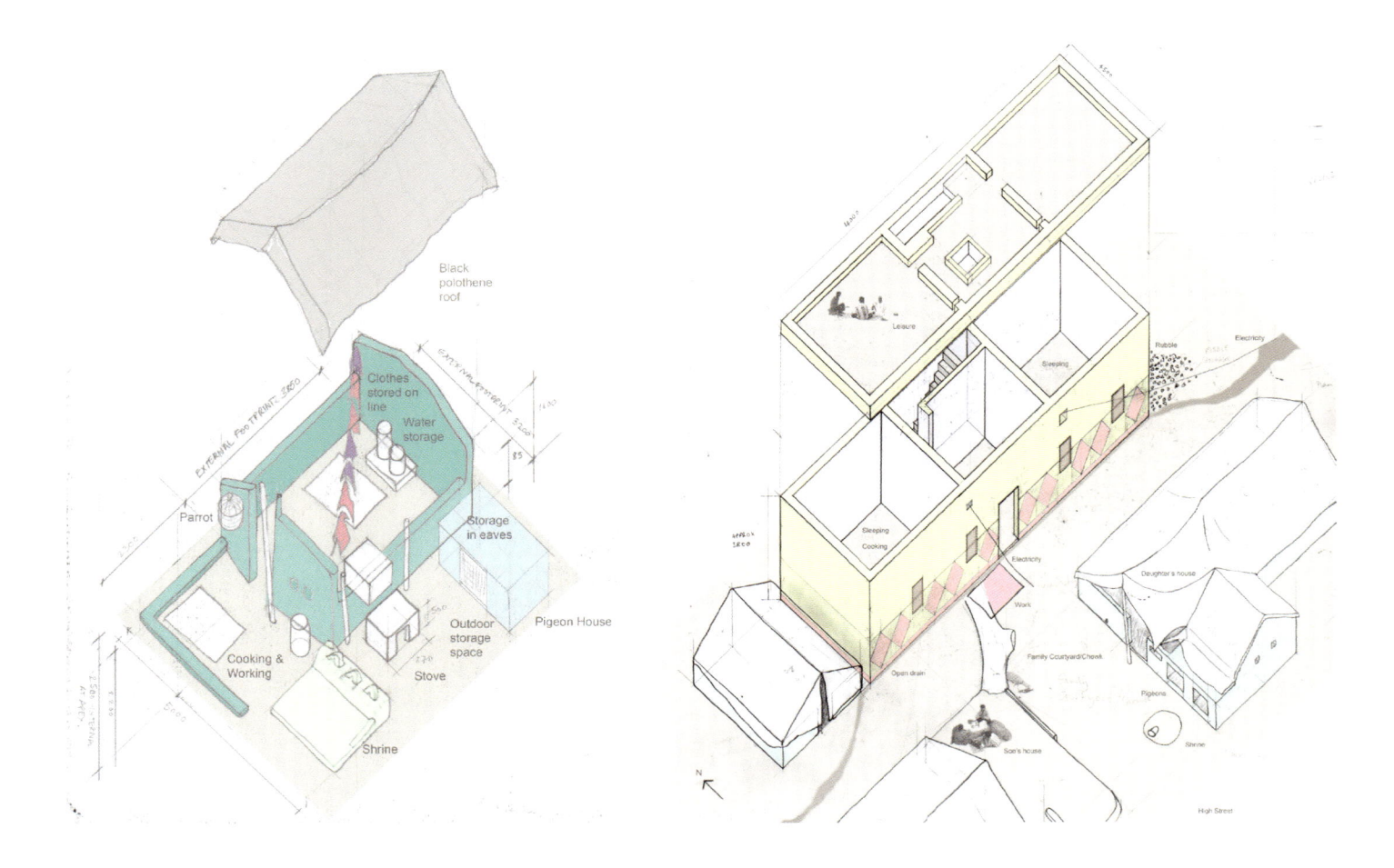

strong evidence that many migrating groups only became known as Marawis after they had left Rajasthan.

The general stereotype of the Marwari businessman is a Hindu or Jain 'baniya' (Vaishya (4) trader or moneylender), carrying nothing but a 'lota' (water pot) and 'kambal' (blanket), who has migrated thousands of miles from poor villages in the dry deserts of Rajasthan to cities and towns all over South Asia (Hardgrove 2004, p. 41). Marwari have combined this tradition of frugal wandering with that of entrepreneurship. In many ways they are a prime example of successful Indian capitalism. Worshiping Lakshmi, the goddess of wealth, they have integrated diligent accounting practices with prayer and religion. Believing that money should be put to good use, dispersed Marwari communities around India are obliged to support other wandering Marwari who turn up at their door with the minimum funds required to set up business. Lakshmi Mittal, a member of the Marwari community resident in the UK, is one of Britain's richest men.

There is a tradition of Marwari leaving the Rajasthani deserts due to famine and droughts, the most severe of which were in the 1850s and the 1930s. Some communities moved over the border into what is now Pakistan (1) but a large proportion migrated across northern India primarily to Kolkata and Mumbai. In the 1920s they were known primarily as wandering traders but later some Marwari became very successful. So much so that they were able buy up the industries left by the English and Scottish after the 1930s depression and the upheavals of Independence in 1947. The wealthy Mumbai Marwari are no longer wandering 'banyiras' and they are reputed on the one hand to have maintained

above left
survey of typical house in Marwari Basti
Emma Curtin
above right
Bhima's House
Emma Curtin
below
Guru Ram Das' yard
Emma Curtin

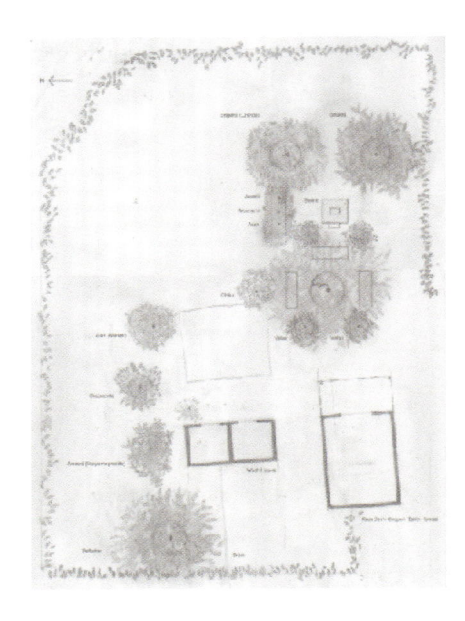

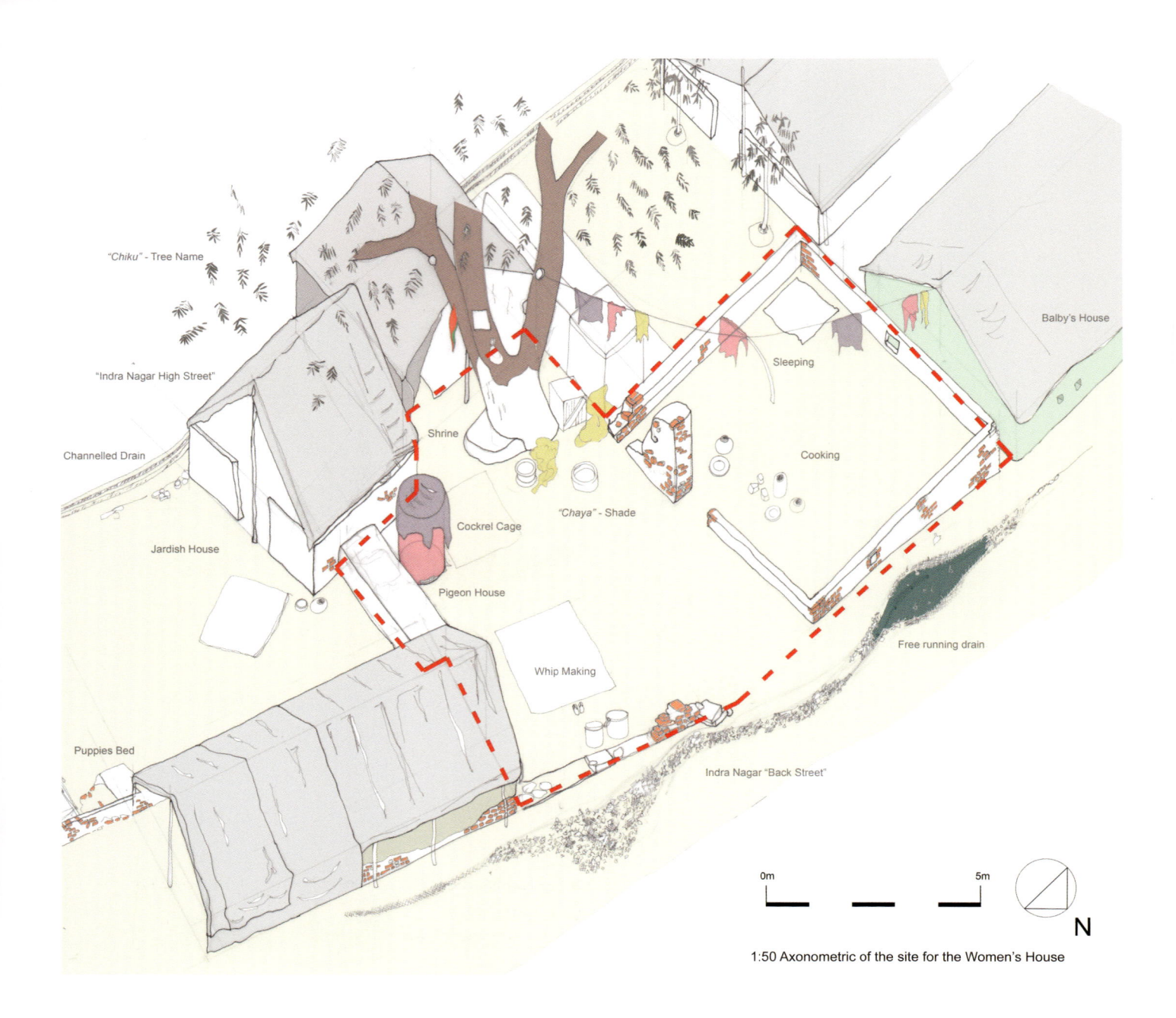

Labels on the axonometric drawing:

"Chiku" - Tree Name

"Indra Nagar High Street"

Channelled Drain

Jardish House

Puppies Bed

Shrine

Cockrel Cage

Pigeon House

Whip Making

"Chaya" - Shade

Sleeping

Cooking

Balby's House

Free running drain

Indra Nagar "Back Street"

0m   5m

N

1:50 Axonometric of the site for the Women's House

site for new women's house
Emma Curtin

their old entrepreneurial tradition of 'rain gambling' (Hardgrove 2004, pp. 136–8) and on the other to have developed a wide range of charitable institutions. They are supportive of schools, hospitals, technology institutes and temples (Hardgrove 2004, p. 12). They also have a distinctive architectural style and are known to support the upkeep of 'ancestral' mansions or havelis in Rajasthan which have richly decorated images painted on the courtyard walls:

... the range in visual themes of the frescoes exceeds the Rajput styles ... the paintings self-consciously appropriate symbols of the modern institutions of European culture, such as the railroad, the motorcar, European women, and the uniformed soldier, and visually deploy these images as a means of suggesting the merchants' own new cosmopolitan outlook (Hardgrove 2004, p. 95).

Legend

- ○ Cockerel Cage
- Tap
- Tap with fabric privacy screen
- Drain
- Bank
- House with pitch of roof and wall type indicated
- Tree

Hindi Glossary

Chaya - Shade
Bagicha - Garden
Pukka - Solid Legal Construction
Kutcha - Temporary often Illegal Construction
Atchi Miti Chai - Good Sweet Chai

survey of Marwari Basti showing family occupation
Emma Curtin

Just as the Marwari of Agra are associated with leather goods (whips for the tourist trade) so the richer Marwari have prospered from this low caste occupation. Dr Prabiha Kaitan, a Marwari from a traditional Kolkata family, has a successful prize-winning company called 'New Horizons' which has been set up specifically to export leather goods (2) and Hermès now have a fashionable leather bag on sale for US$2,000 called a Marwari bag (3).

Clearly, the Marwari brand has been successful in generating livelihoods for its members, both rich and poor and it is understandable if there is a limited desire amongst individuals and families to leave the social comfort of the Marwari community.

Given this situation how can architecture both support the confidence in securing a livelihood given by membership of a nomadic community whilst increasing the opportunity for escape for those who choose to do so?

Before addressing this question let's look at the construction and use of space in Marwari Basti. Let's examine its antecedents and the current relationship to its surroundings both physically and culturally. Then, with reference to precedent, we can go some way towards speculating on what places might be made now which could be of benefit to the Agra Marwari. Furthermore, let's reflect on appropriate shelter for other poor, previously nomadic, urban peoples, whether they choose as a group to remain apart or individually wish to integrate with sedentary society.

Shelter: What to Take with You and What to Leave Behind

(1) Frame and Tent (to take with you)

Many of the nomadic peoples mentioned above, including the Marwari living in Indra Nagar, originated in the deserts of Gujarat and Rajasthan. In November 2002, during the first field trip to India, students travelled to remote villages in Gujarat and observed isolated groups of such nomads. These small, self-sufficient nomadic families wandered slowly but steadily and purposefully along an invisible vector across the hard, arid landscape. During their travelling day they were often grouped around one or two camels which carried their worldly goods. People took it in turns to ride a camel or walk alongside with the camp dogs. The largest and seemingly most ungainly item carried on the back of the camel was the family charpoi. This consisted of either a traditional hardwood or more commonly, a metal, four-legged frame interwoven with a stretched string fabric which provided some level of soft furnishing when used as a bed or sofa. Such charpoi are common throughout India. However, what is remarkable here is that this item of furniture, so comfortable when in use yet so awkward to transport on a camel, should nevertheless be adopted and retained as the largest movable family object.

However, the nomad's charpoi served several other functions in addition to that of bed or sofa. When propped up off the saddle and covered with cloth, it became a palanquin; providing protection to the riders from the sun during the middle of the day. This arrangement allowed the march to continue steadily if somewhat somnolently to the roll of the camel's gait. If forced to stop by the sudden onset of heavy rain or a dust storm, a tarpaulin covered, propped charpoi can provide instant protection when suitably weighted and pegged down. Alternatively, in the heat of the day, if there is no shade available in the vastness of the desert landscape, the charpoi's sturdy frame, perched on rocks against a bank of earth can equally support a brushwood insulated roof and offer a small but cool resting place.

Used in such a way, the charpoi is a rigid travelling frame over which other materials can be stretched and under which people can shelter. It is an element whose effectiveness can be increased if other elements can be found at the site of the day's camp or resting place: such as a wall or an earth bank. The charpoi frame makes use of the camp landscape leaving it as it was found when it is time to move on. In this way the charpoi is a parasitic structure which relies on the ingenuity of the traveller and the happenstance of found materials for place-making.

In Marwari Basti, Agra, roofs are often supported independently of the walls on poles or bamboo frameworks. The leather straps, rubber strips and ropes holding the thatch, black polythene and tarpaulin roof coverings are fixed to the ground like guy ropes with pegs. Like frame tents they are weighted down with rocks or tied through openings low down on the mud walls. As with the truly nomadic, no nails are used. Poles are tied with strips of cloth, rope and string as if primed for re-use. Roof fabrics are under a great deal of tension which needs to be maintained and adjusted depending on the heat and humidity, so the anchors have to be sound (often deeply buried) and the ropes tied in such a way that they are capable of adjustment.

More rudimentary versions of such houses without earth walls can be seen at the edge of the settlement where ridge poles have been supported on both pre-existing perimeter

above
photograph and sketch of community platform and school
Emma Curtin
below
camel boy and charpoi, Gujurat

walls and attached to live trees. Such trees are respected. As before, lateral poles are tied, not nailed, as if the tree is expected to have a longer life than the dwelling. The location of the tree within the settlement identifies the location of the dwelling: a known tree amongst other known trees. The tree type itself may have significance within the culture lending its mythical or physical attributes to dwelling and dweller alike.

All these tented dwellings have the hallmarks of temporary parasitic abodes, making full use of the local landscape and appearing ready to be moved on at a moment's notice leaving just a few crumpled earthen mounds in their wake. This is despite the fact that the Marwari are reputed to have been there since another form of nomadic tribe, the British Army, vacated the site some considerable time ago. Contrary to the temporary appearance however, at least one of the houses is claimed to be 100 years old.

(2) The Moulded Earth Wall and Threshold (to leave behind)

Apart from the occasional charpoi there are no substantial items of furniture in Marwari Basti dwellings: no cupboards, tables or chairs. Instead alcoves, shelves, seats, tables, beds and window openings are all formed out of earth. The low walls are sculpted by the inhabitants to carve out familiar shapes and spaces, thresholds and platforms. Sometimes traditional objects, such as religious shrines, are made of mud and incorporated within the domestic earth mini-landscape. Elsewhere, conversely, earth is moulded to fit around and display more alien objects imported to the culture from the modern world such as television sets or hi-fi speakers. In one case, a large, carefully-shaped, mud recess faced with a barred grill, caged a vociferous green and yellow parrot.

above
internal view of Marwari Basti house
Marco Sosa
below
stored charpoi, Delhi

Alongside the Gujarati nomads observed by students in 2002, permanent desert villages are located where water can be found or collected. Traditionally these village dwellings are also constructed with earth walls extended to form cupboards, shelves, beds and other

raised platforms around a standpipe
Marco Sosa

furniture. The residents of rural vernacular Gujarati homes are renowned for their skills in forming and decorating such items with incised plasterwork decoration, small glass sequins and coloured paint washes. Marwari Basti appears to be a slimmed-down version of this tradition.

From a nomad's point of view, when a decision to move is made, then what to take with you and what remains can be crucial. It is no wonder perhaps, that the artistry embodied in decorating the sedentary mud houses of Gujarat is focused instead by the nomads on their mobile artefacts. In the case of the Marwari in Agra this has been transferred to the easily transportable whips, stools and lanterns which they manufacture for sale.

Mud architecture needs constant maintenance and rebuilding: justified perhaps when a summer camp has to be remade after a winter trek, but less desirable when you are not moving out. More long term settlement implies more permanent construction. Such ambitions for change are not shared in Marwari Basti. Perhaps their way of life depends on their remaining in a permanent state of readiness to move on: a permanent state of impermanence.

Two dwellings have however been transformed into rectangular solid brick constructions with stone roofs. These belong to the richest two members of the community and ironically they house the families of those who travel the most: connecting with other Marwari communities, collecting raw materials and taking manufactured products for sale elsewhere.

Settling in

(1) Public and Private Space

Just as within a Gujarati nomad's camp, dogs abound in Marwari Basti. Just as they sniff
out and warn off strangers from a wandering band, so do they also monitor the public
and private spaces of Marwari Basti. They bark at the unfamiliar, wag their tails as they
recognise a visitor and lie fast asleep for everyone else.

Tented dwellings are grouped around pockets of open space. Connections between
these pockets are made by line of sight, smells and sounds. Each pocket is characterised
by the particular uses to which it is put by the occupying families: making chairs or whips
or the location of cock fights for example; whether or not it has a tap and an open drain;
whether there is a shrine and if so to what god? One pocket was regarded as 'cool'
because music was played constantly. Another was known as the place where the Teno
family was always working: 'look there under the Lymn tree' (5).

Space is divided within the pocket as and when necessary. Women pull their saris and
perhaps an extra cloth around themselves for privacy as they slowly and carefully wash
themselves at the public tap. Temporary fabric screens on sticks are sometimes employed
for more comprehensive showering. The height and covering of the ground surface is
a key to its function and level of intimacy. The concrete hardstanding surrounding a tap
with its sharp edges acts as a ground level, communal, waterproof basin. Working areas
are defined by spreading out a mat on the floor with stretched fabric overhead providing

shade. Sometimes a formal public meeting area can be defined by simply spreading out a carpet.

The more private area in front of a dwelling entrance is defined by a slightly elevated (by about 100mm) earth platform where guests are received and artefacts are produced. Family meals are cooked and eaten here squatting around a fire or cooking pot. On the edge of the platform older family members take extended periods of rest stretched out on an earth bench raised a further 500mm off the ground. The interior of the house is divided into two: shrines and stored goods are located nearest the door whilst the back of the house is reserved for the most intimate and private activities. The more private the floor area, the more often it is swept and cleaned. In contrast to the endlessly polished surfaces of the raised domestic platforms the routes through and circulating around the edge of the settlement are made up of rough, uneven, unmaintained surfaces, littered and unclean.

Whilst the house interiors are sparse and tidy, often richly coloured and hung with cloths, the views of the settlement from outside are of a lower key. The mud walls are usually brightly painted with blues, reds and greens but once the noise of children playing, dogs barking and the birdsong has died away, if you turn around, there is not much left to see. In the hollow of the land below the raised road from which the settlement is entered, the blacks and greys of the roof tarpaulins seem huddled together in a low, dishevelled jumble almost hidden under the tree canopy.

How can a life based on the pretence of mobility and separation from settled society be squared with the need, when you settle yourself, to have a positive ongoing relationship with the immediate neighbourhood?

(2) The Neighbourhood at Large
In this part of Agra, each neighbourhood appears to have its own distinct cultural and physical identity. To the west, the square brick houses of Shambhu Nagar are home to city workers. This is a growing settlement of square, small, two-storey courtyard houses interlaced with pedestrian streets. To the south are arable fields owned by farmers from the settlement of Nangla Devjeet, located half a kilometre to the east. Settlements to the north are cut off by the raised embankment of the Agra to Kolkata railway. Exchanges between all these communities and the Marwari appear to be minimal.

A few buffalo, kept by a couple of families at the southern edge of Marwari Basti provide milk and kanda (dung pats) (6). A few goats are also kept for milk and young male goats are sometimes sold to neighbours. These few buffalo and goats graze amongst the eucalyptus trees surrounding the nalla (natural watershed) lower down, which discharges into the river beside the dhobi ghat (riverside laundry). However this eucalyptus grove is also the location for defecation and in this sloping long wooded space Marwari compete with dhobi wallahs (laundry workers) for space and privacy. Once a year the monsoon sweeps away refuse and night soil into the river. There are no toilets in the settlement itself and this is an increasing problem as the surrounding land becomes developed and less public land is available for piecemeal sanitation.

Relationships between the Marwari and the authorities appear rather mysterious and marked by paper evidence often stored in a sack or box in some dark recess of the tented houses and produced as deemed necessary to justify a point or counter any

top
scheme for pukka houses adjacent to tents: plan
Emma Curtin
middle
scheme for pukka houses adjacent to tents: end elevation 1
Emma Curtin
bottom
scheme for pukka houses adjacent to tents: end elevation 2
Emma Curtin

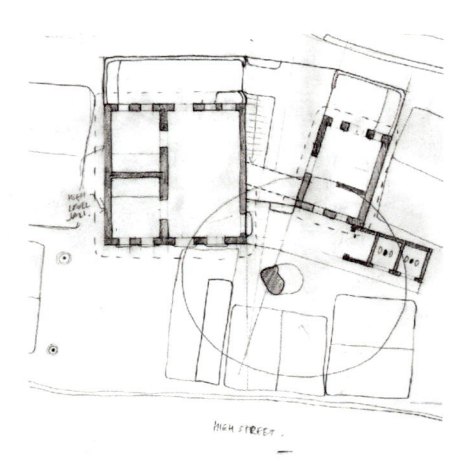

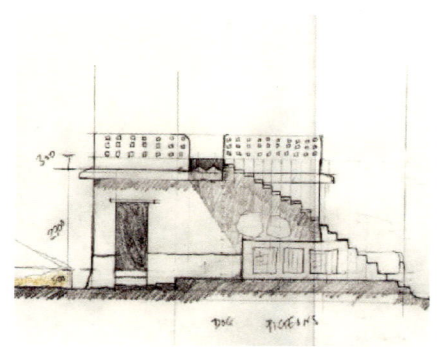

scheme for pukka houses adjacent to tents: front elevation
Emma Curtin

outside challenge. Official documents are often prized for their visual power and assumed to have a very broad legitimacy. Such printed, stamped and sealed evidence is sometimes hoarded to demonstrate status and legitimacy to outsiders even if the documents have only a marginal relevance to the issue under discussion. In trying to understand family relationships and hierarchies within the settlement students found that taking family photographs worked best. Photographs helped students identify family members so that they could draw family trees. At the same time handing over the pictures to the families concerned was a very welcome addition to their printed records.

Running west to east beyond the eucalyptus grove and then turning south on the eastern boundary of the settlement a perimeter road takes tourists to view the rear of the Taj Mahal across the river from the north. These tourists are the prime market for the Marwari products but their point of sale has always been at the main entrances to both the Taj and the Red Fort.

Students engaged with the community to manufacture more modest products such as leather bracelets and constructed a market stall to peddle such products along this eastern road close to the settlement. Due to the energetic participation of the families involved together with the efforts of the students in accosting passing tourists, this exercise was very successful, demonstrating that such smaller objects using less raw materials could be more lucrative than whip production.

But different communities have a different mix of needs and the history of the provision of urban services such as clean water, sanitation, health and education by government and local authorities to such urban communities is not a good one.

Appropriate Amenity Buildings

D'Souza (2001, pp. 42–52) describes how the colonial authorities tried to reform and then integrate groups of itinerant denotified tribes. With fundamentalist Christian groups leading the way, the provision of dowries to enable intermarriage with outside communities, removal of children for separate education and forced labour for the adult males was a familiar agenda. Since Independence, a range of initiatives, funded by a more diverse range of religious and philanthropic organisations has turned to education and

livelihood generation. These initiatives are sited within existing communities, as a way of generating 'improvement' of the community and obtaining the mutual respect of the urban community at large (D'Souza 2001, pp. 53–75).

Despite, rather than because of, such interventions many, if not most, of the recently urbanised migrant communities have settled. They have discovered by a process of trial and error that they can make a living using their singular skills in a particular urban spot. This is clearly the case for the residents of Marwari Basti who have developed a functioning network for the sourcing of raw materials, the financing of the operation and the sale of their products. It is this particularity of location and cultural expression which enriches concepts of place and makes urban nomads so interesting to architects. In addition, the Marwari's situation within a eucalyptus grove, their mixture of colourful clothes, ephemeral shelters and unusual manufactures immediately evoked the curiosity of the students.

Marco Sosa (2008), drew up a comprehensive scheme for a range of amenity buildings to be constructed on the edge of the settlement to support the Marwari in their endeavours.

(1) The Site as a Resource
Marco found that many of the pointers to a suitable design were to be found by studying the existing settlement itself. Just as the Marwari have done, he took advantage of the local landscape. Choosing an adjoining site he proposed to make use of an existing boundary wall with the fields to the west. He chose to intervene in the design of government works to the edge of the tourist road on the higher opposite boundary to provide a transport stop-off and regulated access for visitors.

(2) What to Leave Behind
Marco divided his proposal into temporary (what to take with you) and permanent (what to leave behind) construction. He assumed that function would only be defined when the temporary was installed on the permanent. The range of services and spaces for his programme of increased amenity would need to be more diverse than in the domestic

encampment. The take up and evolution of these services and spaces was, to some extent, unpredictable. Therefore Marco assumed a rather generous supply of permanent landscape, activated when required by occupation signified by colourful temporary installations.

above
a landscape of plinths and thermally massive table structures
Marco Sosa
below
accessible rooftops
Marco Sosa

(2a) Horizontal Surfaces

An indication of the nature of suitable permanent elements was provided by the existing school/temple plinth (activated by the shade of the banyan tree and the shrine) and the two intermittently occupied but permanent houses. Marco's design provided a range of stone plinths and short stairs which led down from the road and elevated group activities off the uneven and occasionally flooded ground.

(2b) Tables, Pavilions and Caves

During the day in July and August temperatures can be as high as 45°C and currently the only relief from this heat available in the camp is provided by the two permanent houses. When openings are firmly closed, thermally massive walls and a flat roof can delay the penetration of daytime heat into the interior. Doors and windows are flung open in the evening and heat is flushed out overnight so that the process can begin again in the morning. In the winter, the opposite is true: the night chills can be ameliorated by laying bare the masonry to heat up during the mild, sunny daytime.

Marco proposed a number of thermally massive flat roofed stone table structures, mounted on parts of the plinths and large enough to shelter a class of pupils or a wide range of workshop activities. These structures could act as thermal caves when closed off or alternatively become open pavilions when required. Their rooftops were to be largely accessible by stairways or directly from the (higher adjacent) road providing opportunity for occupation with a view.

(2c) Courtyards

Plinths were arranged to surround (carve out) spaces and pavilions grouped to provide courts where access might be controlled in case of performance (theatre or exhibition) or the need for privacy (sanitation, laundry) or alternatively become an open public forum.

(3) What to Take with You

The rugged masonry landscape of plinth and pavilion was to be turned into an evolving sequence of places by demonstrative occupation using lightweight colourful materials, similar to those used to make the tented roofs in the settlement. Fabric and mat canopies were to be stretched over bamboo frames to cover plinths and rooftops, enclose workshops and provide privacy screens. Sometimes just the choice of a position within the masonry landscape would be sufficient to activate the space: colourful artefacts arranged for sale or manufacture alone being a vibrant indicator of place.

(4) Social Ownership

The actual take up by Marwari residents of amenities offered in the scheme is, of course, hard to predict. It is not clear for example whether grouping sanitation and laundry facilities together for the whole settlement could be adequately managed to ensure clean and efficient working. Experience elsewhere with more individualised communities suggests otherwise. Whilst Marwari community cohesion might suggest that grouping sanitary facilities was possible here, current water supply and defecation habits suggest that separate and dispersed facilities would be preferred. Similarly, attempts by the students to demonstrate a market on the Marwari's doorstep for smaller leather products was short lived but presumably capable of revival and possible evolution into a craft market. The lack of literacy, particularly amongst the women is especially inhibiting for social mobility but whether the community will embrace substantive education for all community members is not clear. Nevertheless with increasing urbanisation, communities such as the Marwari in Agra will have to make choices. If they do stay where they are and continue to trade on their community identity they will need both to find a solution to their sanitation needs and broaden the market for their Marwari manufactures. In turn this must surely require a degree of vocational training if not a more general education.

In such a situation communal identity will have to be maintained if not reinforced and serviced by amenity buildings such as those proposed by Marco's loose fit approach. The level of engagement by the community will gradually become clearer and the pattern of occupation of the amenity provision more familiar. Then social ownership of the buildings might be indicated by spontaneous addition to, and enclosure of, the more permanent parts initiated by the community themselves. Shrines might be constructed to indicate the establishment of place. Walls might be decorated in the manner of the Marwari's ancestral havelis to reinforce identity. Increased visibility of the community, its culture and manufactures, through tourist visits to the amenity buildings might induce funding of the community's educational programme through the wider Marwari network.

Precedents and Prototypes: Application Elsewhere

Marco's scheme established amenity provision through community occupation of a loose fit, hard landscape of plinths, pavilions and courtyards under three headings: community (education, healthcare and vocational training); sanitation (washing, sanitation and laundry) and showcase (workshops, exhibition and market). To what extent can this approach to design be applied to provide amenity to other urban, recently settled nomadic communities?

puppeteer from the Kathputli Colony, Delhi

Some groups of migrant workers in urban India develop both a permanent and a temporary home. Building workers, for example, might squat in tented dwellings next to their building site and send money home to their village. Such encampments often provide the founding nucleus for illegal slum settlements or J.J. camps which might still maintain a strong connection to the original rural village; the residents migrating between village and J.J. camp dependent on seasonal work. In these cases, unless a distinct community based on a unique way of making a living is established it is unlikely that sufficient community coherence will be generated for a wide-ranging, loose fit, community scheme. In these cases enhanced state provision of education and sanitation would perhaps be more appropriate.

On the other hand, there are groups such as the Pardhi pavement dwellers of Mumbai who perform and beg outside the major hotels, living where they work without an address or even a roof of their own. Here, before wider amenity is considered, the priority must be to secure land for dwellings close to the Pardhi's place of work (7).

Again, another type of urban nomad is represented by the specialised Vedic and Unani medical practitioners who set up small, individual, tented medium-term establishments on pavements near to likely custom. There is no wider local community and no intention for permanent occupation. In these individual cases amenity can only be based on what can be found and latched on to locally.

Then there are other more distinct cultures that have been able to market their unique livelihood speciality and who through their skill and reputation have established themselves in a particular place whilst still lacking basic amenities. Such coherent communities are more likely candidates for Marco's loose fit scheme.

Just such a community is the Kathputli Colony of puppeteers of Bhule Bisre Kalakar (forgotten local artists) Nagar, Shadipur, Delhi. As with the Agra Marwari, they are originally from the deserts of Gujarat, Rajasthan and Haryana. They began to settle at the end of the nineteenth century and have been established on their present site near a disused railway station west of central Delhi, since 1966. The residents live, work, play and make puppets

nomadic Vedic practitioner, Delhi

in the colony. Whilst the call for puppet performances in Delhi has declined due to the advent of cinema and television, the colony gets many commissions from abroad and from the tourist industry. Despite the vibrant creative atmosphere, Kathputli Colony is regarded as a slum by the authorities. It has problems of clean water supply, sanitation and literacy together with alcohol-related issues amongst young men. Nevertheless the colony is firmly established on its land as a coherent and discrete culture of performers who are likely to benefit from the loose fit type of amenity scheme prototyped by Marco in Agra. In this case, however, the showcase (puppet theatre) element of Marco's tripartite mix is likely to predominate alongside community provision (education and health) whilst sanitation may well be dispersed.

Thus, a diverse range of amenity provision is an essential constituent of successful nomadic settlement in India, particularly where nomadic identity is to be reinforced. Such amenity provision is fertile ground for the architectural imagination.

Notes

(1) http://kcm.co.kr/bethany_eng/p_code2/999.html (March 2009).

(2) http://www.tribuneindia.com/2003/20031130/herworld.htm#1 (March 2009).

(3) http://forum.purseblog.com/hermes/a-great-bag-called-marwari-by-hermes-398346.html (March 2009).

(4) Vaishya is the third of the four main Indian castes. They are merchants, artisans and cultivators and those engaged in the specialisation of professional knowledge (Wikipedia, March 2009).

(5) Snippet of conversation with Marwari Basti resident noted November 2006.

(6) Dung pats are used as domestic fuel and to bind the plaster on the low walls of the tented houses.

(7) See Wikipedia (September 2009): Pavement Dwellers; 1985 Eviction Crisis.

chapter 7

Climate, Density and Construction

Passive comfort provision within contemporary illegal and unplanned settlements in India is often sacrificed to the need for high density accommodation. Even the resettlement colonies planned by the Delhi government to re-house slum dwellers, offer plot sizes too small to provide adequate through ventilation. Within this context a modern urban vernacular is emerging: a new architecture without architects (1).

This chapter explores how, in such settlements comfort and conviviality are mixed within this dense urban landscape. It reviews the emergence of a slum house type with its constituent building elements and materials. It assesses the extent to which this type helps alleviate the physical discomfort and overcrowding found in slum settlements and the role it is playing in the construction of a planned government 'site and services' resettlement colony. It questions whether the core skills of architects, those of curiosity, innovation and the manipulation of dimension and fit, do not actually have a significant role to play in the provision of social housing in Delhi.

The Density of Slums

(1) Single-storey Kuchha

Ambedkar Camp, set in the strip of land between the Kolkata-bound railway and the Grand Trunk Road within the east Yamuna Jilmil Industrial Area, is a typical, illegal slum settlement.

Here, clusters of tiny, one-roomed dwellings are packed together within very tight confines. Often a small single room (just 2.5 × 3.0 metres) must accommodate the full range of domestic activity for a family of up to nine people. On the way out of the room, the doorstep provides a raised threshold leading to a shared narrow pedestrian alley, open to the sky and drained by a narrow surface channel. One student, brought up short by the loss of his shoe in such a channel, pondered:

... who decided where the drains would weave their way through the streets and who is unlucky

sketch of room occupation: one circle represents one person
Tze-Ting Mok

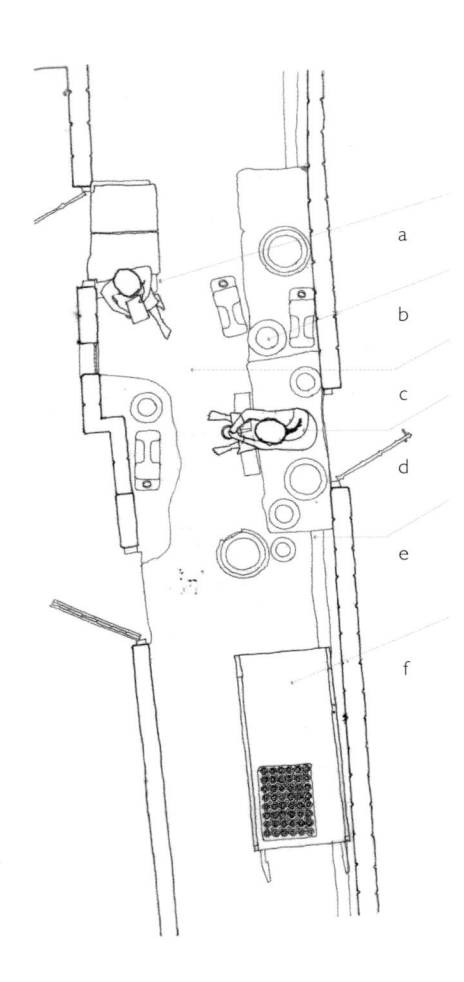

enough to have these drains discharge in front of their doorway when the monsoon comes and floods the homes with dirty water?

Sometimes, the door threshold is enlarged into a verandah providing a place for chores such as sewing and ironing; together with handicrafts, such as weaving and mat-making, taking place to the accompaniment of passing conversation.

Inside each room, security, privacy and protection from the direct rays of the sun is prioritised over daylighting. Windows are small and often above eye level. So rooms are dark. When visited by students these modest sanctums were found to be quiet and comfortable. They were kept very clean and displayed a proud sense of ownership despite being cramped and often poorly ventilated.

After a long day's surveying, one student, feeling hot and tired, was invited into a family's single-roomed dwelling to recuperate. After being ushered inside to perch on the family's bed, she was urged to sit on a special chair placed on the only remaining section of unoccupied floor, under a huge fan embedded centrally within the outside wall. Once activated, this machine dragged outside air through a box filled with wetted ropes at such a speed that the atmosphere within the room became cooled and humidified within just a few seconds. Recovery was instantaneous: the student was left shivering and begging for the machine to be turned off (2).

Normally however, the electricity supply is intermittent or non-existent, due to an overburdened system and this means that children move out of the darkened room to sit on the doorstep or verandah to do their homework in the evening light. In some streets, water is piped along the surface, running past tiny cement lined holes in the ground. These holes, one for each house, act as cisterns filled once or twice a day when the water is turned on by the water authority. In the street alongside the cisterns, outside most homes are small charcoal fuelled cooking stoves (chulha) (3) formed out of plastered brick. Not all these stoves are still in use as now women prefer to cook on gas or petrol stoves within the room. This new practice has lead to an increased fire hazard and health problems associated with petrol and kerosene fumes. Generally ablutions take place away from the home but outside some dwellings, with the agreement of neighbours in the more remote alleys and cul-de-sacs, shower screens have been erected over the surface drain making the narrow alleyways even narrower so that sometimes you have to turn sideways to pass by.

Such tightly-packed domestic activity is possible because of the following three robust multi-valent spaces, each tolerant of change and adaptation: the dark room, raised verandah and narrow, watered and drained, pedestrian public street. In order to carry out their domestic chores with dignity within this tripartite spatial arrangement, women have developed ways to preserve both a public and private face to their lives, which relies on the way they use these three spaces. Faced with such cramped conditions, most use ephemeral techniques such as covering and uncovering, hiding and revealing, to create layers of privacy and establish boundaries of interaction within their day to day routines. Cash and other valuables are squirrelled away at the back of the room whilst lesser, children's treats might be placed behind a familiar object next to the doorway. As well as being closed and locked with a steel shutter when the family is away, at other times doorways can be hung with opaque fabric (which is easily pushed aside) or peppered with a beaded curtain to keep out the flies but let in the daylight; leaving a semi-transparent framed view of the street from inside.

sketch plan of alley occupation, Ambedkar Camp
Stephen Chown:

a Sunhill sits on stone entrance step completing his homework
b water from communal tap stored in buckets and plastic containers for washing and drinking
c the street becomes wet and soapy from the daily washing
d lady washing clothes in front of her house
e stagnant drain filled with litter and rotting matter. It bubbles and smells
f parked cart for selling eggs constricts the street forcing people through a narrower gap

clothes and litter line the roofs to prevent homes becoming excessively hot and to dampen the sound of rain during the monsoon

humidifier set into the wall of a single-storey house

While perched on a doorstep working on an intricate piece of handiwork women who do not want to be disturbed will pull layers of sari cloth around themselves to create an intimate space. Similarly, maintaining privacy whilst washing in the street enveloped in fabric and drying one part of the body after another is effective but tedious, involving long, slow, dance-like movements. Students referred to women shielding themselves in this way as 'conspicuous ghosts' (2):

... [they] would blur the boundaries between public and private to create layers of invisible boundaries. They would conceal their presents [sic] and identity by enveloping themselves with arrangements of street furniture and layers of sari textiles.

Spaces switch genders when husbands come home from work and become more formal. Street furniture is re-arranged to give a spatial hierarchy to the alley, a line of laundry is drawn across the street to obscure outside views and deter through traffic so that neighbours can settle down together to gossip as if they were in a shared living room.

But such ephemeral boundaries are only for adults. Children are the great transgressors of thresholds between public and private, running in and out of each others homes at will, skipping up and down the streets and hopping from rooftop to rooftop. Student photographs are full of images of older children carrying their tiny siblings, entertaining them, whilst mothers are away from home, by seeing just what the students were up to. Within the illegal settlements themselves, small tradesmen have innovated, developed the necessary skills and then set themselves up as businesses to construct and extend dwellings with minimal expense using locally available materials. In this way a local contemporary urban vernacular has evolved to meet the needs of the people with the innovative ingenuity, skills and material resources available locally.

(2) Kuchha Roofs

Example (1) Bamboo, reed mat and rubber sheet roofs manufactured by the Kaur family of Kalyanpuri

Devi Kaur, wife of a roofer in Kalyanpuri Block 19/20 (east Yamuna illegal settlement), weaves chunky reed mats on her doorstep for her husband's business. These mats are spread over bamboo or round pole beams under a black rubberised sheet weighted down with brick to provide an effective roof. The more mat layers installed, the greater the insulation. In another parallel local technology, mats are spread over bamboo stick pergolas providing temporary and movable cool rooftop places. Whether bamboo mats are placed over pergolas or laid over other forms of roof construction as insulating layers, they are particularly effective in moderating the build up of heat during the long hot/dry spring months from April until the monsoon breaks in June during which time the city suffers temperatures up to 47°C together with severe power and water shortages.

The ubiquity of bamboo mat and rubber sheet roofs in the Kalyanpuri area may have something to do with the fact that Kalyanpuri is the market location for the wholesale distribution of bamboo which is brought into Delhi by the lorry load from outside the city. This trade supports a local cottage industry of bamboo screen and ladder making. Bamboo mat and sheet roof technology appears to have been developed by entrepreneurs such as the Kaur family who have taken advantage of the plentiful supply of bamboo at wholesale prices in the area.

The bamboo mat and sheet roofs described above are quite particular to the illegal settlements in the Kalyanpuri area. But they are not the roof of choice in such settlements elsewhere in Delhi. For example, in the illegal settlements distributed amongst the Jilmil Industrial estates not too far away from Kalyanpuri, corrugated asbestos fibre cement sheets on timber or steel purlins are the roof of choice. These materials last longer than bamboo mat roofs and are also manufactured locally, but they are quite brittle and cannot be walked on. To avoid breakages and to facilitate re-use, fibre cement sheets are generally not fixed but simply weighted down with bricks or other layers of debris. To insulate the interior of their homes from extreme internal temperatures residents often overclad their corrugated roofs with brushwood, firewood and/or flattened cardboard boxes.

Example (2)
Nat Horner's insulated fabric roof

As discussed elsewhere, Delhi's waste picking communities use cardboard to clad both bamboo roof frameworks as well as bamboo stud walls. Used as a flat sheet cardboard offers maximum cover for minimum material. In addition, waste pickers often stack cardboard bailed up ready for collection by middlemen, to provide the walls of their temporary shelters. Once the original lower layers of cardboard on the rooftops of such kuchha dwellings are wet, new layers of cardboard are applied to offer more protection from the rain. When a tarpaulin is purchased to cover the cardboard then clearly the roof will last a while longer. In such cases, thick layers of cardboard under the waterproof sheet provide good thermal insulation from the direct rays of the sun.

Picking up the idea of an insulated fabric covered roof, Nat Horner (2005) modelled the performance of an array of waste paper bundles laid out on and fixed to a bamboo grid and covered with lorry tarpaulins as a weathered radiation shield. She engaged an environmental engineer in a discussion of thermal resistance, which was found to relate to the thickness, density, water content and surface properties of such a roof. She explored density by stuffing different quantities of shredded paper into the same sized box to make bales of different weight, which were then tested in a range of temperature conditions. She explored different surface properties by fusing together crisp packets to make a waterproof sheet (even if rather fragile) but concluded that a normal rubberised sheet would be more pragmatic in the circumstances. Nat took her paper bundles to the local

sauna to see how they would behave in the monsoon season and considered the idea
of wetting them at the height of the dry season to increase comfort by humidifying the
atmosphere. After all this investigation she concluded that when her roof was deployed as
a functioning pergola covering a more permanent roof:

*... the top surface of the paper bale roof will absorb the solar radiation reflecting say 50%. This
is less (reflection) than before (when the shiny crisp packet surface was tried) because it will
be rough and will weather to a dark matt finish. So 50% or about 500 watts per square metre
will be absorbed. This will be conducted to the top air stream which will heat up to as much
as 25 degrees Celsius above ambient air temperature. If the bale has a U value of 0.8 then
about 20 watts per square metre will be conducted to the air stream below which will be only
one degree Celsius above the ambient (shaded) air temperature with perhaps four watts per
square metre being radiated to the permanent roof below (Horner 2006).*

Thus such a roof would provide an excellent shading device. Typical bale or matt and
waterproof sheet roofs can be very effective in reducing internal temperatures and
providing comfort in the dry hot season either as a temporary main roof or as rooftop
sunscreen during the day.

Such insulated fabric roofs however can never form the basis of a suspended floor and to
go higher, more permanent heavy and expensive structures are required.

(3) A Second Floor
Kalyanpuri Block 19/20 (described elsewhere in this book) has a few lightweight rooftop
rooms accessed by bamboo ladders. More dwellings in Ambedkar camp have a second
storey accessed by means of a stairway or ladder up the face of the building leading to a

above
section through two-storey houses: Ambedkar Camp
Azedah Mosavi
below
sketch plan showing use of veranda of two-storey house: Ambedkar Camp
Stephen Chown

a small window with decorative metalwork reduces heat gain and improves ventilation
b raised floor level to reduce flooding
c beaded curtain provides privacy with some ventilation
d steel steps to first floor balcony
e electricity pylon
f steps for seating and working
g rainwater drain gets blocked with litter
h curved masonry wall

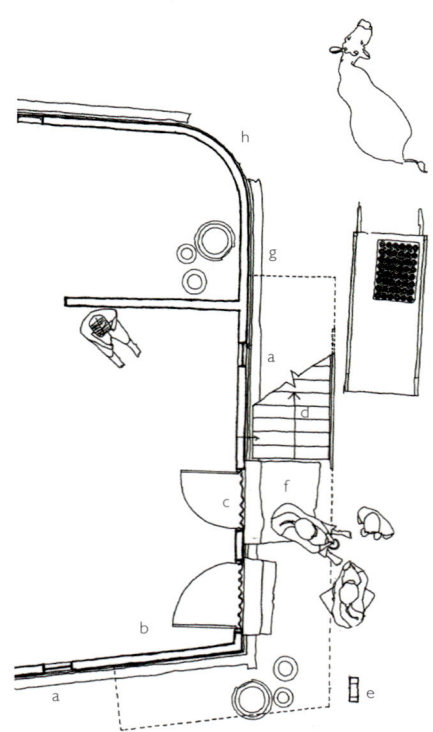

narrow balcony in front of a terrace of other single family rooms. Here, a short terrace of two-storey dwellings presents a colourful green and blue painted façade festooned with laundry and electricity lines, occasional flower garlands and stacked with domestic goods.

In the larger, long-established camps, such as Jagdamba, the tide of development has broken against the established physical boundaries of the settlement and expansion has turned in on itself. If the settlement is big enough to become a significant vote bank then medium term continuity of occupation can usually be assured by the community as a whole adopting a local politician. In this way as the density of the population increases the population acquires the confidence to construct taller buildings with more permanent materials.

Unlike the lighter insulated mat or corrugated fibre cement roofs described above, permanent dwellings employ heavy concrete and masonry suspended floors and roofs which are thermally massive providing, along with their supporting brick walls, a complete thermal enclosure: a cave-like shell of a dwelling discharging skywards onto open habitable rooftops.

In the hot dry summer and in the cooler, but still sunny winter, dwellings which have thermally massive walls, suspended floors and roofs work well to moderate the extremes of temperature especially if they are also provided with some occasional external shading. But in the monsoon season, lacking adequate or indeed any ventilation, such tightly packed sealed dwellings are uncomfortably hot and humid. The tiny dwelling plots, built back to back and side to side, allow no space for adequate ventilation through to a rear courtyard, for example. Whilst the rain is falling, occupants crowd inside their homes to endure a damp and fetid atmosphere. In such circumstances, keeping the rain and flood water at bay has a higher priority than thermal comfort. Even under these conditions dwellings can acquire the thermal mass necessary to moderate the external climate and provide more internal comfort.

Example (3) Steel and flagstone floors and roofs: a contemporary urban vernacular
There are still problems inherent in constructing a solid reinforced concrete suspended floor or roof. In mainstream construction concrete floor and roof slabs account for a high

percentage of the cost of any permanent or pukka house. These costs are high because the prices of cement, steel reinforcement and particularly scarce sawn timber formwork are high. To avoid these pitfalls, a contemporary urban vernacular form has emerged in the illegal settlements.

Here, thermally massive floor and roof construction is based on the support of paving flag type red sandstones, varying in size from roof to roof but approximately 750 × 600 × 30mm thick, on squared timber beams. Such stone floors are built into the walls and screeded to falls with a sand/cement mix to shed the rainfall via a spout through the brick parapet. As timber has become much less plentiful and consequently more expensive it has been replaced with small steel L, T or I sections and the layer of screed thickened and reinforced with mesh to provide a substantial and effective platform which is strong enough over short spans to carry substantial live loads and even a full water tank. Such floors and roofs can be built so as to overhang walls, windows and doorways (eyelids) so as to provide shade and shed rain. This method of construction is also regularly employed to support first floor balcony overhangs which can serve as landings for external stairs and ladders.

Example (4) Toby Pear's filler slabs

Toby Pear (2008/9) set about reducing the quantity of these expensive materials used in conventional heavy suspended floor and roof construction to the minimum by developing the idea of a filler slab from precedents initiated by Laurie Baker in south India (Bhatia 1991).

The principle of the Baker filler slab is to minimise the amount and replace the unneeded reinforced concrete with lighter, cheaper 'filler'. In Kerala this is done by placing doubled up pairs of Mangalore clay tiles (230 × 400 × 60mm thick) spaced 100mm apart on a shutter deck of sawn timber. This filler array of tiles is embedded within a rectangular 350 × 500mm reinforced concrete grid. Using this tried and tested Baker precedent Toby

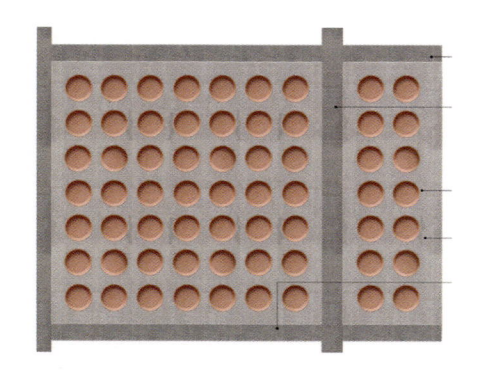

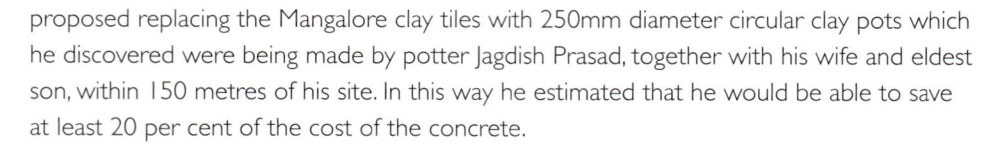

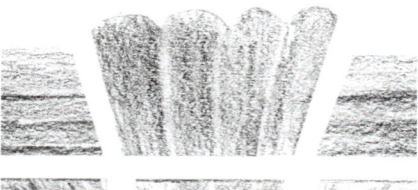

proposed replacing the Mangalore clay tiles with 250mm diameter circular clay pots which he discovered were being made by potter Jagdish Prasad, together with his wife and eldest son, within 150 metres of his site. In this way he estimated that he would be able to save at least 20 per cent of the cost of the concrete.

Toby also explored alternative methods of casting his filler slab. The weight of a cast slab and the tight access to most sites make pre-casting unrealistic. Consequently all slabs must be formed in situ, suggesting the need for expensive customised timber formwork. Unlike Baker's sites in south India where timber is plentiful and cheap, Toby proposed an alternative form of shuttering for Delhi where sawn timber is expensive and scrap oil drums are cheap.

In Delhi, round Sheesham poles, unlike sawn timber planks, are cheap, readily available and used and reused as a form of scaffolding. Toby proposed modular steel trays (750mm x 750mm with a 60mm down-turned rim) as reusable formwork. These modular trays would be supported on horizontal steel angle rails, levelled and bolted to the top of a Sheesham pole scaffolding framework. A folding/cutting pattern for the trays would be inscribed upon and cut out of old oil drums, then beaten flat and turned down at the edges by Omprakash, the steelworker local to Toby's site. In the illegal settlements domestic room spans are small, (3 metres maximum) and heavy suspended floors and roofs made from such filler slabs could be kept to a depth of just 125mm.

Example (5) Odel Jeffries and Henry Lau's troughed ferro-cement vaults

For larger spans of perhaps 4 to 5 metres: those needed for amenity buildings such as schools and clinics, Odel Jeffries and Henry Lau experimented with a permanent first floor shutter of preformed ferro-cement barrel vaults. These troughed structures were to be precast on site or in a nearby workshop with a depth sufficient to span a classroom but light enough be lifted up from the ground without heavy machinery. The vaults, placed side by side, would then be filled and finished from above. Thin (25mm) shell prototype ferro-cement vaults were made successfully in the Department's workshop with a width of 675mm and a depth of 300mm, topped with 100mm of concrete. The concrete topping and fill could be slimmed down and perhaps replaced with less expensive materials such as stabilised earth with a tiled finish. Further refinement could have led to a shallower overall floor depth. Ferro-cement is a labour intensive technology, appropriate where plastering skills are cheap. The materials involved: steel mesh and sand/cement plaster are expensive but used in quite small quantities.

Odel and Henry also investigated ways of inscribing or moulding patterns into the surface of the ceiling, the underside of the vault. They also investigated the idea of embedding

pipes into the floor to extract hot air at ceiling level which would be replaced by cooler air entering the room at low level.

(4) Two Storeys and a Roof Terrace

With their design and construction established by trial and error, two-storey dwellings with thin brick walls and steel and flagstone suspended floors and roofs have emerged as a ubiquitous, everyday, house type. In the densely packed urban context where space is at an absolute premium, back to back terraces of such houses line public ways whether they are broader streets or narrow alleys.

Livelihood craftwork, which in single-storey dwellings is carried out on the verandah, can sometimes expand, in the two-storey version, to take up the whole ground floor which then becomes a workshop or just a plain retail outlet. The women who in single storey houses used to have the run of the alley, the verandah and the house during the day are now usually obliged to retreat to an upper floor, balcony or roof terrace to observe street activity rather passively from the terraces above. Women use the roof for the routines of their everyday life: to dry clothes, wash, make cow dung cakes for domestic fuel and mind

above
opening prototype incised troughed ferro-cement vaullt
Odel Jeffries and Henry Lau

above
two storeys and a roof
Studio Booklet Appendix 08/09
below
women manufacturing incense sticks on a
rooftop
Shamoon Patwari

the children whilst they chat with neighbours over the parapet. Women visit each other by taking shortcuts over the roof or join in loud discussions, shouting from terrace to terrace.

So whilst roofs are essentially the women's preserve social exchange outside the dwelling is left to the men on the street, typically drinking chai (tea) whilst playing card games on the verandah. Of course, such spatial segregation by gender is a generalisation and in the hot season the entire family will sleep on the roof to catch the faintest whiff of a cooling breeze, but the separation of women from public life is reinforced by the introduction of verticality (4). The more enterprising and educated women have organised around this separation of space by gender. The bright, airy roof terraces are used as their shared common ground for cooking, washing and drying clothes. The more comfortable, small but secluded upper floors function as places to visit each other socially and to hold more formal Kitty parties where funds are raised to start new businesses.

(5) Steel Staircases, Doors and Windows
Vertical movement up through the brick, concrete and stone shell of the building is achieved by either a steep steel stairway up the front through a hole in an overhanging

terrace or internally by means of a brick and concrete staircase through the first floor and the flat roof terminating in a masonry enclosure opening on to the rooftop. Approaching the upper floors by way of a frontal stair or ladder is like climbing into a 19th century New York apartment block using the fire escape stairs backwards. It requires the negotiation of small areas of other people's space and an ability to thread your way gingerly up the face of the building using both hands and feet focusing on where to place them on the attendant masonry rather than looking down or away. The internal version is safer. The close tunnel views up the cool enclosed dark steep stairway can be just about hands free. Then as you turn through the doorway and brush past an eyeful of colourful washing, you burst out into the bright, warm light and a long view over the city.

Steel has replaced nearly all timber for construction and this is true for windows and doors as well as stairs. Sometimes the lower stairs are still built of brick but as you go higher and the structures become more slender, the lightness of steel angle make this the material of choice. Steel angle and iron rods are cut and welded locally by metalworkers and blacksmiths who have replaced carpenters as the main 'dry' trade. So stairs, windows and doors are designed, made to measure and fitted in place directly by local craftsmen.

As ventilation in these small, tightly packed dwellings is rarely adequate, very little glass is used. To maximise air flow, window openings take the form of grilles which filter the light and offer layers of privacy as well as security.

Example (6) Pau Ling Yap's steel and bamboo screens

Pau Ling Yap explored roof top realms, largely inhabited by women. She was concerned to provide rooftop enclosures which still allowed a view out and residual ventilation whilst screening out the sun and prying eyes. Her exquisitely wrought screens offered layers of privacy with a hint of mystery.

Pau Ling developed a lightweight, woven willow panel in the Centre for Alternative Technology (CAT) workshop and explored its performance as a privacy screen in the full size model built by all the students at CAT. Her second prototype built in the ASD workshop consisted of an even lighter 2 x 1 metre steel bar and angle panel in-filled with woven split bamboo. In her final scheme she proposed assembling these panels on a primary structure of polished timber scaffolding poles as both vertical screens and horizontal sun protection for enclosing roof terraces and balconies. Employing this system alone her design scheme developed enclosures for a range of rooftop spaces which mediated between the cave like qualities of the interior and the open glare of the unprotected rooftop. For balconies and terraces leading off first floor rooms these screens were adapted for use as carefully fitting and removable (perhaps sliding) sun baffles associated with pot plants and window seats: a snug hideaway for contemplating the street below.

The development of the slum house from single storey kuchha to two-storeys and a roof has been reviewed above. Emerging from the slums, the two storeys and a roof type has also provided the basis for owner built, back to back, terraced housing in the resettlement colonies where it has achieved legitimacy: a pukka house on a legal plot. The remainder of this chapter is a review of this more established house type within the resettlement colony of Savda Ghewra.

top
stair entry, thin brick walls and steel and flagstone overhanging suspended first floor: Ambedkar Camp
above
stair access to upper floor: Ambedkar Camp

The Density of Resettlement

Savda Ghewra, located in arid farm land 50 km northwest of central Delhi, was laid out in 2006 as a self-build, site and service scheme to legitimately house residents of illegal settlements who were to be displaced to make way for the 2010 Commonwealth Games. In November 2008 there were 7,000 families occupying the 250 acre site and this is expected to rise to 20,000 by the time of the games.

(1) House Types at Savda Ghewra

Unfortunately poor planning meant the plot sizes were only marginally larger than those in the slums: $18m^2$ (3.0 × 6.0 m) for those who can prove residence in their previous home from before 1990 and $12.6m^2$ (3.0 × 4.2 m) for those who cannot. As such, they are still not deep enough to install a rear courtyard which would facilitate the through ventilation necessary for passive cooling in the monsoon season. Residents are sold a five year license, hardly long enough to provide security of tenure. So both the single-storey kuchha house and the 'two storeys and a roof' pukka house type which have emerged in the slums and been described above have provided a precedent for self builders in Savda Ghewra.

There has however been some attempt at codification. Whilst the authorities allow two storeys this has been widely interpreted in Savda Ghewra to mean two storeys and a roof terrace. This makes it possible to construct toilet and washing cubicles on the terrace itself. In addition self builders are not supposed to maximise the size of the first floor by projecting forwards over the ground floor or to construct balconies and terraces but this is ignored adding a healthy dynamism to the streetscape.

Within these two minimal footprints (18 or $12.6m^2$) two rooms per floor is typical. The smaller room at the front forms an entrance area used for cooking and washing with a steep staircase to the upper floor. Ground floor rear rooms are slightly larger and used primarily for sleeping and living. The upper floor is used mostly for sleeping but when separate generations of the same family share the house then it is also used for cooking.

(2) Water and Sanitation

The supply of mains water to the settlement has not been forthcoming. Provision in Savda Ghewra of this essential commodity is worse than in the slums the residents have left.

above
roof top realm with woven willow screens
Pau Ling Yap
below
steel framed woven bamboo panel
Pau Ling Yap

There, at least, they had piped water for two hours a day. Water for drinking and washing is, in fact, supplied by tanker twice a week. These lumbering bowsers, spilling their precious cargo as they trundle slowly down the road, are met with frantic activity as people push and shove to get access to the very limited supplies. This scene of a desperate scramble for water is repeated in many slum areas throughout India:

Young men scrambled on to the back of the tanker, jamming green plastic pipes through the hole on the top, passing them down to their wives or mothers waiting on the ground to siphon the water off in whatever they had managed to find: old cooking containers were popular, but even paint pots were pressed into service. A few children crawled beneath the tanker in the hope of catching the spillage (5).

Whilst there are a few communal sanitation blocks, these are inadequate and often out of service so the poorer inhabitants of the single-storey kuchha houses have constructed timber pole frame and fabric washing cubicles on the edge of the settlement. Here residents bathe and launder their clothing. Planting has begun around these stick structures to provide more privacy.

Some of the wealthier inhabitants, usually those who have managed to construct a two storey house, have sunk tube wells and extracted brackish water for washing. Quite a few houses have rooftop water tanks filled from the street level delivery using a household pump. On the roof itself the water tank is perched on top of the two solid brick toilet and washing cubicles. With the communal sanitation blocks only partly functional and the total absence of mains sanitation, residents are left mostly to defecate in the surrounding countryside.

There are few job opportunities in Savda Ghewra as, apart from building, there are no properly established businesses in the settlement of any size. There are of course market stalls selling fresh vegetables, meat and fish and recently a small craft industry producing artifacts for religious festivals has started up. Despite this a significant proportion of residents still maintain the daily journey back to their previous inner city settlements to sustain their once thriving livelihoods where they can still make a greater profit.

In the settlement itself there is a growing sense that a diverse new community is being established, where women are more prominent in the working and public life of the settlement. NGOs have acted as facilitators of development, connecting residents with the relevant government departments. They have organised training courses for masons and one NGO, SEWA is active in promoting female handicrafts and marketing women's produce.

Example (7) Savda Ghewra Cooperative Housing Scheme

Working with the Indian NGO CURE, ASD Projects Office has been developing a proposal for a pilot Cooperative Housing Project in Savda Ghewra. This project aims to integrate the lessons learned from the study of high density housing in the Delhi slums, recent experience with the installation of internal toilets and local treatment of sanitation in Kuchhpura in Agra (see Chapter 8), with the opportunities for the effective sharing of resources made possible by cooperative endeavour.

The evolving pukka house type design has been modified to provide internal stairs up the back of the house. The upper stairs and rooftop stair housing are constructed of steel

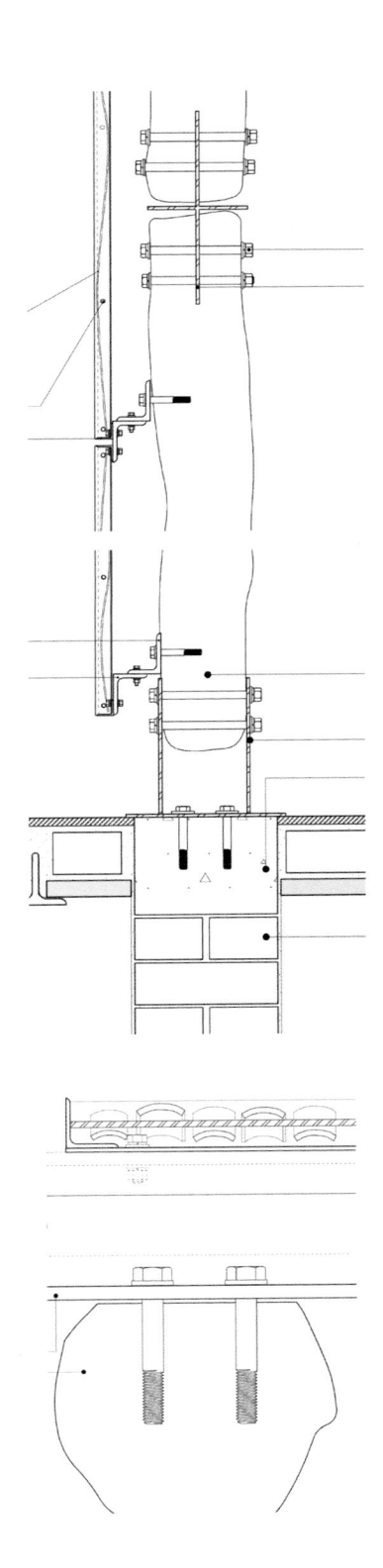

woven bamboo in steel frame wall and roof screen
Pau Ling Yap:

top
vertical section showing screens fixed to horizontal steel rails and vertical timber poles
bottom
horizontal section showing screen and rails fixed to timber poles

angle and mesh allowing stack ventilation in the summer and a cooler, more comfortable, interior. Construction of the suspended floors and roof has been carefully designed to reduce the quantity of reinforced concrete currently employed and avoid the need for extensive timber formwork thus saving costs and improving performance.

As, at the moment, houses are built at different times, each house has a perimeter wall built up to the edge of three sides of the plot. Each of these walls on its own would be sufficient to carry all the loads from both sides. So these perimeter walls are twice as thick as necessary. To share party walls in the UK, legal agreements between neighbours are necessary; called Party Wall Awards. These are unknown in Savda Ghewra. Using the cooperative society as a forum to agree codes for construction, however, one single dividing wall can be agreed, saving 50 per cent of the cost of three of the four perimeter walls and adding over 10% to the floor area for no reduction in performance.

Sanitation for the cooperative is based on experience gained installing new household

toilets in Kuchhpura, Agra, as described in Chapter 8. Each house would be provided with two linked septic tanks buried beneath the verandah discharging treated effluent into the surface water drain. In this way the solid waste is removed immediately and only treated liquid waste needs to drain away. The solid waste is to be pumped out of the septic tanks every few years or so and sold as fertiliser outside the settlement. The above proposals have been made to fit within the 18 square metre back-to-back gridded plots laid out in Savda Ghewra. However a cooperative structure would also provide the opportunity for managing larger multi-occupied courtyard houses taking up several plots. This would allow better ventilation and a more comfortable interior.

Summary

Ashok Lall, Dean of Studies at Delhi's TVB School of Habitat Studies tells how he once set his students to study the population density of an illegal slum settlement in south Delhi. Having assessed the current density he then asked the students to take the same site and design a housing scheme with the maximum density possible within the current building regulations including the option to build high. He found that even the most tightly packed student scheme provided only 50 per cent of the density pertaining in the slum (6).

Here lies the problem for architects. Accepting that the primary issue is lack of land for building in a suitable location how can architects contribute to the improvement of social housing when they are not allowed by regulation to build at the densities necessary or to contribute to the gradual upgrading of existing slums and their slow de-densification as resources permit, on a case by case basis? In the current political and economic circumstances 40 per cent of new migrants cannot build their homes within the regulations and are therefore classified as 'slum dwellers'. Why deny them the benefit of architectural services?

Curiosity in examining unfamiliar circumstances, design innovation and skill in manipulating dimension and fit, make up the essential tool kit of an effective architect. Currently these

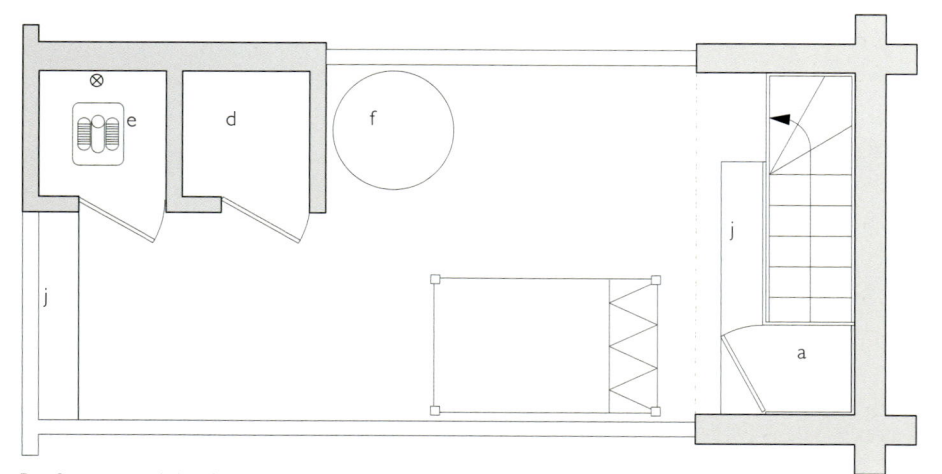

Roof storage and sleeping

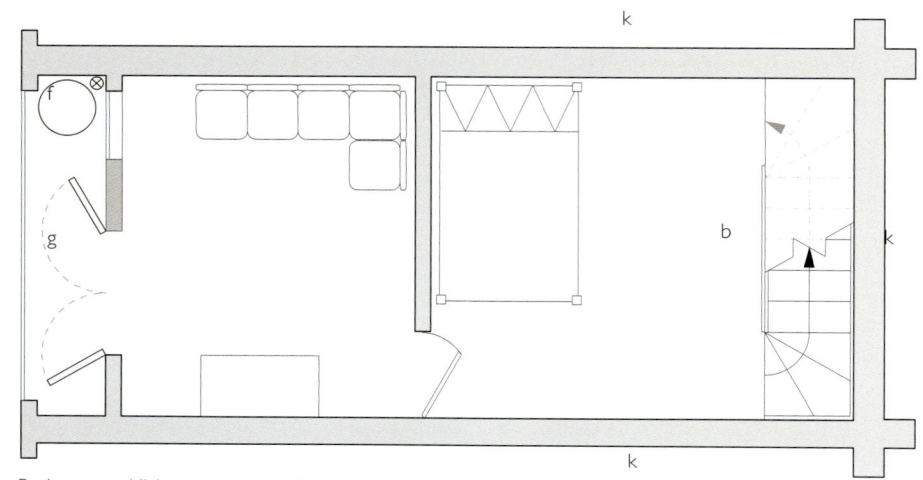

Bedroom and living space

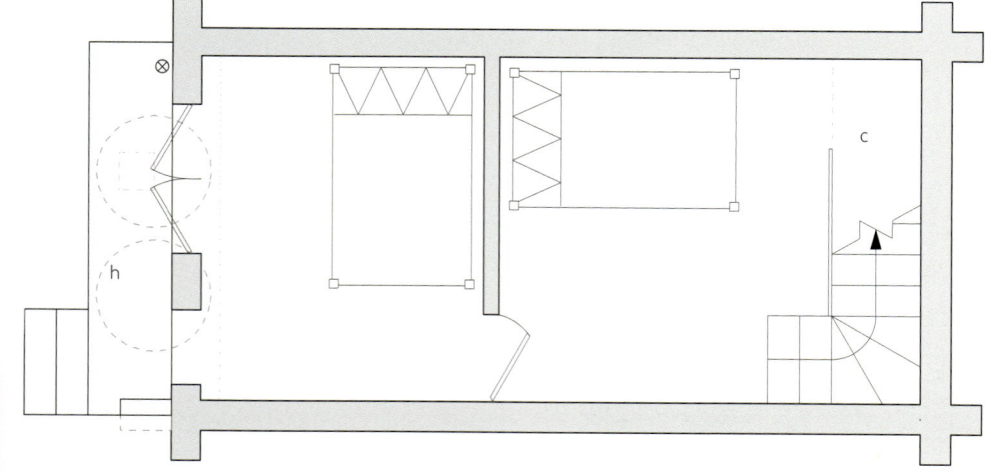

Two bedroom space

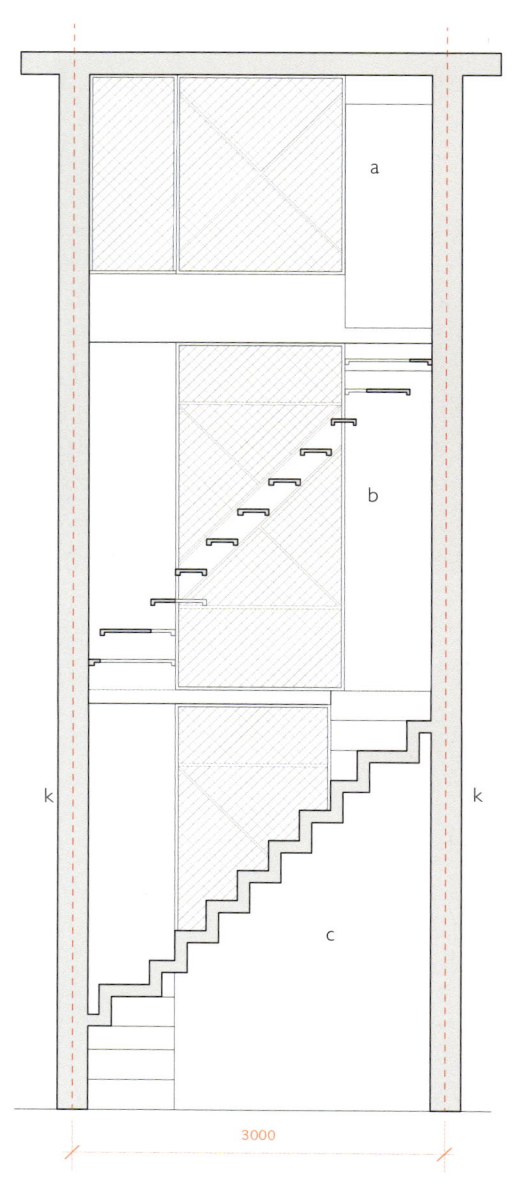

3000

Housing Cooperative Proposal
ASD Projects Office

above
cross section of Co-op House type 1
left
plans of 3m × 6m Co-op House type 1

a roof access and louvred screen with
   removable rain panels
b ventilation mesh and steel stairs on first floor
c ventilation mesh and concrete stairs on
   ground floor
d rooftop washroom
e rooftop toilet
f rainwater catchment and storage
g covered balcony
h septic under front entrance platform
j stone seating
k shared party walls

skills are so circumscribed by planning and other regulations that architects find it difficult to work effectively in slum settlements. Within these constraints self-building, residents rely quite successfully on their own inventiveness and resourcefulness to provide themselves with a home and to connect to whatever infrastructure they can grab hold of: but there is no-one to challenge these constraints by self-conscious design.

This chapter has reviewed the progressive development of a particular housing type derived from the slum experience. It began life as a temporary shack and grew to 'two storeys and a roof' before being adopted (and slightly enlarged), but still confined on three sides, by the new occupants of the resettlement colony of Savda Ghewra.

The design of the physical elements of this house type has been developed through the initiative of slum dwellers using the resources available to them and adapted by iterative endeavour to reduce costs, modify internal climate and to shelter domestic function.

This chapter has, I hope, also shown how student design ideas and experimental models can contribute to the debate about the development of this house type. So, in this way, architectural design skills could have a significant role in challenging and redefining appropriate guidelines.

If the political and economic circumstances within which this house type is currently being built were to shift noticeably to allow a lower population density then the type would probably become redundant unless it could be combined with its neighbours to allow a substantial through draft in the monsoon.

Whether de-densification were to proceed by upgrading existing slums to provide more open space and a greater number of larger rooms or simply to increase the plot size available in planned site and service schemes, then other more convivial house types, allowing through ventilation and internal courtyards would no doubt emerge. An intelligent social housing policy for Delhi and its surroundings would be informed by a study of the house types first developed in the slums and now carried over into resettlement schemes. It would explore ways to improve the sustainable construction of these house types and discover the alternative dimensional plot configurations which would permit a gradual improvement in the space standards and climatic response of these houses. It would also examine the potential role of core architectural skills in the design of these houses.

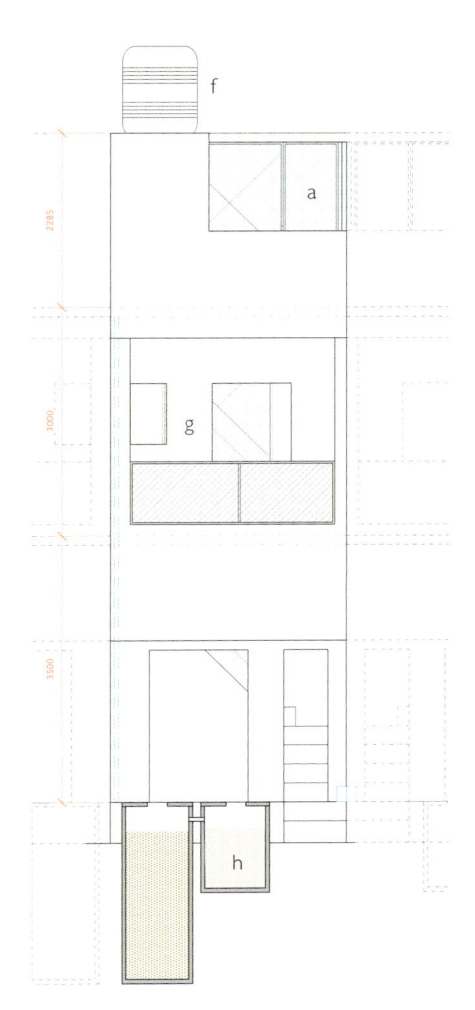

street elevation of Co-op House type 1
ASD Projects Office

Notes

(1) Tze-Ting Mok (2007) surveyed one block in Kalyanpuri Block 19/20 and calculated that for one block where one hundred and eleven people lived they had just 2.58m² of internal space per person.

(2) East Yamuna Exchanges: Delhi Field Trip Booklet, November 2007.

(3) See http://www.dezeen.com/2009/08/29chulha-by-philips-design (September 2009) for the results of a competition to redesign chulha stoves to make them less polluting and less dangerous.

(4) This is amply illustrated by Pau Ling Yap's review (2008/9) of life around Kumar Chowk in Chirag Delhi reviewed in Chapter (5) Havelis.

(5) Chamberlain, G. (12 July 2009) 'India prays for rain as water wars break out', Report in *The Observer* newspaper, London.

(6) Shaili Gupta studied the Bhumiheen squatter settlement near Govindpuri in South Delhi. She

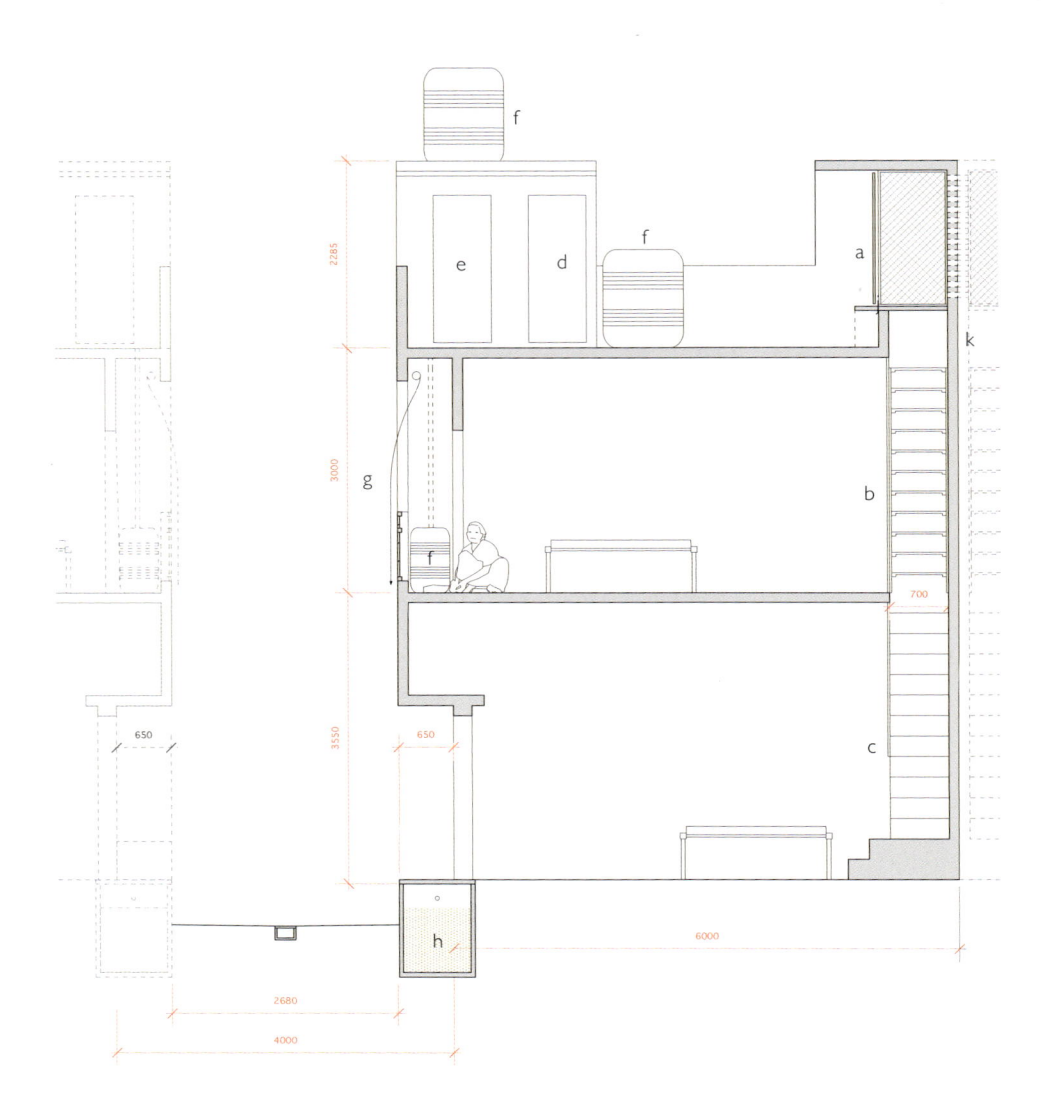

long section of Co-op House type 1
ASD Projects Office

a roof access and louvred screen with
  removeable rain panels
b ventilation mesh and steel stairs on first floor
c ventilation mesh and concrete stairs on
  ground floor
d rooftop washroom
e rooftop toilet
f rainwater catchment and storage
g covered balcony
h septic under front entrance platform
j stone seating
k shared party walls

looked at 2 hectares of the existing camp which housed between 2,000 and 3,000 households (1,000 to 1,500 households per hectare) in mostly single-storey kuchha dwellings. These were on plots of 11m², housing families of between 7 to 10 people. This camp was adjacent to a one hectare site comprising community buildings and toilets. Shaili proposed a social housing scheme which also involved the provision of schools and health clinics as well as green spaces, community spaces and local shops within the combined three hectare site. The houses could be expanded by the residents as and when required and would be up to four storeys high (Ground floor plus three storeys was the height limit as this was considered a reasonable maximum distance to walk up when no lifts were installed). Shaili's houses were larger than the existing dwellings at 39m² per dwelling housing the same number of people (7 to 10) per family and achieved a density of just 333 dwelling units per hectare or 1,000 dwelling units over the whole 3 hectare site. The Delhi Masterplan requires a density of 500 dwellings per hectare for EWS housing (Economically Weaker Sections of society) and to achieve this Shaili would need to either reduce the unit size or increase the ground coverage (and thereby reduce the community and green spaces). Even so, a density of 500 dwellings per hectare is at least 50 per cent less than the current density of Bhumiheen squatter settlement at 1,000 to 1,500 households per hectare.

chapter 8

Place, Space and Services

The dumb assemblage of the infrastructure of architecture whether it is the natural landscape swept regularly by the seasons and irregularly by natural cataclysm or the manufactured kind, provides a skeleton to be inhabited. To imbue a corner of this landscape with a sense of place, transient or enduring requires a timely appropriation at the scale of the inhabitants. The insistence of local identity pealed out from church bells (the Cockney) or regular calls to prayer (mosque or monastery) contribute to a sense of belonging. The identity of everyday places can be built up by methodical inhabitation. A local system of measures of weight and distance; colloquial terms, the memory of foundation, the marking of family and community events with festivals, inscriptions and publications, the adoption of colours and marks; all help to create a local identity of place.

Places as small as an entrance threshold can carry the annual measurements of the height of the children of the family, as they grow taller into adulthood or the marked levels of the annual flood as it laps up the steps each rainy season.

In India place making is a duty to be performed on occupation and by daily puja thereafter. Furniture is positioned, flowers are placed in a niche, and wall plaster is painted and inscribed with the family patterns. Renewal is a duty, habit is refined and celebrated. Place is evoked in a timely fashion and works at different scales. But, of course, different cultures proclaim their own particular way of evoking place. For example in the classical Mediterranean cultures, the Greeks were primarily concerned with placing their cities in the natural landscape and with the view of their meeting places and temples from a distance. They were demonstrably open, transparent and democratic places whilst, in contrast, their Roman successors were fascinated with a sense of the interior as a confined, mysterious place for intrigue.

The, 'in your face', short view of the Hindu household puja (colourful, organic and sweet smelling) might be contrasted with the long, axial, stargazing poetry of the Mughal pleasure

left
entrance threshold
right
courtyard placemaking

street nursery school, Soami Nagar J.J. camp,
south Delhi
Yanira de Armas-Tosco and Rahul Bajaj

garden. Incense, bright yellow saffron, non-assertive, vegetarian and crowded into a warm walled, coloured, deep sunlit courtyard (but dappled with foliage) can be compared with a night scene where Sufi poetry is declaimed to a small group of friends under a starlit sky with a long view over water seated high on a pavilion roof putting the world to rights.

Elsewhere in this book we have discussed how places can alternate between male and female by changing the furniture or pulling a screen of washing across an alley. Similarly a seemingly secular space can be given spiritual, religious or even mystical significance by the addition of a small niche filled with flowers or the passage of a procession.

Joseph Rykwert makes a distinction between form, space and place. He sees form as a product of natural or artificial manufacture and by itself inert and without life. To appreciate space a human aesthetic sensibility is required, whilst to enliven form, to give it meaning and resonance, human occupation is necessary. So occupation, human activity and performance are the processes by which form and space are transformed into place (Rykwert 2000).

It is clearly necessary for architects, involved in place making, not only to understand these processes but also to find a way of intervening and innovating so that form and space can be adapted to fit the contemporary processes for which they are designing. There are perhaps two particular skills required. Firstly a spatial compositional sensibility is necessary to facilitate the manipulation of the established relationships between known spaces and replace them with an altered view which somehow represents the current ambition. Secondly an ability to innovate and introduce new ways of using materials is required to subvert normative values and reconfigure resources efficiently and effectively.
It is suggested in Chapter 2 (Methods) that the architect might be the new artisan,

working with familiar technologies to create new innovative assemblies to suit changing circumstances. In designing buildings, mainstream architects choose products from the internet or from manufacturers' catalogues. Sometimes they might take time to familiarise themselves with a new or alien material or technology and include it within their tried and tested palette/lexicon; but only very occasionally will they work from first principles with materials which they find on site to be immediately available. In contrast the architect/ artisan must know the materials which are available locally because these are the materials with which they must work and with which they add value, by their input, to the specific places they are making for their individual clients. One of the great differences between the innovative small practice or studio and its multidisciplinary counterpart is the ability of the smaller practice to produce really different buildings quite specific to place rather than just repeating an in-house style. Such studios/practices do not choose their materials and components straight from a manufacturers' catalogue, but extemporise and innovate within the situation studied.

In this process the status of known materials is enhanced through the promotion of a high standard of workmanship and the robust and occasionally iconoclastic reinterpretation of these materials within the framework of the project. So the newness or uniqueness of innovation, allows a response to the changing circumstances which imparts an immediacy and originality to the project. Available skills are rapidly adapted and habits of occupation are adjusted so that a new place is born.

In the context of the rapid urbanisation of Delhi and Agra within which the studio has been working, the introduction of the technologies associated with the provision of clean water and adequate sanitation have been the most pressing and urgent agents of spatial change and have provided a primary impetus for the ongoing reconfiguration of place within poor urban communities. Here are a few examples:

edge place Soami Nagar J.J. camp, south Delhi

Soami Nagar

Soami Nagar is a 65-year-old J.J. Camp (1) in south Delhi whose history and circumstances are discussed in Chapter 3. It consists of about one hundred single storey kuchha dwellings wedged into a triangular space between two middle class housing estates and a Muslim graveyard. Here we are concerned with the actual and potential effect on place of providing a clean water supply and effective sanitation.

When students surveyed the area in 2005 the Metropolitan Corporation of Delhi (MCD) had built separate male and female communal toilet blocks at the edge of the settlement which discharged into a cesspit in the graveyard. These were not public toilets. The community had to programme the use of the communal latrines and be effective in keeping them clean for the use of Soami Nagar residents alone. By the following year the MCD had constructed an open drain to take the effluent from the communal toilets but general waste water still ran into the cesspit. Whilst adults used these toilet blocks, children washed and defecated in the open drains. There was a general misconception that, as young children were only imbibing their mothers milk, their faeces were not polluting.

Water was supplied to two taps in the community for two hours a day: the only supply for the whole settlement. In common with other such J.J. Camps, the community had to organise itself to collect clean water from these taps in the short time available each day. Individually, each family had to procure a number of large usually brightly coloured plastic water containers and galvanised metal buckets to collect water from the taps, transport it back home through the narrow alleys and store it inside for later use.

The spatial configuration of most J.J. Camps consists of an emergent conglomerate matrix (2) of single roomed, single storey dwellings grouped in back to back terraces along narrow pedestrian alleys. At Soami Nagar the first terraces were laid out along pre-existing pedestrian routes leading to an asymmetrical form with dwellings to the rear grouped around cul-de-sacs. Each alley has an open drain connecting to neighbouring alleys and discharging to a natural outflow and then on to the cesspool on the edge of the settlement. All alleys are solely pedestrian being far too narrow to admit motor vehicles and this works well in terms of child safety allowing young people to wander at will without fear of motor accident.

Yanira de Armas-Tosco (2004–05) studied this settlement and empathised with the wishes of the residents to privilege incremental improvement of the settlement over the wholesale resettlement of the community. The vague and looming threat of resettlement outside Delhi had hung over the community for a number of years and was currently blighting further investment in their homes by the residents themselves. Yanira chose as her clients the Soami Nagar residents themselves rather than the public authority and set about producing a scheme which aimed to minimise disturbance to the residents whilst introducing positive changes to their homes.

Yanira's proposals were loosely phased to suit each resident's emerging timetable. The settlement was divided into pols (neighbourhoods) around shared alleyways and family groups. Construction was to begin with the provision of shared three storey towers containing toilets, bathrooms and a laundry for each 'pol'. The towers were made up

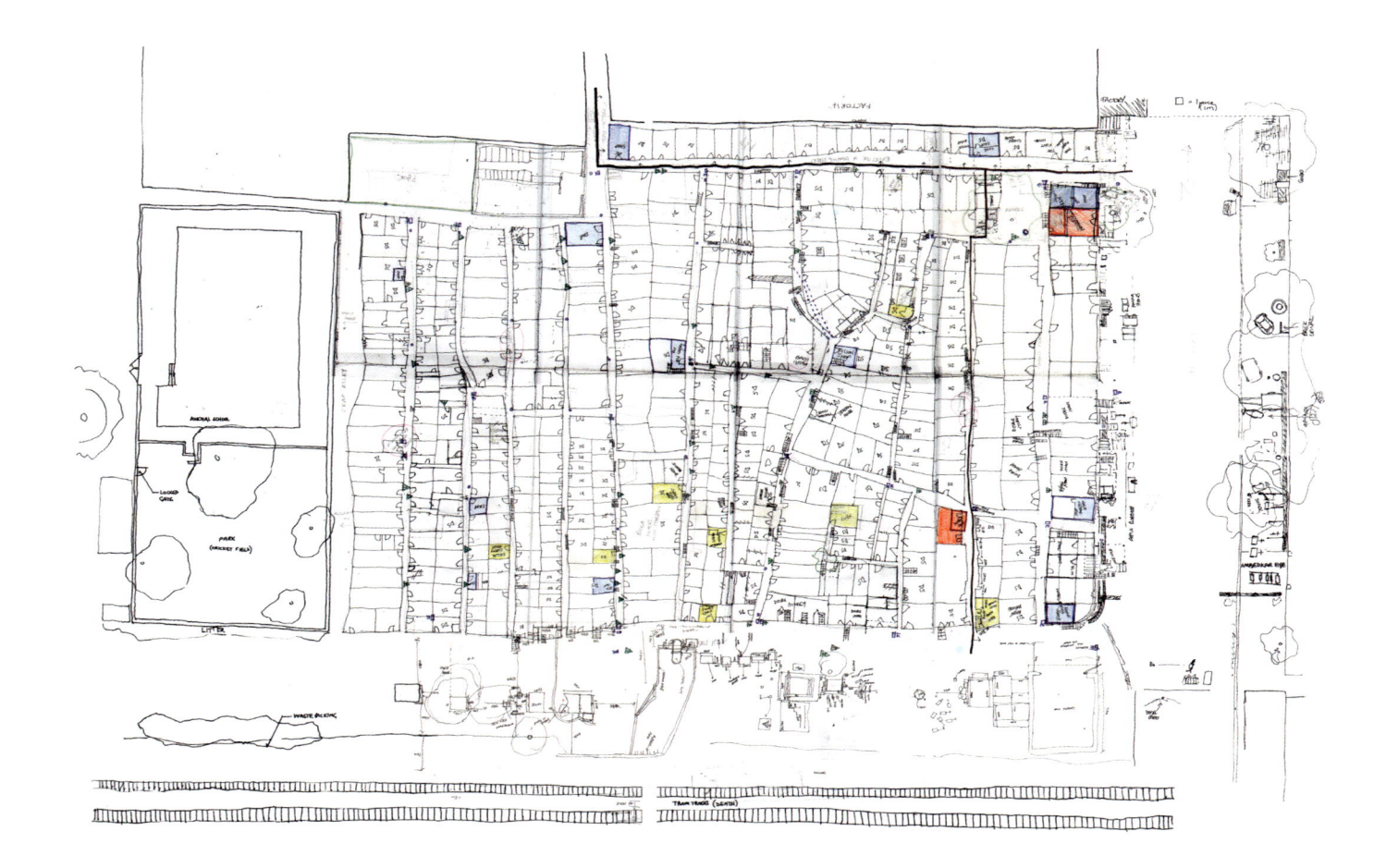

of reinforced concrete frames sitting astride existing structures which in later phases provided access to further framed structures bridging over existing structures. So multi occupied dwellings were to be built largely on the footprint of the existing shacks at the individual family's own chosen pace (3).

The places and spaces made possible by this approach remain child friendly and familiar, building on the places and pathways which went before and retaining a steady engagement with changes to everyday life as the works progress over many years. But these proposals also provide clean water and sanitation and more private space whilst fostering community cohesion without significantly disrupting livelihood patterns.

Ambedkar

Each J.J. Camp in Delhi has a dedicated open space usually on the edge of the settlement which is accessible to motor vehicles and often contains communal facilities. Soami Nagar has such a place on the southern edge where a minor vehicular road separates the settlement from the cesspool. The rather more pleasant public open space associated with Ambedkar camp in east Delhi attracted students to study this settlement in 2007. Ambedkar provides homes for seasonal workers in the Jilmil Industrial Area and consists of the usual back to back terraces. Whilst the first dwellings followed existing paths and therefore had some asymmetry of plan the newer part of the settlement was arranged orthogonally on what was then cleared land.

sketch plan of Ambedkar Camp, east Delhi showing the 'High Street' at the bottom of the sketch running above the railway line
Studio Booklet 07/08

The open space favoured by students is contained between the settlement and the east-west railway embankment to the south. Students called this space the High Street and enjoyed its air of serenity and calmness. It was here where residents congregated, especially in the evening after work and exchanged conversation:

Amongst the many activities which take place along this hub are waste picking, worshipping, Kista (a version of hopscotch), washing, shaving (a shack has become home to barbers) and a man who keeps chickens. This street is a delight and changes character with almost every footstep (Mosavi 2007, p. 29).

Whilst it contained a Hindu temple, it had a secular feel with shady trees small businesses and a few shops, a waste collection point, a recycling yard, a chicken shack and a water cistern. It was here that rationed food was distributed by government to those with ration cards and where students built a temporary shelter to shade those queuing patiently for their daily hand-out.

Unlike Soami Nagar, however, communal toilets were not located in the High Street. Those that had been provided by the Delhi authorities were placed in a remote corner of the settlement and were blocked, filthy and abandoned. So residents had to find an alternative location to defecate and often this was along the rail line. In Chapter 1, I describe how every year, some children lose their lives to a spectral, silent ghost train which appears out of the morning mist to run them down whilst they are pre-occupied with defecation.

Stephen Chown (2007) sought out an appropriate way of bringing safe sanitation to the Ambedkar community. He was reluctant to disturb the dense orthogonal alleyways, finding that whilst there was little room to provide internal toilets the surface water from showers and kitchens drained naturally enough through these passageways to the High Street where they ran to waste without polluting the immediate neighbourhood. He was also reluctant however, in the current circumstances, to propose communal or public

children playing in the 'High Street' at Ambedkar Camp, east Delhi

facilities in the High Street which he felt would either become dirty and unused like the current facilities or, even if properly used, would probably reduce the street's attraction as a place to stroll and relax.

But during the course of his fieldwork Stephen made an important observation. After dusk artificial lighting, whether by kerosene lantern or cooking fire, transformed the outside landscape of the High Street. The boundary of each group activity was defined by discrete pools of artificial light. Individuals seemed to pass rather silently between each illuminated spot. Emboldened by daytime familiarity Stephen made his way one evening beyond the High Street to visit friends in the alleyways. Just one or two domestic electric light sources were visible from the street and these rather significantly shone in homes where visiting tutors held forth to groups of paying students both children and adults.

Remembering that this was the settlement in which one mother had related how she had sold one of her kidneys to pay for her child's education, Stephen became intrigued by the extent of the drive by the residents to improve educational achievement within Ambedkar and the entrepreneurial energy associated with this. Stephen discovered that the primary school attended by the children of the settlement was located at some distance on the far side of the railway line. This required a long diversionary trek by schoolchildren to the nearest safe crossing point and resulted in poor school attendance.

Put together as a narrative design idea Stephen established that the polluted railway embankment was a physical barrier to education as well as a boundary to the High Street. His proposal involved an extensive communal toilet and shower facility hosted by and maintained within an adult education building which formed the settlement side of a bridge from the High Street over the railway giving easier access to the primary school buildings beyond.

By combining toilets and education within an inhabited bridge, Stephen's project potentially broke down the physical boundary to education and provided a respectable front to the toilet facility; thus enhancing conviviality and increasing the use of the High Street. Nevertheless whilst in the short term Stephen's scheme allows sanitation without demolition of houses, if the settlement is to develop in situ, piped sewers will still need to be laid down the main alleyways so that when houses are upgraded or replaced they can be provided with internal toilets and sewer connections.

But, if this were to happen, where would the sewerage run to? For most J.J. Camps the outflow is a cesspit rather than the mains sewer. But what if the sewerage is treated locally and used as compost to grow trees, bushes, plants and vegetables? It was a scheme for the treatment of waste water and the cultivation of a bamboo grove along the railway embankment which won Valerie Saavedra Lux (2007), a commendation for the RIBA Bronze Medal in 2008.

Rykwert (2000, p. 246) describes, how in such a situation, 'sobriety and effective action' by individuals and urban groups with their 'little plans' are needed to shape cities effectively:

To understand the city as a dynamic three-dimensional figure, to follow and inflect its process of self-generation, to knit and extend its fabric requires a humane discipline, an understanding of how built forms are transformed into image by experience.

Valerie imagined a client NGO capable of provoking and coordinating the individual ideas of the owners of the various enterprises within the High Street. Linked to women's education and a community centre built from the bamboo grown on the railway embankment, this scheme, which is illustrated in the catalogue at the end of the book, transforms and enhances the relaxed and wholesome nature of the High Street by integrating the little plans of residents, waste pickers and recyclers, street walkers and vendors, those queuing for rations and water, and temple supplicants into a coherent whole which communicates a sense of real place to the occupants.

Kuchhpura

The first live project carried out by the studio was to provide internal toilets and local treatment of sewerage within the settlement of Kuchhpura in Agra.

Kuchhpura is a settlement with 448 households and a population of 2,780 (2006) situated, on a low rise, across the Yamuna river from the Taj Mahal. The old part of the settlement (Purani Basti) was founded about 500 years ago by the king of Kuchh, Raja Maan Singh and today clusters around Humayun's mosque (1520). One hundred years ago the village consisted of just 60 farmer's huts but it has grown steadily since that time. Whilst the settlement is registered as a 'slum' with the Agra authorities and has been incorporated within the city limits, the buildings are soundly constructed in brick and have an attractive air of settled permanence about them.

There is an established irony in the way the village is occupied. Whilst the population is predominantly Hindu, it has grown around the oldest mosque in Agra. Muslim

worshippers at Humayun's mosque live a stones throw away to the north in the village of Garhi Chandi which is the site of an important Hindu temple that in turn services the religious needs of the people of Kuchhpura. So there is a long established mismatch in the creation of religious place-making.

the Mehtab Bagh with the Taj Mahal in the distance across the river Yamuna

Kuchhpura's local economy relies heavily on the Agra shoe making industry for which the village acts as a workers dormitory (5). This industry provides jobs for more than half the adult males of the village. The rest of the population farms the land which slopes down gently to the river. In addition some income is gained from tourism based on proximity to the Mehtab Bagh (Black Taj), a Mughal Garden on axis with the Taj Mahal but on the Kuchhpura side of the river just below the village.

(1) Student Work

Both student and live projects were begun in association with the NGO CURE (4) who hosted the studio field work in Agra in 2006. With their help the studio focused its projects for the year in Kuchhpura (and three other settlements in the area) where student place making proposals for change arose as in previous years, from their local investigations. Within their wider programme for improvements to the area, CURE had set up a women's self help group in Kuchhpura. Each month around 15 women from the village met up to discuss their problems. The group collects 10 to 15 Rupees at each meeting and they then decide as a group to give the money to the member most in need that month. The first issue identified by this group was the increasing problem of sanitation, particularly for women (see below). Two young women from the self help group were particularly helpful to the students; providing in depth information about the village, inviting female students for sleepovers and dressing them in saris, discussing issues

room with a view of the Taj Mahal
Jaroslaw Engel

related to modernity and independent living for women, and translating Bollywood hits.

The students carried out a range of mapping activities and cultural exercises. Anthony Corke's use of a cricket match, played between LMU students and a combined team from Kuchhpura and Garhi Chandi to tease out a narrative structure to his investigations is mentioned in Chapter 2 (Methods). Student mapping involved measured surveys, corrections to an inaccurate government tax map and insights derived from a copy of a map used by the women's self-help group to record pregnancies. Levels were estimated by observing the flow of water in the surface channels and measured more accurately where appropriate with the use of a specially prepared marking stick and theolodite made with the help of a bicycle repair man and a carpenter.

Many residents welcomed the students into their homes and up on to their rooftops. Children were the most willing helpers. Responding in some cases to only hand gestures, they held the tape measure in the correct position, counted bricks, recounted the names of trees and generally opened doors both literally and metaphorically.

Student proposals for Kuchhpura included a linked series of public open spaces, sheltered provision for older people, adult vocational training and a women's bath house. Apart from the live sanitation scheme described below, Jaroslaw Engel's (2007) hypothetical student scheme for tourist accommodation located within village houses was picked up for realisation by some house owners with the help of CURE. Now two years later there are several simple, attractive rooms with a view of the Taj Mahal which have been added to the top of village houses for short stay tourist accommodation.

The rest of this chapter investigates the impact of irrigation pathways, surface water drainage, and the live sanitation scheme on place making within Kuchhpura and sets it within the context of the wider exploration of place provoked by student projects.

(2) Surface Drainage, Irrigation and Male Place-making

For most of the year water for drinking, cooking, washing and irrigation appears to be plentifully supplied from wells. Hand pumps supply water for domestic use within the village and, outside the monsoon season, large powered pumps on the periphery of the settlement provide water for irrigation.

A large open, earth banked surface drain runs north west to south east across the north east corner of the village taking about two thirds of Kuchhpura's waste water together with a similar amount from other villages further north. On both banks of this drain are groups of houses which form the new part (Nai Basti) of the village. Houses currently turn their backs on this drain but it provides a useful, if litter strewn, shortcut for pedestrians. Spencer Owen's (2007) scheme involved covering this drain to provide a series of linked secular public open spaces with communal toilet, laundry and washing facilities arranged along this new backbone.

The large mass of polluted water in this primary outflow drifts sluggishly down the raised drainage channel following the gentle contours through the fields. Farmers open the banks at strategic points to divert some of this water for irrigation and then close them up again when sufficient water has been distributed on to their field. In places along the drain more extensive water storage ponds have been dug against the drain and under trees to reduce evaporation. These shaded pond edges are the site of day time male repose: a place (Place

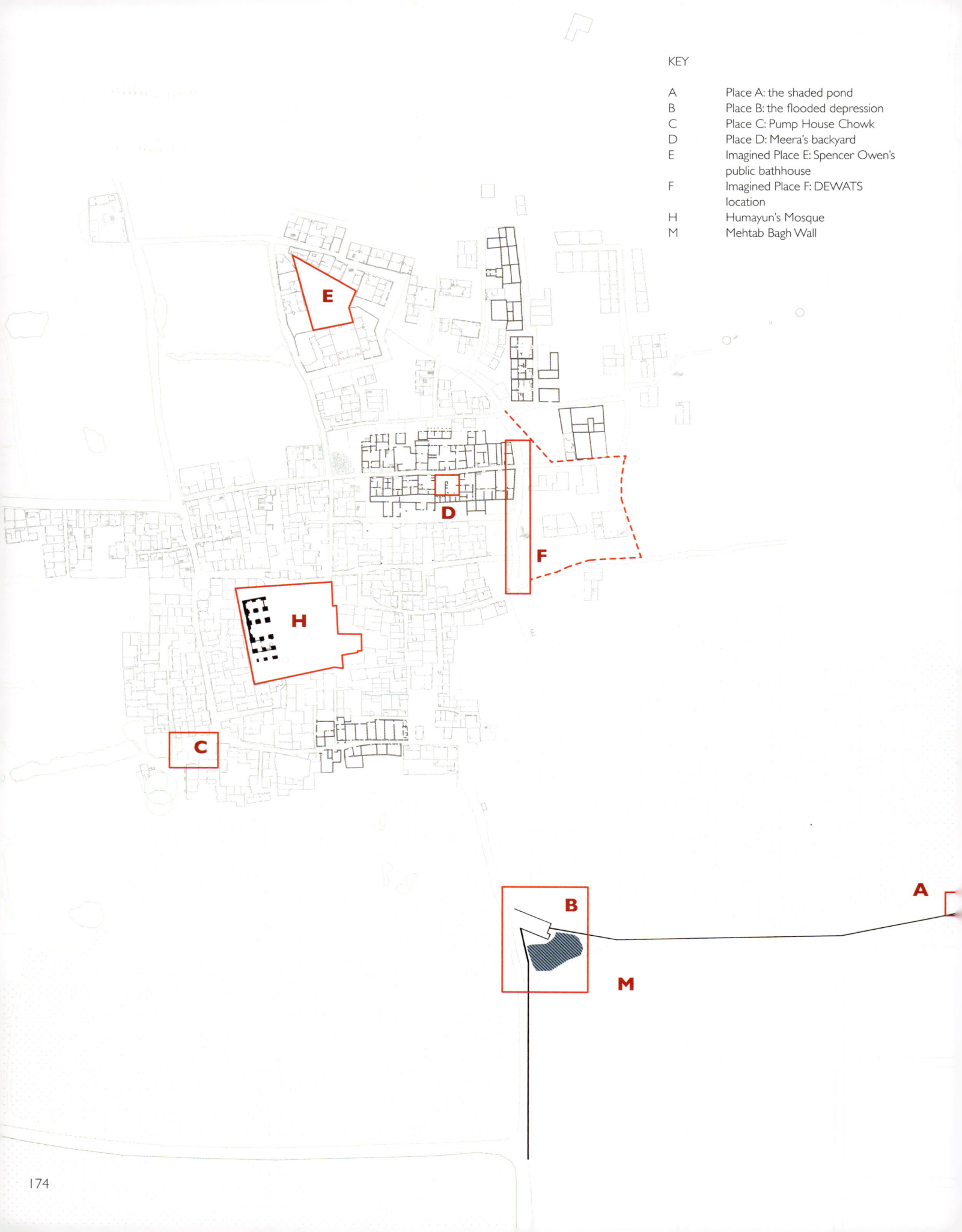

KEY

A	Place A: the shaded pond
B	Place B: the flooded depression
C	Place C: Pump House Chowk
D	Place D: Meera's backyard
E	Imagined Place E: Spencer Owen's public bathhouse
F	Imagined Place F: DEWATS location
H	Humayun's Mosque
M	Mehtab Bagh Wall

A: the shaded pond) for a farmer's lunch and relaxed conversation. Eventually the drain penetrates the boundary of the Mehtab Bagh Mughal garden and swings sharply east and then south to enter the Yamuna River further downstream.

The other one third of Kuchhpura's wastewater runs east through a smaller drain across the southern boundary of the village before turning to follow the road south and then discharging into a shallow depression in a field up against the north west corner of the Mughal garden (Place B: the flooded depression).

This secondary drain starts in the rather neglected south west corner of the village where farmers and shoe workers gather in the evenings in an open space beside a pump house in a community of mutual livelihood support (Place C: pump house chowk). Cradled between the buildings at the periphery of the village and the raised waterways which, fed by the pump, discharge into the surrounding crop fields, this place hums with all manner of emergent activities. Some congregate around the pump house whilst others sit on the raised community platform in the shade of a grove of Neem trees. It is here that factory workers dream of setting up their own shoe making business and where, more prosaically, famers arrange with their neighbours a programme for sharing pumped water to their fields. Being at the head of the run, Place C does not currently need further drainage and it serves well as an unpolluted convivial secular space.

At the other end of the secondary drain (Place B: flooded depression/village entrance), where the flood settles and stagnates against the wall of the Mehtab Bagh, with nowhere

above
place A: the shaded pond
facing page
map of Kuchhpura, places and drains
Studio Booklet 06/07

else to fall to, the local authority has, in its wisdom, built a community toilet. This facility, intended to ameliorate sanitation problems associated with increased population density associated with rapid urbanisation, floods in the monsoon, despite being raised on a brick plinth. Consequently it has been neglected and disused for some time and is now a ruin. This place is adjacent to the main southern entrance road to the village. The unsightly and pungent nature of this abandoned convenience together with that of children's faeces scattered at the side of the adjacent road deters tourists from entering this otherwise very attractive village on their way back from viewing the Taj Mahal across the river.

(3) Sanitation and Female Domestic Place-making

In the past, farming families have defecated on the cultivable land surrounding the village: this being the normal sanitary provision in rural areas. As the local population has grown to include a majority of industrial workers and the city of Agra has encroached on the surrounding farmland open defecation is increasingly untenable. Maintaining privacy and convenience has been correspondingly difficult. Consequently women now wait until nightfall to go out into the fields to find a place to defecate in private. The lack of freedom to defecate in the daytime has led to medical problems for women as well as an increased fear of being attacked during their night time journeys. Women no longer had a convenient place of their own.

Women spent most of their time either on the threshold between their house and the street or in their backyard (Place D: Meera's backyard). In both these locations women worked alongside neighbours and friends. Here students observed women's mutually

two examples of a house entrance threshold
being a women's place
Studio Booklet Appendix 06/07

supportive labour in the hard task of keeping a household together, and, apart from these more substantive tasks, also observed women helping each other wash their hair, choose clothes and make up; demonstrating, in this way, their close relationships with one another. Backyards were still quite spacious and clearly under the control of the woman of the house. Here domestic chores such as cooking, clothes washing and drying were performed. Here water was stored and trees or canopies provided shade. There was adequate room in these yards for two more cubicles (toilet and shower) and there were several precedents. CURE reported that 5.6 per cent of households already had private toilets linked either to septic tanks and/or with outfalls to the primary drain mentioned above (CURE 2007, p. 6). Existing toilets and showers were located either in a courtyard or on the roof of a house. In Soami Nagar the communal toilets at first discharged into a cesspit across the road, but later the MCD made a piped connection into the roadside drain. At Kuchhpura the communal toilet was built adjacent to and sometimes within the stagnant water. The pooled water is at the lowest point of a hollow, too low to connect to the primary drain further to the east and without any opportunity for future connection to a mains sewer network. It is not surprising therefore that the communal toilet at Kuchhpura has been abandoned.

Fortunately Kuchhpura is not yet quite as dense as the Delhi J.J. Camps and there was still space to construct toilets and showers in the back yards of dwellings. In the first phase of the Kuchhpura live sanitation project carried out by four students (6) over the summer of 2008 the women householders of 9 houses in one street in the northern part of the village chose to install a toilet and shower with the associated septic tanks. Meera was the

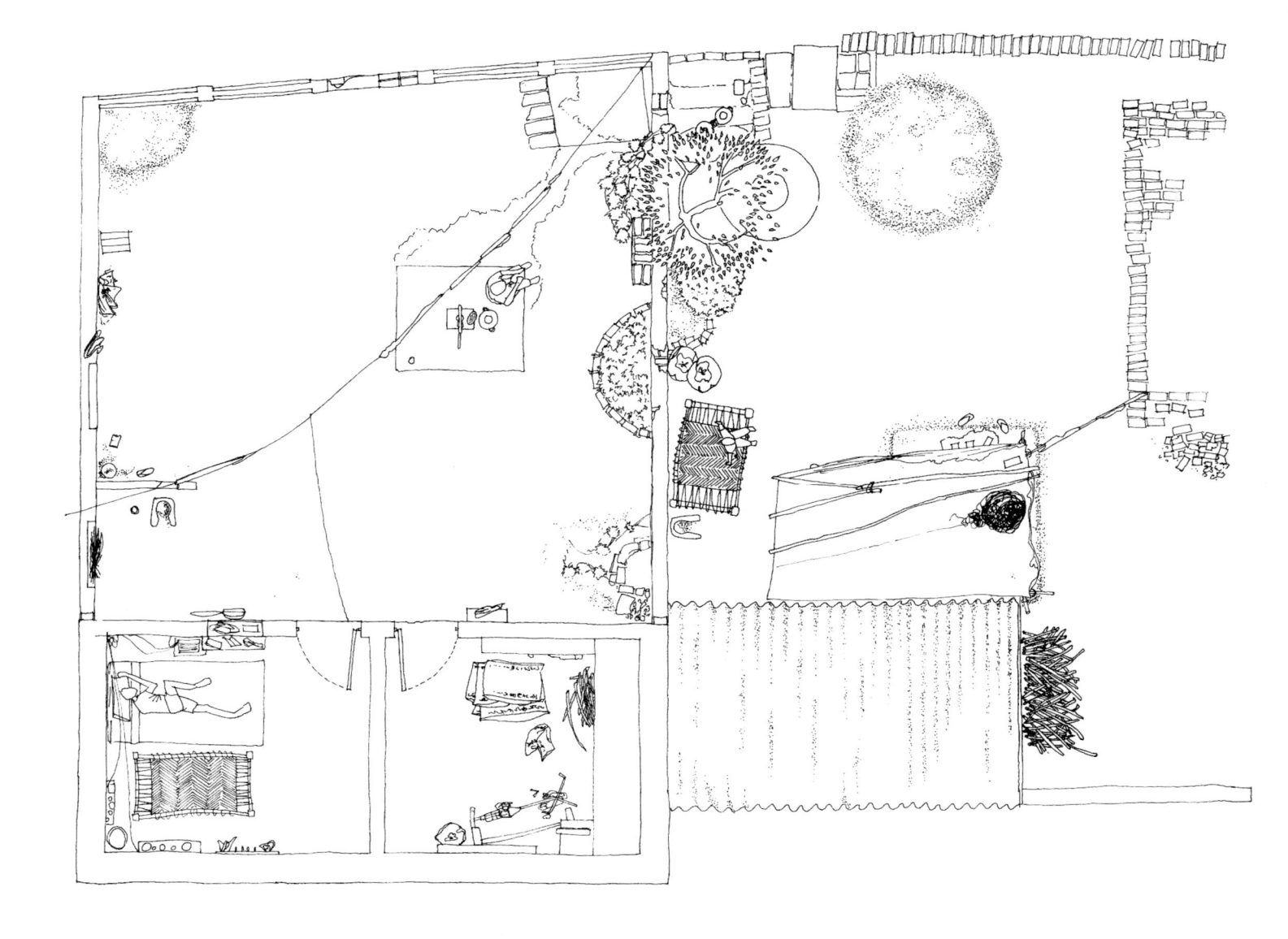

plan of Meera's backyard
Shamoon Patwari

first householder to have an improved septic tank toilet system fitted into her courtyard. Her pregnant neighbour was the next. A knock on effect took place with seven other householders in the street installing toilets and as a result the street was renamed 'swatch gali' (clean street). The success of these early prototypes prompted a steady take up elsewhere in the village. Led by the women's self help group and helped by loans and a revolving Community Credit Fund a number of Toilet Savings Groups were established by village women. By April 2009, 65 such improved individual family toilets had been installed in domestic yards.

What effect did the installation of sanitary cubicles have on the rear yard as a place? Brick built toilet and shower cubicles and their attendant underground precast reinforced concrete septic tanks connected by a waste pipe to the surface drain in the street, are not furniture to be moved around like cooking pots, washing lines or water storage jars. They are a fixed and very visible part of the infrastructure of the home. In order to avoid food contamination and for effective use the new toilets and showers required the acquisition of a new set of hygiene habits, ergonomic procedures and adjustments to domestic spatial configurations. The toilets themselves need to be cleaned after each use and the septic tanks emptied every year or two. This meant putting aside savings for operation and maintenance and providing access to outside contractors.

above
sketch of Meera washing pots in her backyard,
Bo Tang
below
woman signing loan agreement for internal wc,
Shamoon Patwari

Just as children played a major part in the student's survey work they played a key role in developing the village's engagement with the issues necessary for the sustainability of the scheme. Students ran a number of hygiene awareness workshops within the village school which resulted in children taking the message home to their families encouraging a broader and more explicit discourse on the project within the village as a whole. Students were also physically involved in the process of septic tank manufacture and cubicle construction for the first few installations; streamlining the process and making adjustments to the design to help them fit the slightly different locations.

Pride in the new sanitary installation and cleanliness went hand in hand. Cubicles were painted in bright colours, their doors and screens decorated; their insides were regularly swilled out and shown off to outside visitors and inquisitive neighbours interested in signing up to the revolving loan scheme. For a few months at least the backyard was transformed into a 'front room'.

(4) Upscaling: The Effect on Place of Decentralised Wastewater Treatment

Back yard sanitary installations, even when the effluent is treated in two consecutive septic tanks, can still result in liquids containing some pathogens running into the open surface drains in the street. The open drains in Meera's (place D) street run directly into the polluted primary open drain, described above, which meanders through the fields, skirting the Mehtab Bagh and finally discharges into the Yamuna. Working with CURE, students planned to treat this water locally before it was used for irrigation in the fields below the village using a system called DEWATS developed in India and Germany for decentralised waste water treatment.

This is a highly organised root zone system (7) which consists of a linear array of brick

lined open chambers built into the ground. Currently (January 2010) this DEWATS system is being constructed alongside the primary drain as it skirts to the east of the village. The primary drain is to be diverted to run through these chambers which are filled with sand and gravel and support tall reed growth to capture and treat the pathogens. The clean water emerging from this array is to be diverted back into the existing drain which will then supply the shady agricultural ponds (Place A) and run, as now, into the river. In this way the water in the pond/reservoirs will be cleaner and their edges a more pleasant place to sit and have lunch.

The problems associated with the water filled depression (Place B) are more difficult to address. Whilst currently the redundant toilet has been abandoned and the farmer has recovered his field for production, the local authority planned at first to rebuild this facility in the same location despite the fact that the field still floods in the monsoon. A second experimental small scale DEWATS is planned by CURE/ASD to clean the water running from the village into the depression and children can perhaps be persuaded to avoid

Meera's completed toilet
Bo Tang

defecating on the road edges but there is no prospect of the effluent from any communal toilet on this site discharging other than into the flooded field. There is still a strong pressure from the local population for communal sanitary facilities for the poorer families who have not yet been able to acquire an internal toilet. But to provide such a facility it would be easier to change the location of the toilet than drain the flooded field. Perhaps the best location for communal toilets and showers would be on the (to be covered) primary drain to the north of the village, perhaps combined with a laundry and child nursery as envisaged by Spencer Owen. This would allow place B to fulfill its primary role as an attractive promenade from the motorised road up the hill to the village.

A more ambitious public bath house such as this, to the north of the village, would provide a hub of conviviality (imagined place E) at the start of a new leisurely walk along the covered primary drain past the narrow 'backs' of Nai Basti to emerge at the tall reeded banks (imagined place F: DEWATS location) where you might stop for a while to enjoy the long view over the fields towards the Mehtab Bagh before continuing your walk along the now open and cleaned surface channel to its river junction and the classic rear view of the Taj Mahal.

Summary

It is perfectly natural to want to avoid defecating in one's own house. That such polluting and smelly practices should be kept well away from home makes perfect sense in a rural situation. However, when rural changes to urban, individualised internal flush toilets are preferred by house owners over any other type. In this context the provision of communal toilets to the Soami Nagar and Ambedkar J.J. camps was always a stop gap solution. In these camps space was so tight that installing toilets and showers to each dwelling would have been impossible without a reduction in density. The operation, cleaning and maintenance of communal toilets in any circumstances is problematic and requires unusually close and friendly cooperation between the families involved.

Public sanitary facilities, of any size larger than those shared intimately by a few cooperating families, need on-site, minute to minute, cleaning and caretaking to survive neglect and rejection by the community. For public toilets to be sustainable they need to be associated with convenient and convivial places. In this regard they might best be combined with other public provision such as pumped water supply, bathing and laundry facilities.

The cost of installing a conventional underground piped sewerage system is very high especially when combined with a conventional treatment plant. In addition such conventional systems are difficult to install retrospectively without significant damage to the established places through which they will run. Where such upheaval is already underway, for example whilst density is being increased, upgraded infrastructure provision can be phased alongside the building programme to reduce disruption as in the case of Yanira's scheme for Soami Nagar.

Alternatively the treatment of polluted water locally, within and alongside existing drainage channels, saves time and resources and also helps to sustain and upgrade the quality of existing places which have their own history and set of memories for their occupiers. Yanira retained the established building footprints to maintain familiarity during densification at Soami Nagar. In the same way the current live scheme at Kuchhpura

fosters modernity in existing backyards and cleans up water in places already established by use in the fields. In contrast, Place B at the entrance to the village was not place functional and in this case radical relocation, not conservative surgery (8), is proposed (9). Any initiative aimed at upgrading infrastructure locally at minimal construction cost requires a detailed knowledge of local conditions and the ability to balance and accommodate a range of local opportunities and resistances in order to design for and manage change effectively.

Notes

(1) J.J. Camps is an abbreviation for Jhuggi-Jhopari Camps meaning settlements composed of temporary huts and lean-tos.

(2) Conglomerate Matrix is a term used to describe the largely built-up, dense complex mass of buildings making up a historical settlement where buildings adjoin and it is difficult to determine from the outside where one property starts and its neighbours begin. It derives from the term 'conglomerate ordering' used in Smithson (1993).

(3) On 11 May 2009, a similar hypothetical scheme for incremental upgrading of slums into permanent urban districts through a process of gradual improvement to existing dwellings instead of demolition and rebuilding in Mumbai has been posted on the web by Filipe Balestra and Sara Goransson. http://www.dezeen.com/2009/05/05/incremental-housing-strategy-by-filipe-balestra-and-sara-goransson/.

(4) The NGO CURE India is a development NGO that works with poor communities and

above left
septic tank construction
Bo Tang
above right
open street drains, Kuchhpura

imagined place F: site for the new DEWATS construction

local governments on pro-poor policy reforms, improving access to basic services, inclusive and participatory governance and the building of Community Based Information Systems. CURE organises and empowers low income communities, especially women and young people in urban areas to access water supply, sanitation, power, livelihoods, education, health care and housing. It works at all levels of government — national, state and local.

(5) The leather off-cuts from this same Agra-based shoe industry support the Marwari Basti community's leather whip making, see Chapter 6 (Nomads).

(6) Bo Tang, Shamoon Patwari, Spencer Owen and Kasia Banak.

(7) DEWATS stands for Decentralised Wastewater Treatment System. Details can be found at http://www.borda-net.org/modules/cjcontent/index,php?id=29#background.

(8) A reference to Patrick Geddes' method of diagnostic survey followed by conservative surgery (Stephen 2004).

(9) In November 2009 we learned that the old communal toilet at the entrance to the village had been demolished and the local authority had agreed to rebuild a new communal toilet in a new location adjacent to the main drain well away from the village entrance.

chapter 9

The Relevance for Architectural Education in the UK

As a profession and as an academic subject, architecture in the UK has struggled to establish its identity by bridging pairs of juxtaposed ideas which are often in conflict with one another. The opposition of tradition with modernity in design approach, of artistic with scientific endeavour together with hand to eye experiential learning with deductive methodologies have made the subject difficult to define. To engage with these dichotomies educators have sought to produce generalists equally familiar with process and product, balancing the rigour which must be applied to the resolution and delivery of a particular building project with the study of its relevance in a global world. Some would say that the modern architectural profession was founded on the need to bridge such conflicting scenarios. For example, in the early 19th century, a gentleman client, loathe to muddy his boots, needed an architect, not only for his ability (and it invariably was a man) to design buildings but also for his capacity to be at ease both in the gentleman's parlour when pouring over the design drawings as he was on the building site discussing details of construction with the building foreman.

We have to go back to the Middle Ages to find a world without an architectural profession as such. At that time master masons and carpenters had sufficient imagination, technical skill and experiential knowledge to design and construct major buildings. But since the time of Wren and Hawksmoor, architects have acquired their design skills in the drawing office rather than by hands on experience on the building site. Furthermore, since the Industrial Revolution drawing skills have become increasingly important to architects as a means not only to communicate with the builder but also to sell architectural ideas in an increasingly competitive environment. Today it is possible to practice architecture in an office culture where the design process is quite remote from involvement in the actual construction process.

Currently, in the UK, a large part of the building industry is focused on the factory production of new building components for rapid dry assembly on site by technicians rather than crafts people. Indeed the opportunity for crafts people to make decisions on site using their own reasoning or initiative is increasingly being limited to works to existing buildings whether these buildings are listed or just simply out of date. By 2007 at the height of the liberal capitalist boom in UK cities, the craft approach to designing and constructing buildings with its heady mix of experience and experimental, on-site innovation had been all but sidelined. The result has been an over determined, mass produced, architecture of consumption micro managed by the building companies for the benefit of their shareholders. For these buildings the process of experimentation and reasoning in design has been divorced from operations on site.

How did this situation come about? In the nineteenth century, once the profession had established itself with an Institute and a Royal Charter (1) it sought to raise standards and limit entry by attempting to surround vocational practice with an aura of academic respectability. By the 1924 Congress on Architectural Education, some university schools had been established but the majority of architects were still trained in offices, through pupilage or apprenticeship schemes. By the 1958 Oxford Conference (2) on Architectural Education, however, there was rising confidence in a professional identity remote from site. 'Getting their hands dirty' was no longer part of the curriculum (3). Entry requirements for architectural education were raised to university level and most schools of architecture were absorbed into one university or another. The two A level examination subjects preferred for entry to an architectural undergraduate course were fine art and a science subject:

The profession of architecture was pervaded by a sense of certainty; certainty about the redemptive power of architecture, the structures within which the profession worked, and the positive belief in a narrowish set of paradigms. This certainty is almost entirely absent five decades later ... [this] is a reflection of the schisms within and without the profession, the fractures and shakes in the fabric of a once solid and unassailed western belief system and the evidence that our cities now reflect pressures so complex and baffling we may prefer not to acknowledge them (4).

In the last decade, as a result of these 'schisms', architecture schools and the profession have witnessed a resurgent debate on alternative types of practice and their relationship with intellectual endeavour. In the early 2000s, Cambridge University reopened the question of whether architecture could claim to be a subject worthy of postgraduate study (5). In the current recession, a significant minority of architecture graduates faced with work as a 'CAD monkey' (6) at best, and long term unemployment at worst, have taken the matter into their own hands challenging professional orthodoxy. These students and graduates are once more looking to design and build projects with their own hands. In the process they are finding that the location of experimental construction is not limited to high tech laboratories associated with factory production but that students themselves can innovate in the school workshop and on site (7).

It might be said that students are all 'modernists' now. But that does not mean that they do not embrace iterative experience and experimental innovation as part of their design process. For these students and graduates hand to eye practice is a large part of the empirical basis for intellectual thought. Output is drawn, written ... and built. However such architects/craftspeople are still a minority of those passing through the schools. In reviewing the end of year architecture show at the Royal College of Art (2009) Will Hunter (8) characterises the split:

... the terms (traditionalist and modernist) are evolving fresher meanings. At their most extreme a much younger generation of reactionaries is producing projects conceived almost entirely in brick ... work concerned with place-making, materiality, light and shadow – while the youthful progressives look to be abandoning context and inhabitation altogether in an explosion of the digital/parametric.

Much of this on-site experimental student building work is driven by the desire to respond to the problems of environmental sustainability (the green agenda), an increasing scarcity of resources, rapid social, technical and economic changes and the associated humanitarian agenda which mainstream methods have so comprehensively failed to address. They are thinking global and acting locally on their own initiative.

The idea of architectural study at postgraduate level was also initiated at the 1958 conference. It was recognised that the competence of the profession, and indeed its claims to be a valid profession at all, depended on the advancement of knowledge by the study of a much broader range of subjects than that considered necessary in the past for the design of buildings:

... knowledge is not merely an ornament to a profession [nor] a substitute for architectural imagination: but it is necessary for the effective exercise of imagination and skill in design. Inadequate knowledge ... depresses the general level of design (9).

So if knowledge by research is not the same as design but is, on the other hand, its life blood, is research, architecture? Most postgraduate research since 1958 is not concerned with the architectural imagination or the making experience but with subjects linked to architecture which can be advanced using established scientific methods such as day lighting, material science or airport passenger flows. In academic research environments, bounded as they are by the western scientific paradigm, the continuing split between what is design and what is research still inhibits the acceptance of architectural design as a legitimate academic subject (5).

However one of the new research subjects of the 1950s, tropical architecture (10), opened minds to the comprehensive study of context. As rainfall, temperature and humidity can be measured, the subject could be studied as a science. In a reductionist manner studies divided the world up into a range of climate types and showed how building design had in the past, and could in the future, be influenced by the local climate.

In the 1960s, this singular emphasis on passive response to climate as the sole indicator of context was diversified to include interest in the relationship between vernacular architecture, locally available resources, culture and society (11). Increasingly such studies showed that whilst linkages between culture, climate, availability of local resources, and building form could be established, the final form could not be predicted. As the evidence mounted it became abundantly clear to some that good design involved an intense engagement with the particularities of each situation rather being limited to the arbitrary application of predictable and quantifiable variables to a reduced view of context.

The ideas which transformed notions of context into those of time sensitive situation have been influencing architectural education for perhaps the last two decades. These, along with the other ideas discussed in Part 1 of this book, including those of detective, author and craftsperson are derived from literary, philosophical and fine art sources, as well as empirical studio experience, rather than scientific orthodoxy.

Curiously, those students who become more 'hands-on', who regard the site context as a resource, also seem to be those who would like their design work to respond to the situation in which the local people, who occupy the site and its surroundings, find themselves.

Several studio critics have asked why the studio bases its work in India when there are plenty of disadvantaged groups to design for in the UK. The response is threefold.

The first is that lack of familiarity is an aid to learning. When students are embedded in their own everyday context they are loaded down with a plethora of mostly irrelevant information and unquestioned assumptions. It is much easier for the independent minded student to tease out, recognise, represent and abstract experience from a particular unfamiliar situation (and thereby enrich their architectural imagination) than by reworking familiar territory.

The second is that, looking back to the optimism of the 1958 conference, and its emphasis on scientific truth and tendency to exclude un-measurable variables, experience shows that seeking to avoid complexity by narrowing the reach and application of architectural insights to the UK context risks undermining the legitimacy of the profession and 'depresses the quality of design' (8). It also hinders the acceptance of architecture as a subject worthy of postgraduate study within the wider academic community.

The third is that such pragmatic local situationism is a good broad preparation for architectural practice throughout the globalised workplace. The wider the experience, the more hands-on and innovative the approach and the more reflective the thinking; the richer and more appropriate the architectural imagination is likely to be.

Notes

(1) The Royal Institute of British Architects (RIBA) was founded by Royal Charter in 1834 and is the professional body for UK architects with a membership of about 40,000 (2009). This has increased from 8,218 in 1938, 10,706 in 1948 and 18,175 in 1958.

(2) Leslie Martin (1958) The 1958 RIBA Conference on Architectural Education. Report by RIBA Chairman: http://www.oxfordconference2008.co.uk/1958conference.htm.

(3) Tom Woolley, Professor of Architecture, Centre for Alternative Technology, Wales (2008). Viewpoint on the 2008 Oxford Conference: http://www.oxfordconference2008.co.uk/tomwoolley.htm.

(4) David Gloster, Director of Education, RIBA (2008). Viewpoint on the 2008 Oxford Conference: http://www.oxfordconference2008.co.uk/davidgloster.htm.

(5) The Cambridge School of Architecture had its Diploma School closed in 2003 because the research output from the school was not considered to be high enough by the university at large, raising questions at the highest level as to whether architecture was a suitable subject for academic study.

(6) A 'CAD monkey' is defined as an architectural graduate who spends all their time at work in front of a computer inputting other people's designs and making alterations to those designs and who never has the opportunity to meet the client or visit the site.

(7) This urge to innovate on site for oneself is not limited to students however. Professors Jeremy Till (the Straw House), Tom Woolley (hemp/lime construction of father's house) and Susan Roaf (Oxford Eco House) all found it necessary to experiment and innovate with their own funds within the green agenda to further their research and understanding.

(8) Hunter, W. (10 July 2009) 'The show must go on'. Review in *Building Design* of the 2009 Royal College of Art end of year architectural exhibition.

(9) R. Llewellyn Davies (1958) 'Deeper Knowledge: Better Design'. Paper presented to the 1958 RIBA Conference on Architectural Education.

(10) Seminal in this regard are:

Maxwell Fry, E. and Drew, J. (1964) *Tropical Architecture* (New York: Reinhold).

Koenigsberger, O. H. et al. (1974) *Manual of Tropical Housing and Building: Part One: Climate Design* (London: Longman).

Givoni, B. (1969) *Man, Climate and Architecture* (Amsterdam: Elsevier Publishing Co. Ltd).

(11) Seminal in this regard are:

Rudofsky, B. (1965) *Architecture Without Architects* (New York: John Wiley and Sons).

Rapoport, A. (1969) *House Form and Culture* (Englewood Cliffs, NJ: Prentice-Hall).

Oliver, P., ed. (1997) *Encyclopedia of Vernacular Architecture of the World* (3 volumes) (Cambridge: Cambridge University Press).

theme 1

Slums, Sanitation, Amenity and Housing

Angela Hopcraft
Widows' Refuge, Jagdamba Camp, South Delhi

Haveli type accommodation for widows, new pedestrian access to the linear slum from higher road level, community classroom with impluvium under, blacksmiths' workshops and associated garden sanctuary all built over newly-culverted main drain.

Runner-up for RIBA Silver Medal 2006
See Chapter 2, Example (2)

view of new entrance to Jagdamba Camp alongside the Widows' Refuge

east–west section through Widows' Refuge

1 resting within the community
2 lifting expectations
3 a class for the Jagdamba children
4 hermetic seal
5 rituals

6 a conversation with the landscape
7 leaving the sanctum
8 life in the refuge
9 building relations
10 the east bridge: connections and exchange

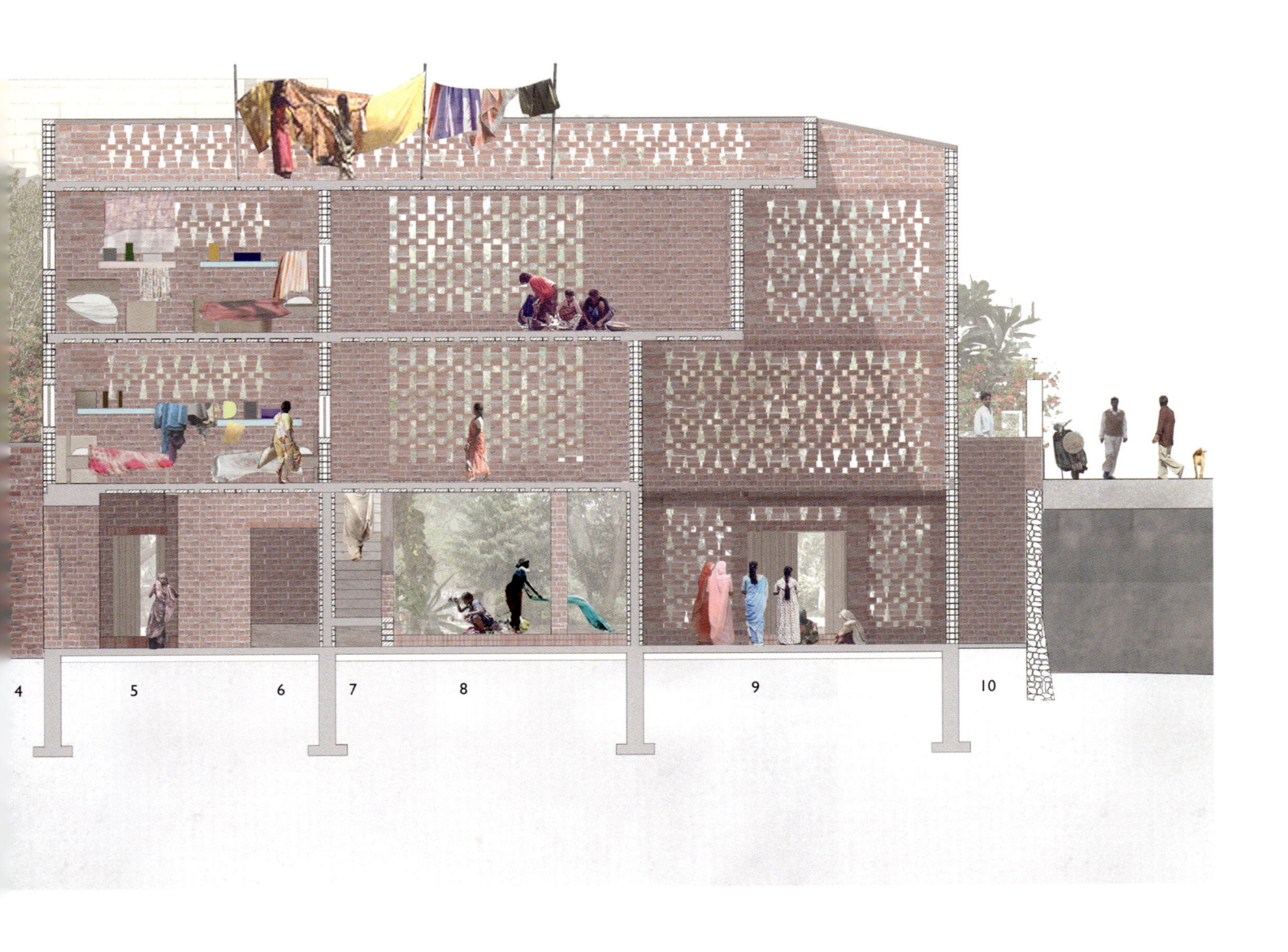

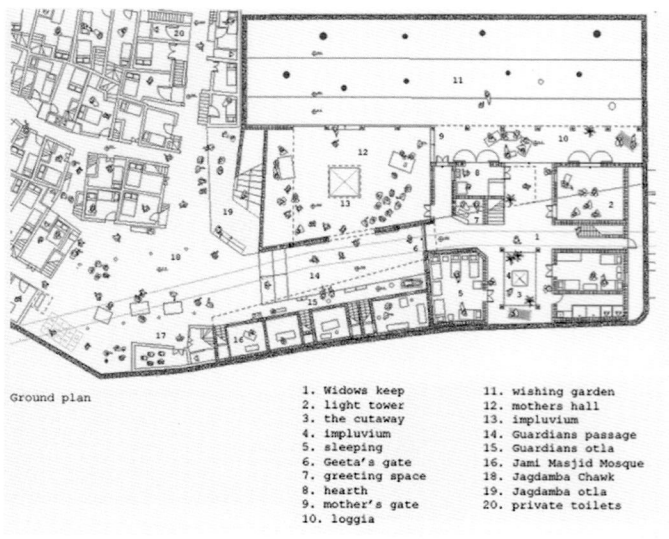

Ground plan

1. Widows keep
2. light tower
3. the cutaway
4. impluvium
5. sleeping
6. Geeta's gate
7. greeting space
8. hearth
9. mother's gate
10. loggia
11. wishing garden
12. mothers hall
13. impluvium
14. Guardians passage
15. Guardians otla
16. Jami Masjid Mosque
18. Jagdamba Chawk
19. Jagdamba otla
20. private toilets

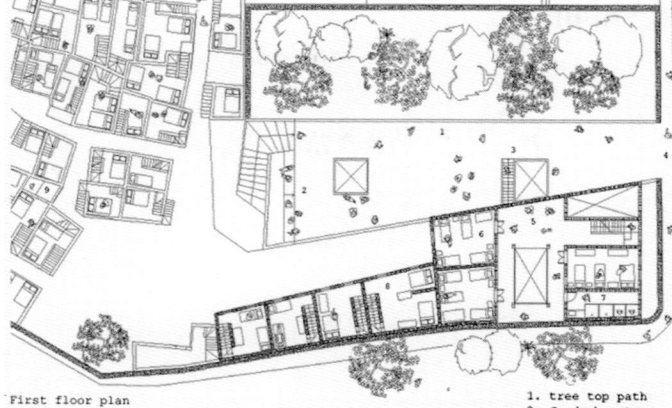

First floor plan

1. tree top path
2. Jagdamba steps
3. widow's pass
4. East bridge
5. the look out
6. sleeping
7. bathing
8. Guardians rest
9. private toilets

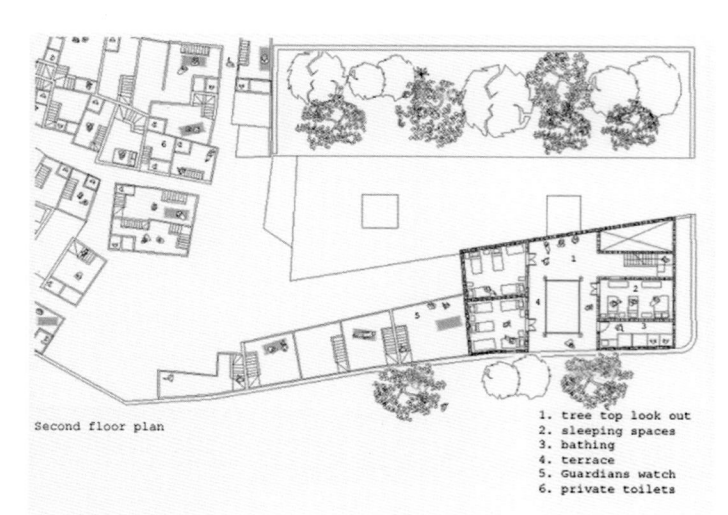

Second floor plan

1. tree top look out
2. sleeping spaces
3. bathing
4. terrace
5. Guardians watch
6. private toilets

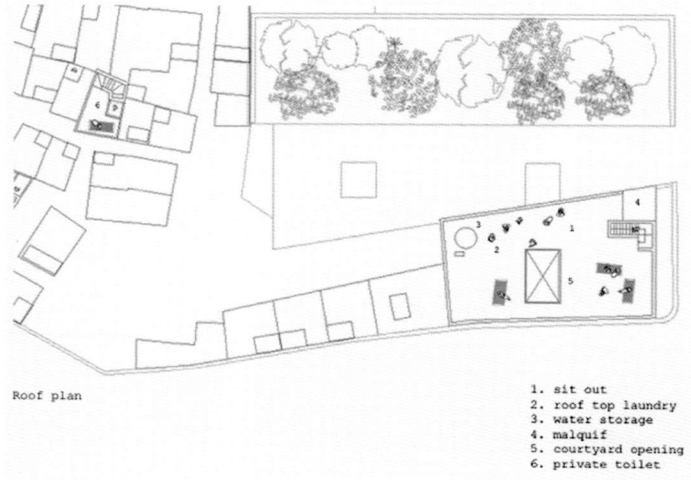

Roof plan

1. sit out
2. roof top laundry
3. water storage
4. malquif
5. courtyard opening
6. private toilet

top
ground, first, second and roof plans of Widows' Refuge
bottom
north–south section through Widows' Refuge

top
interior view to garden
middle
external view of entrance from Jagdamba Camp
bottom
west elevation from Jagdamba Camp

Yanira De Armas-Tosco
Slum Upgrading and Provision of Sanitation Towers, Soami Nagar J.J. Camp, South Delhi

Reinforced, concrete-framed and serviced infrastructure towers providing water and sanitation to each street extended over time to service new flats built on the existing footprint over and replacing existing kuchha housing.

See Chapter 1, Mapping: Physical Surveys (1) Accuracy, and Chapter 8, Soami Nagar.

left
existing camp divided into pols
main
student survey of Soami Nagar J.J. Camp

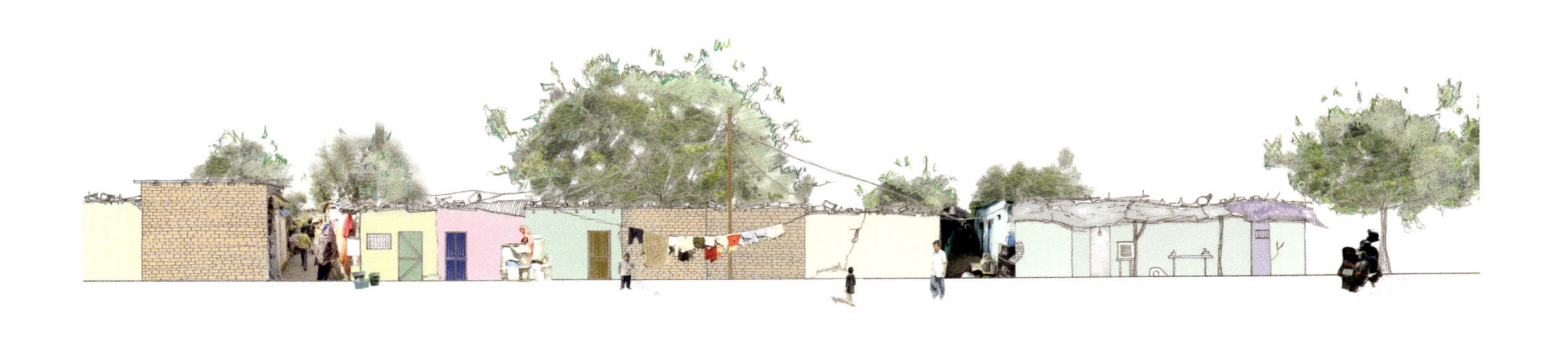

top
elevation of existing dwellings
middle
elevation of existing dwellings with basic tower
structure inserted
bottom
reconstruction and upgrading of surrounding
dwellings

199

left
section through sanitation tower and surrounding houses
below
plans and section through sanitation towers showing water supply and drainage

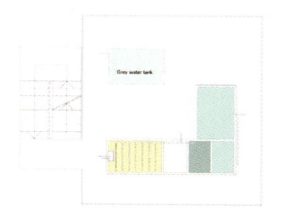

water tanks

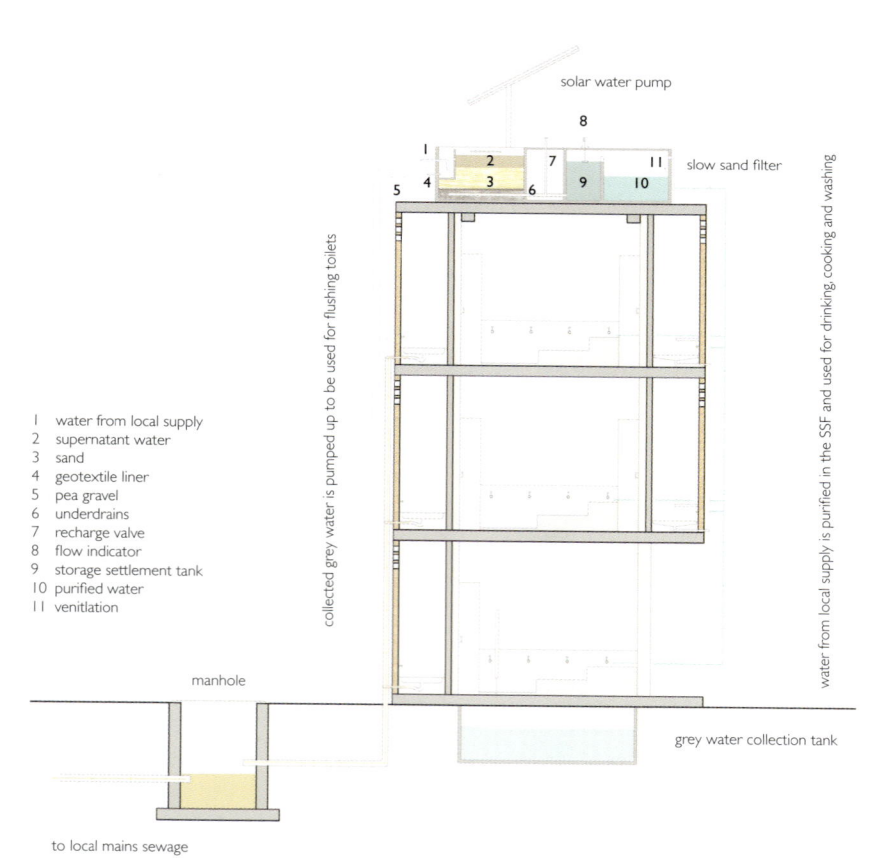

solar water pump

8

slow sand filter

1 water from local supply
2 supernatant water
3 sand
4 geotextile liner
5 pea gravel
6 underdrains
7 recharge valve
8 flow indicator
9 storage settlement tank
10 purified water
11 venitlation

collected grey water is pumped up to be used for flushing toilets

water from local supply is purified in the SSF and used for drinking, cooking and washing

manhole

grey water collection tank

to local mains sewage

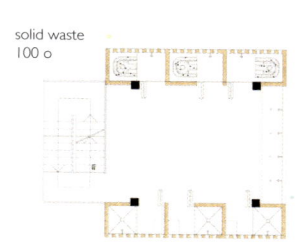

solid waste
100 o

female floor

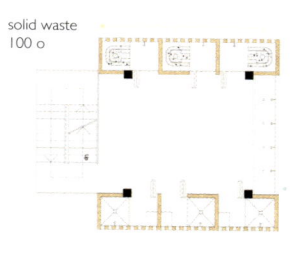

solid waste
100 o

male floor

manhole

solid waste
100 o

kids floor

200

Valerie Saavedra Lux
Community Centre, Bamboo Workshop and Public Space, Ambedkar Camp, East Delhi

An urban micro-plan integrating bamboo production, water conservation, the reuse of redundant land and the construction of a women's community centre using recycled bricks and locally sourced bamboo.

Commendation for RIBA Bronze Medal 2008.
See Chapter 7, The Density of Slums, single-storey kuchha for a description of Ambedkar Camp and Chapter 8, Ambedkar, for a description of the 'High Street'.

left
upgraded public space: the High Street; Ambedkar Camp
below
sketch survey of Ambedkar Camp
Studio Booklet 07/08

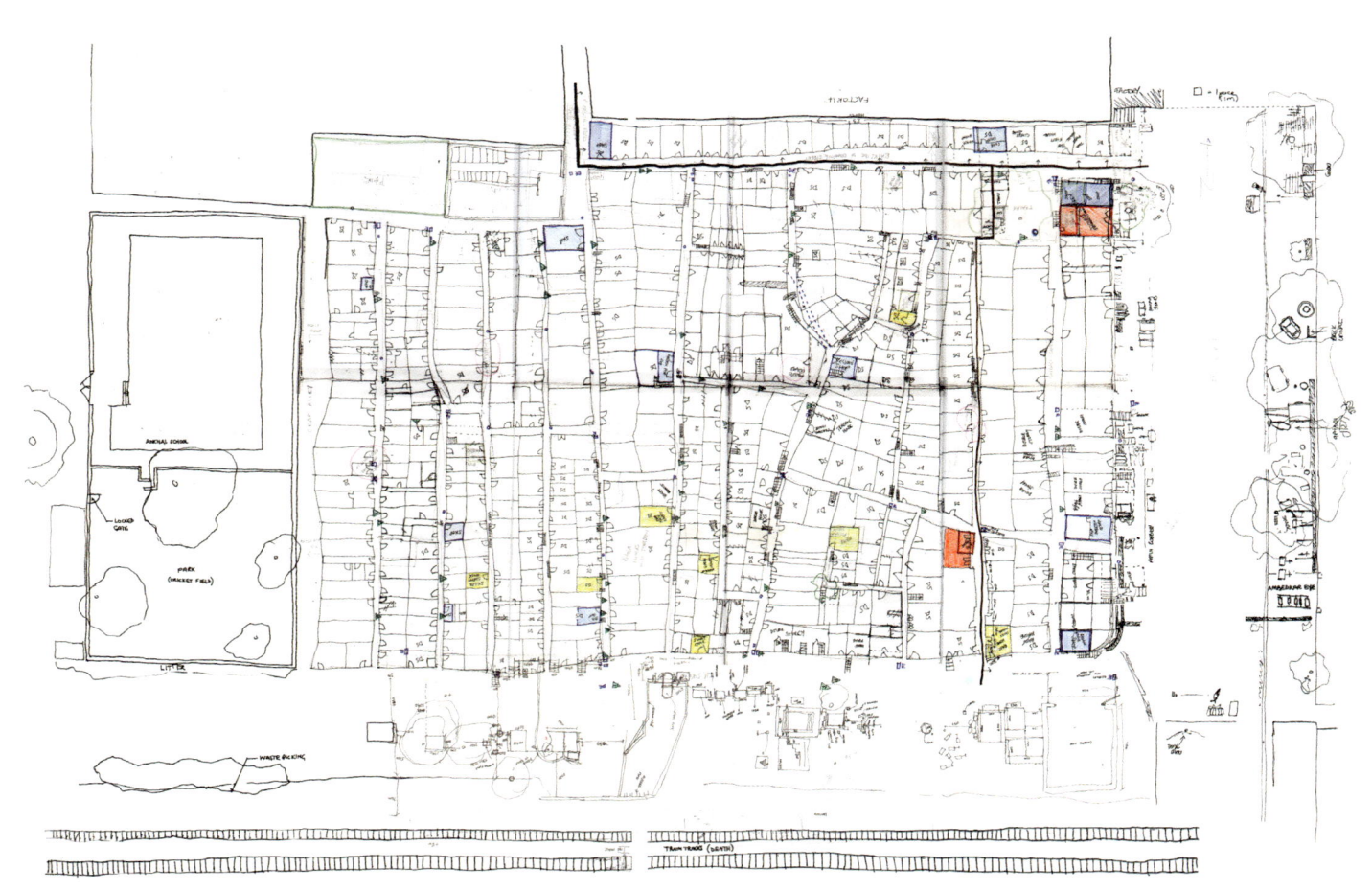

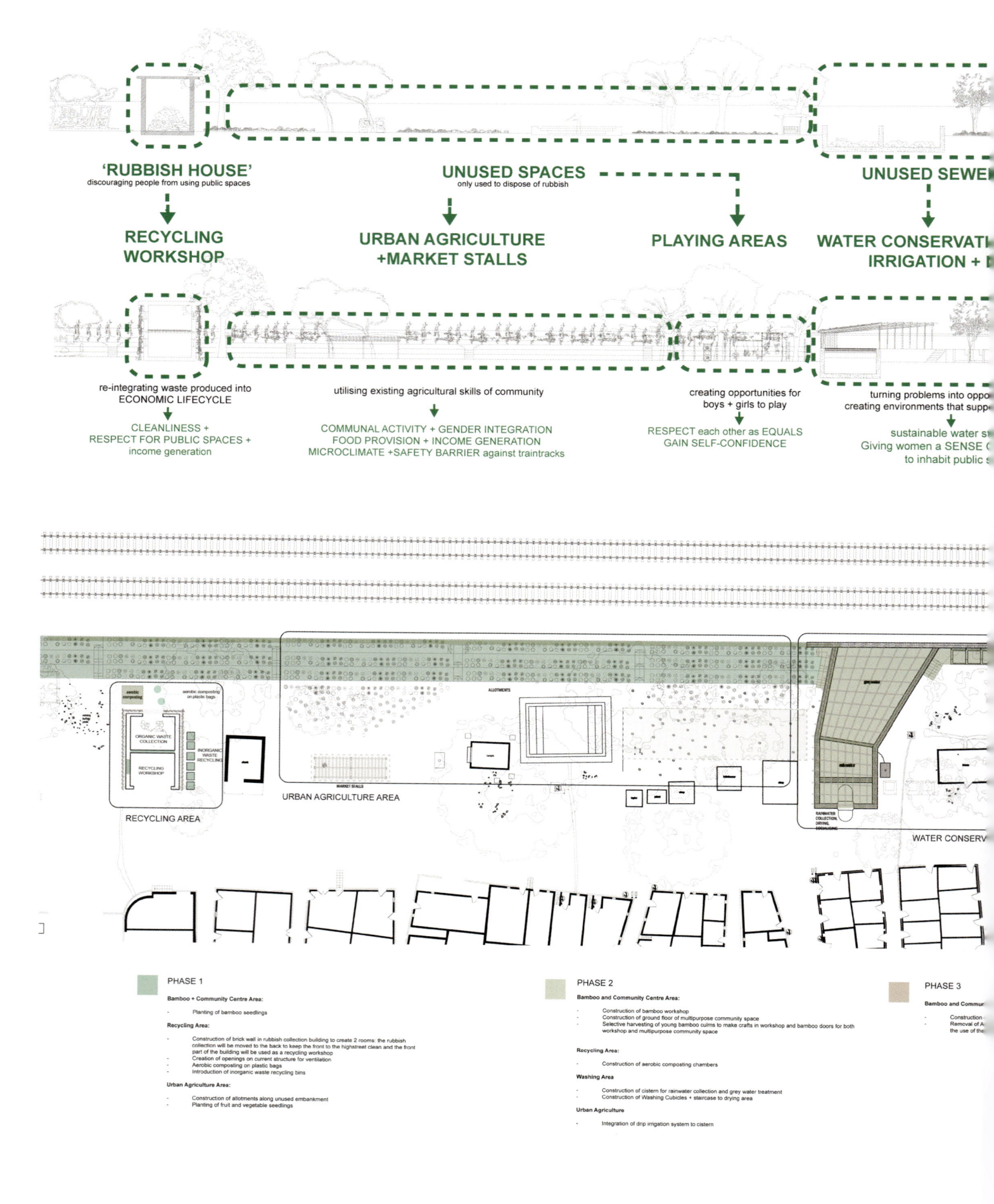

'RUBBISH HOUSE'
discouraging people from using public spaces

UNUSED SPACES
only used to dispose of rubbish

UNUSED SEWE

↓

↓

↓

↓

RECYCLING WORKSHOP

URBAN AGRICULTURE +MARKET STALLS

PLAYING AREAS

WATER CONSERVATI IRRIGATION + I

re-integrating waste produced into
ECONOMIC LIFECYCLE

utilising existing agricultural skills of community

creating opportunities for
boys + girls to play

turning problems into oppo
creating environments that suppo

↓

↓

↓

CLEANLINESS +
RESPECT FOR PUBLIC SPACES +
income generation

COMMUNAL ACTIVITY + GENDER INTEGRATION
FOOD PROVISION + INCOME GENERATION
MICROCLIMATE +SAFETY BARRIER against traintracks

RESPECT each other as EQUALS
GAIN SELF-CONFIDENCE

sustainable water s
Giving women a SENSE
to inhabit public s

RECYCLING AREA

URBAN AGRICULTURE AREA

WATER CONSERV

PHASE 1

Bamboo + Community Centre Area:

- Planting of bamboo seedlings

Recycling Area:

- Construction of brick wall in rubbish collection building to create 2 rooms: the rubbish collection will be moved to the back to keep the front to the highstreet clean and the front part of the building will be used as a recycling workshop
- Creation of openings on current structure for ventilation
- Aerobic composting on plastic bags
- Introduction of inorganic waste recycling bins

Urban Agriculture Area:

- Construction of allotments along unused embankment
- Planting of fruit and vegetable seedlings

PHASE 2

Bamboo and Community Centre Area:

- Construction of bamboo workshop
- Construction of ground floor of multipurpose community space
- Selective harvesting of young bamboo culms to make crafts in workshop and bamboo doors for both workshop and multipurpose community space

Recycling Area:

- Construction of aerobic composting chambers

Washing Area

- Construction of cistern for rainwater collection and grey water treatment
- Construction of Washing Cubicles + staircase to drying area

Urban Agriculture

- Integration of drip irrigation system to cistern

PHASE 3

Bamboo and Commu

- Construction
- Removal of A
- the use of the

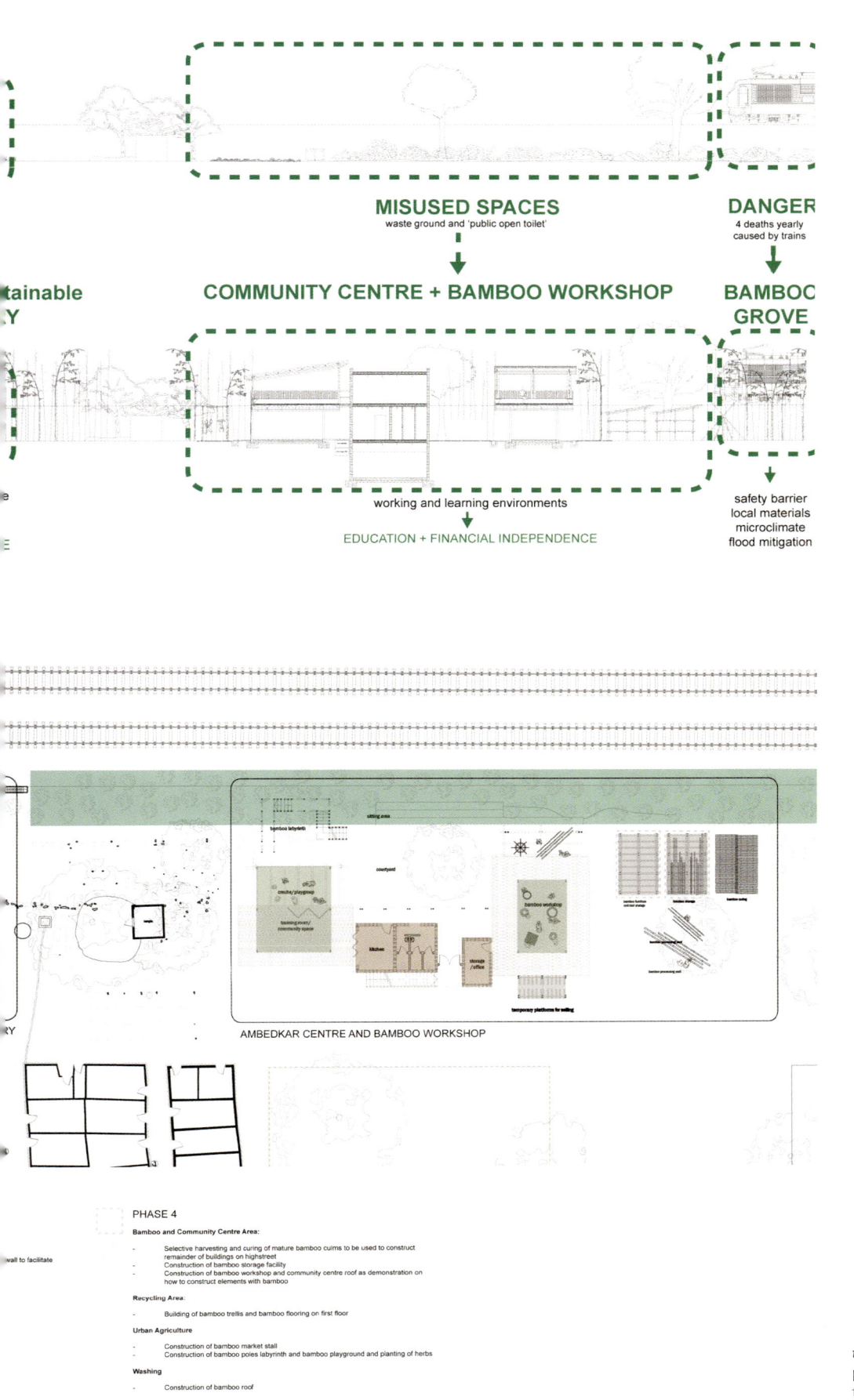

MISUSED SPACES
waste ground and 'public open toilet'

DANGER
4 deaths yearly
caused by trains

tainable
Y

COMMUNITY CENTRE + BAMBOO WORKSHOP

BAMBOO
GROVE

working and learning environments

EDUCATION + FINANCIAL INDEPENDENCE

safety barrier
local materials
microclimate
flood mitigation

AMBEDKAR CENTRE AND BAMBOO WORKSHOP

PHASE 4

Bamboo and Community Centre Area:

- Selective harvesting and curing of mature bamboo culms to be used to construct remainder of buildings on highstreet
- Construction of bamboo storage facility
- Construction of bamboo workshop and community centre roof as demonstration on how to construct elements with bamboo

Recycling Area:

- Building of bamboo trellis and bamboo flooring on first floor

Urban Agriculture

- Construction of bamboo market stall
- Construction of bamboo poles labyrinth and bamboo playground and planting of herbs

Washing

- Construction of bamboo roof

top
plan showing overall strategy for spatial
transformation
bottom
plan of phased proposal

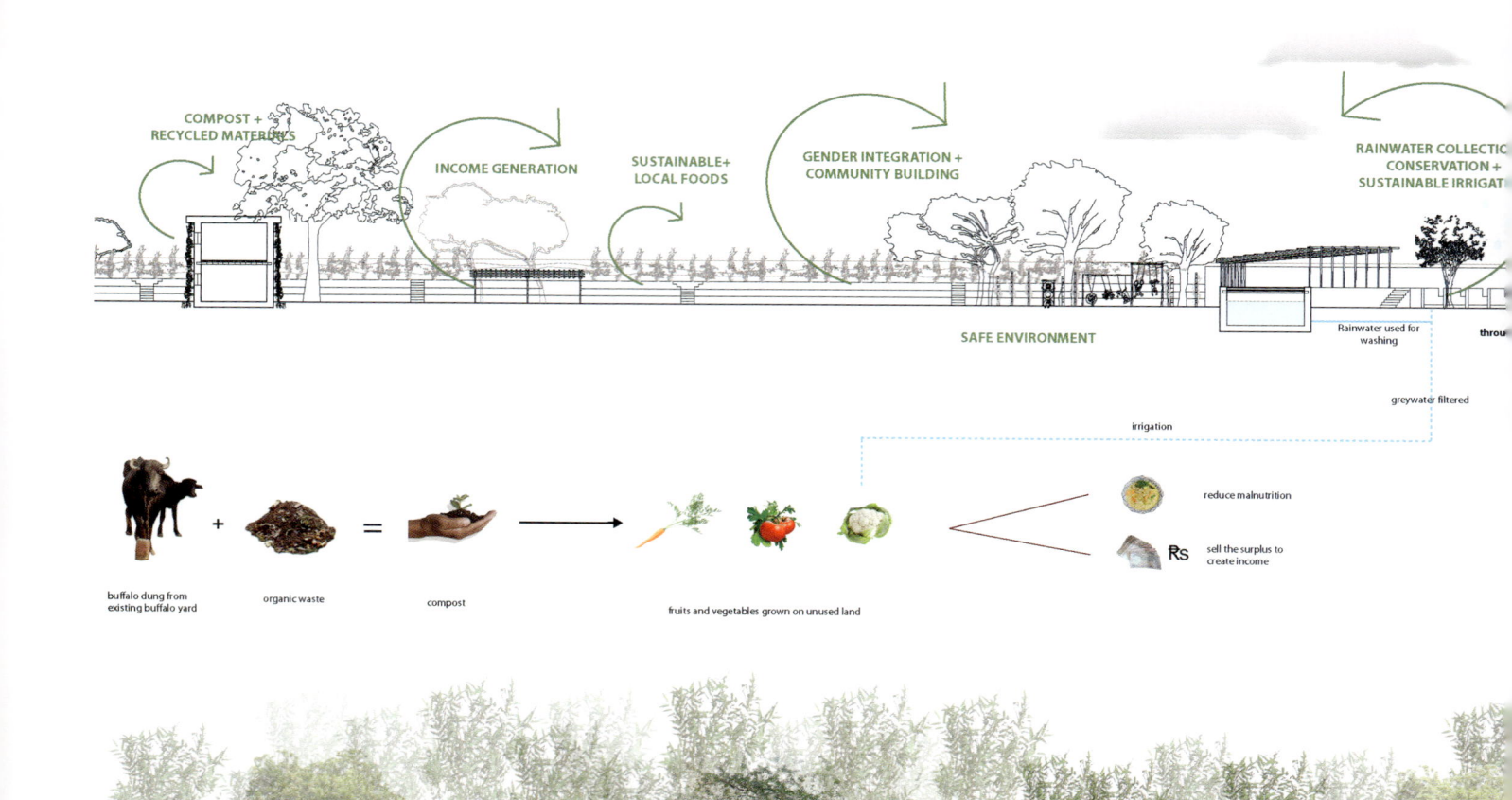

COMPOST + RECYCLED MATERIALS

INCOME GENERATION

SUSTAINABLE + LOCAL FOODS

GENDER INTEGRATION + COMMUNITY BUILDING

RAINWATER COLLECTION CONSERVATION + SUSTAINABLE IRRIGATION

SAFE ENVIRONMENT

Rainwater used for washing

through

greywater filtered

irrigation

reduce malnutrition

Rs sell the surplus to create income

buffalo dung from existing buffalo yard

organic waste

compost

fruits and vegetables grown on unused land

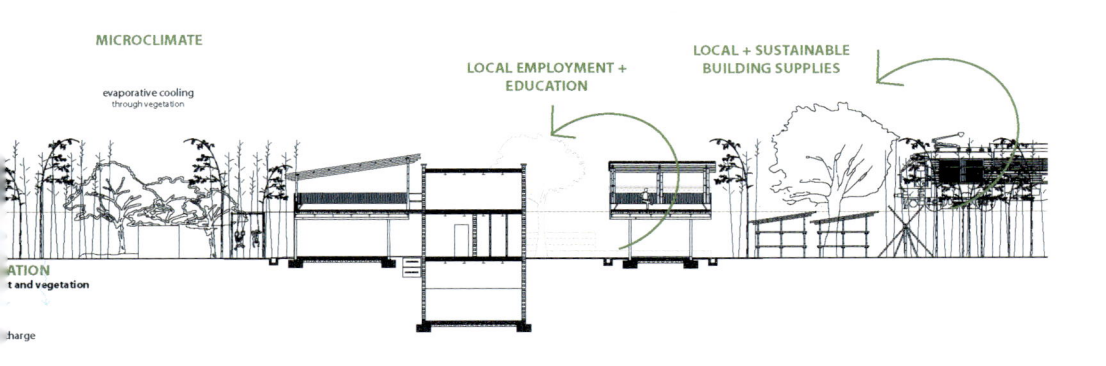

MICROCLIMATE

evaporative cooling
through vegetation

LOCAL EMPLOYMENT +
EDUCATION

LOCAL + SUSTAINABLE
BUILDING SUPPLIES

ATION
t and vegetation

harge

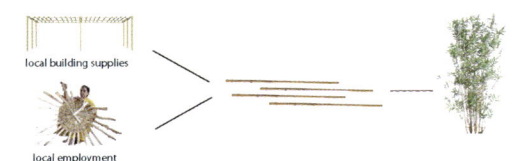

income generation

local building supplies

local employment

bamboo grown on unused land

this page:
top
section showing strategy for social sustainability
middle
east–west elevation of community centre from
the High Street
bottom left
view from the community centre upper terrace
bottom middle
view along the High Street beside the community
centre
bottom right
view of the community centre and bamboo
production

overleaf:
east–west section through the community centre

top
north–south section showing environmental
strategy
bottom
north–south section through the community
centre

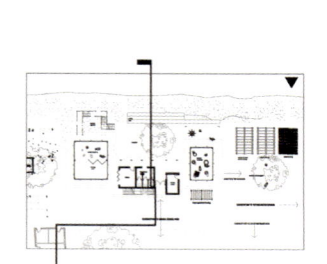

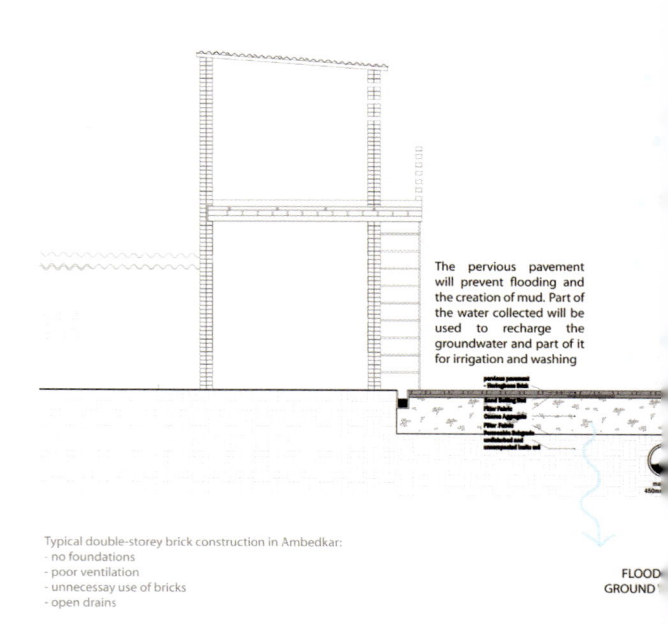

The pervious pavement
will prevent flooding and
the creation of mud. Part of
the water collected will be
used to recharge the
groundwater and part of it
for irrigation and washing

Typical double-storey brick construction in Ambedkar:
- no foundations
- poor ventilation
- unnecessay use of bricks
- open drains

FLOOD
GROUND

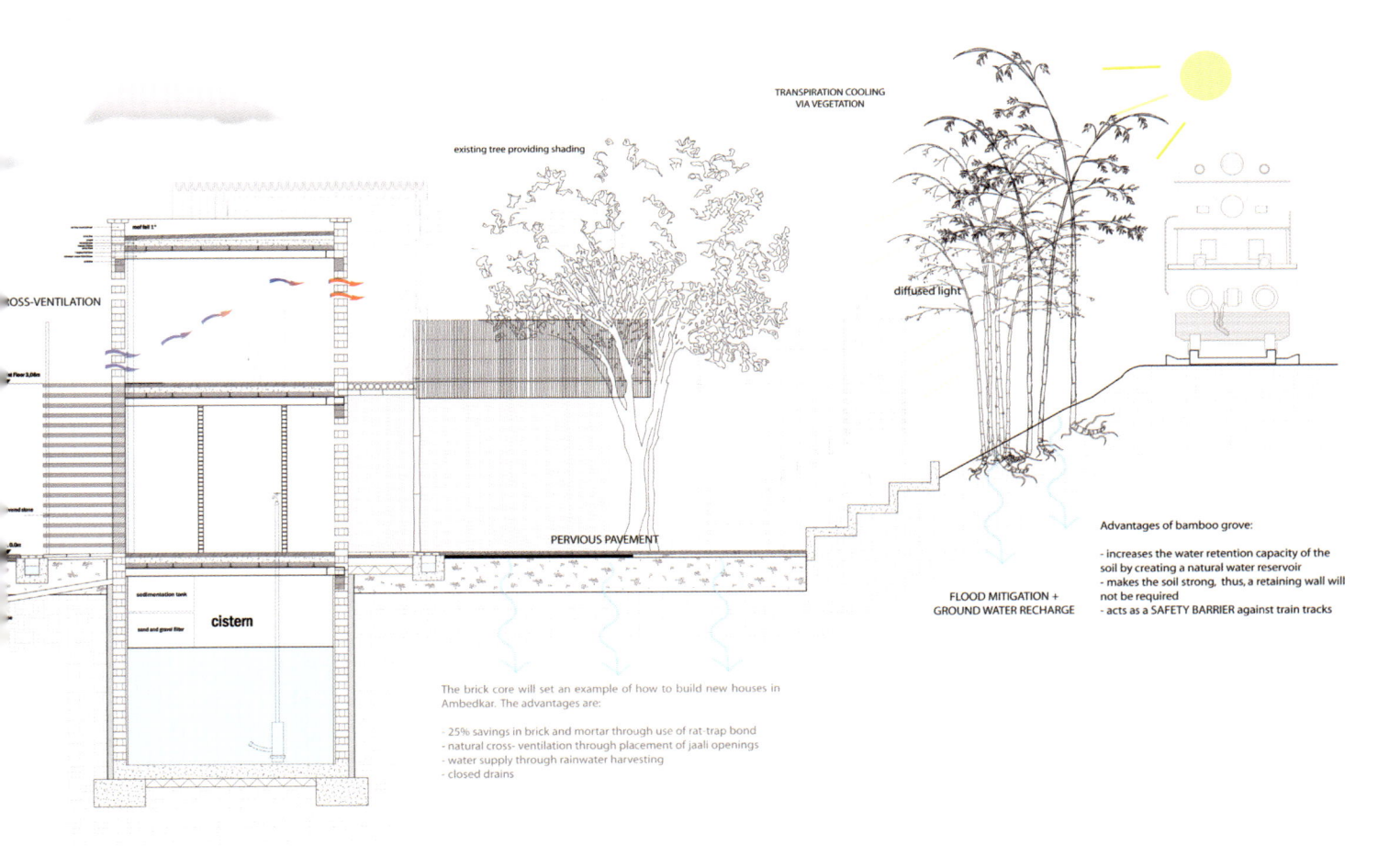

TRANSPIRATION COOLING
VIA VEGETATION

existing tree providing shading

CROSS-VENTILATION

diffused light

PERVIOUS PAVEMENT

cistern

FLOOD MITIGATION +
GROUND WATER RECHARGE

Advantages of bamboo grove:

- increases the water retention capacity of the soil by creating a natural water reservoir
- makes the soil strong, thus, a retaining wall will not be required
- acts as a SAFETY BARRIER against train tracks

The brick core will set an example of how to build new houses in Ambedkar. The advantages are:

- 25% savings in brick and mortar through use of rat-trap bond
- natural cross- ventilation through placement of jaali openings
- water supply through rainwater harvesting
- closed drains

Victoria Wagner
Plant Nursery, Cinema and Community Place, North Jagdamba Camp, South Delhi

Reacting to the young people of Jagdamba Camp's expressed desire for a place for leisure activities together with the commercial opportunity for a plant nursery, this building offers a counterpoint to the claustrophobic J.J. Camp by providing accessible open spaces outside the camp.

See Chapter 3, A Landscape of Walls (3) Retaining Walls: Jagdamba Camp for a description of Jagdamba Camp.

main image
north–south section through cinema, new housing and existing Jagdamba Camp

above:
east–west section through cinema and nursery showing water management

facing page:
view of Jagdamba Camp from tower

street level

Stephen Chown
Sanitation, Education and Public Space, Ambedkar Camp, East Delhi

The adult literacy building is accessed from the 'High Street' and bridges over the railway to the south of the settlement. It provides communal sanitation and a safe route to school for the children.

See Chapter 5, The Conglomerate Matrix and the Modern Vernacular, for a description of the settlement. See Chapter 8, Ambedkar for description of this scheme. See Chapter 2 for an illustration of a model of Stephen's experimental construction detail.

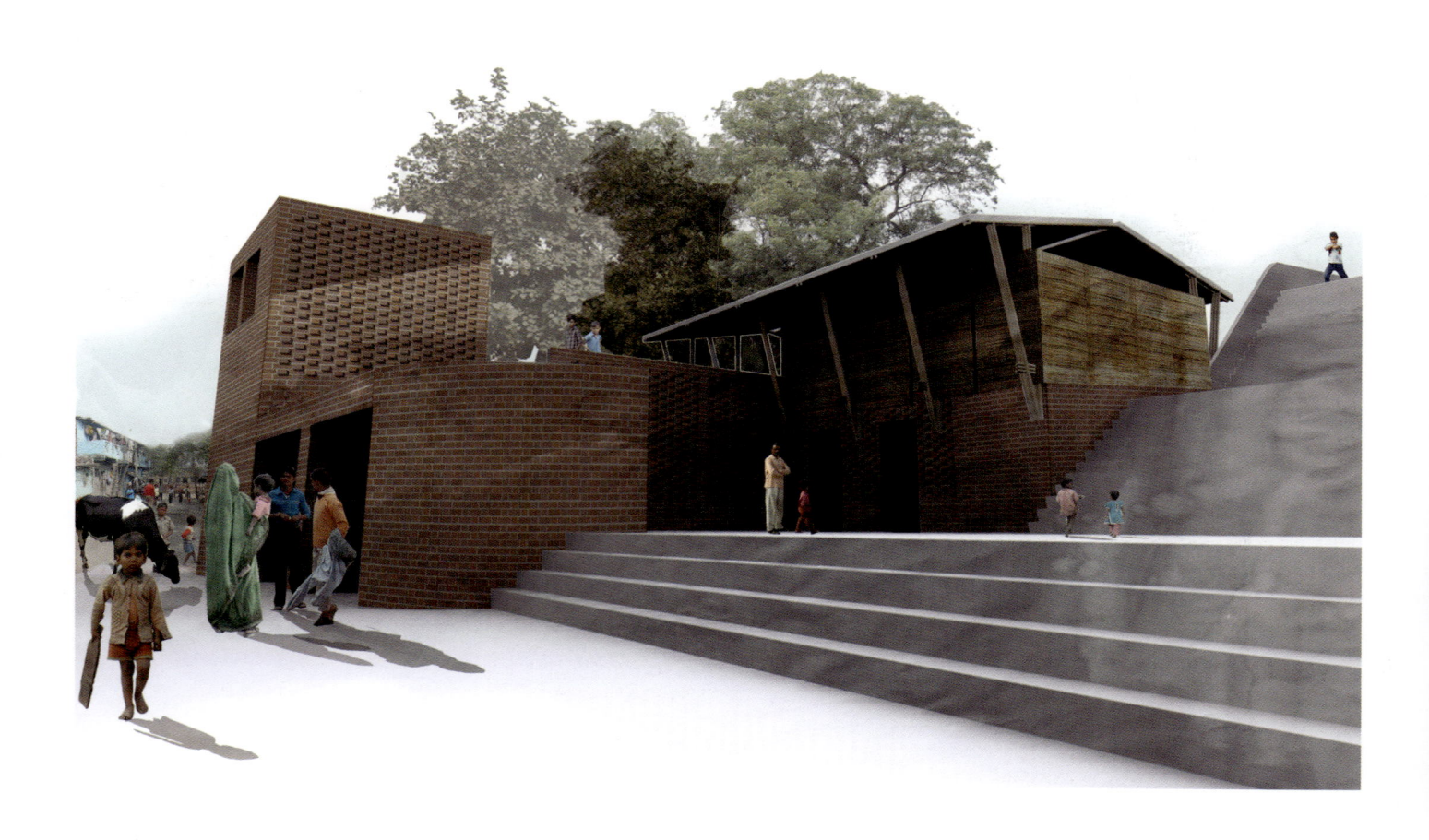

main image below
north–south section showing proposed
education bridge over railway

this page:
left
view crossing education bridge over railway
at night
above
High Street Temple at entrance to education
bridge over railway

facing page:
view of adult literacy building at the side of steps
to new railway bridge

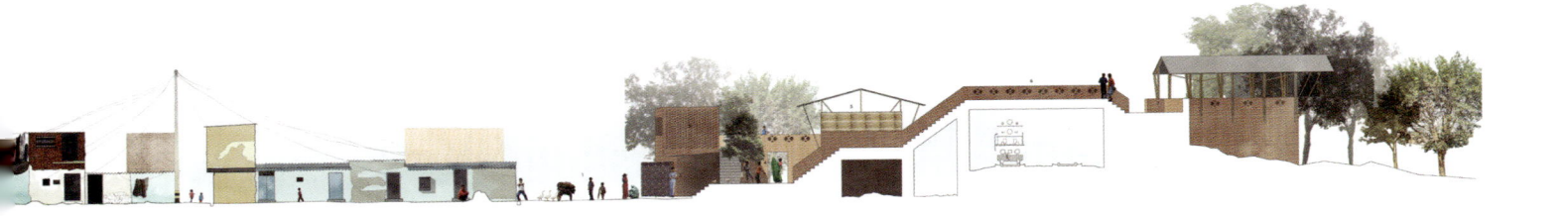

Nick Maari
Upgrading Kalyanpuri Block 19/20, East Delhi

Development of house and shop types for upgrading existing single storey housing stock.

See Chapter 1 (2) Morphological Tales for Nick's first impressions of the settlement. See Chapter 3 (5) Backs to the Wall, for a description and history of the settlement.

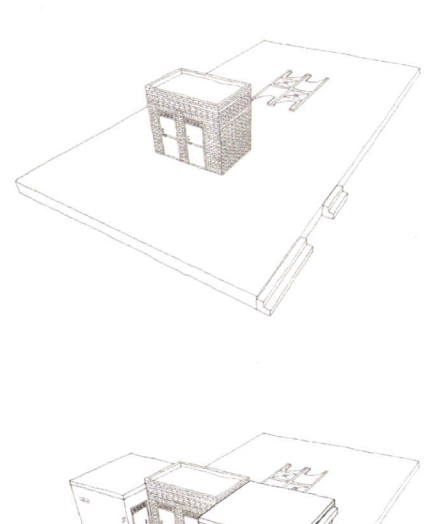
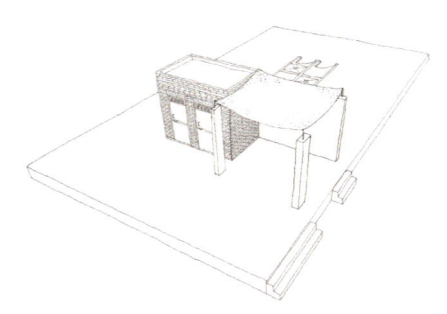
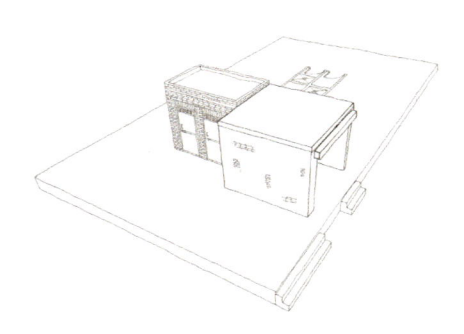

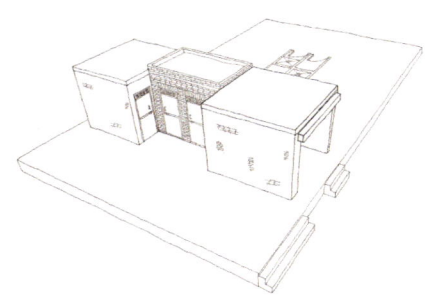
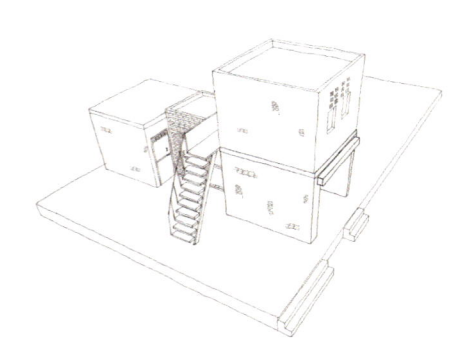
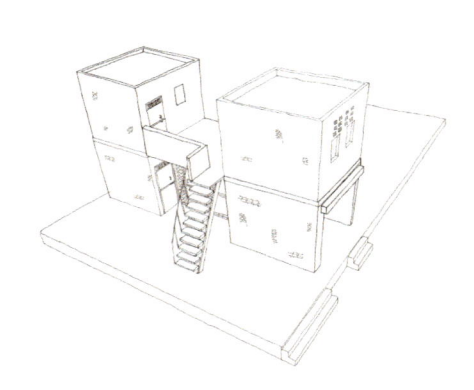

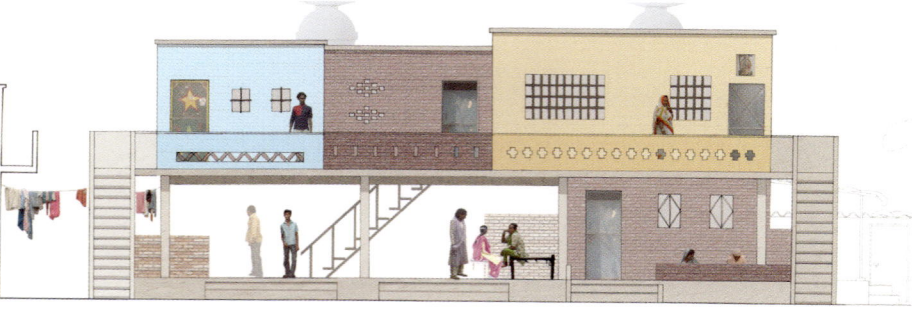

top
diagrams of proposed phases of house construction
left
proposed phased shop house: front elevation
bottom left
view of proposed phased shop house
bottom right
view of proposed shop house from the street

Amelia Rule
Upgrading Kalyanpuri Block 19/20, East Delhi

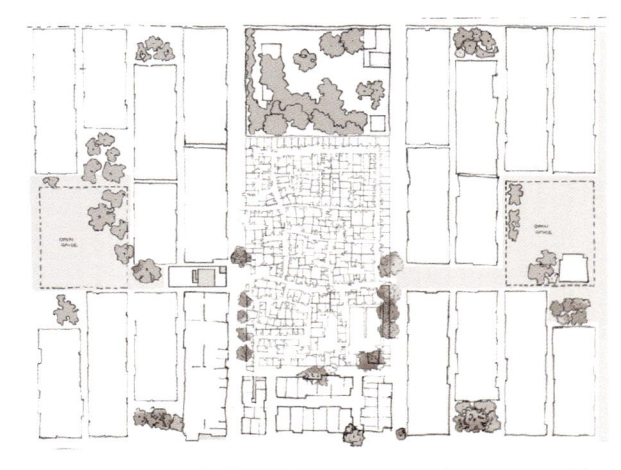

The intensification and rehabilitation of an existing pedestrian route through an illegal single-storey settlement to create a bazaar street, community centre and three-storey phased houses and workshops.

See Chapter 2 (5) Validity, Legitimacy, Characters, Friends for quote. See Chapter 3 (5) Backs to the Wall for a description of the settlement. See Chapter 7 (2) Kuchha Roofs, Example (1) for roof making in the settlement.

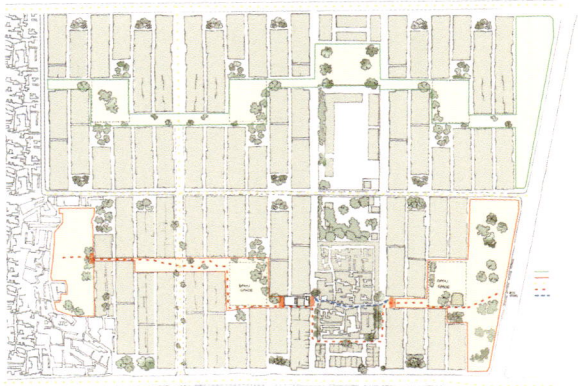

top
location plan and student survey of settlement of Kalyanpuri Block 19/20
middle
plan of proposed new route through Kalyanpuri
below
existing section along through route
bottom
detailed plan of existing through route

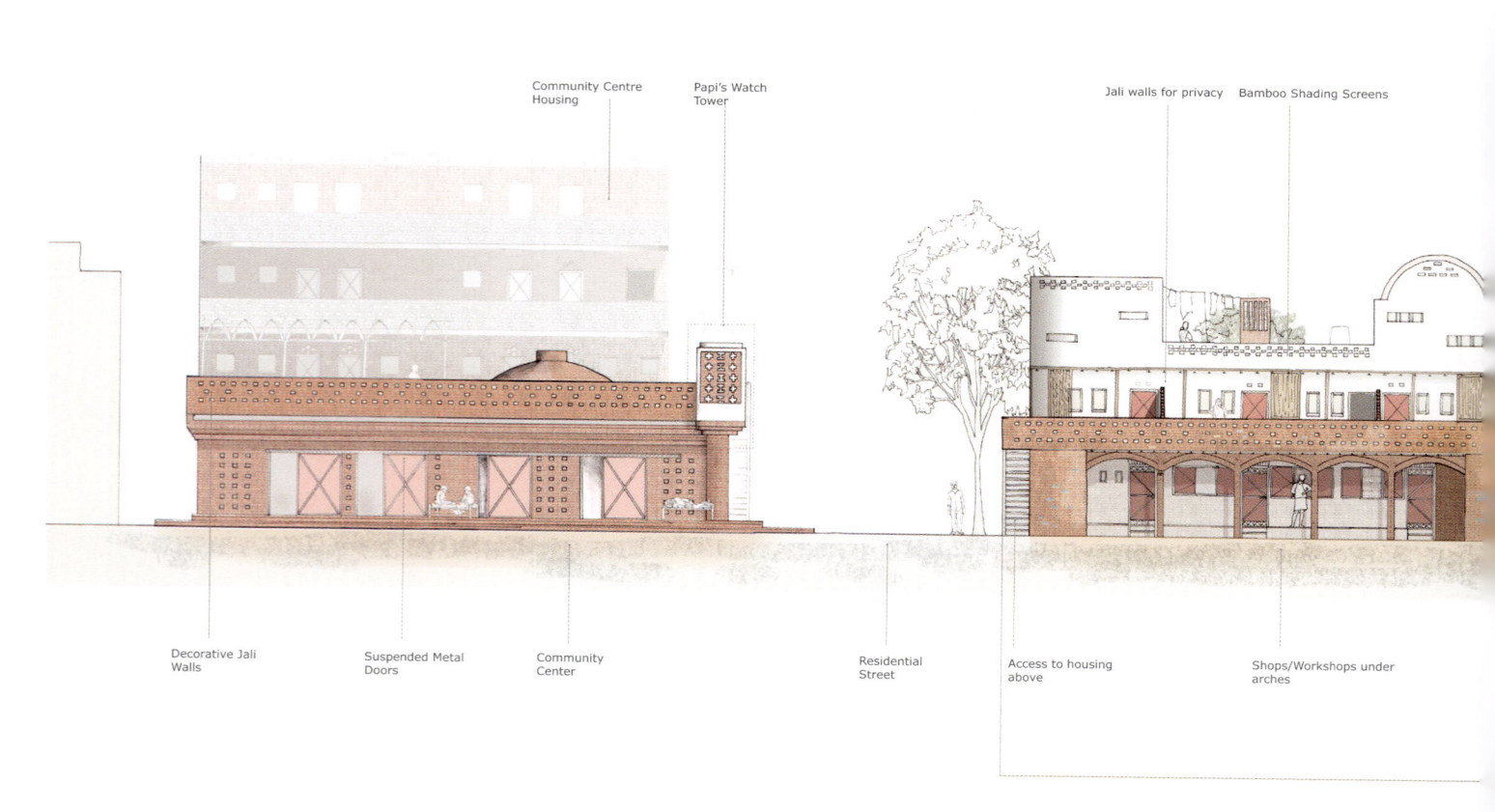

Community Centre Housing

Papi's Watch Tower

Jali walls for privacy

Bamboo Shading Screens

Decorative Jali Walls

Suspended Metal Doors

Community Center

Residential Street

Access to housing above

Shops/Workshops under arches

main image below
proposed High Street elevation

this page:
proposed section through Community Centre

facing page:
proposed part plan of High Street and
Community Centre

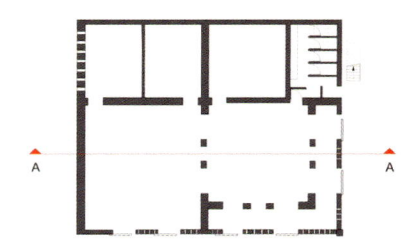

A ◄——————————————► A

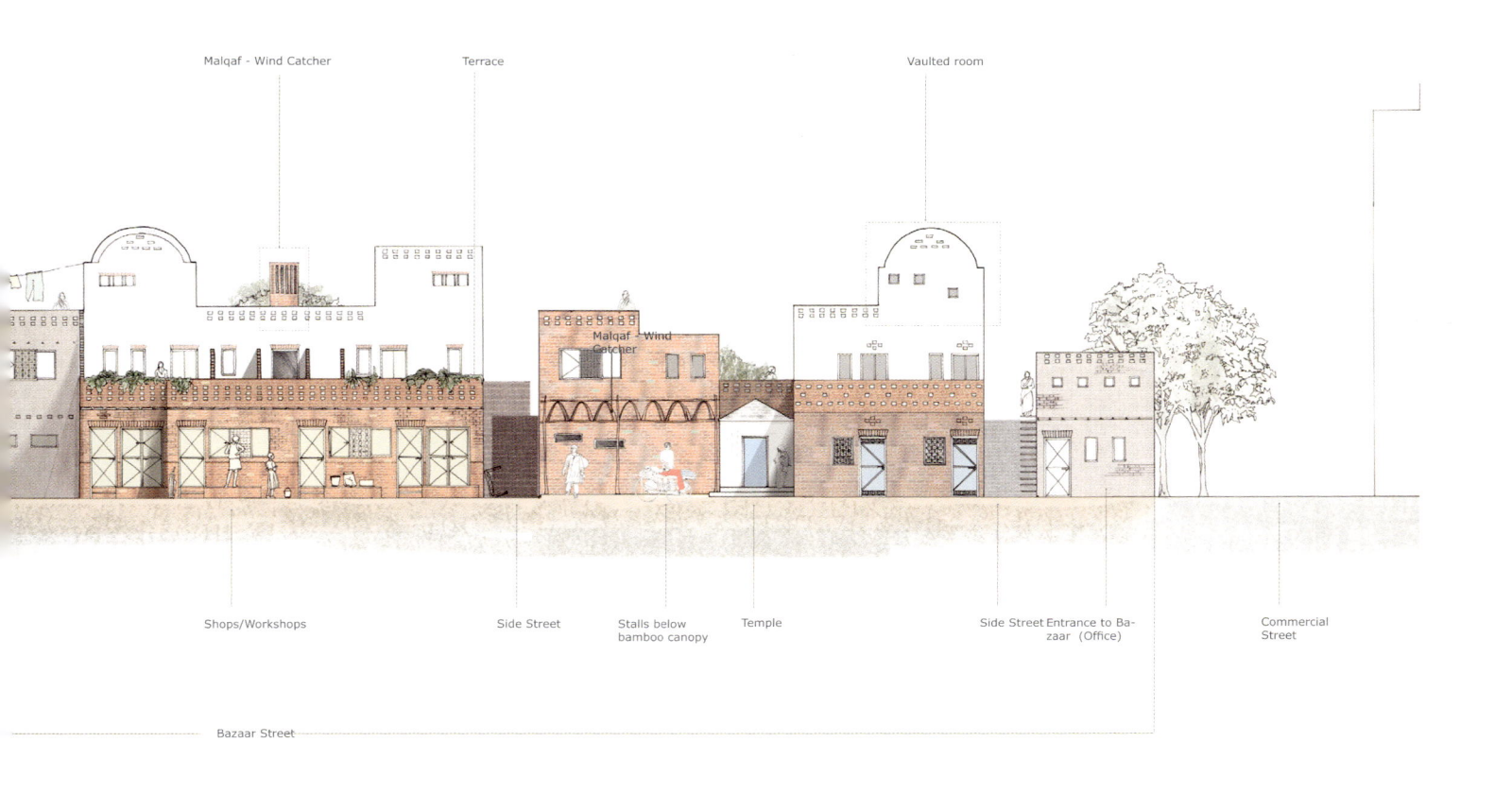

Malqaf - Wind Catcher   Terrace   Vaulted room

Malqaf - Wind
Catcher

Shops/Workshops   Side Street   Stalls below   Temple   Side Street Entrance to Ba-   Commercial
                                          bamboo canopy   zaar (Office)   Street

Bazaar Street

Azedah Mosavi
Sanitation, Education and Public Space, Ambedkar Camp, East Delhi

Densification of an illegal settlement with provision of more public spaces through partial removal, giving identity to each newly-formed chowk (public space) through focused activity. Construction of new social housing to provide for demolished houses.

See Chapter 7 (1) Single-storey Kuchha for description of settlement.

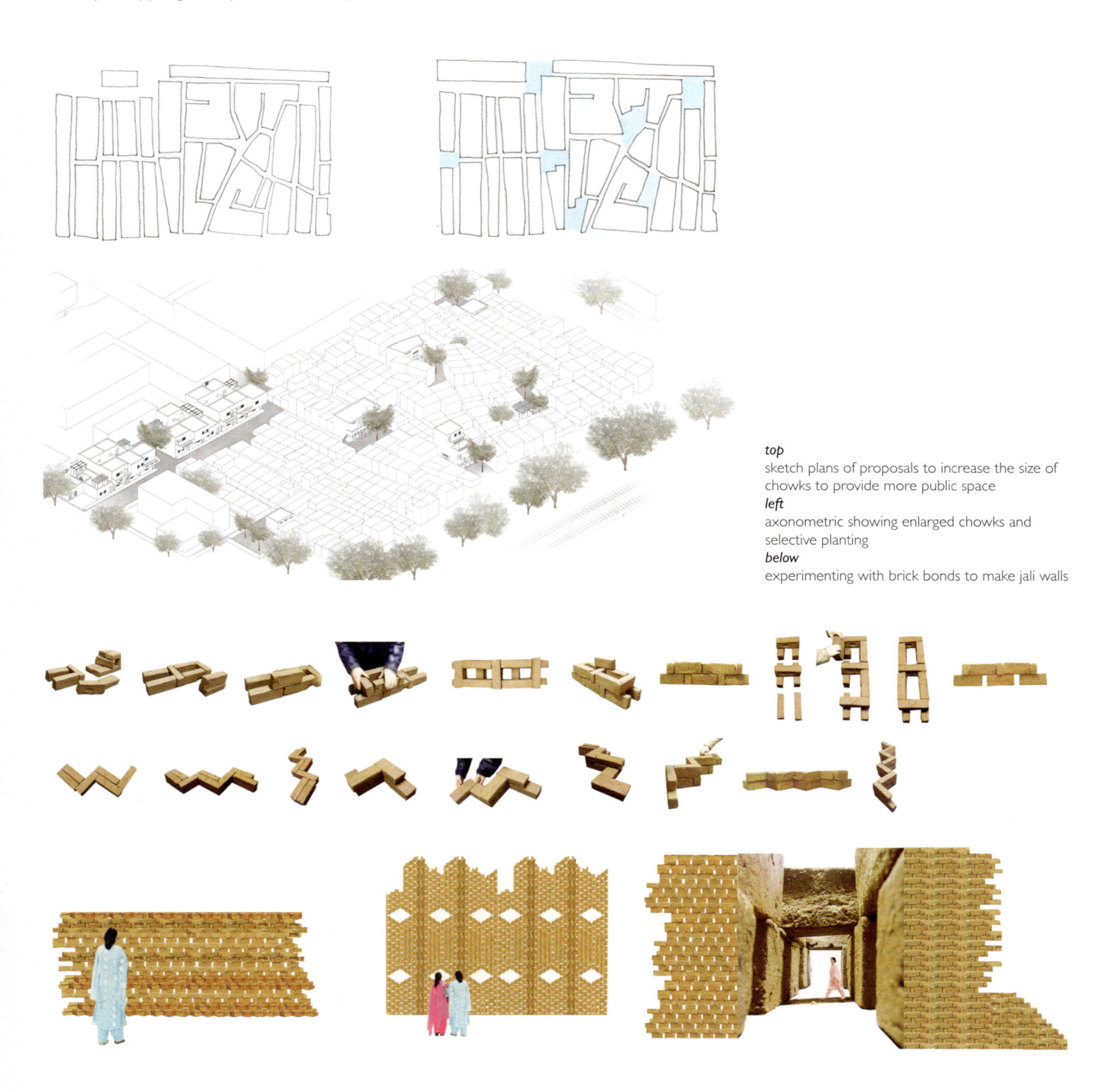

top
sketch plans of proposals to increase the size of chowks to provide more public space
left
axonometric showing enlarged chowks and selective planting
below
experimenting with brick bonds to make jali walls

theme 2

Waste Picking

Sam Bentil-Mensah
Waste Picker Shophouses, Panchsheel Vihar, South Delhi

A scheme based on the comprehensive upgrading of six existing waste picker yards using brick and bamboo construction.

See Chapter 4 for other images of this scheme.

left
proposed plan of phased improvements
below
sketch design idea for dwellings over workshops and yards
bottom
view of improvements in progress

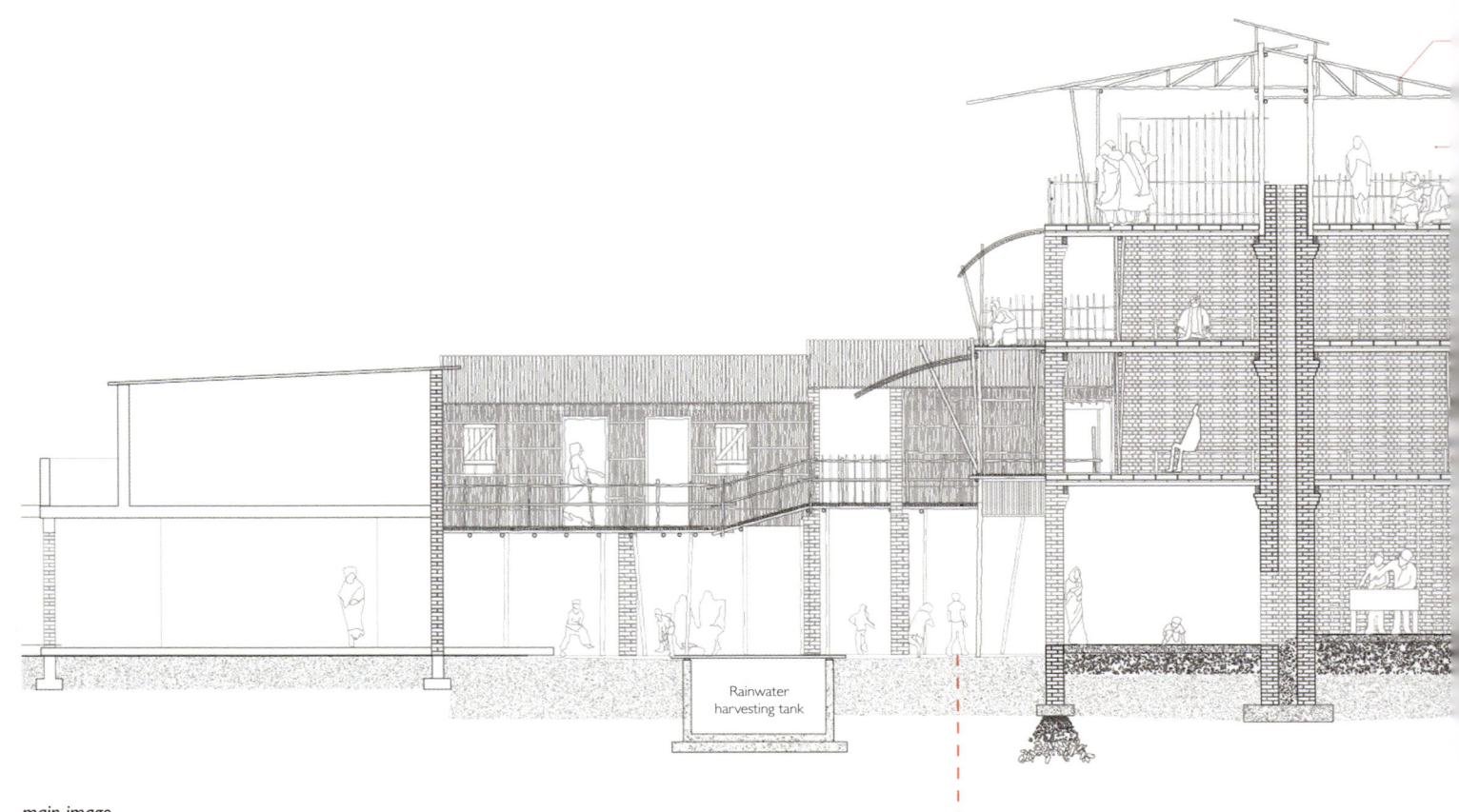

Rainwater harvesting tank

main image
section through two improved waste picker yards

this page:
bottom left
analytical sketch of heating and cooling in a proposed upper floor room
bottom right
sketch showing access to upper floor rooms

facing page:
part elevation of proposed waste picker workshop houses

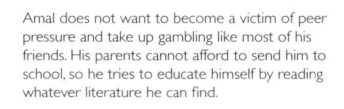

Amal does not want to become a victim of peer pressure and take up gambling like most of his friends. His parents cannot afford to send him to school, so he tries to educate himself by reading whatever literature he can find.

I would very much like to start my own business when I grow up, and help my family out of poverty.

The only space we have available to hang out is the jungle, which is often overcrowded and means we cannot play any cricket.

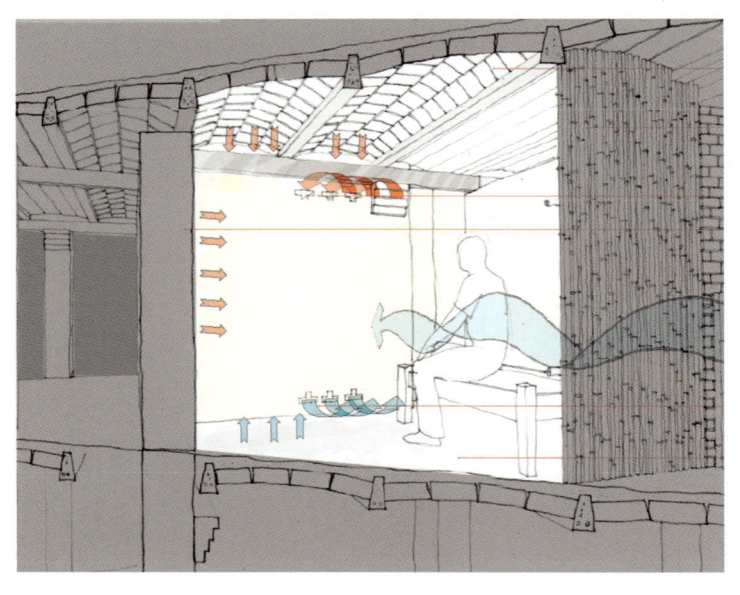

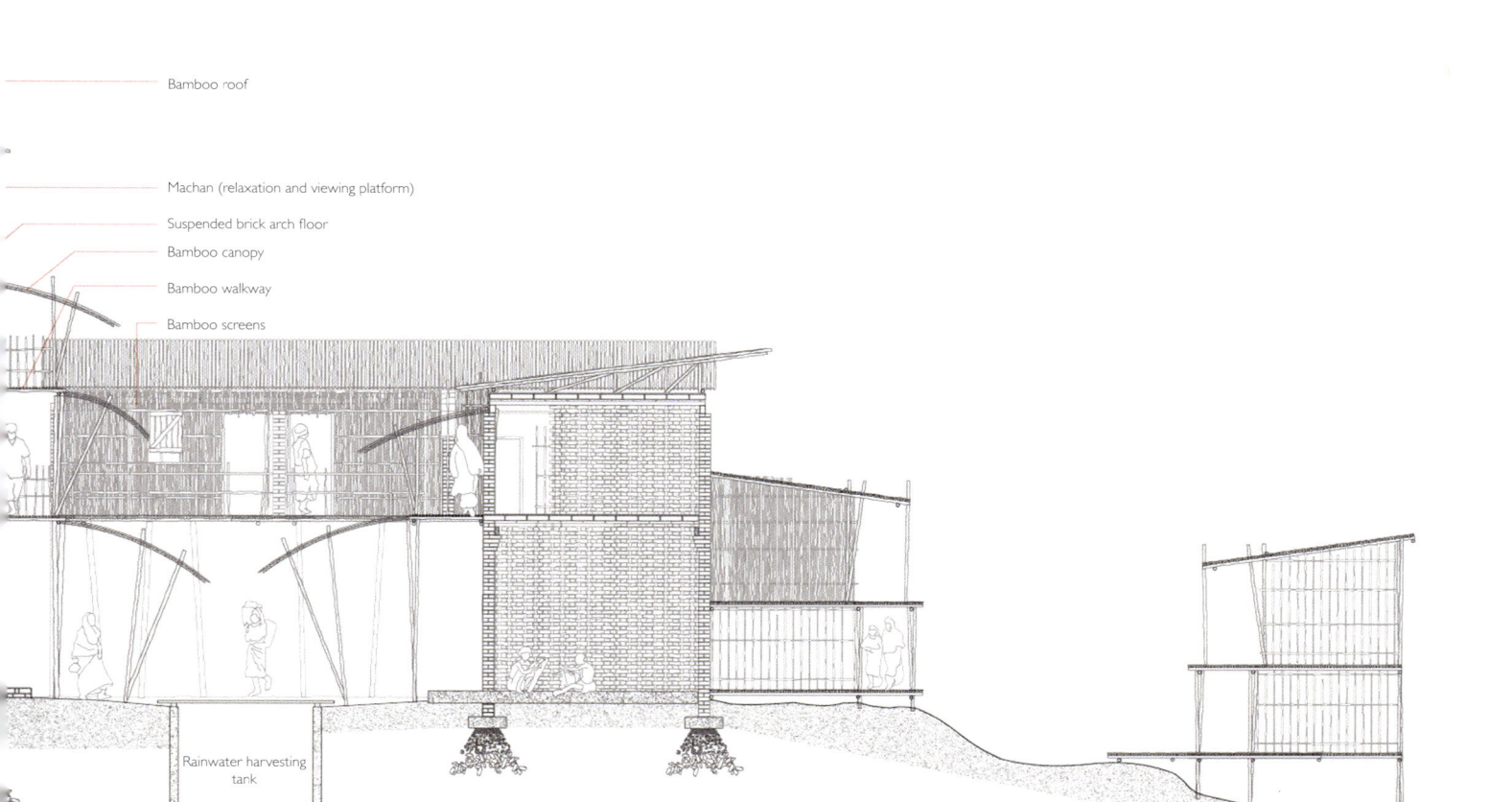

Bamboo roof

Machan (relaxation and viewing platform)

Suspended brick arch floor
Bamboo canopy
Bamboo walkway
Bamboo screens

Rainwater harvesting tank

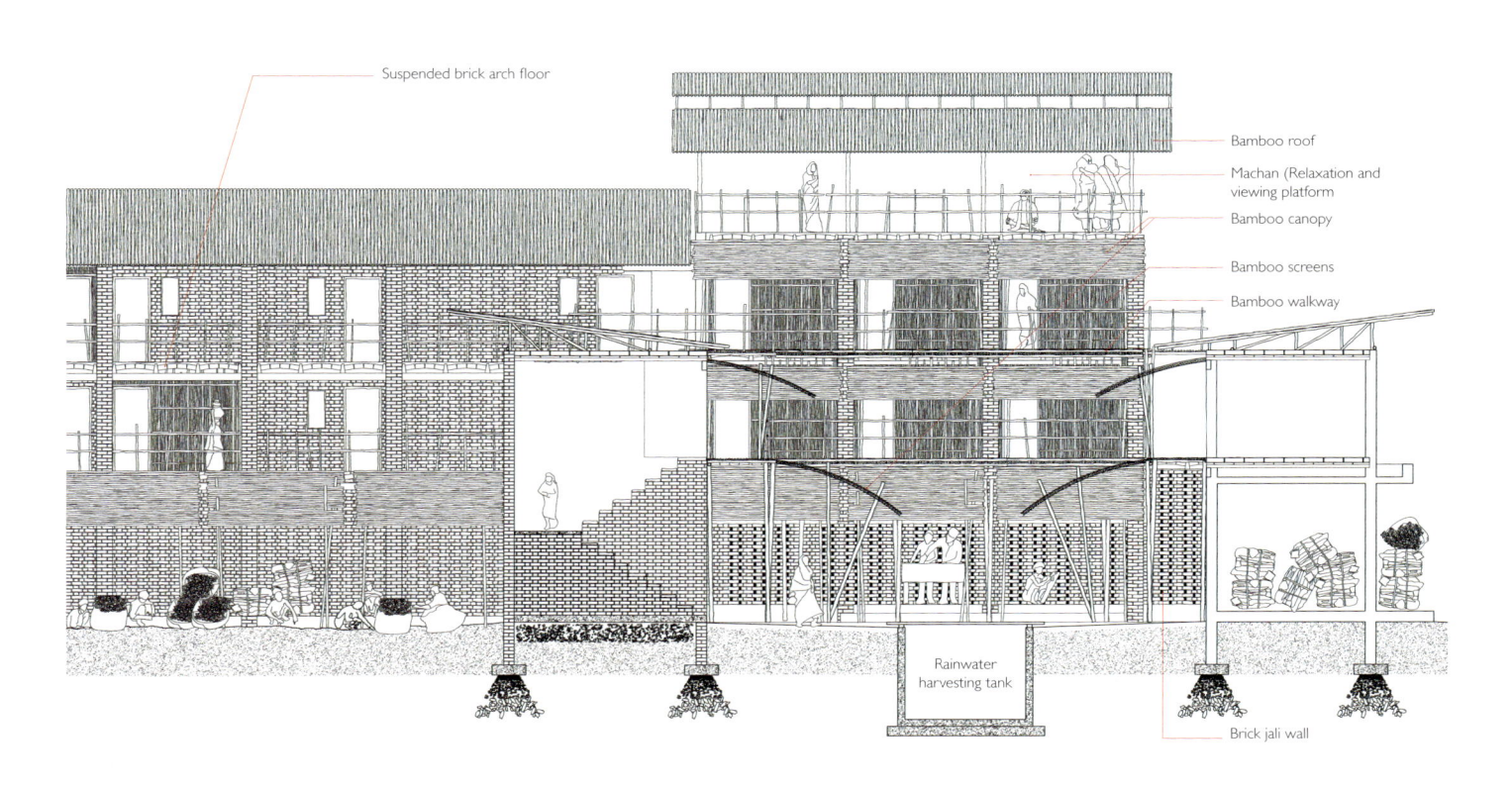

Suspended brick arch floor

Bamboo roof

Machan (Relaxation and viewing platform

Bamboo canopy

Bamboo screens

Bamboo walkway

Rainwater harvesting tank

Brick jali wall

Natasha Reid
Waste Picker Amenity Building, Panchsheel Vihar

A scheme for the self-improvement of the waste picking community through education and cooperative endeavour. Based on an idea for the inhabitation of the flood plain and the construction of a school hall and tower with a nursery and workshops.

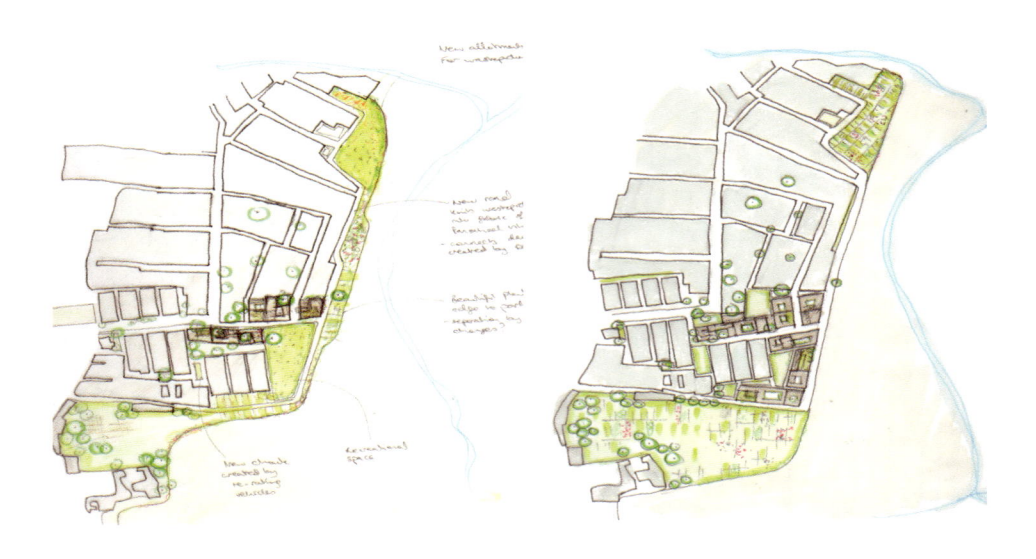

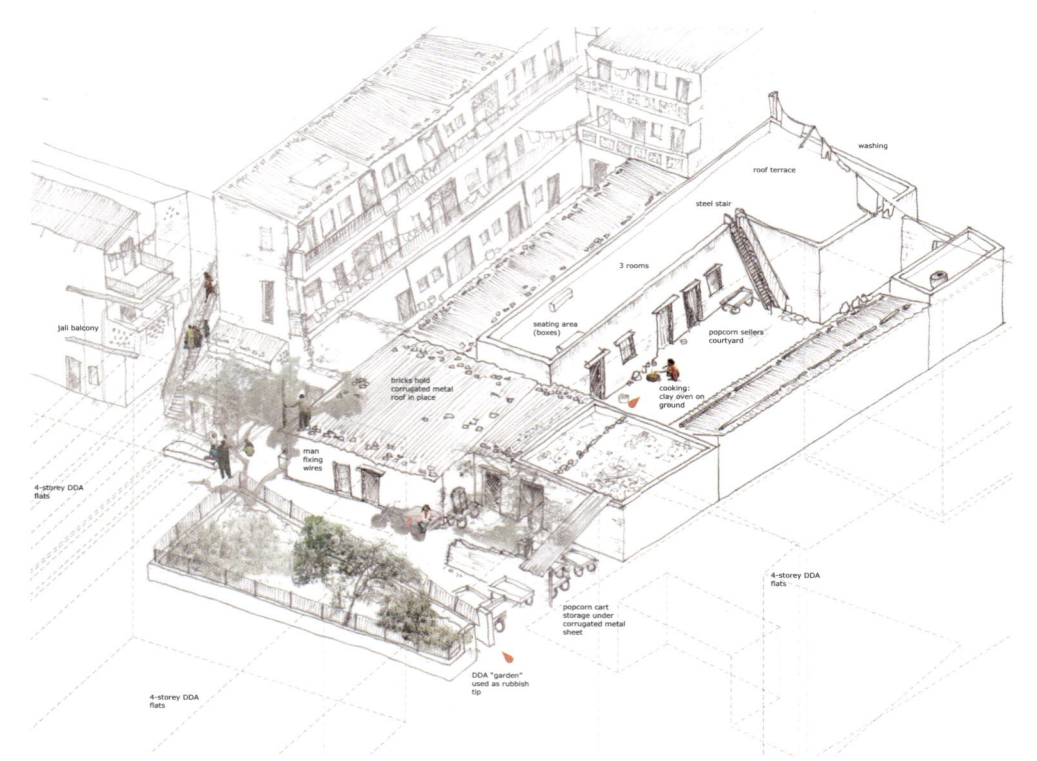

above
projected growth of Panchsheel Vihar into the nala
left
sketch of existing waste picker house on proposed site
below
brick pillar construction for waste picker community hall

below left
view inside community hall at the foot of the tower stairs
below middle
idea for a garden on the community hall roof
below right
street level view of community hall
bottom
view of part of the waste picker community hall used as a classroom

overleaf
view over waste picker amenity building showing tower (containing water filtering system), community hall, roof pergola and resurfaced pedestrian chowk at street level

Cristina Monteiro
Waste Pickers Re-working the Marginal Land, Panchsheel Vihar, South Delhi

An idea for inhabiting the flood plain along bamboo walkways and two-storey brick workshop/houses.

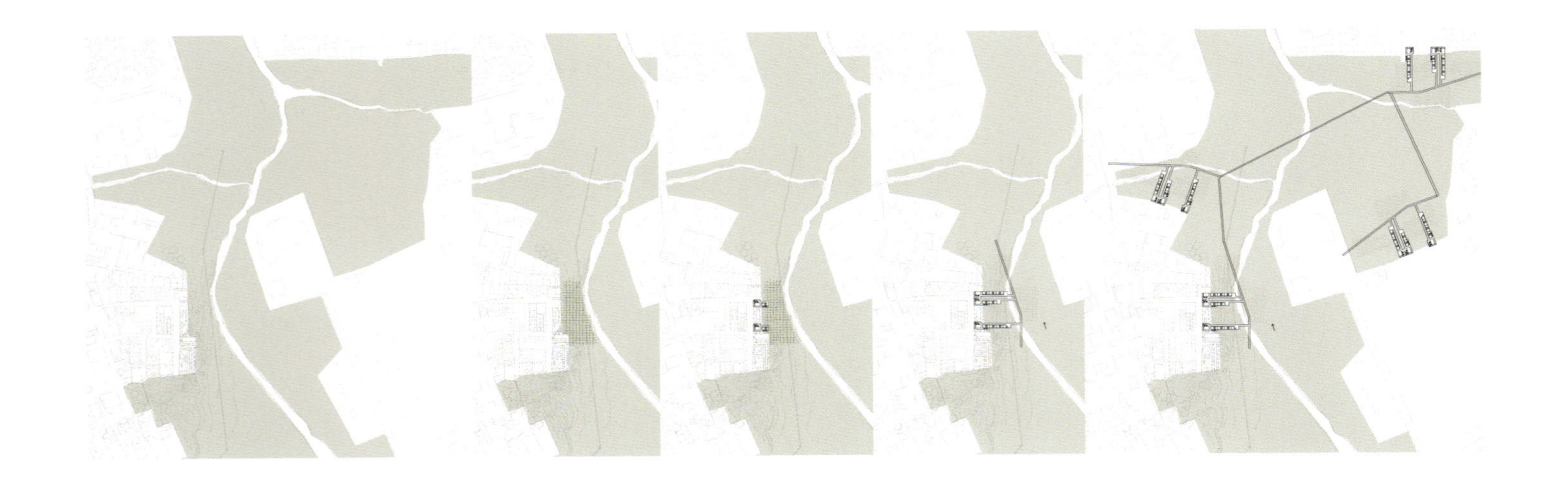

this page:
above left
view from bamboo walkway at the side of a workshop/
house towards the nala
above right
section through brick workshop/house
below
axonometric of one brick workshop/house in pier
extension

facing page:
top
plans showing phasing of pier extensions linked to
footpaths which cross the nala
bottom
elevation of brick and bamboo pier extension into nala

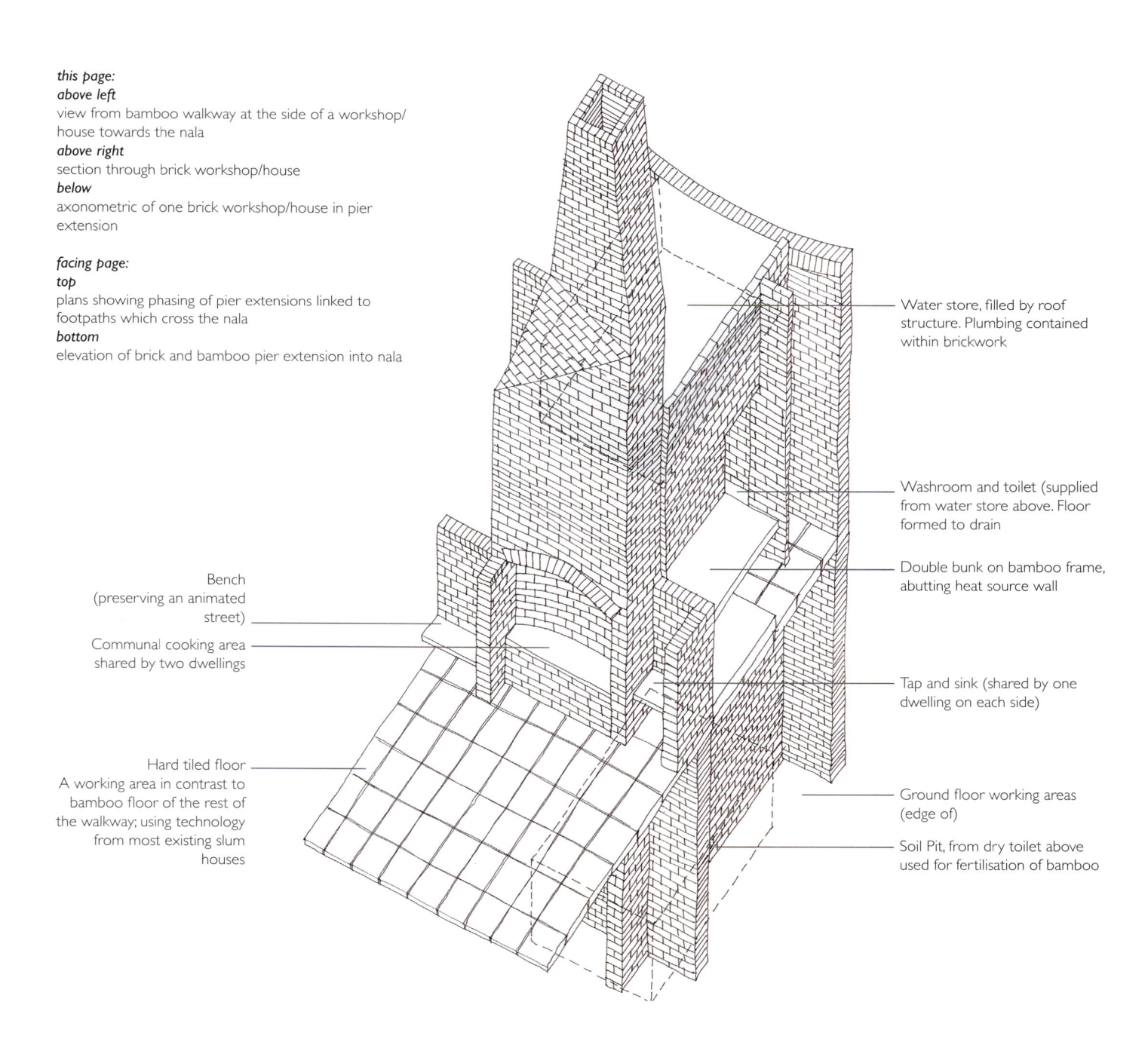

Water store, filled by roof
structure. Plumbing contained
within brickwork

Washroom and toilet (supplied
from water store above. Floor
formed to drain

Double bunk on bamboo frame,
abutting heat source wall

Tap and sink (shared by one
dwelling on each side)

Ground floor working areas
(edge of)

Soil Pit, from dry toilet above
used for fertilisation of bamboo

Bench
(preserving an animated
street)

Communal cooking area
shared by two dwellings

Hard tiled floor
A working area in contrast to
bamboo floor of the rest of
the walkway; using technology
from most existing slum
houses

Dawn Keatley
Waste Pickers' Housing, Workshops and Paper Factory, Panchsheel Vihar, South Delhi

Cooperative waste paper recycling factory owned by the waste pickers on the edge of the flood plain. The paper can be picked and sorted for sale to a junk dealer next door or processed to make papier mâché pots. The shed is made of a lightweight bamboo framework with open sides to encourage ventilation.

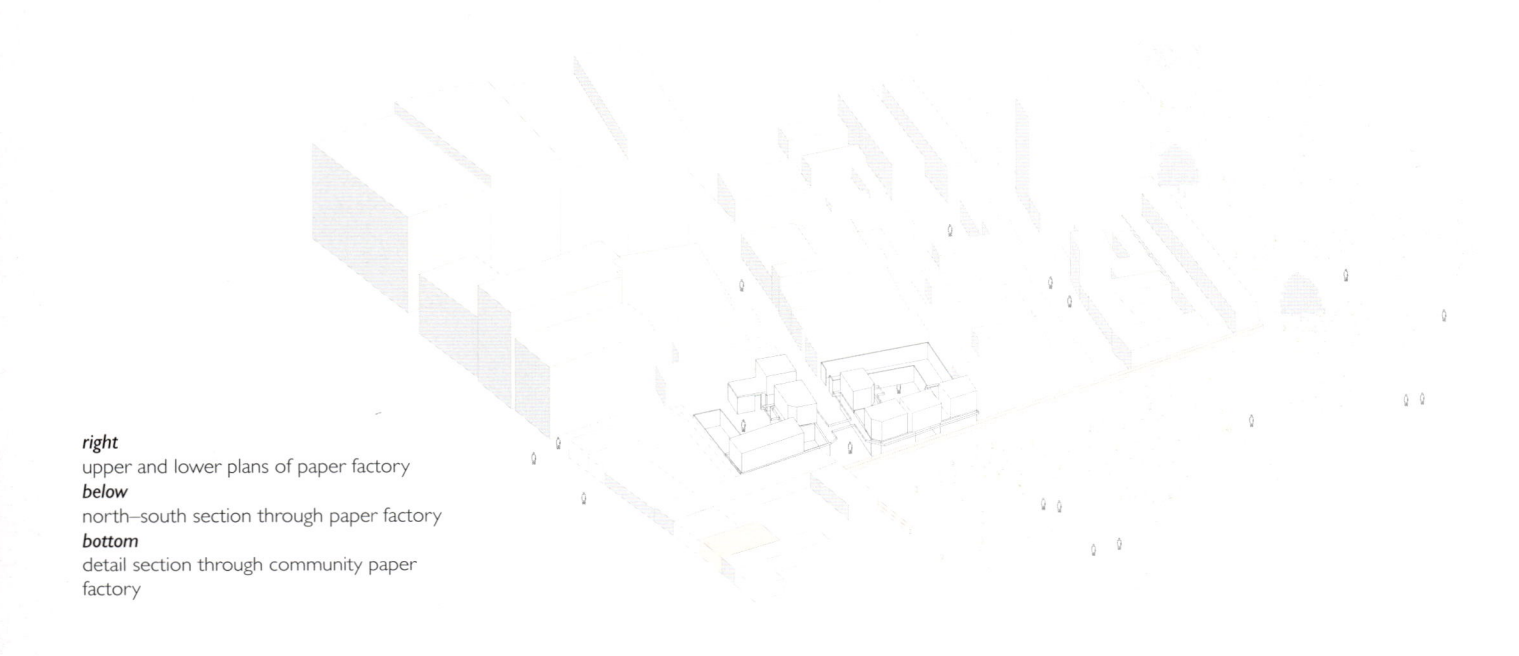

right
upper and lower plans of paper factory
below
north–south section through paper factory
bottom
detail section through community paper factory

theme 3

Havelis

Pau Ling Yap
Women's Rooftop Escape Routes and Havens, Chirag Delhi, South Delhi

See Chapter 5, Example (1) for a description of the scheme.

Dargah Chowk

Medical Chowk

Male Chowk

Motor Vehicle Chowk

plan of Chirag Delhi showing main chowks

top
plan of rooftop routes and havens, upper level, see Chapter 5, Example (1)
middle
long section through rooftop routes and havens
bottom
view of haven accessed from above

facing page:
view called Redemption: making up after a marital split in a bamboo screened courtyard

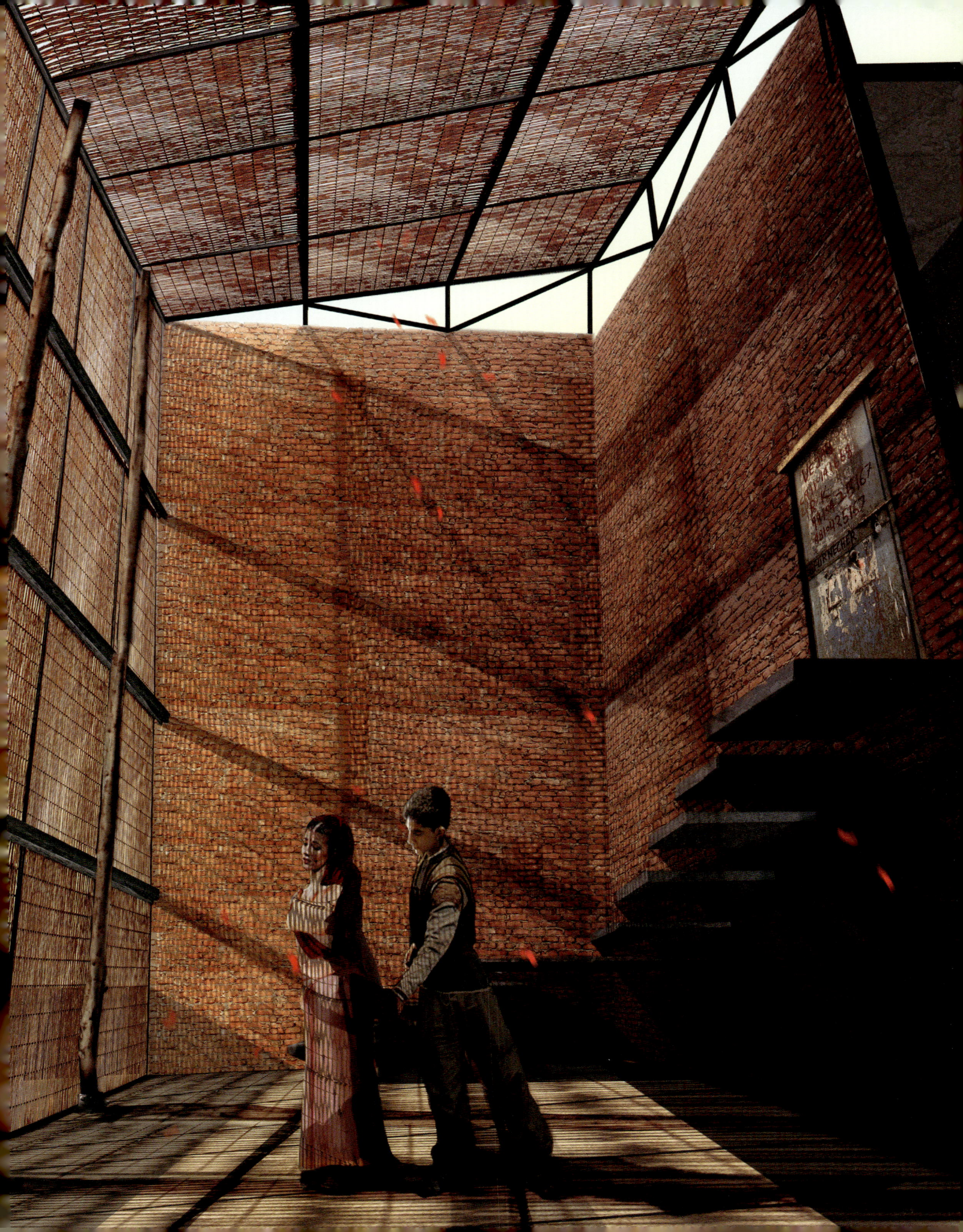

Toby Pear
Dargah Library, Tower and Madrassa, Chirag Delhi, South Delhi

Reinvigorating Chirag Delhi by providing a public library and student accommodation.

See Chapter 5, Example (4) for a description of this project.

below left
imagined reconstruction of the 14th century Dargah complex
below right
view of Qutub Minar from proposed tower
bottom left
plan of Dargah chowk
bottom right
view of proposed library tower at night

this page:
left
rooftop view of proposed tower
middle
elevation of tower and library courtyard
bottom
front elevation of Madrassa fronting on to Dargah chowk

previous page:
view into library courtyard

Emre Turkmen
Peacock Corner, Rooftop Streets and Workshops accessed through Water Towers, Khirki Village, South Delhi

A scheme for a craft market along a rooftop route accessed by water filtration towers, thus providing public space and clean water for the local inhabitants.

See Chapter 5.

right
view of Khirki rooftops showing use by both women and men
below
view of rooftop children's drawing workshop

the mosque is now highly visible and the 'bat tower' trumpets Khirki's street in the sky

children's theatre group comes every week ... local kids gather round to watch their antics

views from the top of the tower are spectacular ... try not to disturb the bats

anyone can wonder round Khirki mosque ... take care to miss flying cricket balls

it is cool and quiet inside the mosque and breezy above it ... the roof is used as a park ... the old men play cards ... women collect water from the local well on Peacock Corner

above
elevation of Peacock's Corner showing Khirki Mosque and new access and water tower
below
view of Peacock's Corner

top
section through Peacock's Corner showing water tank, new
access and water tower and roof top street
bottom
view of rooftop artists' studio

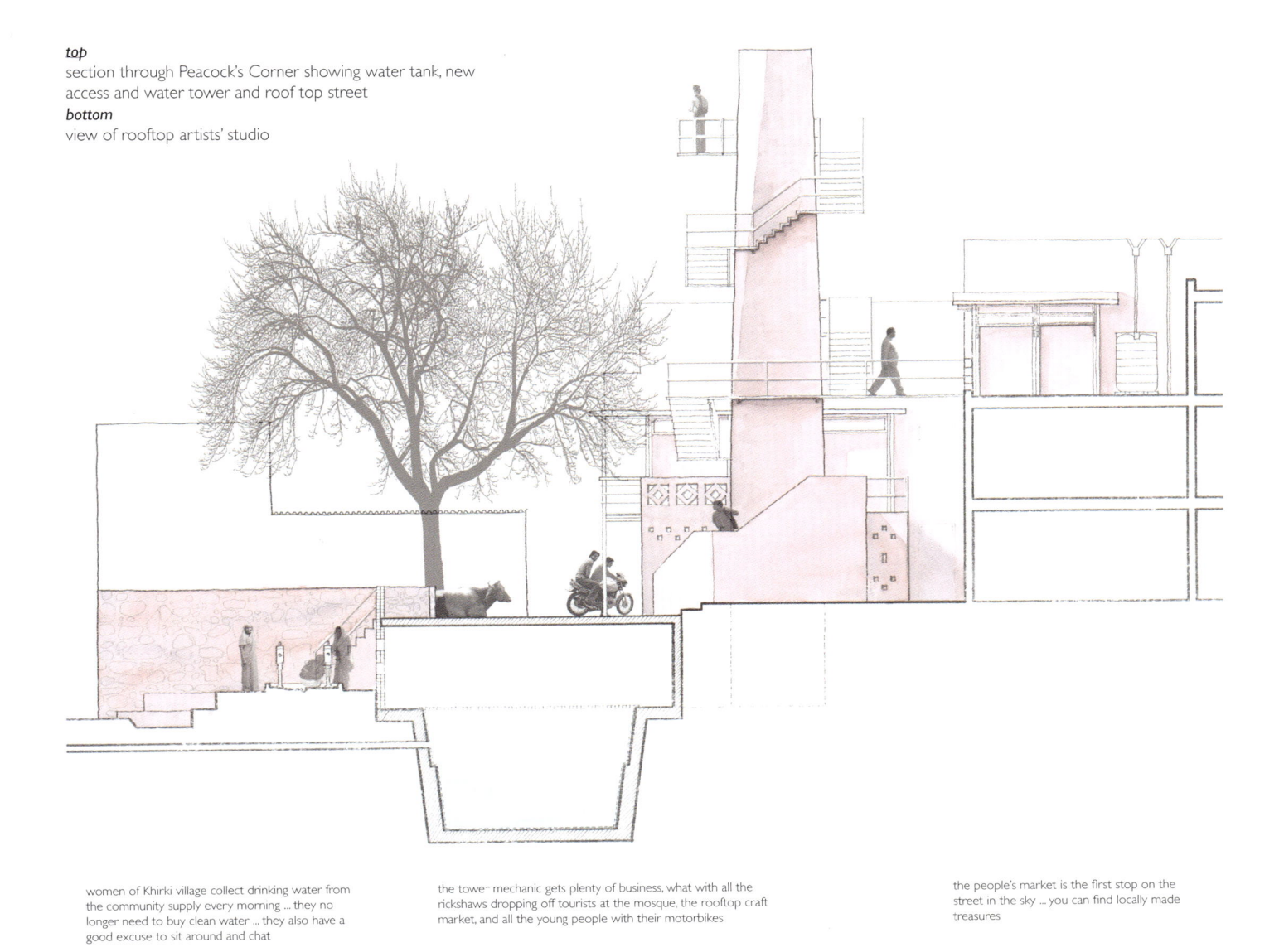

women of Khirki village collect drinking water from
the community supply every morning ... they no
longer need to buy clean water ... they also have a
good excuse to sit around and chat

the tower mechanic gets plenty of business, what with all the
rickshaws dropping off tourists at the mosque, the rooftop craft
market, and all the young people with their motorbikes

the people's market is the first stop on the
street in the sky ... you can find locally made
treasures

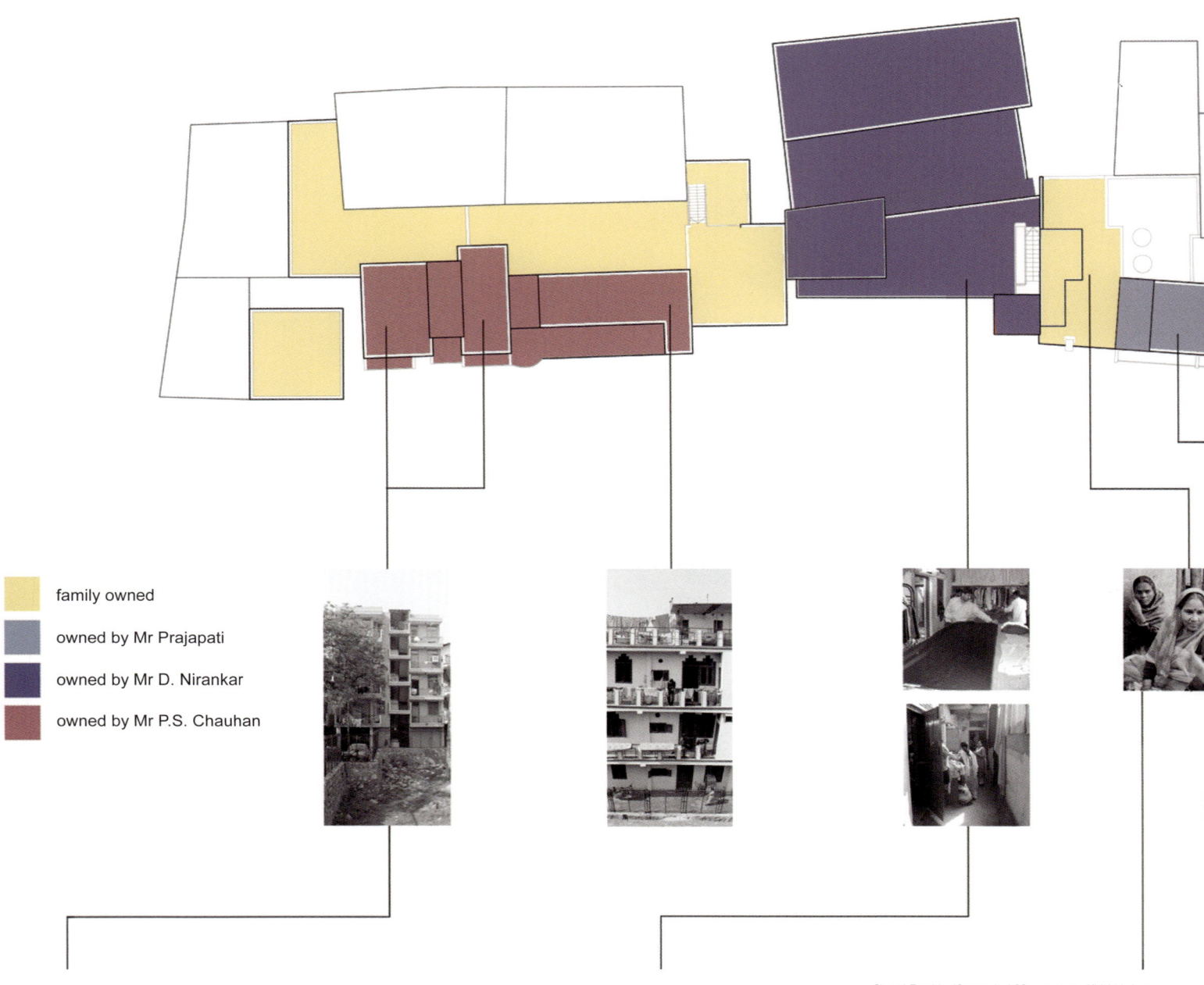

family owned

owned by Mr Prajapati

owned by Mr D. Nirankar

owned by Mr P.S. Chauhan

Mr P. S. Chauhan lives in the northeast corner of the mosque at no. KK55 with his wife Usha (sunray), mother, daughter and son who is top of the class because he only sleeps four hours a night and is going to do IT engineering at college.

They acquired their plot in 1996 and built a five-storey house. Mr Chauhan owns five other properties in Khirki village, one of which is this large block. He also owns a fast-food place in Noida which opened last month and he is hoping to open another in the next year.

Mr Chauhan was pleased about the new District Centre being built nearby because it will increase his property values and improve the area.

The fashion factory

Nadia is 22 and just graduated from the Delhi College of fashion. She is the principal and sole fashion designer for Nyx, a clothes manufacturing company. Nadia's designs are all original and hand made by 20 people working at no. 157 Khirki Village. Here there are two floors and a roof which also has two rooms. Clothes are made on the first floor and administration is on the ground floor.

Mr Nirankar, the landlord, is one of the four major property owners in the village but does not live there. He owns three back-to-back plots.

Clothes are sold elsewhere as the building is not suitable for sales.

Shanti Devi is 48, married 32 years ago. Khirki is her husband's ancestral home. She has two daughters and two sons. her elder married daughter lives with her husband elsewhere. The other three children, all young adults, live with her.

She gets up at 7am, prepares breakfast and wakes the kids. During the day the boys look for work. Her husband leaves for work and she finishes the housework and then goes outside to sit in the sun. At about 2:45 the shade swallows up the outside so she goes to sit with other ladies of the neighbourhoods elsewhere.

Shanti knows very little about the old mosque but thinks children should be allowed to play there. This will be banned once the government cleans up the space. She likes the idea of having a market nearer as she has to travel to Madangir to shop.

The painters

There are 5 graduates from the Delhi College of Art living in Khirki. Kamal Kumar Dora, Ankur Rana and Yati Jaiswal are painters whilst Hardeep Dhayal and Raghubir Singh run their own events company. They also moonlight as photographers working for the national television company.

They each rent out a studio flat on separate floors for 1800 rupees per month from Mr Prajapati. They have lived here for a year since graduating and regularly exhibit in local galleries. They have problems finding space to paint. Ankur and Kamal like to paint on the roof in the evening and through the morning. With rising prices they will be driven out and need opportunities to supplement their income and space and light to paint.

Morika is 20 years old and lives at the end of the main alley entrance from the west of the mosque. She lives with her parents and older brother in KK239 on the second floor.

At roof level there is a shower room and a wall mounted sink with some corrugated plastic for shade. In her room she studies for her fashion course. She is in her first of two years at Delhi University. She is in western dress.

On the balcony she displays a sign for Tae Kwon Do lessons. She was a champion of this sport but had to quit because of injury. She misses it but now spends her spare time going to the cinema in the nearby PVR complex.

main image
patterns of ownership, phase one buildings, potential participants in the streets in the sky project

this page:
top
patterns of ownership for buildings surrounding Khirki Mosque
middle
plan of existing buildings surrounding Khirki Mosque at rooftop level

Bo Tang
Kite Centre and Haveli Campus, Chitli Qabar Bazaar, Old Delhi

See Chapter 5, Old and New Delhi: The Conglomerate Order Contained and Fragmented for a description of the site and context.

this page:
right
view of cycle rickshaw being loaded with commercial printed matter in alley
below
plan of the mohalla in 2007

facing page:
top left
view looking down on mohalla from adjacent building
top right
view of goats feeding
middle
section from mohalla through to Chitli Qabar Bazaar
bottom
existing sectional elevation across mohalla looking towards Chitli Qabar Bazaar

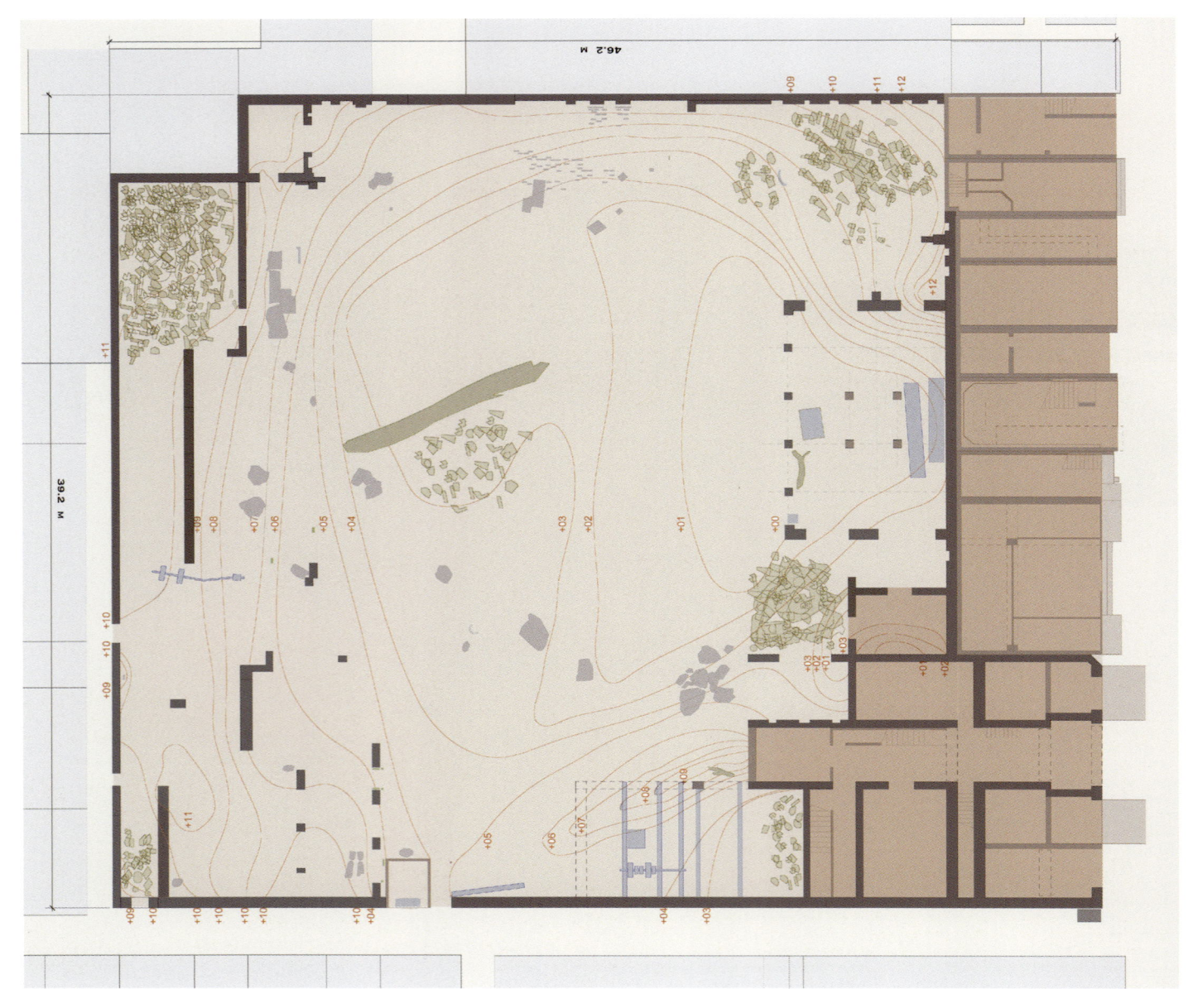

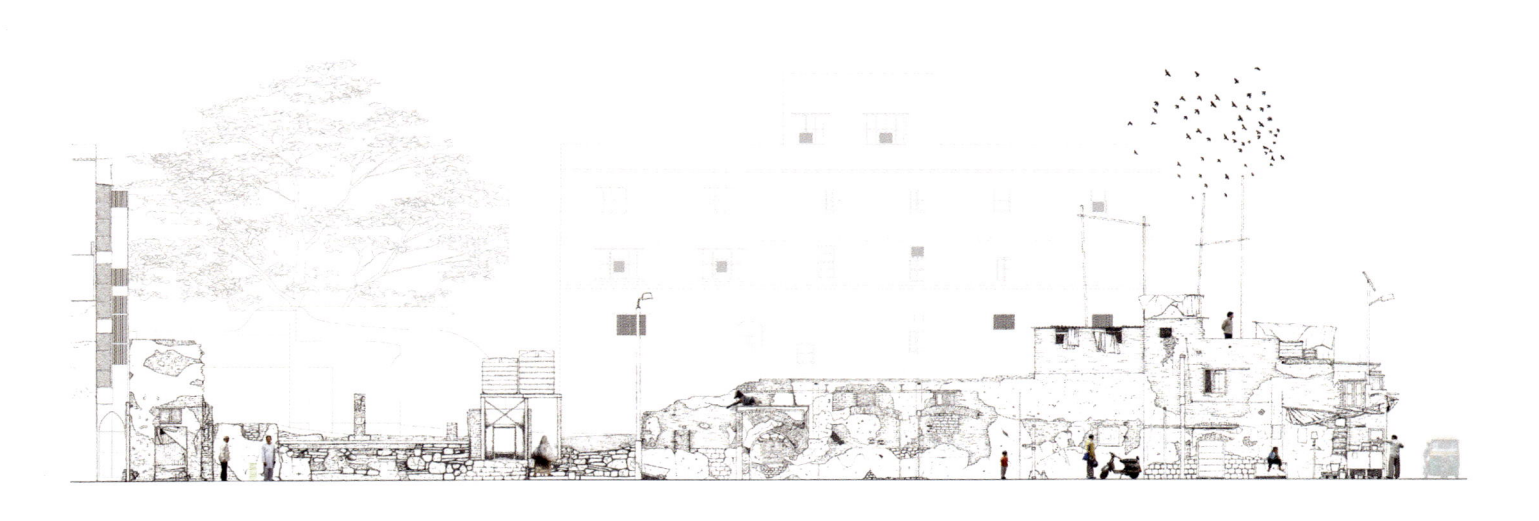

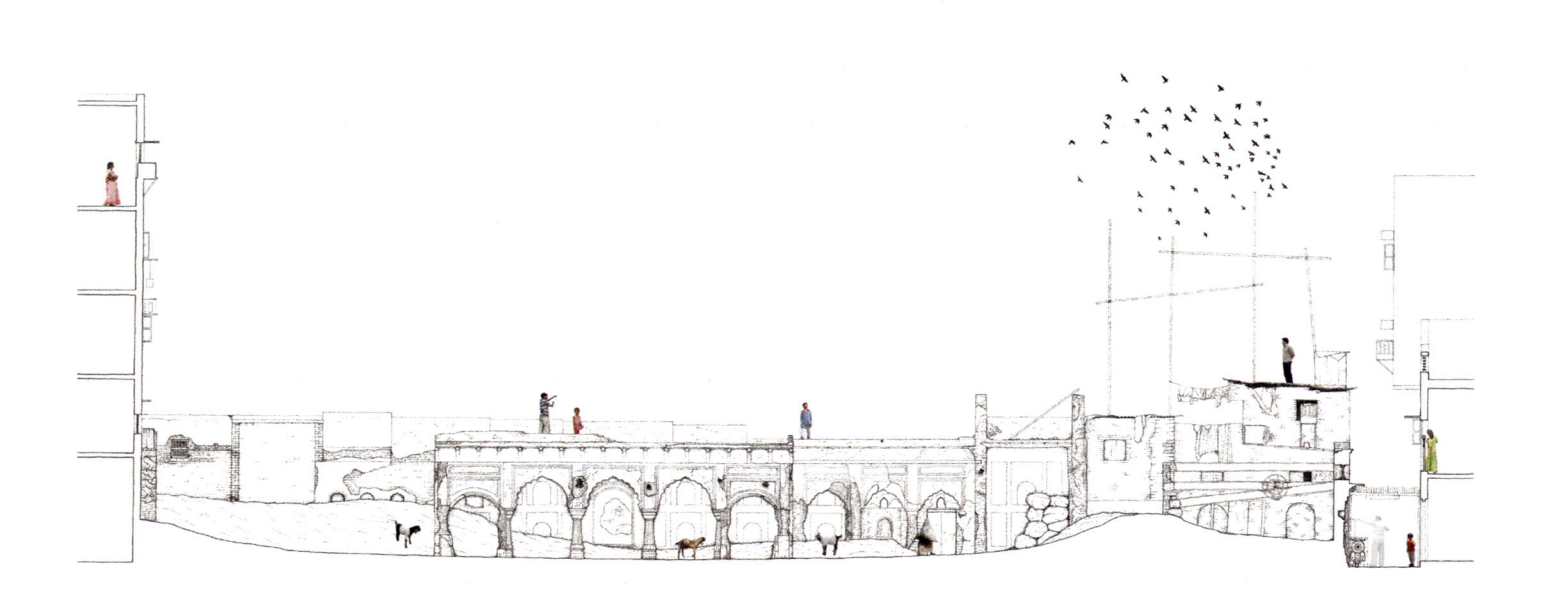

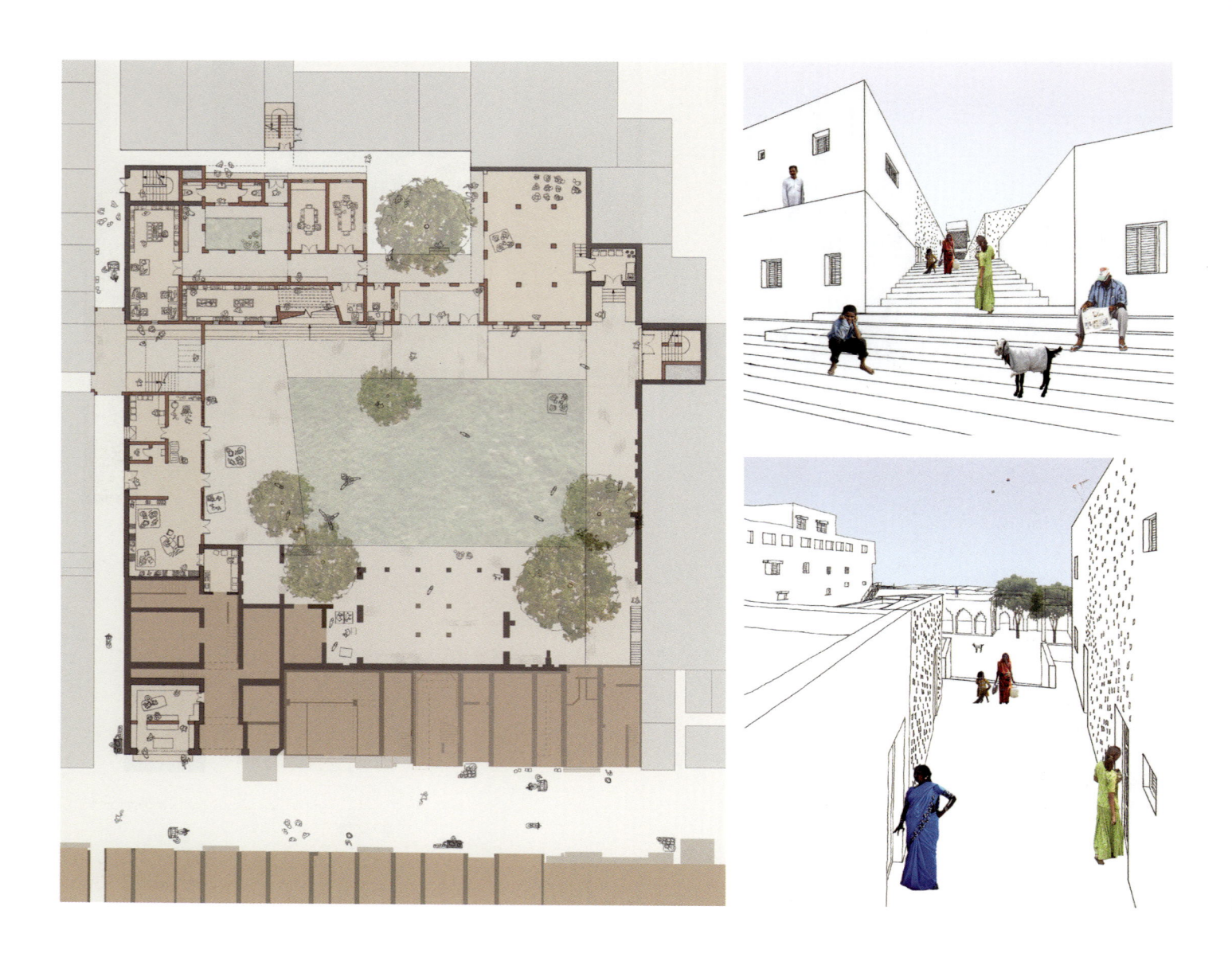

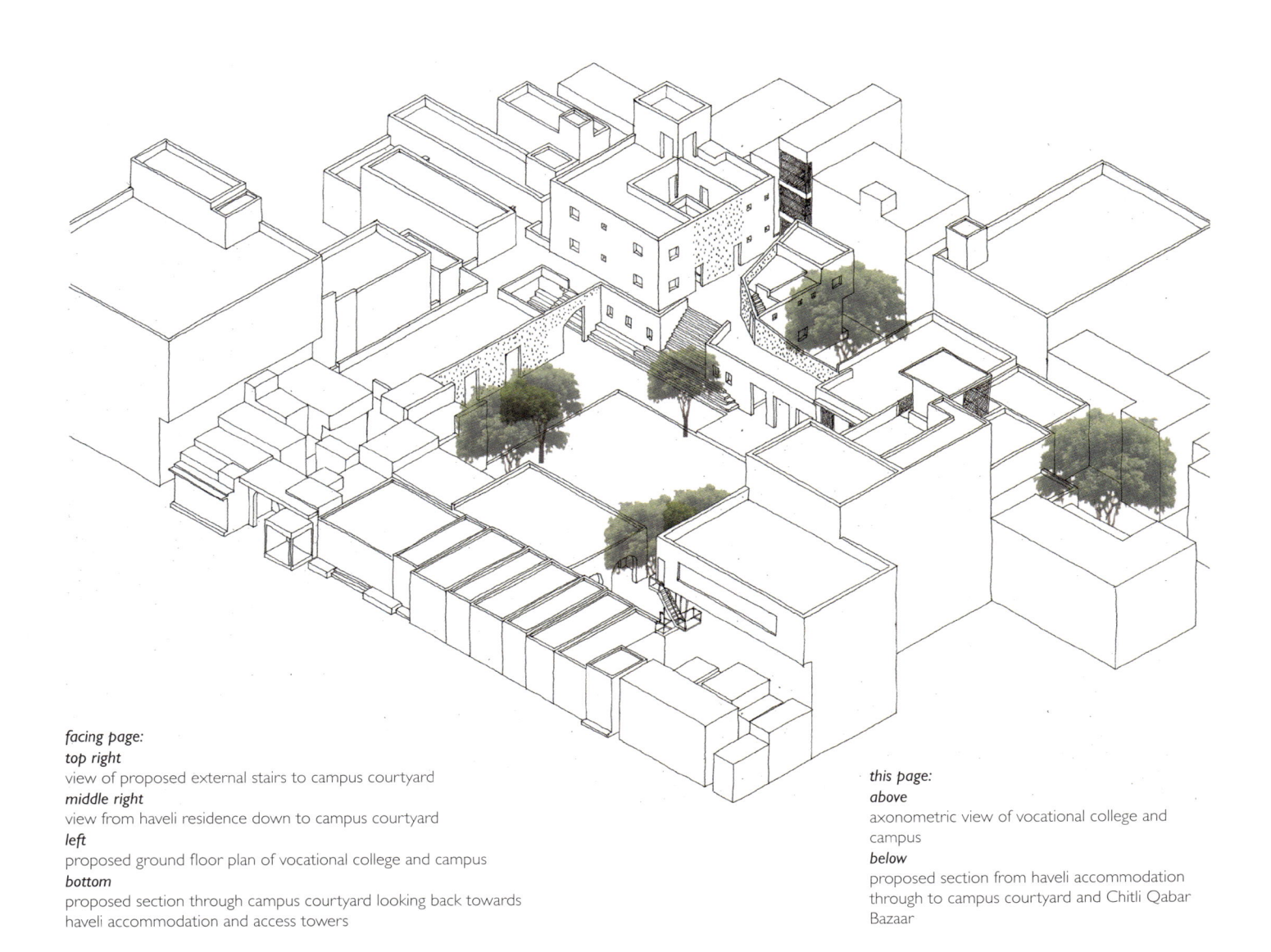

facing page:
top right
view of proposed external stairs to campus courtyard
middle right
view from haveli residence down to campus courtyard
left
proposed ground floor plan of vocational college and campus
bottom
proposed section through campus courtyard looking back towards
haveli accommodation and access towers

this page:
above
axonometric view of vocational college and
campus
below
proposed section from haveli accommodation
through to campus courtyard and Chitli Qabar
Bazaar

Shamoon Patwari
Sorting Office, Summer School and Indoor Souk, Chitli Qabar Bazaar, Old Delhi

See Chapter 5, Old and New Delhi: The Conglomerate Order Contained and Fragmented for a description of the site and context.

below
plan of the proposed haveli summer school, sorting office and indoor souk
right
sketch of the hidden Baq'ullah Khan haveli entrance

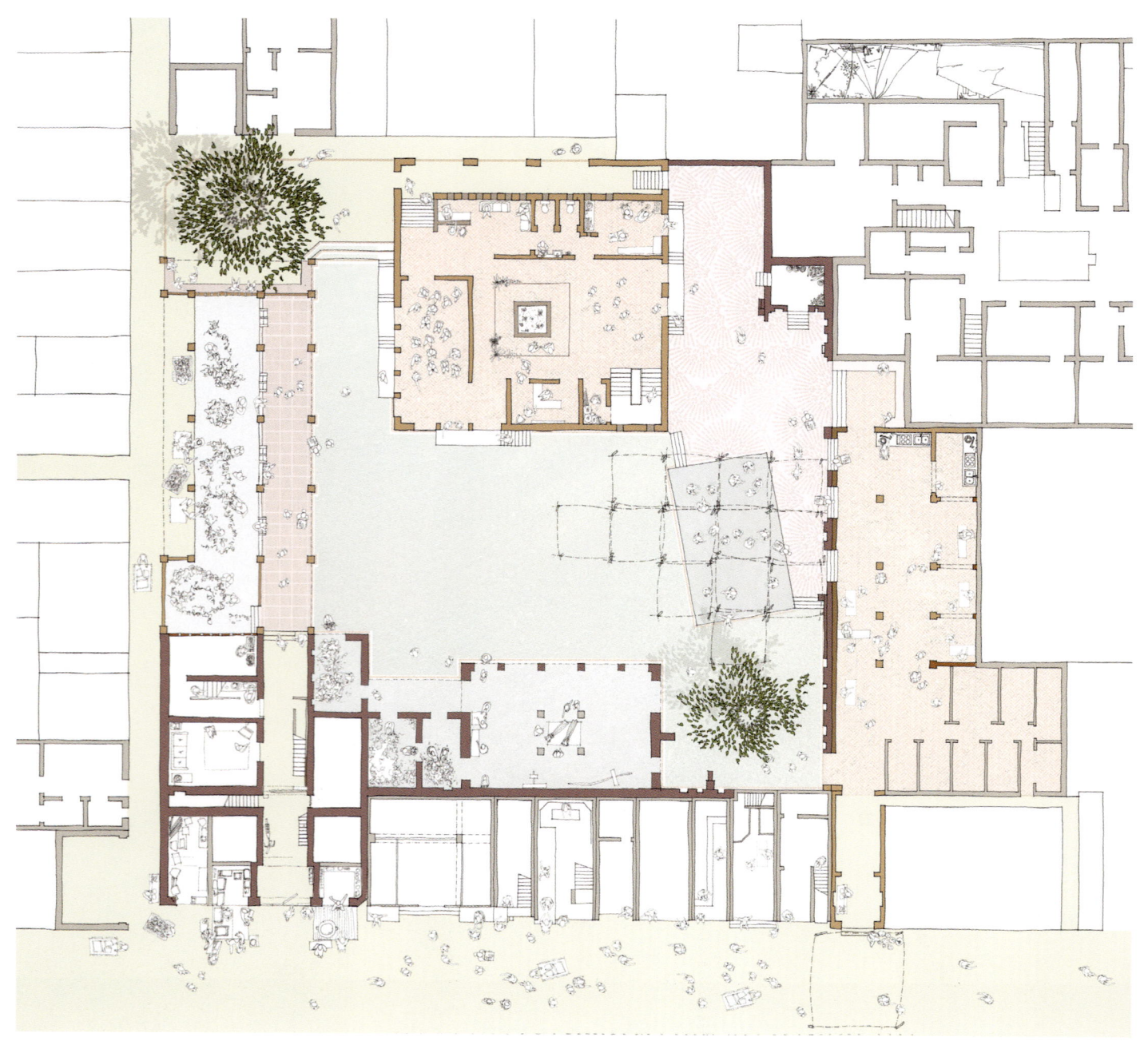

left
sketch section through squatters' residence
at the entrance to the old haveli
below
proposed section through souk, restored
haveli and sorting office
bottom
proposed section through haveli, souk and
Chitli Qabar Bazaar

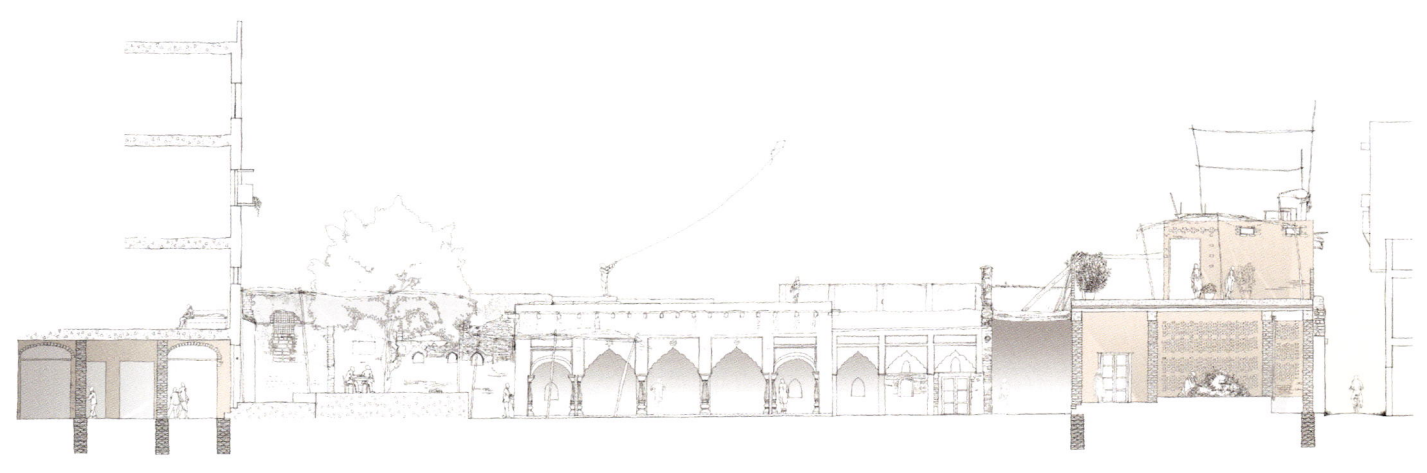

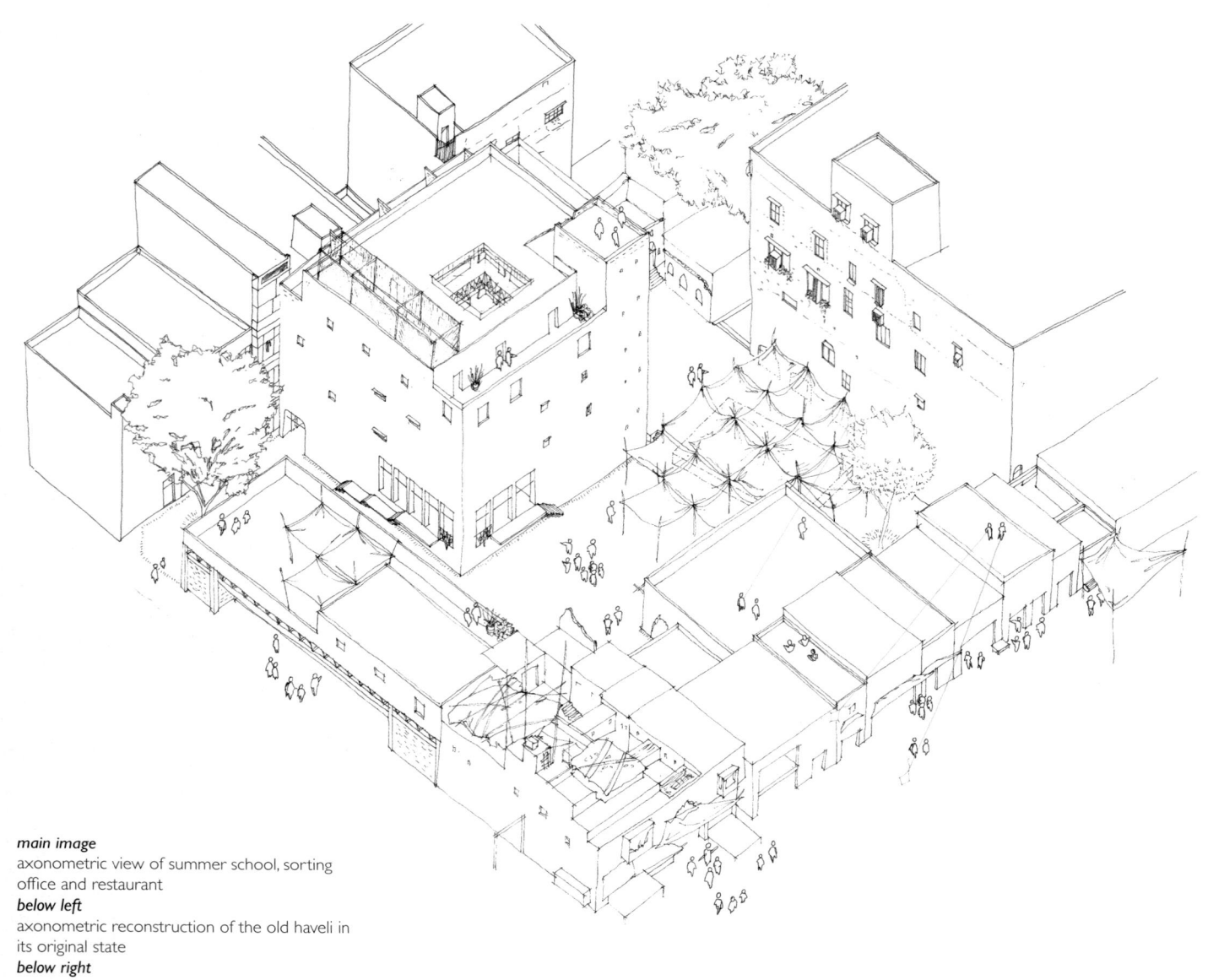

main image
axonometric view of summer school, sorting office and restaurant
below left
axonometric reconstruction of the old haveli in its original state
below right
axonometric of the ruined haveli today

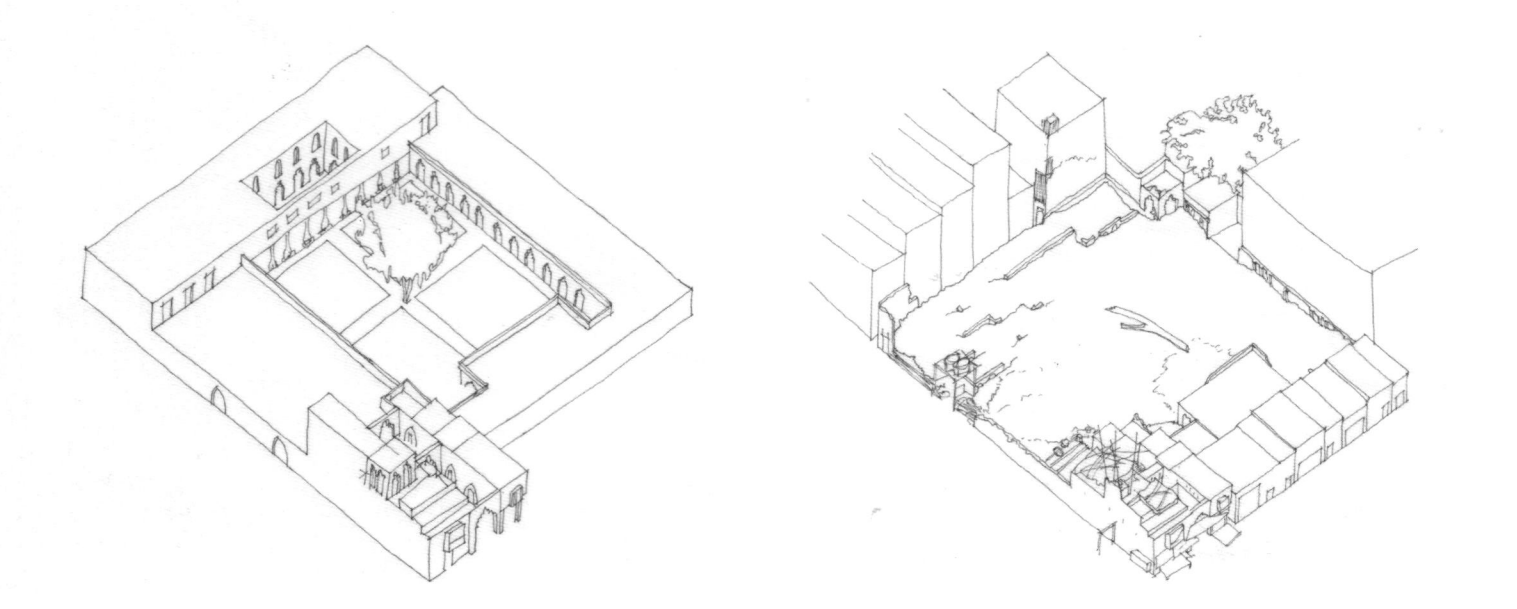

theme 4

Urban Nomads

Emma Curtin
New Houses and Education Space, Marwari Basti, Agra

See Chapter 6 for more illustrations of this scheme.

this page:
main image
detail plan of existing settlement showing water
(supply) pipe and drainage
below
plan of new temple school
bottom
axonometric of new temple school

overleaf
plan of proposals for two new houses for Bhima
and Balby and for a new Temple School

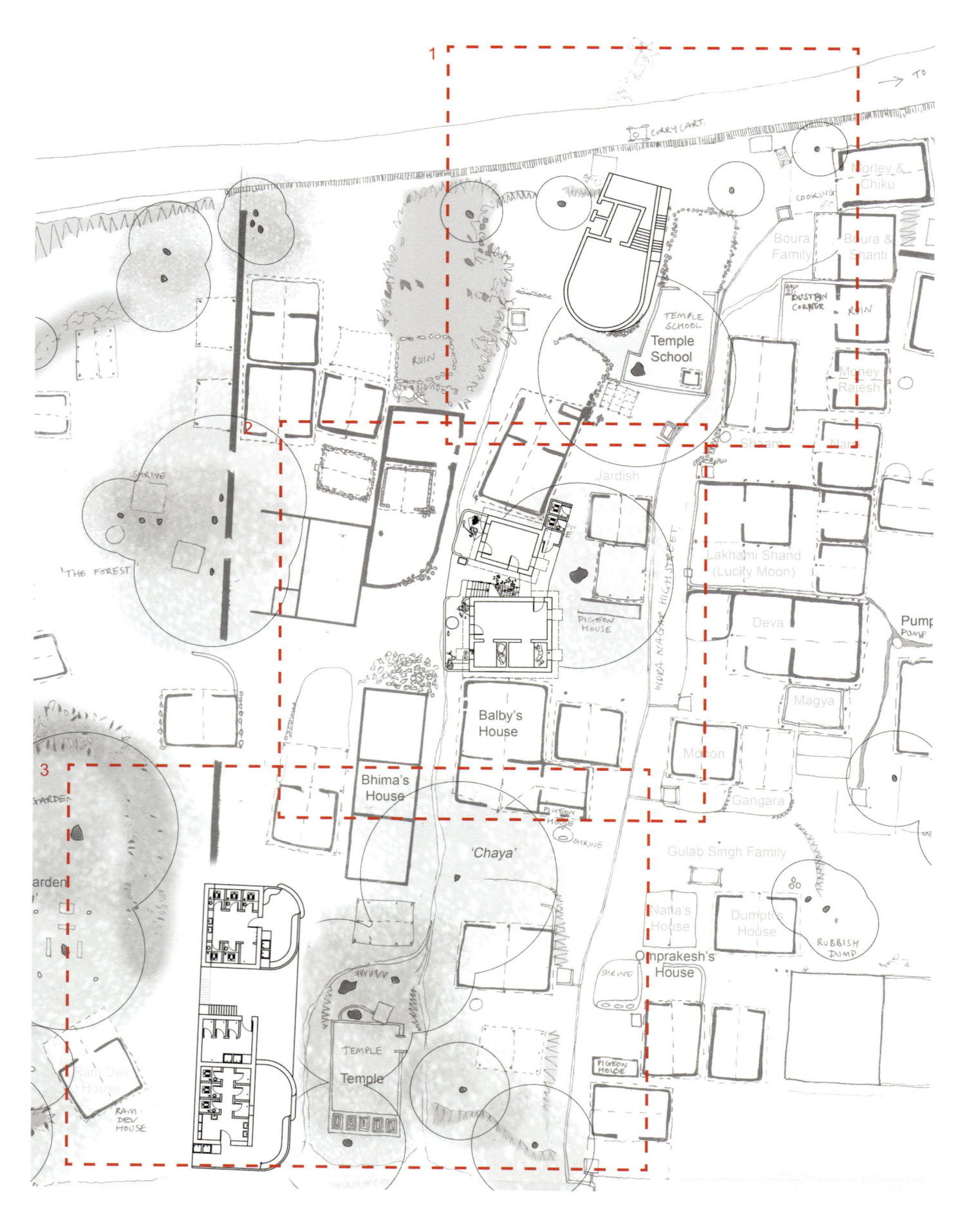

Marco Sosa
Cultural and Amenity Places, Marwari Basti, Agra

Landscapes of Change. A scheme to provide basic amenities (sanitation, education, healthcare, market and workshops) for an urban nomadic community.

See Chapter 6, Appropriate Amenity Buildings, for a description of this project.

top
aerial view of part of existing settlement
middle
north–south section from road through
proposed visitor entrance to open courtyard
bottom
view of colonnade and open courtyard showing
rooftop terrace

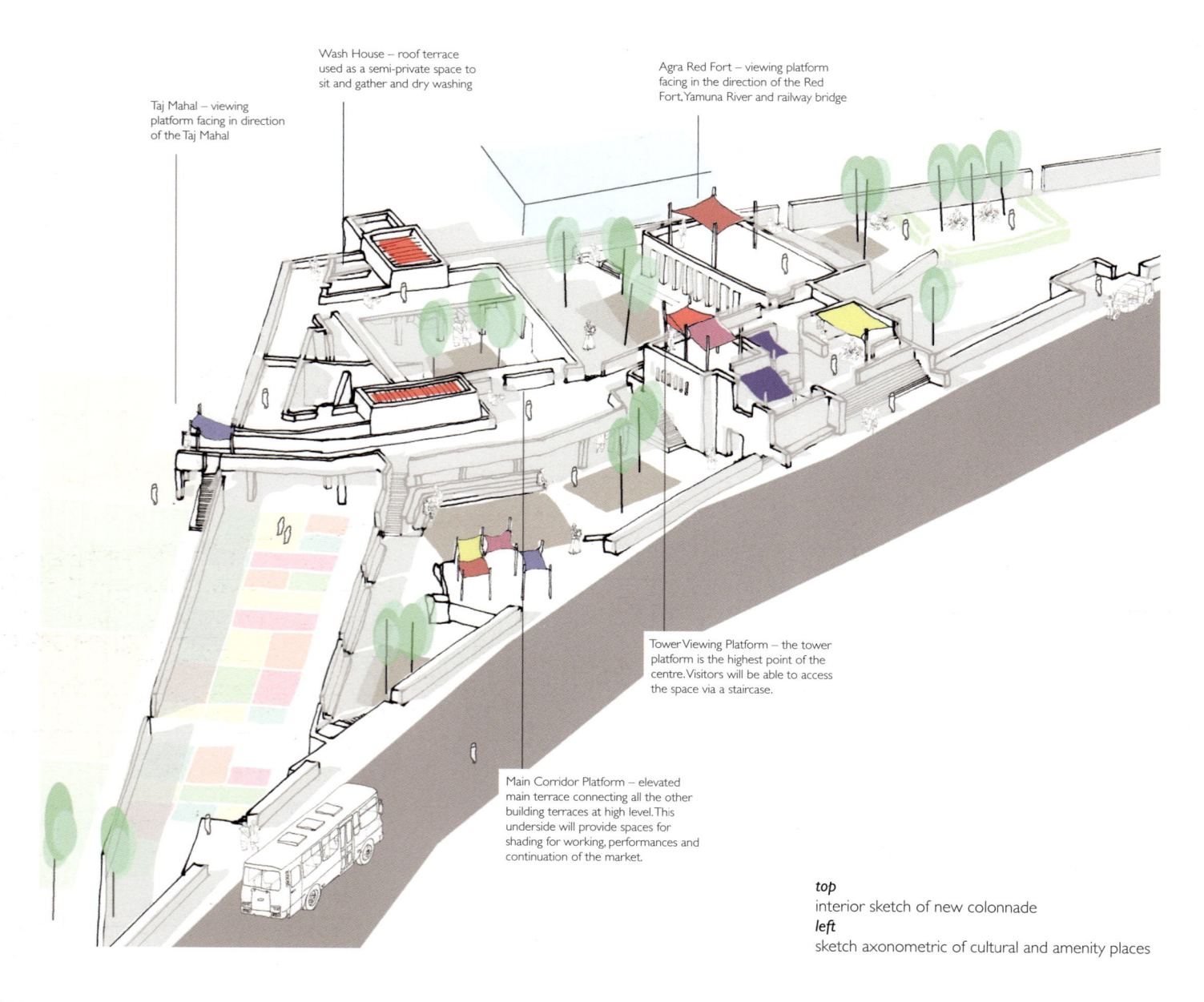

Taj Mahal – viewing platform facing in direction of the Taj Mahal

Wash House – roof terrace used as a semi-private space to sit and gather and dry washing

Agra Red Fort – viewing platform facing in the direction of the Red Fort, Yamuna River and railway bridge

Tower Viewing Platform – the tower platform is the highest point of the centre. Visitors will be able to access the space via a staircase.

Main Corridor Platform – elevated main terrace connecting all the other building terraces at high level. This underside will provide spaces for shading for working, performances and continuation of the market.

top
interior sketch of new colonnade
left
sketch axonometric of cultural and amenity places

theme 5

Leisure and Livelihoods

Nat Horner
Work/Shop Houses for Waste Pickers, North Panchsheel Vihar, South Delhi

An opportunity for waste pickers to move to permanent residence and waste recycling. The development of a new 'High Street' lined with shop houses. Experimentation with a rooftop prototype pergola made from bamboo frames and waste paper bundles.

See Chapter 7, Example (2) for an account of the development of the pergola roof. See Chapter 4 for waste pickers and a description of the site and context.

four phased plans showing the assembly of a high street for shop houses along the nala flood plain

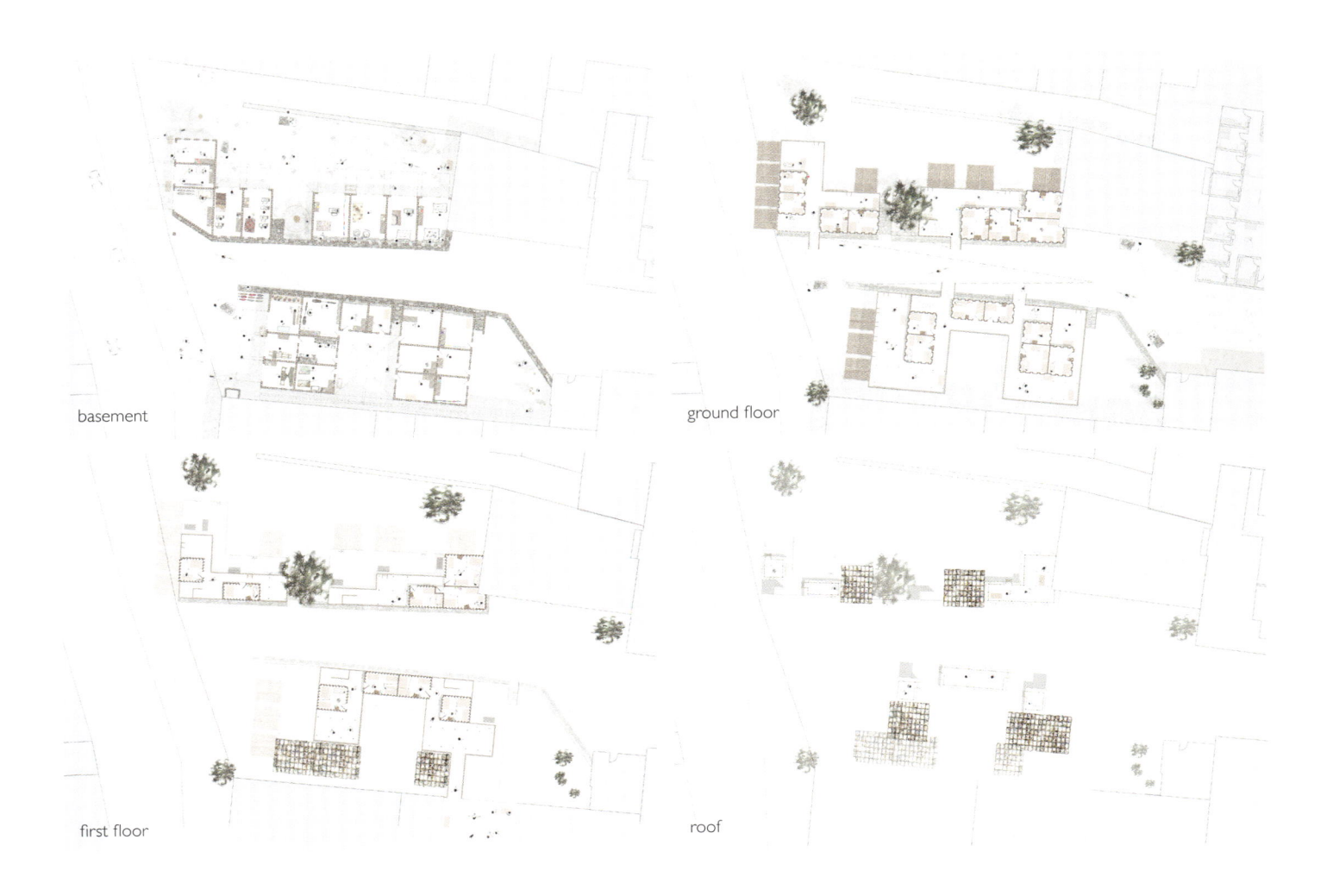

basement

ground floor

first floor

roof

facing page:
top
view inside paper and bamboo roof canopy
bottom
elevation of workshops and courtyards

this page:
above
four plans showing basement, ground floor, first floor and roof levels of courtyard work/shop house
below left
view of basement workshop
below middle/right
two axonometric views of phased construction of shop house

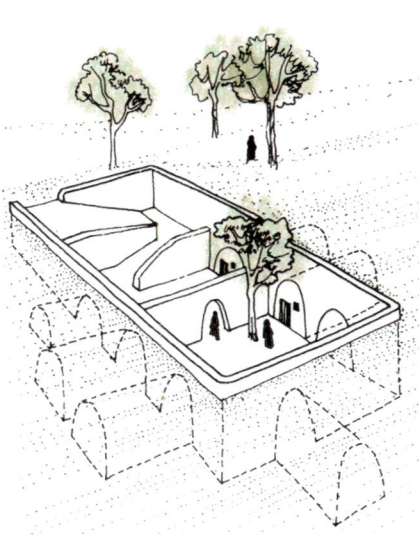

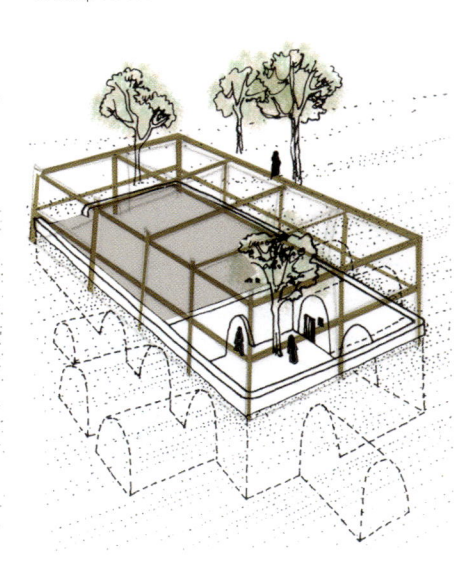

Francesca Pont
Open Air Cinema and Lovers' Tower, Brahmpuri, Meerut

Raised on a stepped plinth to avoid flooding, providing conviviality and sanctuary to the young; sandwiched between a rickshaw driver's rest stop and an urban dairy, this building would transform the backstreets of suburban Meerut.

See Chapter 6, Appropriate Amenity Buildings for a description of this project.

main image
roof plan of cinema
below
view of cinema entrance

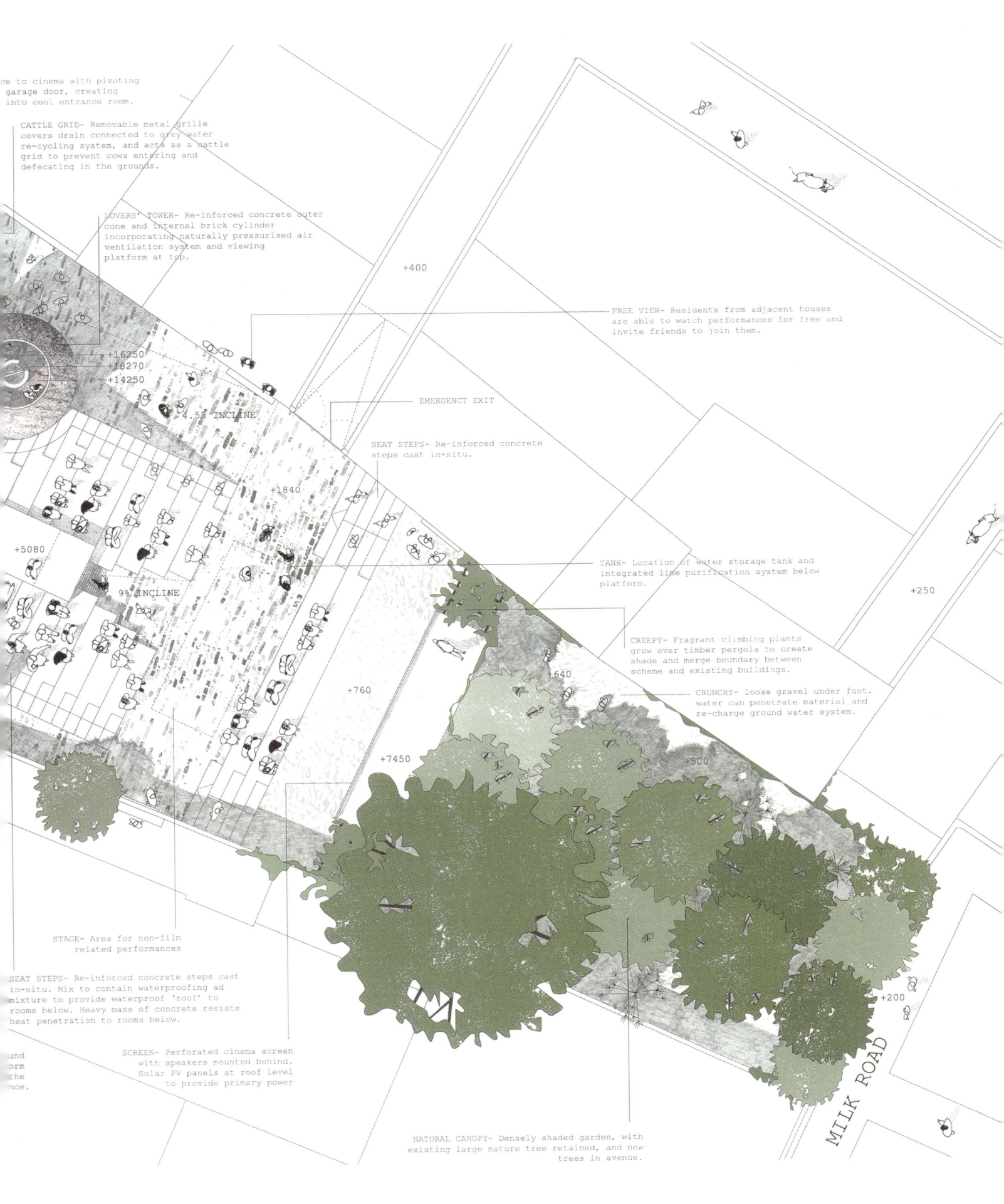

...e to cinema with pivoting garage door, creating into cool entrance room.

CATTLE GRID- Removable metal grille covers drain connected to grey water re-cycling system, and acts as a cattle grid to prevent cows entering and defecating in the grounds.

LOVERS' TOWER- Re-inforced concrete outer cone and internal brick cylinder incorporating naturally pressurised air ventilation system and viewing platform at top.

+400

FREE VIEW- Residents from adjacent houses are able to watch performances for free and invite friends to join them.

+16250
+18270
+14250

4.5% INCLINE

EMERGENCT EXIT

SEAT STEPS- Re-inforced concrete steps cast in-situ.

+1840

+5080

9% INCLINE

TANK- Location of water storage tank and integrated lime purification system below platform.

+250

CREEPY- Fragrant climbing plants grow over timber pergola to create shade and merge boundary between scheme and existing buildings.

+1640

CRUNCHY- loose gravel under foot. water can penetrate material and re-charge ground water system.

+760

+500

+7450

STAGE- Area for non-film related performances

SEAT STEPS- Re-inforced concrete steps cast in-situ. Mix to contain waterproofing ad mixture to provide waterproof 'roof' to rooms below. Heavy mass of concrete resists heat penetration to rooms below.

+200

...und ...orm ...che ...ce.

SCREEN- Perforated cinema screen with speakers mounted behind. Solar PV panels at roof level to provide primary power

MILK ROAD

NATURAL CANOPY- Densely shaded garden, with existing large mature tree retained, and new trees in avenue.

263

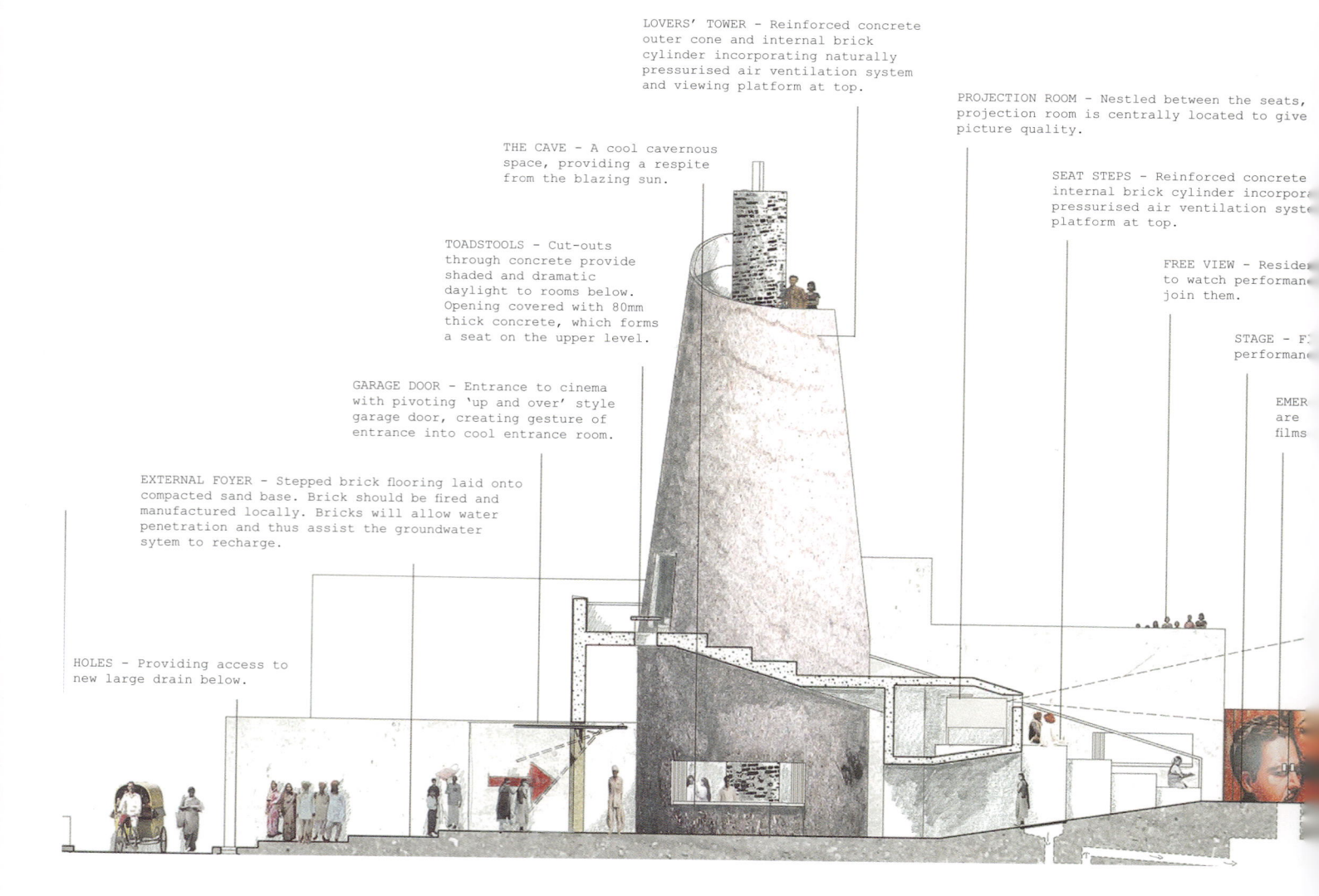

LOVERS' TOWER - Reinforced concrete
outer cone and internal brick
cylinder incorporating naturally
pressurised air ventilation system
and viewing platform at top.

PROJECTION ROOM - Nestled between the seats,
projection room is centrally located to give
picture quality.

THE CAVE - A cool cavernous
space, providing a respite
from the blazing sun.

SEAT STEPS - Reinforced concrete
internal brick cylinder incorpora
pressurised air ventilation syste
platform at top.

TOADSTOOLS - Cut-outs
through concrete provide
shaded and dramatic
daylight to rooms below.
Opening covered with 80mm
thick concrete, which forms
a seat on the upper level.

FREE VIEW - Reside
to watch performan
join them.

STAGE - F
performan

GARAGE DOOR - Entrance to cinema
with pivoting 'up and over' style
garage door, creating gesture of
entrance into cool entrance room.

EMER
are
films

EXTERNAL FOYER - Stepped brick flooring laid onto
compacted sand base. Brick should be fired and
manufactured locally. Bricks will allow water
penetration and thus assist the groundwater
sytem to recharge.

HOLES - Providing access to
new large drain below.

264

and
ly
ng

acent houses are able
and invite friends to

non-film related

3 metre high metal doors
with scenes from famous

ion of water storage tank and
ime purification system below

SCREEN - Perforated cinema screen sized for both wide-screen and 'normal' film sizes. The screen is mounted on a three storey structure providing accommodation for migrant and nomadic workers. Shaded by planting Solar PV panels at roof level to provide primary power.

PICNICS - Beneath the canopy conversations and snoozes take place.

CREEPY - Fragrant climbing plants grow over timber pergola to create shade and merge boundary between scheme and existing buildings.

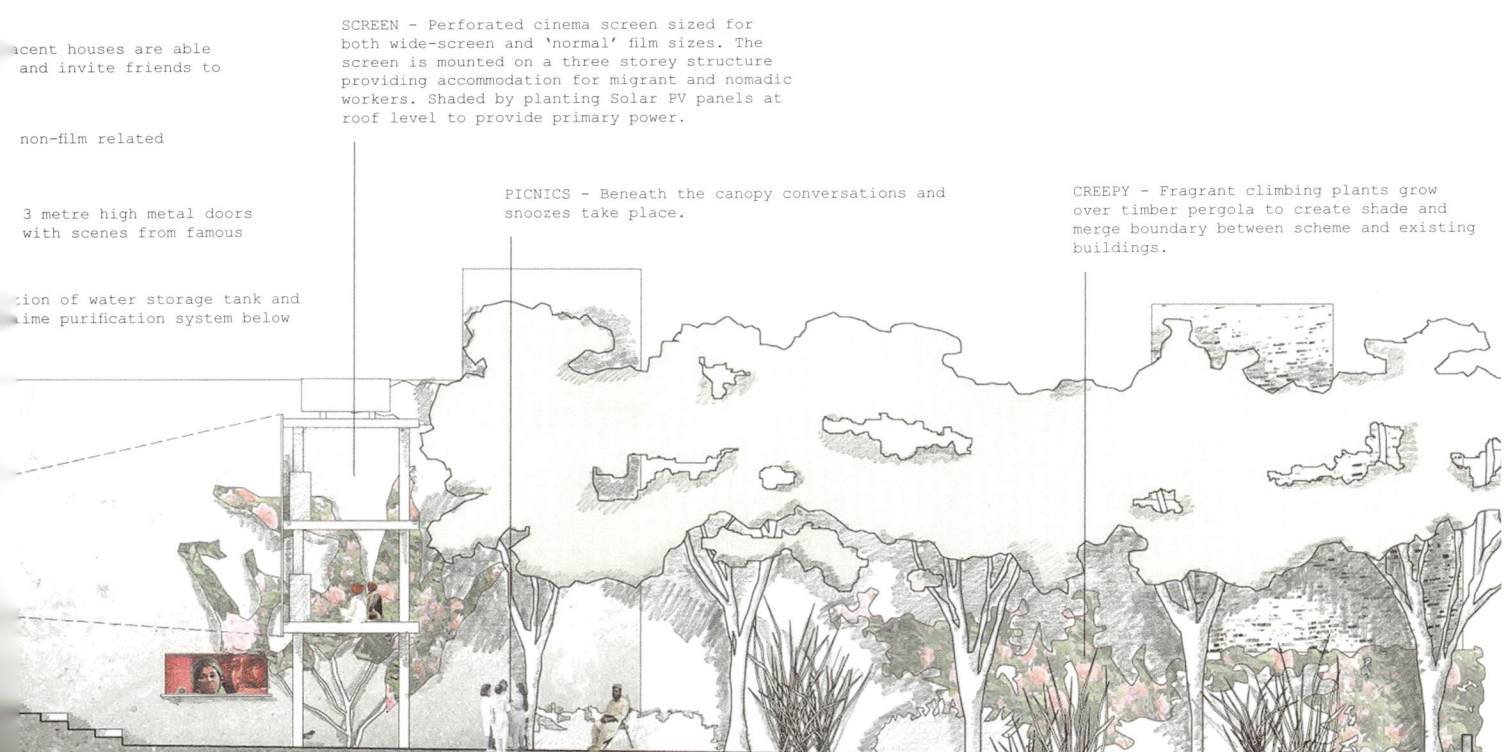

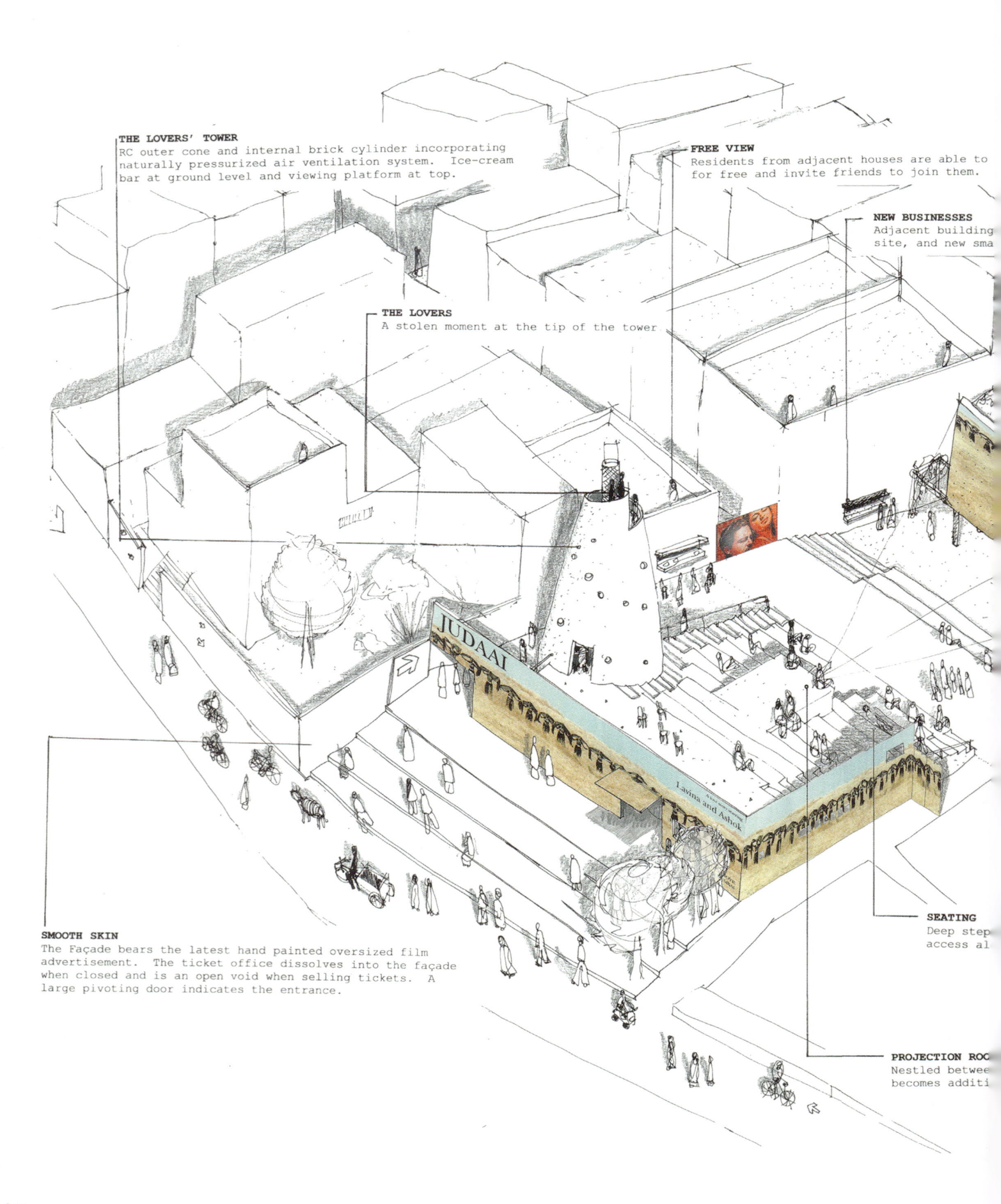

THE LOVERS' TOWER
RC outer cone and internal brick cylinder incorporating naturally pressurized air ventilation system. Ice-cream bar at ground level and viewing platform at top.

THE LOVERS
A stolen moment at the tip of the tower

FREE VIEW
Residents from adjacent houses are able to for free and invite friends to join them.

NEW BUSINESSES
Adjacent building site, and new sma

SEATING
Deep step access al

PROJECTION ROO
Nestled betwee becomes additi

SMOOTH SKIN
The Façade bears the latest hand painted oversized film advertisement. The ticket office dissolves into the façade when closed and is an open void when selling tickets. A large pivoting door indicates the entrance.

JUDAAI

Lavina and Ashok

LOVERS' TOWER – Reinforced concrete outer cone and internal brick cylinder incorporating naturally pressurised air ventilation system and viewing platform at top.

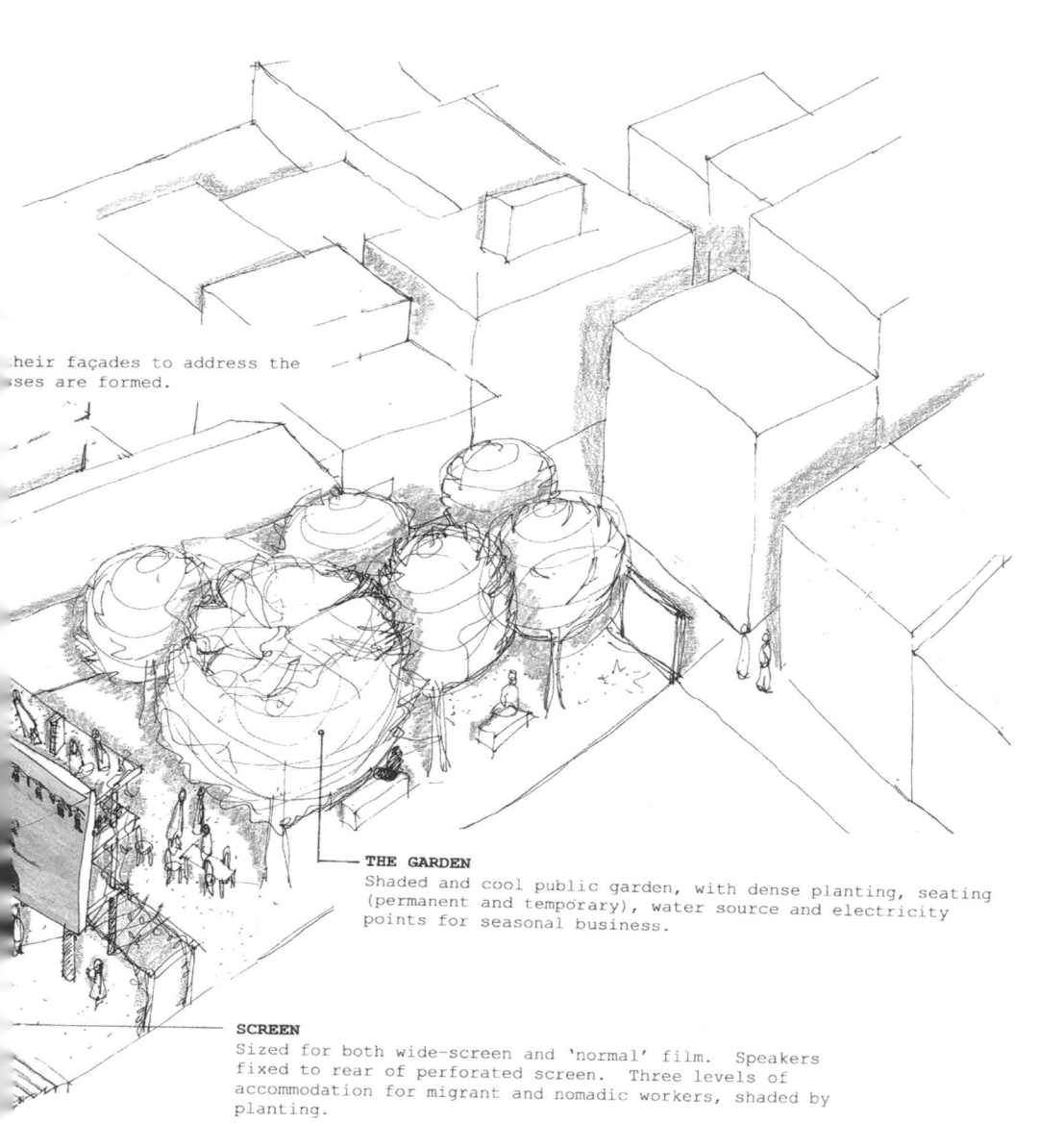

heir façades to address the
ses are formed.

THE GARDEN
Shaded and cool public garden, with dense planting, seating (permanent and temporary), water source and electricity points for seasonal business.

SCREEN
Sized for both wide-screen and 'normal' film. Speakers fixed to rear of perforated screen. Three levels of accommodation for migrant and nomadic workers, shaded by planting.

THE PLATFORM
Flat area between seating, which allows access to all seating areas and emergency exits. It can be used for marriage ceremonies and other non-film related presentations.

both sitting (and reclining) and

of seats, the top of the room
g.

 N

main image
axonometric of cinema, tower and garden behind
above
detail plan of lovers' tower

Anthony Corke
Vocational College and Cricket Ground, Kuchhpura, Agra

See Chapter 2, Example (1), for a description of this scheme within its context.

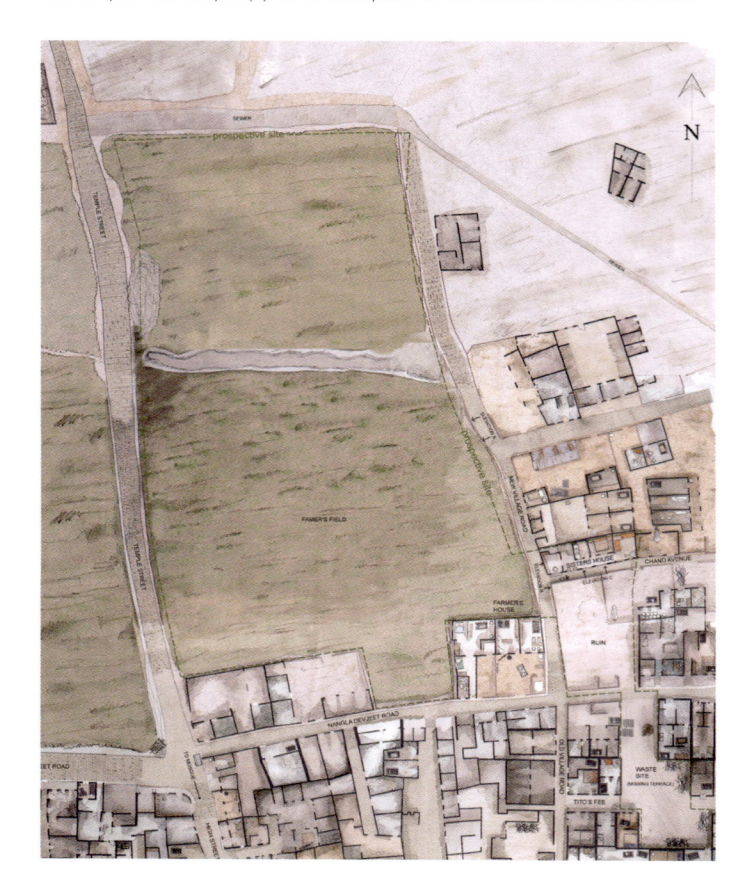

above left
plan of existing site for cricket ground and vocational centre
above right
proposed plan of cricket ground and vocational centre
left
the surveyor's plans for field irrigation
below
two projections showing alternating irrigation plans for the cricket ground

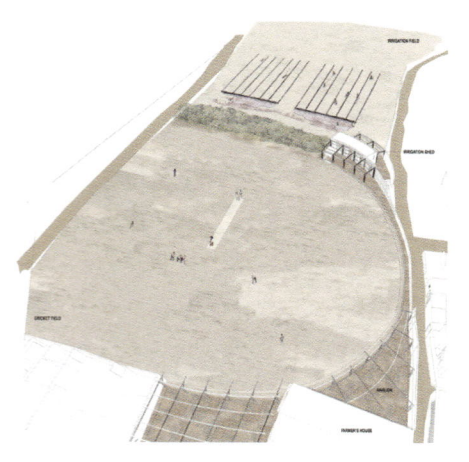

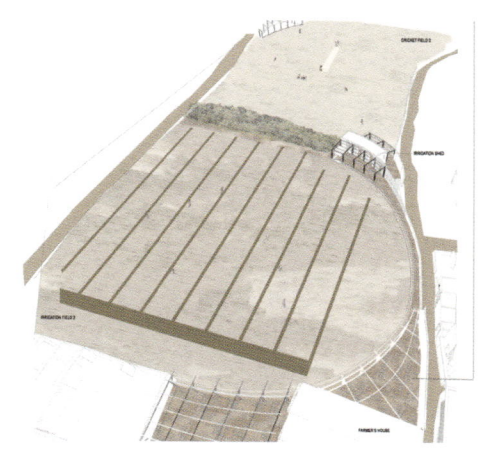

left
children who helped students draw up a
survey of the village
below middle
proposed elevation showing tower extension
to surveyor's house
bottom
proposed elevation of vocational college
and surveyor's house as cricket score board
tower

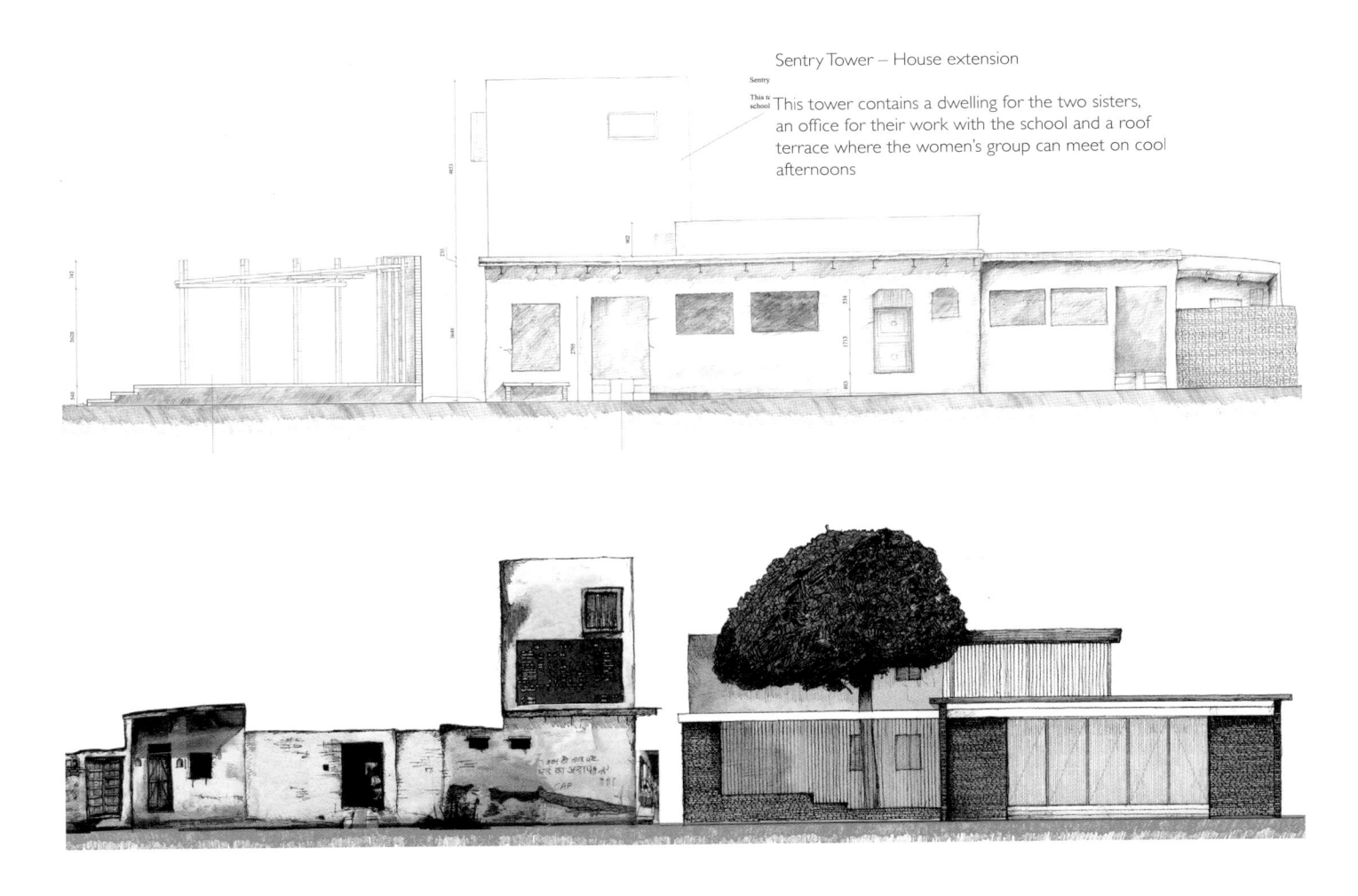

Sentry Tower – House extension

This tower contains a dwelling for the two sisters,
an office for their work with the school and a roof
terrace where the women's group can meet on cool
afternoons

269

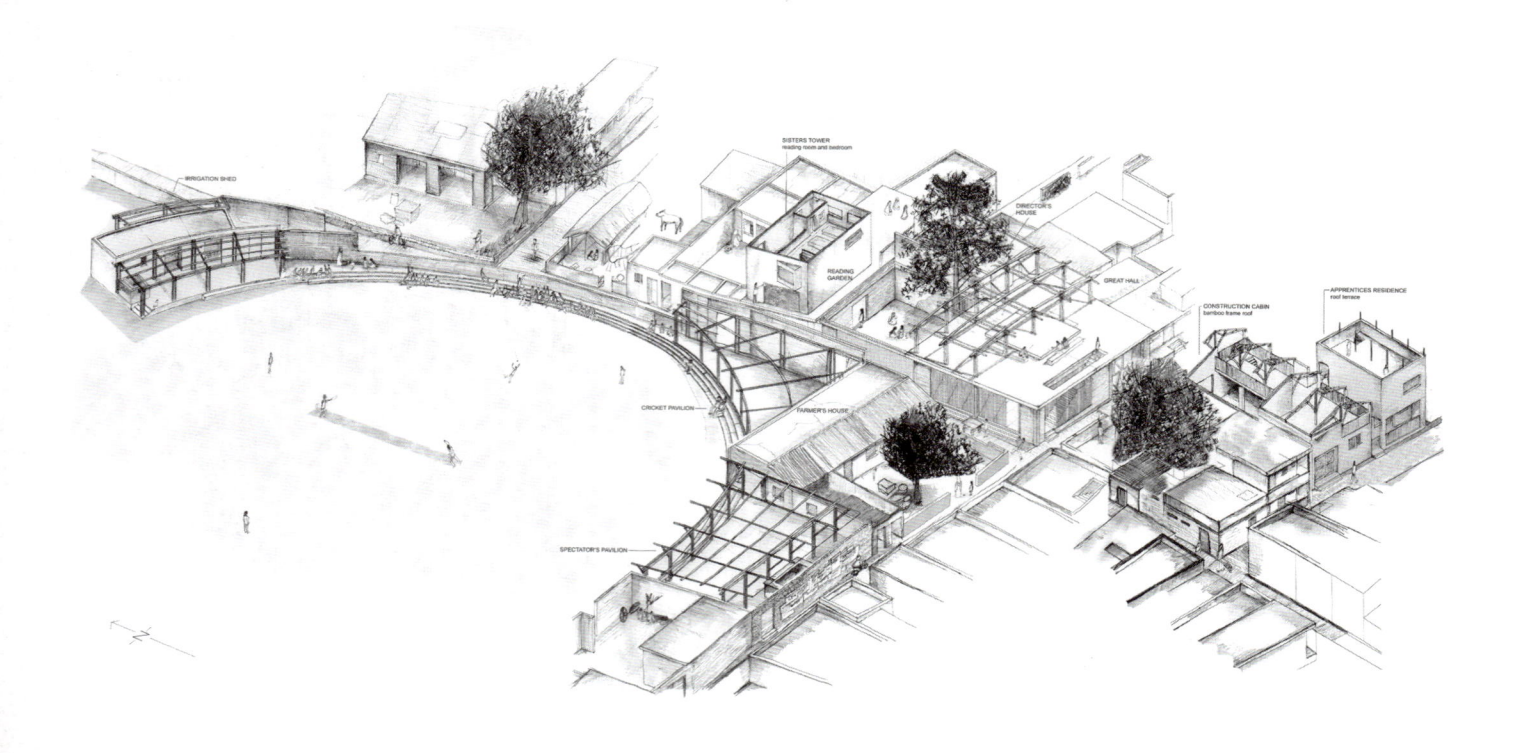

above
proposed axonometric projection of cricket ground and vocational college
right
sketches of students surveying
below left
aerial block view of vocational college integrated with settlement pattern
below middle
plan of godfather's house
below right
plan of vocational college and corner of cricket ground

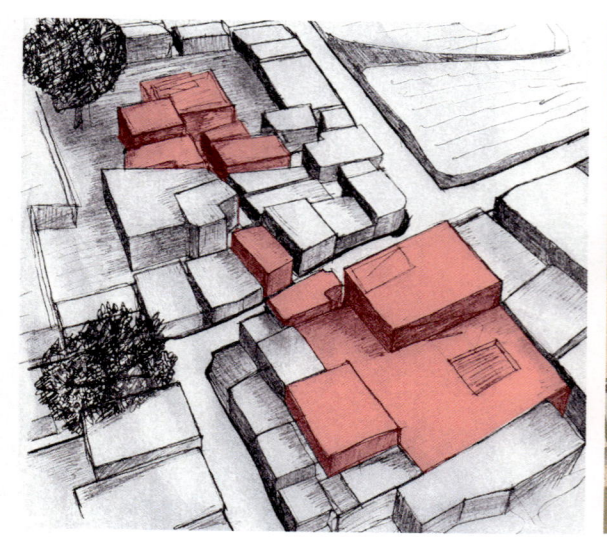

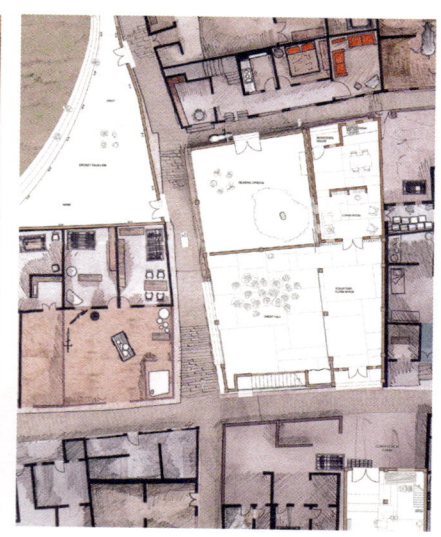

theme 6

Live Projects

Kuchhpura Sanitation Upgrading Project, Agra

See Chapter 8 for a full description and further illustrations of this scheme to provide household toilets and washrooms for the population of Kuchhpura.

this page:
right
schoolchildren attending a hygiene awareness workshop highlighting issues caused by open defecation
Shamoon Patwari
below
meeting of Kuchhpura Panchayat (village council) attended by students

overleaf:
top
plan of Meera's street, the first to have household toilets installed
amended from Studio Booklet 06/07
bottom
plan of Kuchhpura village showing location of toilet sites
amended from Studio Booklet 06/07

NISHA'S HOUSE

RASHMI'S HOUSE

MEENA'S HOUSE

MEERA'S HOUSE

SUNITA'S HOUSE

POOJA'S HOUSE

SONU'S HOUSE

GEETA'S HOUSE

TAJGANJ

SITE 3

SITE 1

HUMAYAN MOSQUE

SITE 2

100M RESTRICTION ZONE AROUND MOSQUE - PLANNING PERMISSION REQUIRED FROM ARCHAEOLOGICAL SURVEY OF INDIA (ASI) FOR ANY CONSTRUCTION WORK IN THIS AREA

MAIN SEWER

SHARING A SEPTIC TANK BETWEEN TWO HOUSEHOLDS

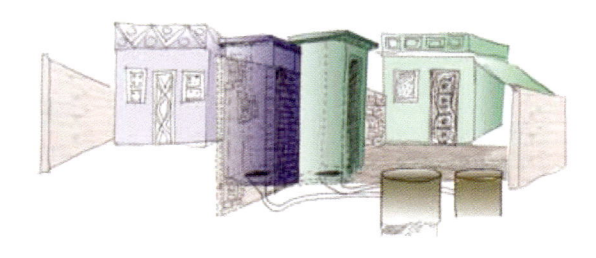

MAINTENANCE

right
sketches showing how a septic tank works, is
maintained and how it can be shared
Katarzyna Banak
below left
excavating the pits for the proposed decentralised
waste water treatment system
CURE
below right
plan showing analysis of existing surface water
drainage in the vicinity of Kuchhpura in preparation
for proposals for the installation of a treatment
system
amended from Studio Booklet 06/07

HOW A SEPTIC TANK WORKS

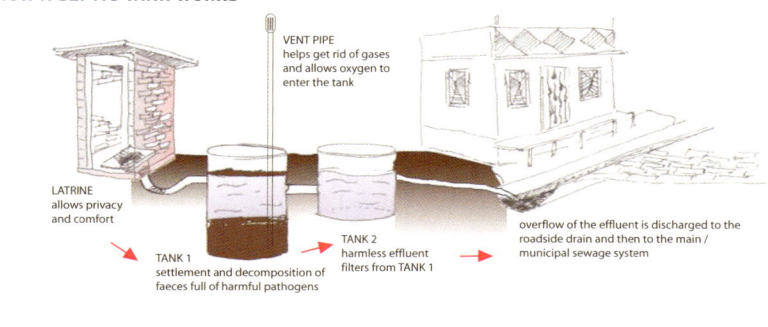

VENT PIPE
helps get rid of gases
and allows oxygen to
enter the tank

LATRINE
allows privacy
and comfort

TANK 1
settlement and decomposition of
faeces full of harmful pathogens

TANK 2
harmless effluent
filters from TANK 1

overflow of the effluent is discharged to the
roadside drain and then to the main /
municipal sewage system

1   Primary New Kuchhpura drain
2   Secondary Old Kuchhpura drain
3   Junction of primary and secondary drains
4   Junction where secondary drain meets community toilet structure
5   Combined drain leading to Yamuna river
6   Assumed forced drain flooding field A
7   Point of broken primary drain flooding field A

A   Flooded field (seasonal)
B   Low lying flooded area within Mehtab Bagh wall

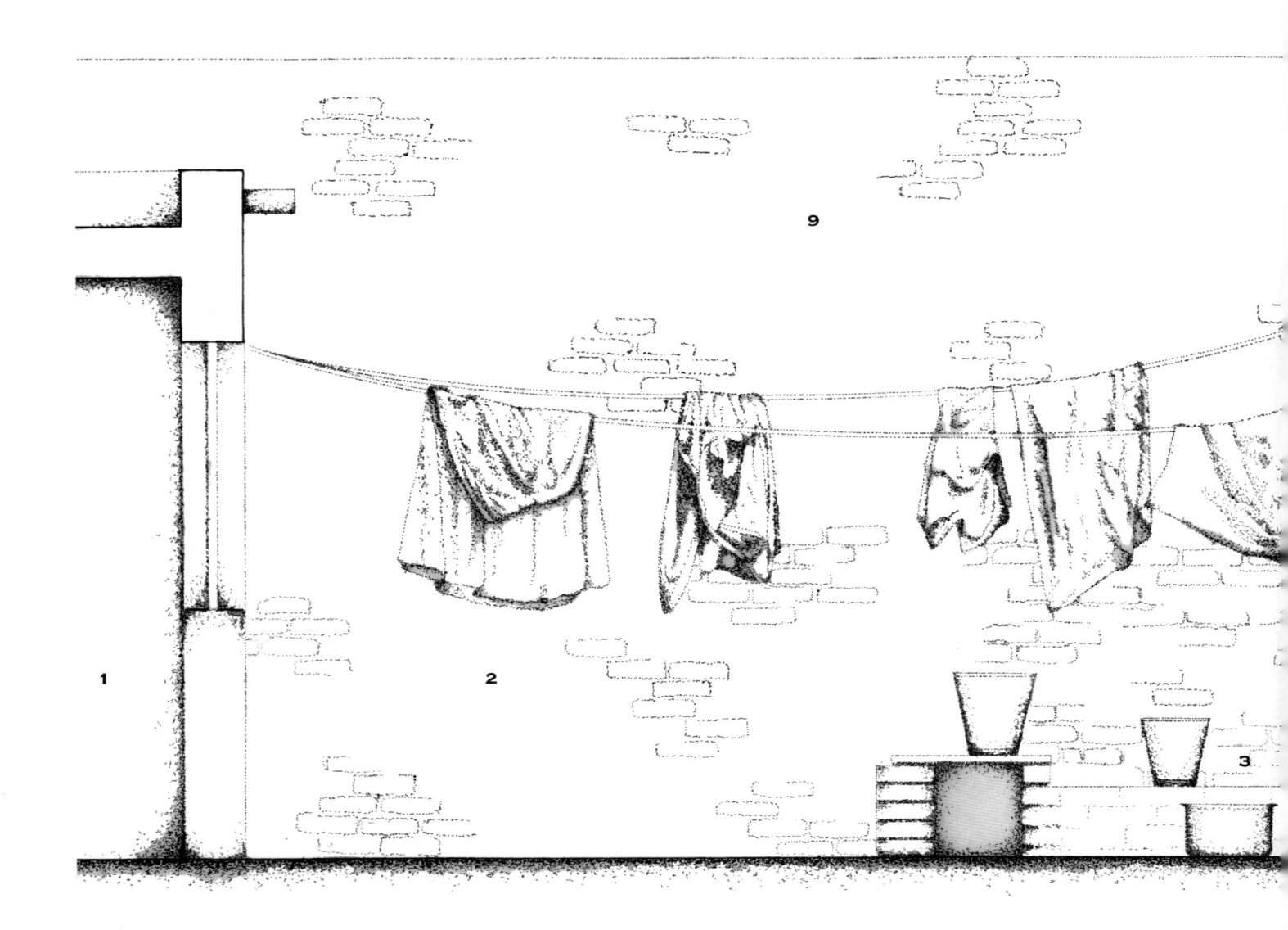

section through Meera's back yard showing newly installed septic tank and toilet
Bo Tang

1. Meera's House
2. Courtyard
3. Washing platform
4. Extended bricks - potential for extension to structure
5. Toilet
6. Precast concrete septic tank I (primary) – 8ft deep
7. Precast concrete septic tank II (secondary) – 4ft deep
8. Temporary curtain awaiting door
9. Existing brick wall
10. Outflow pipe
11. Existing drain
12. Access hatch to septic tank I for maintenance
13. Inflow pipe
14. Lamp post

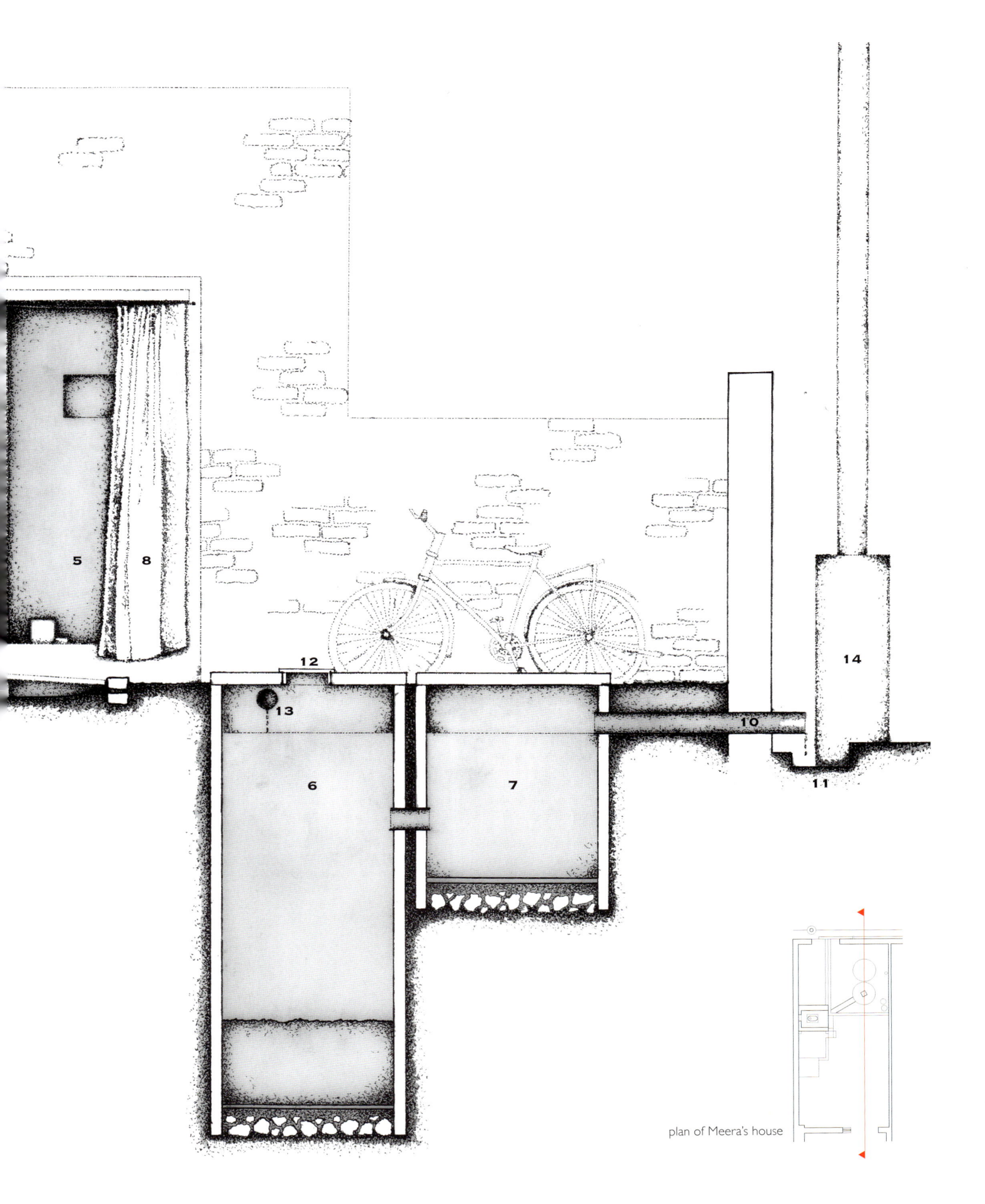

plan of Meera's house

Quarry Community Classrooms, Navi Mumbai

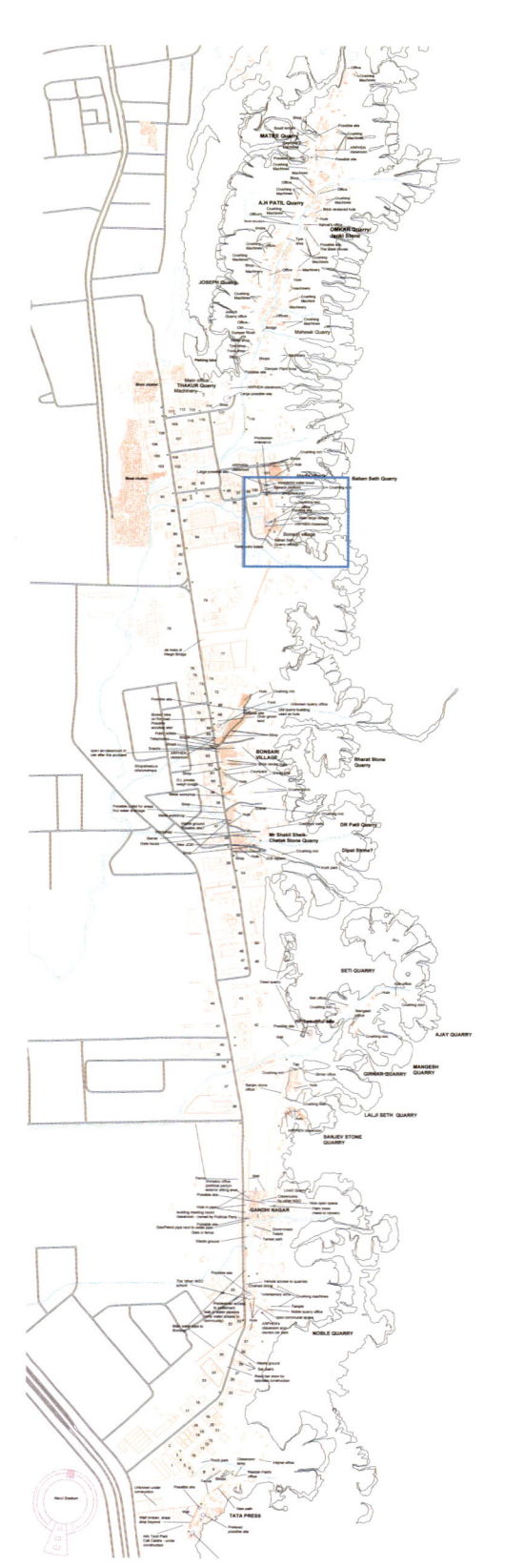

The stone quarry communities of Navi Mumbai are on the periphery of a booming industrial zone. Within the 6km stretch of the Thane-Belapur quarry belt there are 84 working, individually-owned quarries. NGO ARPHEN has been working in these communities for over 20 years, successfully creating bridge classes enabling children of quarry workers to enrol in the mainstream government education system.

To date, two community classroom buildings have been constructed using local skills, techniques and materials to create permanent formalised community spaces and classrooms for the quarry worker families. The first classroom in Baban Seth quarry was built by Project Assistants Shamoon Patwari and Bo Tang over a period of five weeks in March 2009. They built the second classroom in Tata Press quarry in November 2009 with 5th year students as part of the diploma course.

left
plan of Navi Mumbai ridge showing location of
family run stone quarries
Paul Watson and Valerie Saavedra Lux
below
detail plan showing location of community
classroom in Baban Seth quarry settlement
Paul Watson and Valerie Saavedra Lux

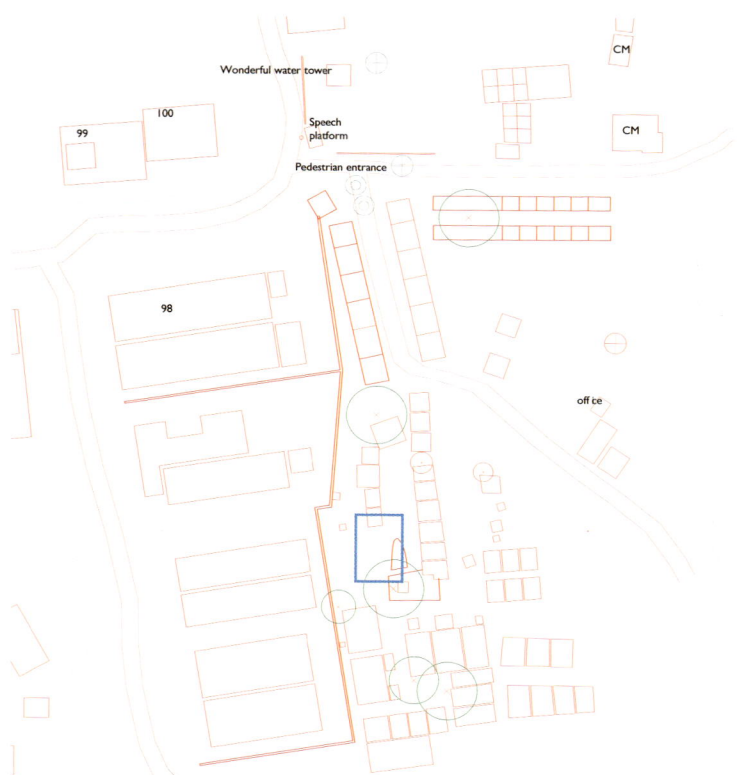

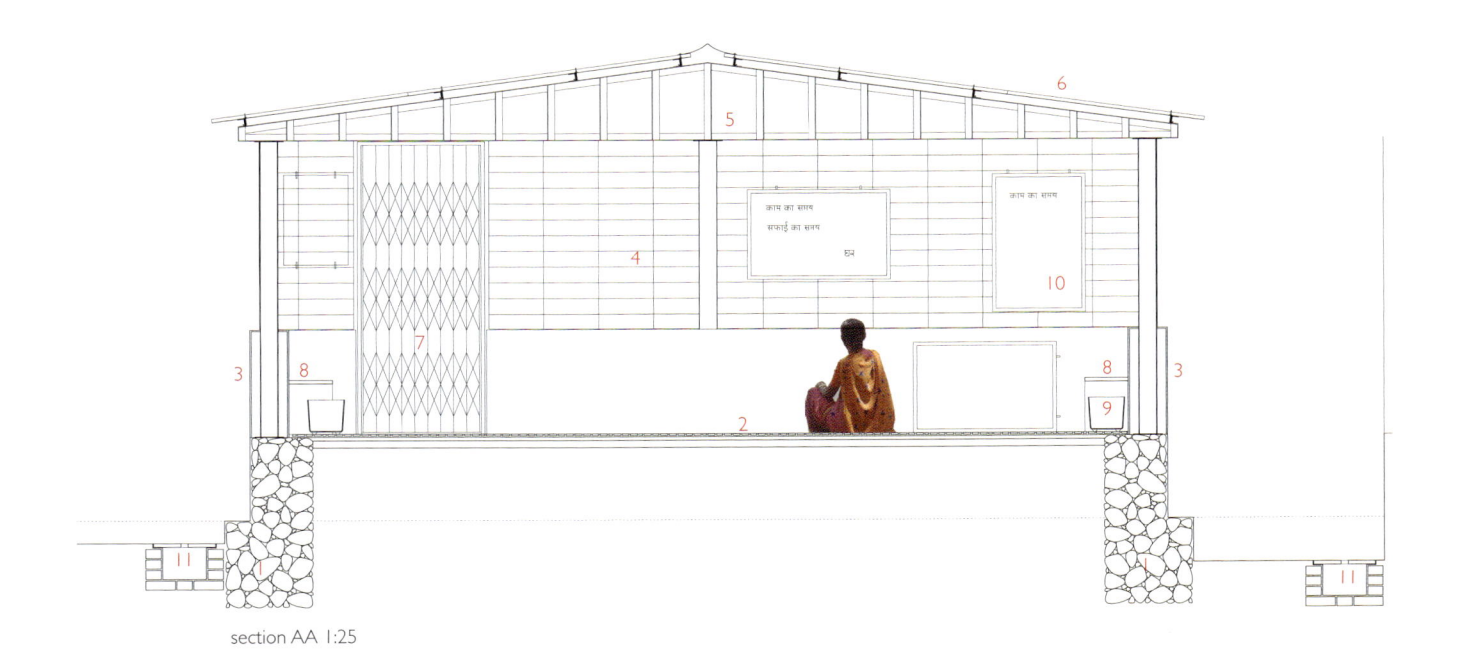

section AA 1:25

section BB 1:25

sections through community classroom
ASD Projects

Key

1. Stone foundation (donated by quarry owner)
2. Floor - Reclaimed marble off cuts
3. Rendered brick wall
4. Steel security grill
5. Steel roof frame
6. Corrugated plastic roof sheeting
7. Door
8. Seating - Black stone slabs
9. Storage buckets under seating
10. Blackboard
11. Covered brick drain
12. Rendered brick steps

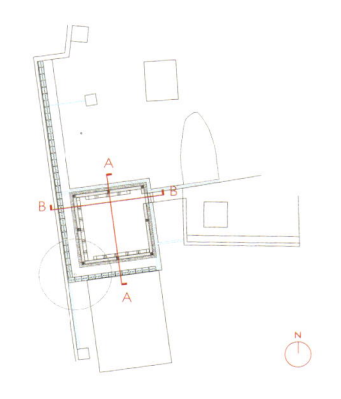

top left
view of community classroom during
construction from adjacent high rise block
Shamoon Patwari

top right
view of community classroom during
construction showing steelwork framing
Shamoon Patwari

below
view of upgraded community classroom
March 2010
Bo Tang

left
view of community temple from inside new classroom
Bo Tang
below
view of community classroom completed for the opening ceremony in March 2009
Helena McDermott

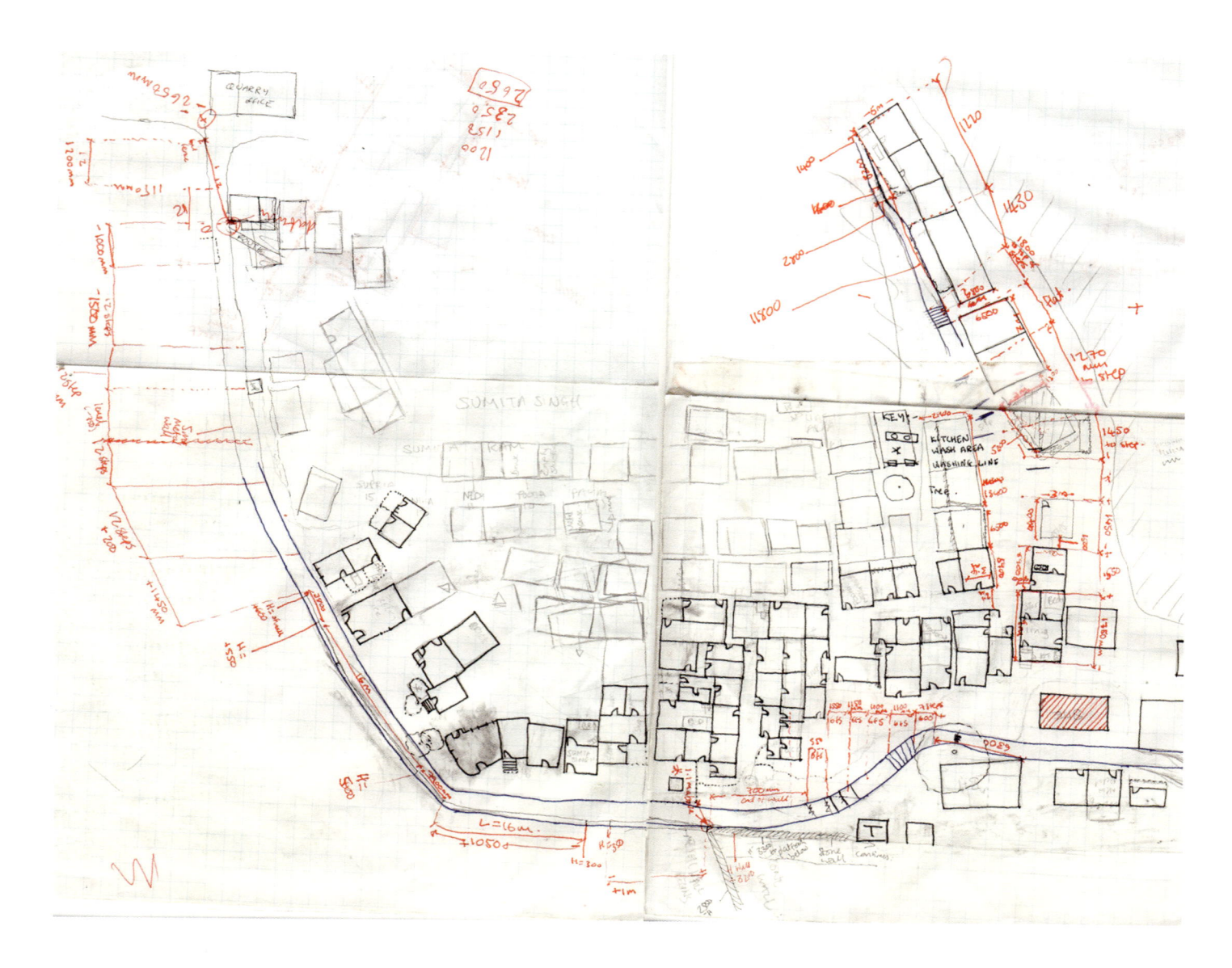

top
survey drawing of Tata Press community
Hawar Sargalo
right
view of completed Tata Press classroom
within the community
Odel Jeffries

282

Students and Projects 2002–2010

Year / Name	Project	Location	Metaphor
Studio 02/03 Gujarat			
Heesun Lim	Women's Vocational Centre	Datrana	Ruins and Reunited
Niccolo Manco	Bus Station	Verahi	Water Tower Plaza
Olga Sieczewicz	Women's Refuge	Datrana	Hakki Transcripts
Tanja Eichenauer	Marriage Shelter	Verahi	Canvas over Bazaar
Heidi Moxon	Lorry Stop	Verahi	Truck Stop
Karen Crequer		Patanka	Nomadic Landscape
James Stuart		Patanka	Adobe Seismic Construction
Visham Purbnoo		Patanka	Regeneration after Earthquake
Kathryn Manning		Patanka	Connections Across Boundaries
Mano Pooth		Patanka	Collapsible Canopy
Alex Martinez		Patanka	Growth towards and from Water
Sam McDermott		Patanka	Hub Cap
Studio 03/04 Meerut			
Carolos Efstathiou	Rooftop Summer School	Meerut Old Town	
Konstantinos Poulopoulos	Rooftop Farm	Meerut Old Town	
Chris Gilbert	Music School	Meerut Gate / Clock Tower	
Eunah Kim	Women's Refuge	Outside Meerut	
Francesca Pont	Cinema	Outside Meerut	
Kaori Luchi	Women's Vocational Centre	Meerut Old Town	
Youjung Park	School in Haveli	Meerut Old Town	
Studio 04/05 South Delhi			
Emre Turkmen	Rooftop Crafts / Water Filtration	Khirki	
Yanira de Armas-Tosco	Sanitation Towers	Soami Nagar J.J. Camp	Community Life
Amy Penford	Housing and Shops by Mosque	Khirki	
David Wannerton	Water Filtration and Reservoir	Jagdamba Camp	Over the Top
James Crosse	Laundry	Jagdamba Camp	A Game of Cricket
Leo Thomson	Ecological Centre	Chirag Dilli	The Inner Periphery
Terri Whitehead	Tower	Khirki	
Robert Johnson	School	Khirki	
John McCulley	Nomad Housing	East Khirki	
Edwin Chomen		Chirag Dilli	The Edge
Glen Campbell		Chirag Dilli	The Beauty that Shines from Within
Rahul Bajaj		Soami Nagar J.J. Camp	Platform for Living
Simone Kuhniein		Chirag Dilli	Re-use and Recycling
Brinda Sengupta		Chirag Dilli	Residential Spine
Maliha Chaudry		Chirag Dilli	Transient Shelter
Jensil John		Chirag Dilli	Street Theatre

Year / Name	Project	Location	Metaphor
Helen Greenbeck		Soami Nagar J.J. Camp	Sustaining the Spirit
Abishek Mathur		Jagdamba Camp	Greening the Trench
Medha Dixit		Jagdamba Camp	Planning Density
Heha Singh		Jagdamba Camp	Connecting People
John McCulley		Satpula	Nomadic Permanence
Ellyasaq Jamil		Satpula	A Space Sympathetic

Studio 05/06 South Delhi

Year / Name	Project	Location	Metaphor
Yanira de Armas-Tosco	Upgrading	Soami Nagar J.J. Camp	
Mohammed Akmal	Inhabited wall	Soami Nagar J.J. Camp	
Anja Theis	Birthing Centre	Chirag Dilli	Birthing and Health Centre for Women
Angela Hopcraft	Widow's Refuge	Jagdamba Camp	Flexible Community Centre
Natalie Horner	Waste Pickers	Panchsheel Vihar	The Recycling Camp
Chloe Talbot	Waste Pickers	Panchsheel Vihar	Transient Lives and Livelihoods
Judith Ben-Tovim	Waste Pickers	Panchsheel Vihar	If you really care for us, then help us
Cristina Monteiro	Waste Pickers	Panchsheel Vihar	Waste Pickers' Houses by the Nallah
Sam Bentil-Mensah	Waste Pickers	Panchsheel Vihar	Transient Cycles
Hiromi Yang	Waste Pickers	Panchsheel Vihar	Oil the Rusty Wheel of Recycling Awareness
Tim Sanderson	Health Centre	Jagdamba Camp	Health Centre
Toshitsugo Matsumura	Happy Places	Jagdamba Camp	A Happy Space
Idris Anjay	Sanitation	Jagdamba Camp	Lifting Expectations
Glen Campbell			Healthcare in Changing Densities and Openness
Eoin O'Keefe			Entrance Activities

Studio 06/07 Agra

Year / Name	Project	Location	Metaphor
Bo Tang	Housing / Workshops / Water	Marwari Basti	A Tale of Three Communities
Shamoon Patwari	Vocational School	Katra Wazir Khan	The Death of a Tradesman
Maro Sosa	Amenity Building	Marwari Basti	The Lantern
Ben Smith	Language School	Katra Wazir Khan	Language Exchange
Emma Curtin	Housing	Marwari Basti	Physical Landscape and Cultural Life
James Lloyd-Mostyn	Vocational School	Nagla Devjeet	Saraswati Place
Miu Sze Hung	Ayurvedic Centre	Kuchhpura	Cultural and Health Avenue
Stefanie Rhodes	Women's Radio Station	Nagla Devjeet	Economies of the Everyday
Edward Ridge	Cloth	Nagla Devjeet	Fertile Ground
Iain Smales	Sites and Services	Nagla Devjeet	Waste Pickers' Community
Chris Fletcher	Old People	Kuchhpura	Older Adult Community Support
Anthony Corke	Vocational School / Cricket Pitch	Kuchhpura	Village Academies
Matthieu Dalziel		Marwari Basti	Towards a Community
Dean Foskett		Marwari Basti	Archive
Katarzyna Banak		Kuchhpura	A Grooming Space for Women
Jaroslaw Engel		Kuchhpura	A Room with a View

Year / Name	Project	Location	Metaphor
Je Ahn	Shoe Worker	Kuchhpura	A Doorway
Maria Smith			Shift
Maxine Jackson	Livelihoods	Katra Wazir Khan	
Andrea Carbogno	Paneer Factory and Restaurant	Katra Wazir Khan	Dairy Products in KWK
Spencer Owen	Sanitation	Kuchhpura	Linking the Village together through Communal Spaces

Summer Project Agra 2007

Bo Tang	Sanitation	Kuchhpura	
Shamoon Patwari	Sanitation	Kuchhpura	
Spencer Owen	Sanitation	Kuchhpura	
Katarzyna Banak	Sanitation	Kuchhpura	

Studio 07/08 East and Central Delhi

Bo Tang	Haveli Campus	Old Delhi	Rediscovering Haveli Ruins in Old Delhi
Shamoon Patwari	Sorting and Students	Old Delhi	The Goatherder and the Haveli
Anna Kerrane	Housing	Kalyanpuri	Vibrancy and Vocation
Amelia Rule	Upgrading and Community Centre	Kalyanpuri	A Way Through
Stephen Chown	Sanitation / Educaton / Crossing	Ambedkar	Spectacular High Street
Azedah Mosavi	Upgrading Chowks	Ambedkar	Conspicuous Ghosts
Nicolas Maari	Site and Service	Kalyanpuri	The Wall
Nisha Kurian	Women's Centre	Kalyanpuri	Living in Close Quarters
Tze-Ting Mok	Housing	Kalyanpuri	Life Along the Edge
Yougesh Bhanote	Housing	Kalyanpuri	The Weaving Process
Clinton Jordan	Housing	Ambedkar	Workers' Housing
Stephanie Van der Brandt	Housing	Kalyanpuri	A Roof with a View
Eureka De La Cruz	Re-use of Empty Industrial Blocks	Sonia Camp	Housing and Education
Dan Tambling		Sunder Nagri	Interweaving Weaving and New Recycled Materials
Daria Buhanovska		Sunder Nagri	Spinning Through Life
Sanna Rautio		Sunder Nagri	Variable Spaces
Valeriya Slobodyuk		Sunder Nagri	Health and Ergonomic Issues in a Weaving Place
Emma Ellis	Replanning Houses	Ambedkar	Interrupting Activities
Nicole Bruun Meyer		Sonia Camp	Laundry and the Little Ones
Jon Webb		Sonia Camp	Cricket: A Game of Life
Clinton Jordan		Ambedkar	Worker Housing
Paul Watson		Ambedkar	Manna from Heaven
Toni Frye		Ambedkar	The Big House
Valerie Saavedra		Ambedkar	Towards Better Livelihoods through Equality
Henry Thorold		Kalyanpuri	The K 1920 Co-op Industrial Prod Society
John Turney		Kalyanpuri	Breaking Barriers

Year / Name	Project	Location	Metaphor
Nick Silk		Kalyanpuri	Natural Balance
Yannick Guillen		Kalyanpuri	A Workshop on the Toilet Block

Summer Projects 2008

Year / Name	Project	Location	Metaphor
Bo Tang		Agra, Navi Mumbai, Delhi	
Shamoon Patwari		Agra, Navi Mumbai, Delhi	
Valerie Saavedra Lux	10 Community Classrooms	Navi Mumbai	
Paul Watson	10 Community Classrooms	Navi Mumbai	
Odel Jeffries	Housing and Resettlement	Savda Ghewra	
Phil Lyons	Housing and Resettlement	Savda Ghewra	

Studio 08/09 South Delhi

Year / Name	Project	Location	Metaphor
Henry Lau		Chirag Delhi	Chowk: A Users Manual
Harjeet Suri		Panchsheel Vihar	Soft Wall Mental Boundaries
Yilmaz Korkmaz		Chirag Delhi	Chowk Life
Graham Read		Meharauli	A Cup of Chai, Where's the Water From?
Katherine Edmondson		North Jagdamba	Emerging and Connecting Communities
Victoria Wagner		North Jagdamba	A Garden to Bridge Across Genders
Paul Harvey		Chirag Delhi	Space for Building
Audrey Lematte		Panchsheel Vihar	Breaking Through to the Other Side
Toby Pear		Chirag Delhi	Relighting the Lamp of Delhi
Sally Johns		Chirag Delhi	Chirag Delhi Dairy Arts
Pau Ling Yap		Chirag Delhi	Teapots on Chowk; Pods on Rooftops
Cian Owen McKay		North Jagdamba	A Sense of Calm
Huw Trevorrow		North Jagdamba	Retreat to the Trees
William Notley		Panchsheel Vihar	Back Street
Natasha Reid		Panchsheel Vihar	Breaking Down Boundaries
Odel Jeffries		Mehrauli	A Place to Stay, A Place of Rest
Sadiqa Jabbar		West Jagdamba	Breaking Barriers Uniting People
John Jack		East Jagdamba	Breaking out of JD: The Powerful Potential of Organic Waste
Pavol Svihra		East Jagdamba	Community Product Independency
Dawn Keatley		Panchsheel Vihar	Decay in Growth
Civita Halim		Panchsheel Vihar	Vague Future
Hawar Sargalo		Panchsheel Vihar	Alleviation of Deterioration: Skill and Growth
Evangelos Kolokotronis		Mehrauli	Solid Houses
Chloe Athanasopoulou		Mehrauli	Connections
Simona Grimaldi		Mehrauli	Women's Workshop Terrace
Verde Buliani		Mehrauli	Water is Life
Simon Elliston		Mehrauli	Snakes and Ladders

Year / Name	Project	Location	Metaphor
Viktor Westerdahl		Mehrauli	Do you want to be an Astronaut?
Saki Hajijan		Mehrauli	Memories of Past and Future
Sheldon Roachford		Gaushala	At Last Changes for the Future
Zara Aziz Khan		Gaushala	Holy Traditions
Karamii Clarke		Gaushala	Raising the Standard of Living through Industry
Arman Borhani		Gaushala	Gaushala Hamam
Hasan Abbas		Gaushala	Cow Urine Distillery

Studio 09/10 South Delhi

Year / Name	Project	Location	Metaphor
Alpa Depani	Housing and Density	Haus Rani	Inward Housing
Amy Stevens	Workshops	Haus Rani	Zen and Motorcyle Maintenance
Oliver Beardon	Housing and Sanitation	Haus Rani	The Gudwara Urban Village
Rachel O'Grady	Housing and Density	Haus Ran	Metro, Market and Making
Sally Gray	Plastics Recycling Factory	Haus Rani	
Sarah Jonasson	Library Learning Centre	Haus Rani	
Amanda Rashid	Housing and Density	Lado Sarai	
Antoine Carrier	Tourist's Procession	Lado Sarai	
Benedetta Rogers	Public Spaces	Lado Sarai	Porous Lado Sarai
Eiko Kizu	Sanitation	Lado Sarai	Launderette
Jonathan Buckland	Caravanserai	Lado Sarai	Rest and Relaxation
Louise Ducey	Housing	Lado Sarai	Domestic Landscapes
Michelle Barlow	Creative Forum	Lado Sarai	
Phuntsok Bhutia		Lado Sarai	The Brothers
Valentina Jaen Malmsheimer		Lado Sarai	Free-dom Pockets
Amy Claire Bradley Smith	Cycle Workshops	South Mehrauli	
Claire Osborne	A Women's Dhobi Ghat	South Mehrauli	
Claudia Raurell		South Mehrauli	Interstitial Spaces
Hansol Park		South Mehrauli	
Mariam Marzyeh Gomary		South Mehrauli	Expanding Horizon
Owen Rutter		South Mehrauli	Protection through Development
Thomas Harrison	The Regeneration of the Maidan	South Mehrauli	
Sally Boucher		South Mehrauli	
Vanessa Lee	Workshop Spaces	South Mehrauli	Changing Fabric
Rosa Chan		South Mehrauli	From Floodlands to Women's Hub

Studio 09/10 Navi Mumbai

Year / Name	Project	Location	Metaphor
Harjeet Suri	Women's Refuge	Turbhe	The Myth of Return
Audrey Lematte		Turbhe	Phytoremediation and Landscapes
Toby Pear	Food and Sanitation	Turbhe	Tiffin and Dhobi Wallahs
Odel Jeffries	Street Theatre and Housing	Turbhe	Of Time and the City
William Notley	Routes and Cricket	Chunabhatti	Swadeshi Spine – Catalyst Scheme
Cian McKay	Artisan Quarter	Chunabhatti	

Live Project Mumbai 2009

Bo Tang	10 Community Classrooms	Navi Mumbai	Education
Shamoon Patwari	10 Community Classrooms	Navi Mumbai	Education
Harjeet Suri	10 Community Classrooms	Navi Mumbai	Education
Audrey Lematte	10 Community Classrooms	Navi Mumbai	Education
Toby Pear	10 Community Classrooms	Navi Mumbai	Education
Odel Jeffries	10 Community Classrooms	Navi Mumbai	Education
William Notley	10 Community Classrooms	Navi Mumbai	Education
Cian McKay	10 Community Classrooms	Navi Mumbai	Education

Glossary
Indian Terms and Place Names

Ambedkar Camp	An illegal settlement in east Delhi studied by students in November 2007
Archaeological Survey of India	The Archaeological Survey of India (ASI), within the Ministry of Culture, is responsible for the regulation of archaeological research and the protection and maintenance of the cultural heritage of India
Baithak	Community gathering space
Baniyas	Merchants
Barsati Structure	An open structure or pavilion on top of a roof
Bihar	The modern name for the ancient kingdom of Magadha. It is located to the east of Delhi, part of Bengal, stretching as far as the coast around Kolkotta
Brahmin	Priestly caste
Brahmpuri	A settlement on the outskirts of Old Meerut which some students studied in November 2003
Bouvra Chowk	A public space in Chirag Delhi called the Medical Chowk by the students
Chapati	Unleavened flat bread
Charpoi, Charpoy	Lightweight, timber-framed bed platform strung with a string net mattress for relaxing
Chhatri	Elevated, dome shaped pavilion
Chirag Delhi, Chirag Dilli	An urban village in south Delhi
Choli	Midriff-baring blouse often worn with a sari
Chowk	A place where paths intersect or meet with the emphasis on place
Chulha	Charcoal-fuelled, domestic cooking stove
Commodifying	Transforming objects or services into saleable products
Criticality	A space has a high criticality when it is designed and used for one purpose only. The space is often named after that use (Bedroom for sleeping, kitchen for cooking, for example)
CURE	An Indian NGO with whom the studio has carried out two of its live projects and who have provided access to slum communities. The Centre for Urban and Regional Excellence works in a range of low income, mostly illegal settlements promoting the livelihoods of women.
Dargah	Tomb complex
Diurnal Range	Difference between day and night temperatures
Delhi Development Authority	Created in 1955 under the provisions of the Delhi Development Act to promote and secure the development of Delhi
Delhi Jal Board	Delhi Water Board
Dharamsala	Pilgrims' rest house
Dhobi Ghat	Riverside laundry
Dhobi wallahs	Laundry workers
Flyash	Pulverised Fly Ash (PFA) is a by-product of power stations and is a form of pozzolana (see below)
Google Earth	Computerised mapping software freely available on the web
Gali	Dead-end lane
Haveli	A traditional courtyard house
Impluvium	Found in ancient Greek and Roman domestic architecture, an impluvium is a sunken pool in an atrium or courtyard used for the purpose of collecting and storing rainwater which enters through an opening in the roof or compluvium. Sometimes a cistern is connected to the pool for the longer term storage of drinking water
Indra Nagar	Name of Marwari settlement in Agra which is also known locally as 'Marwari Basti'
Jaal	Grill
Jahanpanah	The fourth city of Delhi

Jama Masjid	Friday Mosque. The Jama Masjid of Delhi dates from the 17th century and is the principal mosque of Delhi
Jainism	A religion associated with, but separate from, Hinduism
Jali	arrays of small openings giving ventilation whilst maintaining privacy
Jagdamba Camp	An illegal settlement situated on a drain in south Delhi
Jats	farmers
J.J. Camp	Jhuggie-Jhonpri or higgledy-piggledy. Refers to illegal settlements which are perceived as being constructed of temporary materials.
Kalyanpuri Block 19/20	A poor illegal settlement in East Delhi
Katra Wazir Khan	An east bank riverside community in Agra
Kanda	Dung pats used as domestic fuel
Khirki Masjid	A 14th century mosque located in Khirki village which was abandoned soon after it was constructed
Khumaris	Potters
Kitty Party	Regular meetings, mostly attended by women where a collection of funds from members is made at each meeting and given to each member in turn as capital to start a business
Kuchha	temporary, short life, reducing in value
Kuchhpura	A village situated to the North of the Taj Mahal in Agra where students studied in November 2006 and where a live sanitation project was carried out by students and the ASD Projects Office
Ladakh	A region within the Indian State of Jammu and Kashmir in the Himalyas
Lal Dora	Area demarcated (the red line on the map) to signify that the settlement within this boundary can grow without the need for government permissions. Often applied to pre-existing (abadi) land associated with old established settlements and urban villages when city expansion engulfs them
Lime	A cement made by heating limestone and slaking the resulting quicklime in water. The cement hardens by contact with the air
Madrassa	Religious school
Marwari	Wandering traders from Rajasthan
Marwari Basti	Settlement of the Marwaris in Agra
Masala chai	A type of spiced tea
Masand	Reclining cushion
Masjid	Mosque
MCD	The Municipal Corporation of Delhi governs nine Districts of Delhi, in the state of Delhi, India. It is one of three municipal corporations in the National Capital Territory of Delhi, the others being the New Delhi Municipal Council, and the Delhi Cantonment Board
Meerut	An ancient city about 40 miles to the North East of Delhi in the state of Uttar Pradesh where LMU students studied in November 2003
Mohalla	Neighbourhood or locality in the cities and towns of central and south Asia
Mughal	A corruption of 'Mongol' and refers to the Empire which dominated northern India from the 14th to the 19th centuries
Multivalent	Refers to spaces which are not differentiated according to function
Nalla, Nala, Nahla, Nallah	Natural water course in an urban area into which sewage and waste water flows from the surrounding area
NGO	Non-government organisation
Otla	A raised threshold or porch at the entrance to a house where residents sit and chat to passers by
Panchsheel Vihar	A part of south Delhi where communities of waste pickers live and work and where students studied in 2004, 2005 and 2008
Pardhis	A particular wandering 'denotified' nomadic community
Pol	The name given to a (sometimes gated) cul-de-sac or neighbourhood in Ahmedahbad. It is

	called a gali in Old Delhi
Post Hoc	After the event
Pozzolanic	A material which when added to Portland Cement will extend its properties of strength and durability. Originally refering to glassy material thrown out during volcanic eruptions, pozzolanic materials include ground up, fired bricks and PFA (pulverised fly ash), a waste product from power stations
Pukka	Permanent, finished, increasing in value
Puja	Many Hindu homes have a personal shrine set aside somewhere in the house that includes pictures of various gods. A daily puja is a ritual which may include offerings such as light, water and incense to the family's personal deity
Rajasthan	The largest Indian state, situated to the West of Delhi and bordering Pakistan
Ranguli	Dry paint patterns placed on the ground
Retrofit	The process of fitting a product after the main construction has been completed so that it is not a part of the critical path of construction and therefore cannot hold up later work
Sheesham pole	A type of timber pole used for scaffolding in Delhi
SEWA	Self-Employed Women's Association, an NGO active throughout North India
Siri Fort	The third city of Delhi
Slums	A term used in India to denote poor, illegal settlements usually built of temporary materials
Soami Nagar	A J.J. camp in south Delhi studied by students in November 2004 and November 2005
Sufism	A mystical, ascetic dimension of the Islamic faith
Terra Incognito	Literally unknown worlds. Used by the students to describe unfamiliar terrain within which they are looking for methods to survey physically and understand culturally
Tabula Rasa	The idea that you can start from scratch with a blank, level site, disregarding what went before both historically and topographically
Tuk tuk	Tuk tuks are auto rickshaws: three wheeled covered vehicles (now usually powered by liquid petroleum gas) which provide the most common form of urban transport in India
TVB School of Habitat Studies	Indian School of Architecture in Delhi with which the students worked in 2004 and 2005
Uttar Pradesh	An Indian state to the north of Delhi
Waqf Board	A trust to administer charitable funds within the Islamic communities, usually associated with a particular mosque

Bibliography

Alexander, C. (1979) *The Timeless Way of Building* (New York: Oxford University Press)

Alexander, C., Ishikawa, S. and Silverstein, M. (1977) *A Pattern Language: Towns. Buildings. Construction.* (Oxford: Oxford University Press)

Andreotti, L. and Costa, X. (1996) *Theory of the Derive and Other Situationist Writings on the City.* Museo d'Art Contemporani de Barcelona

Ben-Tovim, J. (2007) Life and Garbage: Garbage as a tool for growth development and for creating a sustainable environment. Unpublished MA dissertation

Berthon, S. and Robinson, A. (1991) *The Shape of the World. The Mapping and Discovery of the Earth* (London: George Philip Ltd)

Bhatia, G. (1991) *Laurie Baker: Life, Works and Writings* (Harmondsworth: Penguin Books)

Chambers, R. (1983) *Rural Development: Putting the Last First* (Harlow: Longman)

CHINTAN (undated) Space for Waste, Planning for the Informal Recycling Sector. Paper published by Chintan (Indian NGO specialising in the needs of waste pickers)

Cruickshank, D. (1992) 'I Like a Brick', *Architects Journal.* EMAP Architecture

CURE (15 January 2007) Kuchhpura Sanitation Pilot Project: The Cross Cutting Agra Programme Inception Report. Report submitted to TCG International

Davis, D. (2006) *Planet of Slums* (London and New York: Verso)

Dean, A. and Hursley, T. (2002) *Rural Studio: Samuel Mockbee and an Architecture of Decency* (Princeton: Princeton Architectural Press)

De Armas-Tosco, Y. (2005) J.J. Camp S/136 Soami Nagar, Malviya Nagar, New Delhi, India. Unpublished student report

De Berry, J. (2004) 'Rebuilding Kabul: The Role of Young People', *Trialog* 83/2004

De Certeau, M. (1984) *The Practice of Everyday Life* (Berkeley: University of California Press)

Devy, G.N. (2005) http://www.indiatogether.org/2005/may/soc-adinomad.htm

D'Souza, D. (2001) *Branded by Law: Looking at India's Denotified Tribes* (New Delhi: Penguin Books India)

Evans, R. (1997) 'The Rights of Retreat and the Rites of Exclusion: Notes Towards the Definition of Wall' in 'Robin Evans: Translations from Drawing to Building and Other Essays', *AA Documents* 2 (London: Architectural Association)

Grover, A. et al. (2002) 'House form and society in Delhi', in *Seminars in Architecture* (New Delhi: School of Planning and Architecture)

Gupta, S. (2005) EWS Housing, Govindpuri. Thesis project presented to TVB School of Habitat Studies, Delhi 28 May 2005

Gupta, S. (undated) Behaviour of Streets. Distinctions in street character as a component of Physicality and Activity in the inner city of Meerut. Thesis submitted to CENDEP School of Architecture, Ahmedabad, India

Hamdi, N. (2004) *Small Change: About the Art of Practice and the Limits of Planning in Cities* (London: Earthscan)

Hardgrove, A. (2004) *Community and Public Culture: The Marwaris in Calcutta 1897–1997* (New York: Columbia University Press)

Harkness, T. and Sinha, A. (2004) 'Taj Heritage Corridor: Intersection between History and Culture on the Yamuna Riverfront', in *Places: Forum of Design for the Public Realm*, 16(2)

Harvey, D. (1996) *Justice, Nature and the Geography of Difference* (Malden, MA: Blackwell)

Highmore, B. (2006) *Michel de Certeau: Analysing Culture* (London: Continuum)

Horner, H. (2006) Unpublished 4th year submission for Appropriate Technology in Architecture module. London Metropolitan University, Department of Architecture and Spatial Design

Hosagrahar, J. (2005) *Indigenous Modernities: Negotiating Architecture and Urbanism* (London and New York: Routledge)

Hosseini, K. (2003) *The Kite Runner* (London: Bloomsbury)

INTACH (1996) Process for Historic Site Development. Chirag Delhi: A Case Study. Prepared by INTACH in collaboration with Institute of Asian Cultures, Tokyo

Keay, J. (2000) *The Great Arc: The Dramatic Tale of How India was Mapped and Everest was Named* (London: HarperCollins)

King, A. (1995) *The Bungalow: The Production of a Global Culture* (Oxford: Oxford University Press).

Knippers, J. (2008) 'New Building Products from Waste Materials in India', *Detail* Magazine 2008 No. 6

Knutt, E. (2005) 'Building bamboo's reputation', *Building Design* 2 December

Kracauer, S. 'The Hotel Lobby,' in Leach, ed. (1997) *Rethinking Architecture* (London: Routledge)

Kumar, S. (2002) *The Present in Delhi's Pasts* (New Delhi: Three Essays Press)

Lefebvre, H. (1997) 'The Everyday and Everydayness', in Harris, S. and Berke, D. *Architecture of the Everyday* (Princeton: Princeton Architectural Press)

MacPherson, Y. (2007) 'Images and icons: harnessing the power of the media to reduce sex selective abortion in India', *Gender and Development* 15(3) November, Oxfam

Mani, B.R. (1997) *Delhi: Threshold of the Orient* (Studies in Archaeological Investigations)(New Delhi: Aryan Books International)

Miller, S. (2009) *Delhi: Adventures in a Megacity* (London: Jonathan Cape)

Mitchell, M. (1998) *The Lemonade Stand: Exploring the unfamiliar by building large-scale models* (Wales: Centre for Alternative Technology Publications)

Mitchell, M. (2003) *Rebuilding Community in Kosovo* (Wales: Centre for Alternative Technology Publications)

Mosavi, A. et al. (2007) East Yamuna Exchanges. Unpublished Field Trip Booklet, Degree Studio 7 and Diploma Unit 6, ASD, London Metropolitan University

Mumtaz, B. (undated) Reading the City. Notes for students at the Development Planning Unit, University College, London . Photocopy in author's possession

Pallasmaa, J. (2005) *The Eyes of the Skin: Architecture and the Senses* (New York: John Wiley and Sons)

Pandya, Y. (2005) *Concepts of Space in Traditional Indian Architecture* (Ahmedabad: Mapin Publishing)

Parikh, H. (2004) New ways of engineering for developing countries. Text of Happold Memorial Lecture held at Royal Society of Arts, 21 January 2004, London.

Peck, L. (2005) *Delhi. A Thousand Years of Building* (New Delhi: Intach Guides: The Lotus Collection)

Peck, L. (2008) *Agra, The Architectural Heritage* (New Delhi: Intach Roli Guide)

Pickford, J. (1995) *Low-Cost Sanitation: A Survey of Practical Experience* (London: ITDG Publishing)

Prussin, L. (1995) *African Nomadic Architecture: Place Space and Gender* (Washington, DC: Smithsonian Institution Press)

Rai, V. (1998) *Curfew in the City* (New Delhi: Lotus Collection of Roli Books)

Reed, R.A. (1995) *Sustainable Sewerage* (London: ITDG Publishing in association with Water, Engineering and Development Centre)

Rule, A. (2008) IDS Report 2008, Diploma Unit 6, p. 10

Rule, A. (2008) Housing the masses: are resettlement colonies the answer to Delhi's population problem? Unpublished submission January 2008

Rule, A. (2008) IDS Diary 2008. Unpublished submission in part fulfilment of Postgraduate Diploma in Architecture, London Metropolitan University

Rykwert, J. (2000) *The Seduction of Place. The History and Future of the City* (Oxford: Oxford University Press)

Said, S. (1978) *Orientalism* (Harmondsworth: Penguin Books)

Sengupta, N. (2008) 'Use of cost-effective construction technologies in India to mitigate climate change', in *Current Science*, 94(1), 10 January

Sennett, R. (2008) *The Craftsman* (London: Allen Lane)

Shirangan, K. (2000) *Delhi Field Studies and Workshop Appendix 1.* UK Department for International Development (DFID)

Singh, V. (2007) *Master Plan for Delhi with the Perspective for the Year 2021* (New Delhi: Rupa and Co.)

Stephen, W. (ed.) (2004) *Think Global, Act Local: The Life and Legacy of Patrick Geddes* (Edinburgh: Luath Press Ltd)

Stendhal (1995) *The Life of Henry Brulard.* Transl. John Sturrock (New York: New York Review of Books)

Smithson, P. and Smithson, A. (1993) *Italian Thoughts* (Stockholm: Alison and Peter Smithson)

Sosa, M. (2008) How can an architectural intervention facilitate the integration of previously nomadic communities into the modern Indian city? Unpublished Masters Thesis

Tang, B. (2008) IDS Diary 2008. Unpublished submission in part fulfilment of Postgraduate Diploma in Architecture, London Metropolitan University

Tschumi, B. (1994) *The Manhattan Transcripts* (London: Academy Editions)

Tschumi, B. (1996) *Architecture and Disjunction* (Cambridge, MA: The MIT Press)

Vidler, A. (2000) *Warped Space: Art, Architecture and Anxiety in Modern Culture* (Cambridge, MA: The MIT Press)

Wagstaff, S. (2004) *Edward Hopper.* Exhibition Catalogue (London: Tate Publishing)

Index